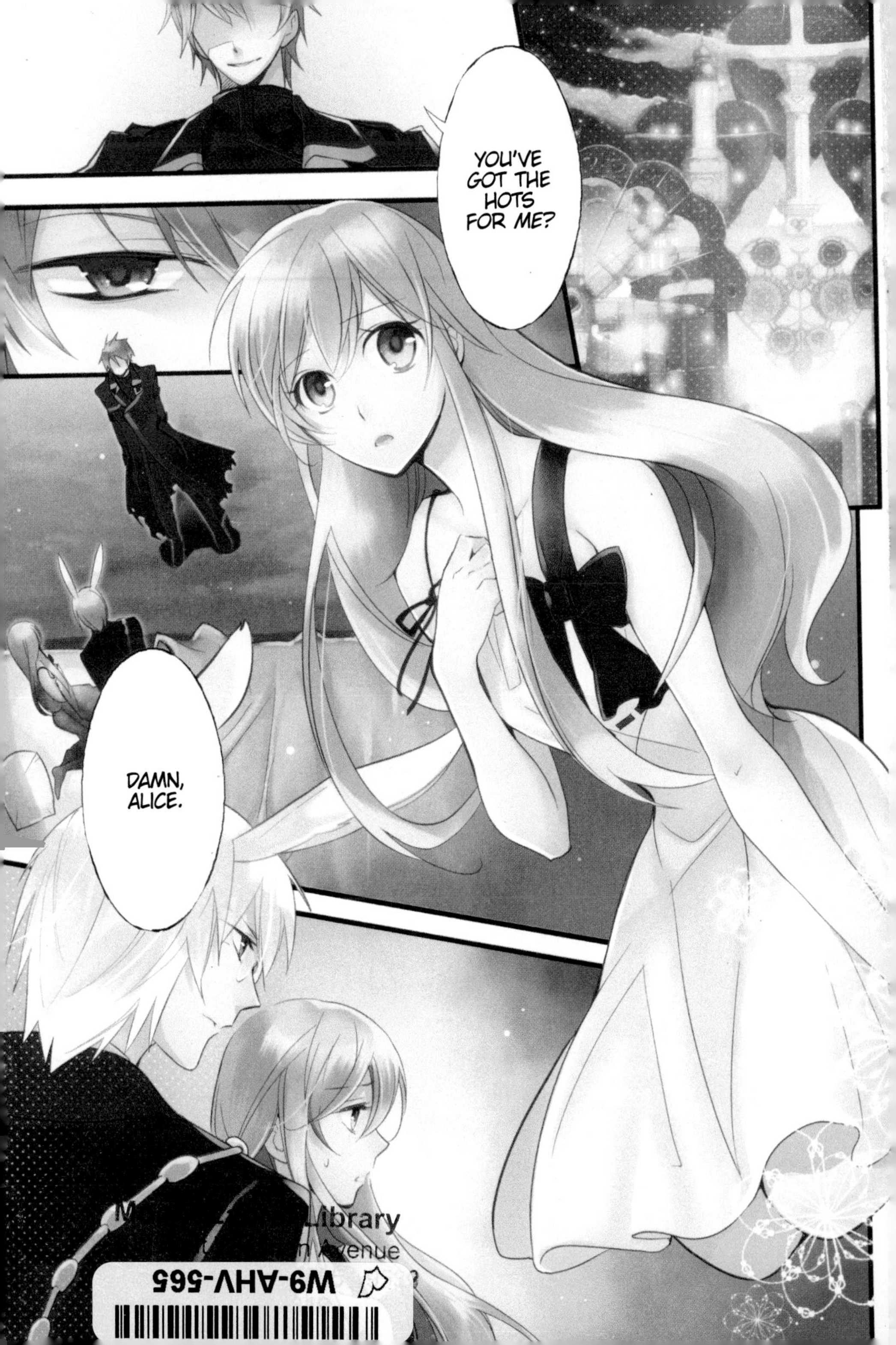
YOU'VE GOT THE HOTS FOR ME?
DAMN, ALICE.

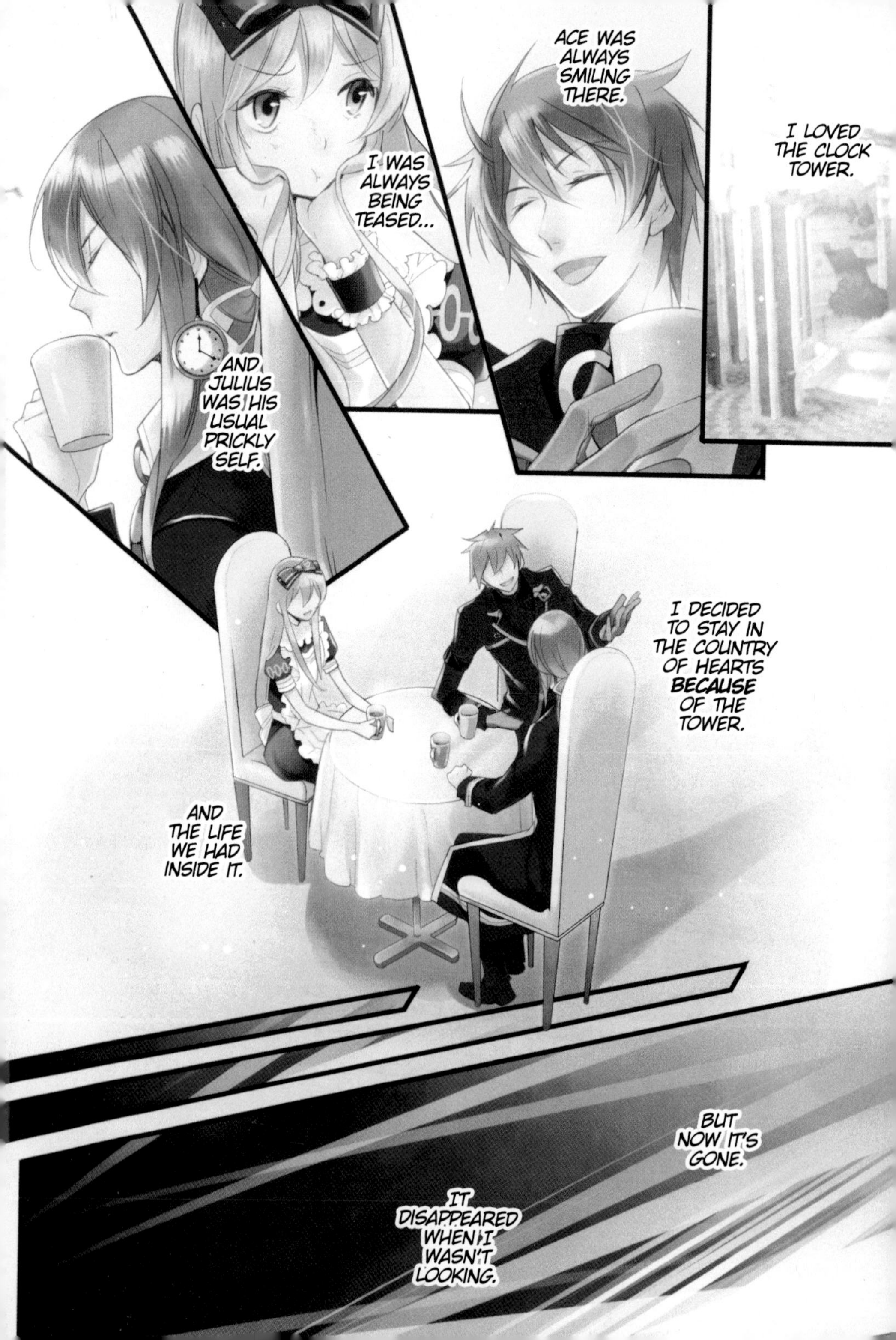
I LOVED THE CLOCK TOWER.
ACE WAS ALWAYS SMILING THERE.
I WAS ALWAYS BEING TEASED...
AND JULIUS WAS HIS USUAL PRICKLY SELF.
I DECIDED TO STAY IN THE COUNTRY OF HEARTS BECAUSE OF THE TOWER.
AND THE LIFE WE HAD INSIDE IT.
BUT NOW IT'S GONE.
IT DISAPPEARED WHEN I WASN'T LOOKING.

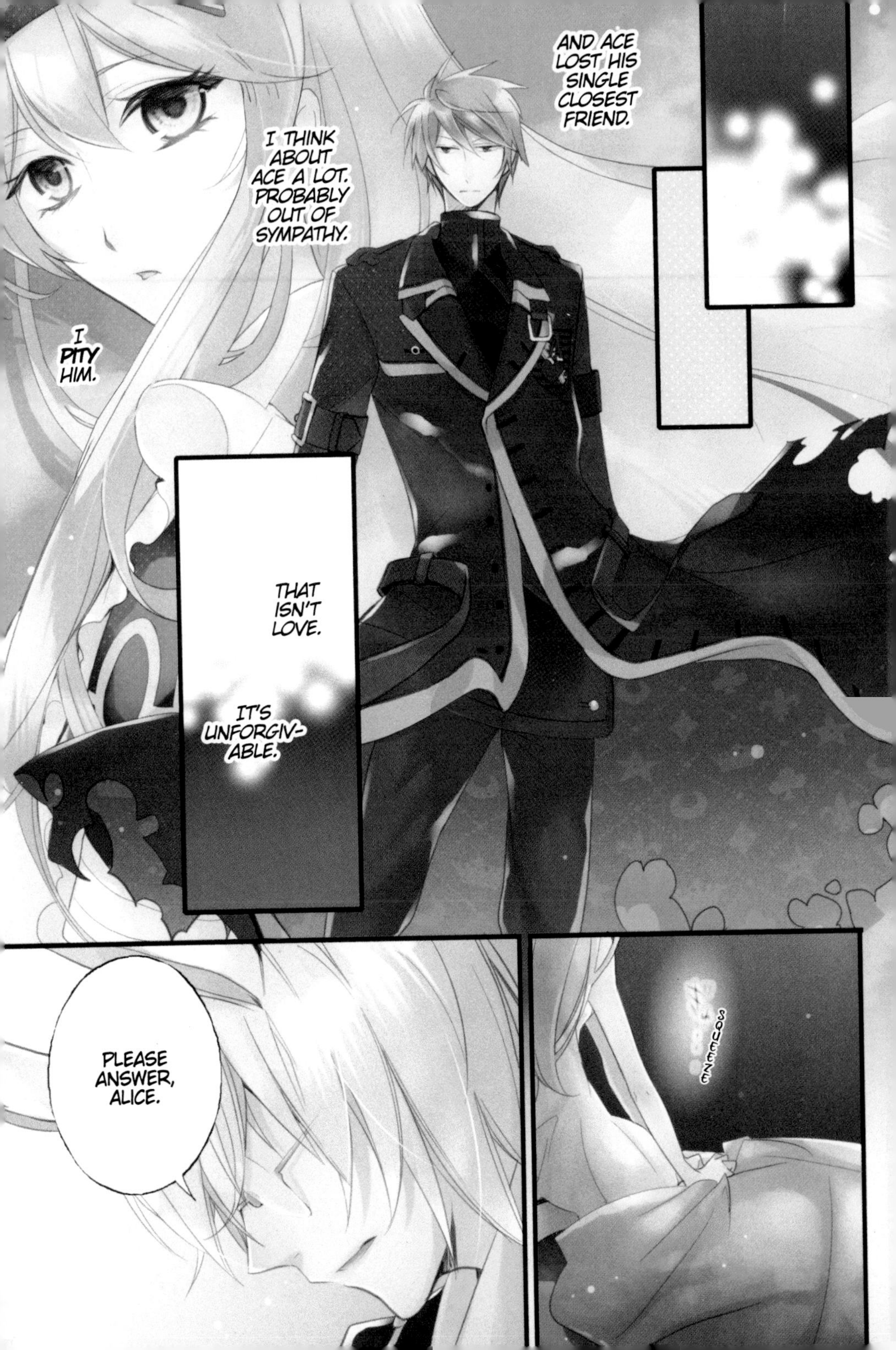
AND ACE LOST HIS SINGLE CLOSEST FRIEND.
I THINK ABOUT ACE A LOT. PROBABLY OUT OF SYMPATHY.
I PITY HIM.
THAT ISN'T LOVE.
IT'S UNFORGIV-ABLE.
SQUEEZE
PLEASE ANSWER, ALICE.

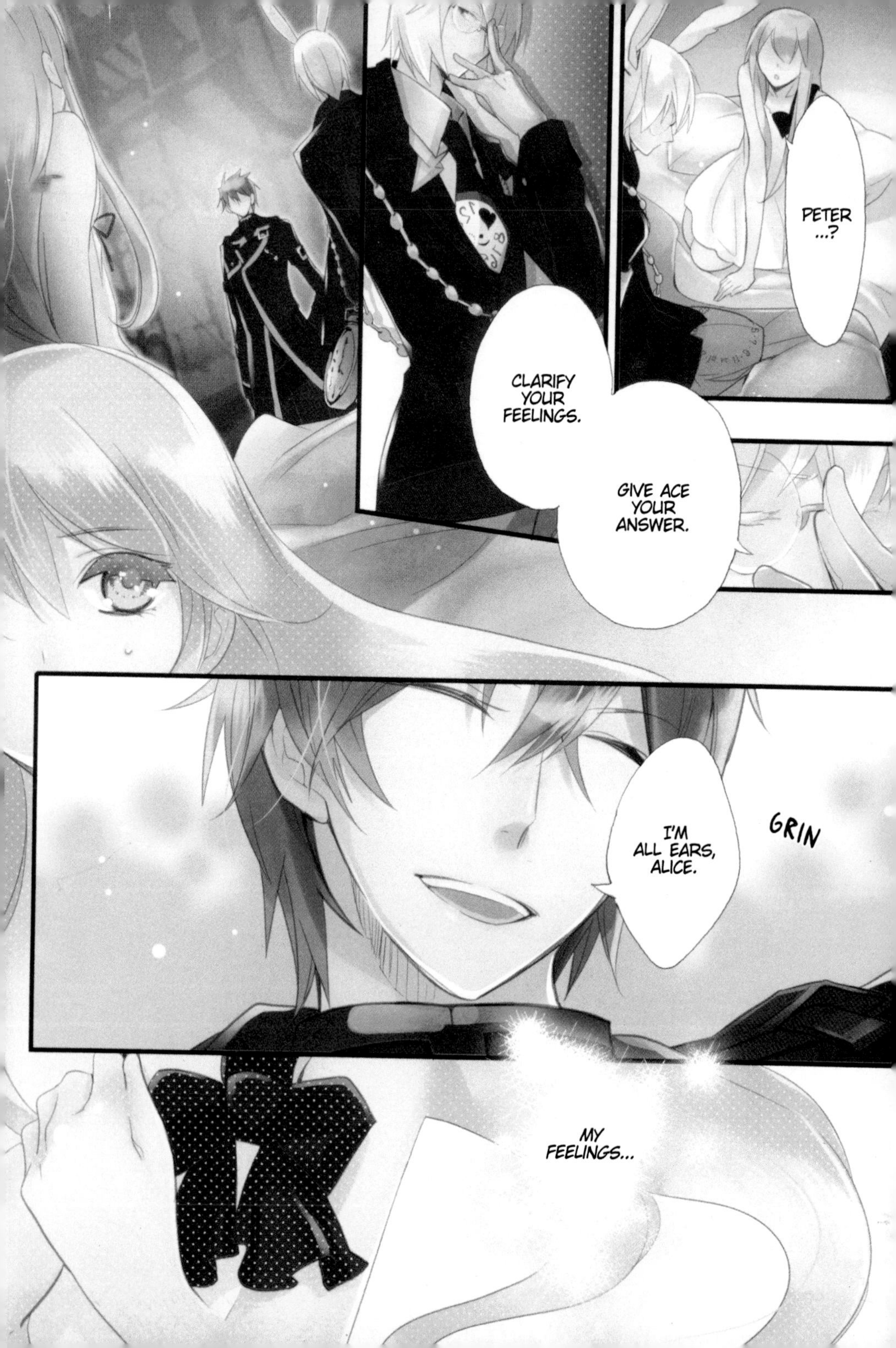
PETER ...?
CLARIFY YOUR FEELINGS.
GIVE ACE YOUR ANSWER.
I'M ALL EARS, ALICE.
GRIN
MY FEELINGS...

ALICE IN THE COUNTRY OF CLOVER 2
~Knight's Knowledge~

SAI ASAI

浅井 西

SEVEN SEAS ENTERTAINMENT PRESENTS

Alice in the Country of Clover

KNIGHT'S KNOWLEDGE VOL.2

art by SAI ASAI / story by QUINROSE

TRANSLATION
Angela Liu

ADAPTATION
Lianne Sentar

LETTERING AND LAYOUT
Laura Scoville

LOGO DESIGN
Courtney Williams

COVER DESIGN
Nicky Lim

PROOFREADER
Rebecca Scoble
Conner Crooks

MANAGING EDITOR
Adam Arnold

PUBLISHER
Jason DeAngelis

ALICE IN THE COUNTRY OF CLOVER: KNIGHT'S KNOWLEDGE VOL. 2

First published in Japan in 2012 by ICHIJINSHA Inc., Tokyo.
English translation rights arranged with ICHIJINSHA Inc., Tokyo, Japan.

Seven Seas books may be purchased in bulk for educational, business, or promotional use. For information on bulk purchases, please contact Macmillan Corporate & Premium Sales Department at 1-800-221-7945 (ext 5442) or write specialmarkets@macmillan.com.

ISBN: 978-1-626920-63-7

Printed in Canada

First Printing: September 2014

10 9 8 7 6 5 4 3 2 1

FOLLOW US ONLINE: *www.gomanga.com*

READING DIRECTIONS

This book reads from ***right to left***, Japanese style. If this is your first time reading manga, you start reading from the top right panel on each page and take it from there. If you get lost, just follow the numbered diagram here. It may seem backwards at first, but you□ll get the hang of it! Have fun!!

1
2
3
4
5
6
7
8
9

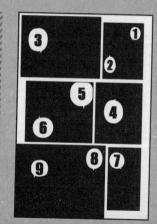

Alice in the Country of Clover
クローバーの国の
アリス
~ Wonderful Wonder World ~

- STORY -

In *Alice in the Country of Clover*, the game starts with Alice having not fallen in love, but still deciding to stay in Wonderland.

She's acquainted with all the characters from the previous game, *Alice in the Country of Hearts*.

Since love would now start from a place of friendship rather than passion with a new stranger, she can experience a different type of romance from that in the previous game. Her dynamic with the characters is different because of this friendship—characters can't always be forceful with her, and in many ways it's more comfortable to grow intimate. The relationships *between* the Ones With Duties have also become more of a factor.

In this game, the story focuses on Heart Castle. Alice attends the suited meetings (forcefully) and gets involved in various gunfights (forcefully), among other things.

Land fluctuations, sea creatures in the forest, and whispering doors—it's a game more fantastic and more eerie than the first.

Will our everywoman Alice be able to have a romantic relationship in a world devoid of common sense?

Alice in the Country of Clover
Character Information

Elliot March
VA: Tsuguo Mogami

Blood's right-hand man has a criminal past... and a temperamental present. But he's not as bad as he used to be, so that's something. Joining Blood has been good(?) for him.

Blood Dupre
VA: Katsuyuki Konishi

The head of the mafia Hatter Family, Blood is a cunning yet moody puppet-master. Alice now has the pleasure of having him for a landlord.

Alice Liddell
VA: Rie Kugimiya

A normal girl with a bit of a chip on her shoulder. Deciding to stay in the Wonderland she was carried to, she's adapted to her strange new lifestyle.

Vivaldi
VA: Yuuko Kaida

The beautiful Queen of Hearts has an unrivaled temper—which is really saying something in Wonderland. Although a picture-perfect Mad Queen, she cares for Alice as if Alice were her little sister...or a very interesting plaything.

Tweedle Dum
VA: Jun Fukuyama

The second "Bloody Twin" is equally cute and equally scary. In *Clover*, Dum can also turn into an adult.

Tweedle Dee
VA: Jun Fukuyama

One of the "Bloody Twin" gatekeepers of the Hatter territory, Dee can be cute when he's not being terrifying. In *Clover*, he sometimes turns into an adult.

Boris Airay
VA: Noriaki Sugiyama

This riddle-loving cat has a signature smirk—and in *Clover*, a new toy. One of his favorite pastimes is giving the Sleepy Mouse a hard time.

Ace
VA: Daisuke Hirakawa

The unlucky knight of Hearts was a former subordinate of Vivaldi and is perpetually lost. Even though he's depressed to be separated from his friend and boss Julius, he stays positive and tries to overcome it with a smile. He seems like a classic nice guy... or is he?

Peter White
VA: Kouki Miyata

The Prime Minister of Heart Castle—who has rabbit ears growing out of his head—invited (kidnapped) Alice to Wonderland. He loves Alice and hates everything else. His cruel, irrational actions are disturbing, but he acts like a completely different person (rabbit?) when in the throes of his love for Alice.

Gray Ringmarc
VA: Kazuya Nakai

Nightmare's subordinate in *Clover*. He used to have strong social ambition and considered assassinating Nightmare... but since Nightmare was such a useless boss, Gray couldn't help but feel sorry for him and ended up a dedicated assistant. He's a sound thinker with a strong work ethic. He's also highly skilled with his blades, rivaling even Ace.

Nightmare Gottschalk
VA: Tomokazu Sugita

A sickly nightmare who hates the hospital and needles. He has the power to read people's thoughts and enter dreams. Even though he likes to shut himself away in dreams, Gray drags him out to sulk from time to time. He technically holds a high position and has many subordinates, but since he can't even take care of his own health, he leaves most things to Gray.

Pierce Villiers
VA: Souichirou Hoshi

New to *Clover*, Pierce is an insomniac mouse who drinks too much coffee. He loves Nightmare (who can help him sleep) and hates Boris (who terrifies him). He dislikes Blood and Vivaldi for discarding coffee in favor of tea. He likes Elliot and Peter well enough, since rabbits aren't natural predators of mice.

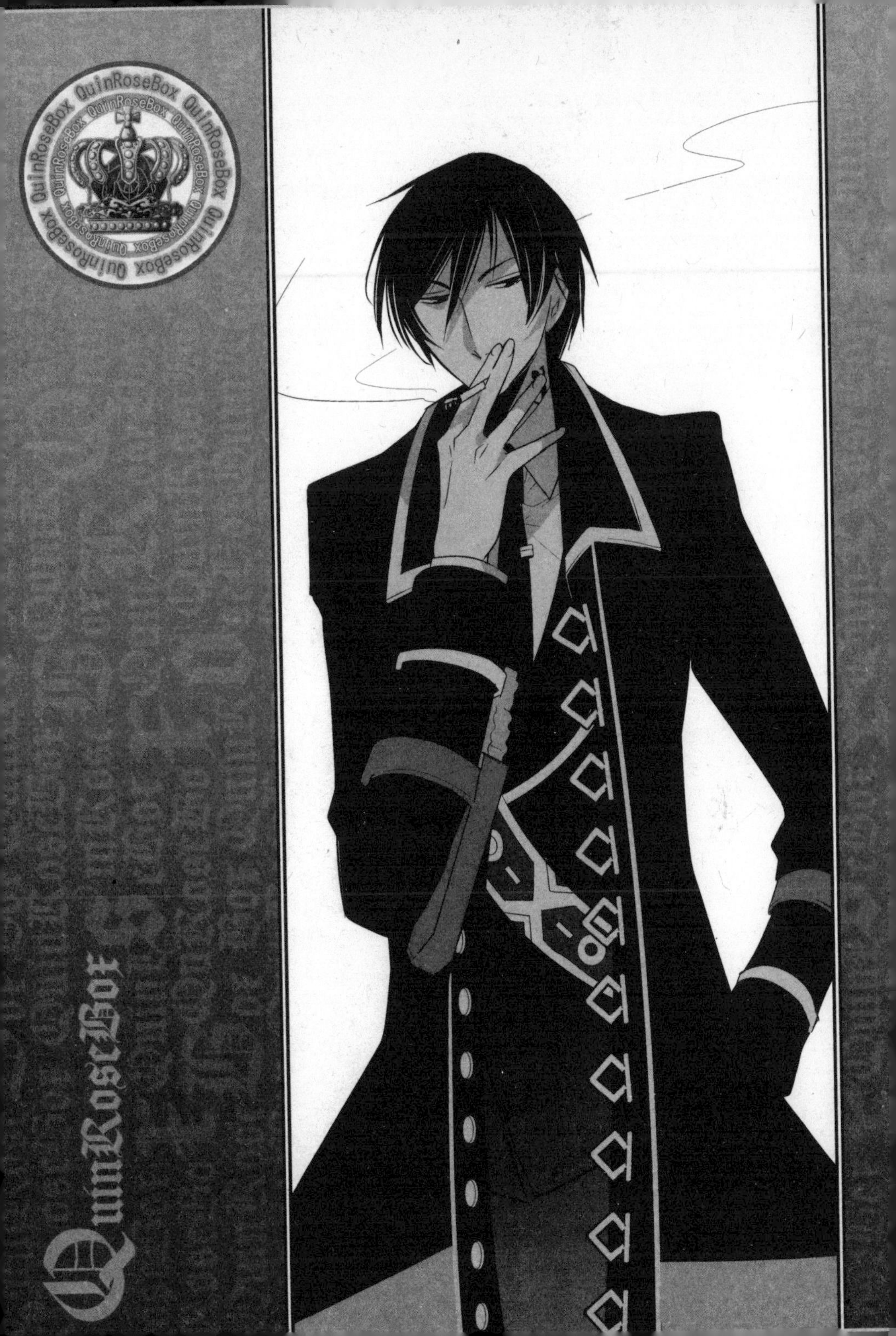
QuinRoseBox

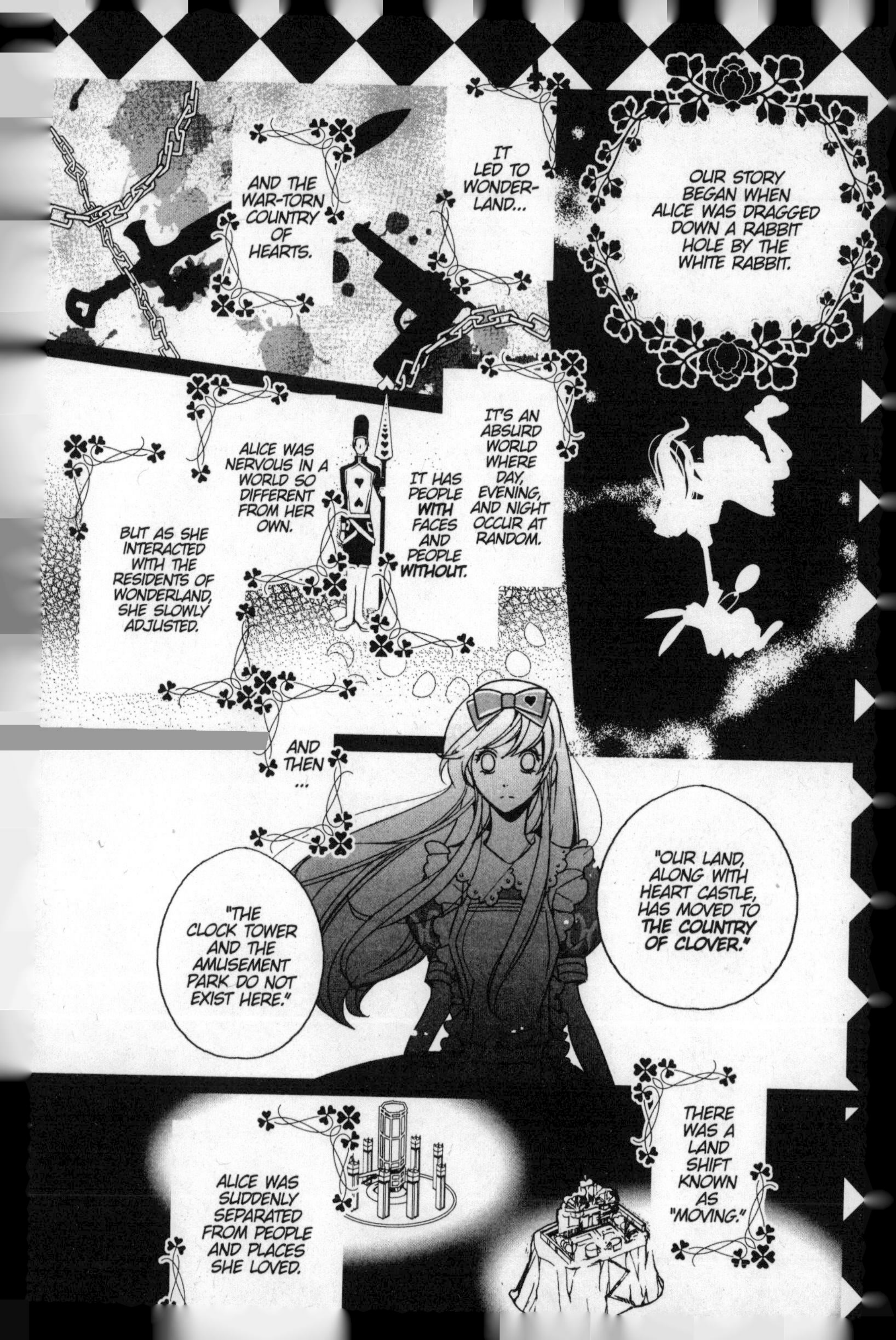
OUR STORY BEGAN WHEN ALICE WAS DRAGGED DOWN A RABBIT HOLE BY THE WHITE RABBIT.
IT LED TO WONDER-LAND...
AND THE WAR-TORN COUNTRY OF HEARTS.
IT'S AN ABSURD WORLD WHERE DAY, EVENING, AND NIGHT OCCUR AT RANDOM.
IT HAS PEOPLE **WITH** FACES AND PEOPLE **WITHOUT**.
ALICE WAS NERVOUS IN A WORLD SO DIFFERENT FROM HER OWN.
BUT AS SHE INTERACTED WITH THE RESIDENTS OF WONDERLAND, SHE SLOWLY ADJUSTED.
AND THEN ...
"OUR LAND, ALONG WITH HEART CASTLE, HAS MOVED TO **THE COUNTRY OF CLOVER.**"
"THE CLOCK TOWER AND THE AMUSEMENT PARK DO NOT EXIST HERE."
THERE WAS A LAND SHIFT KNOWN AS *"MOVING."*
ALICE WAS SUDDENLY SEPARATED FROM PEOPLE AND PLACES SHE LOVED.

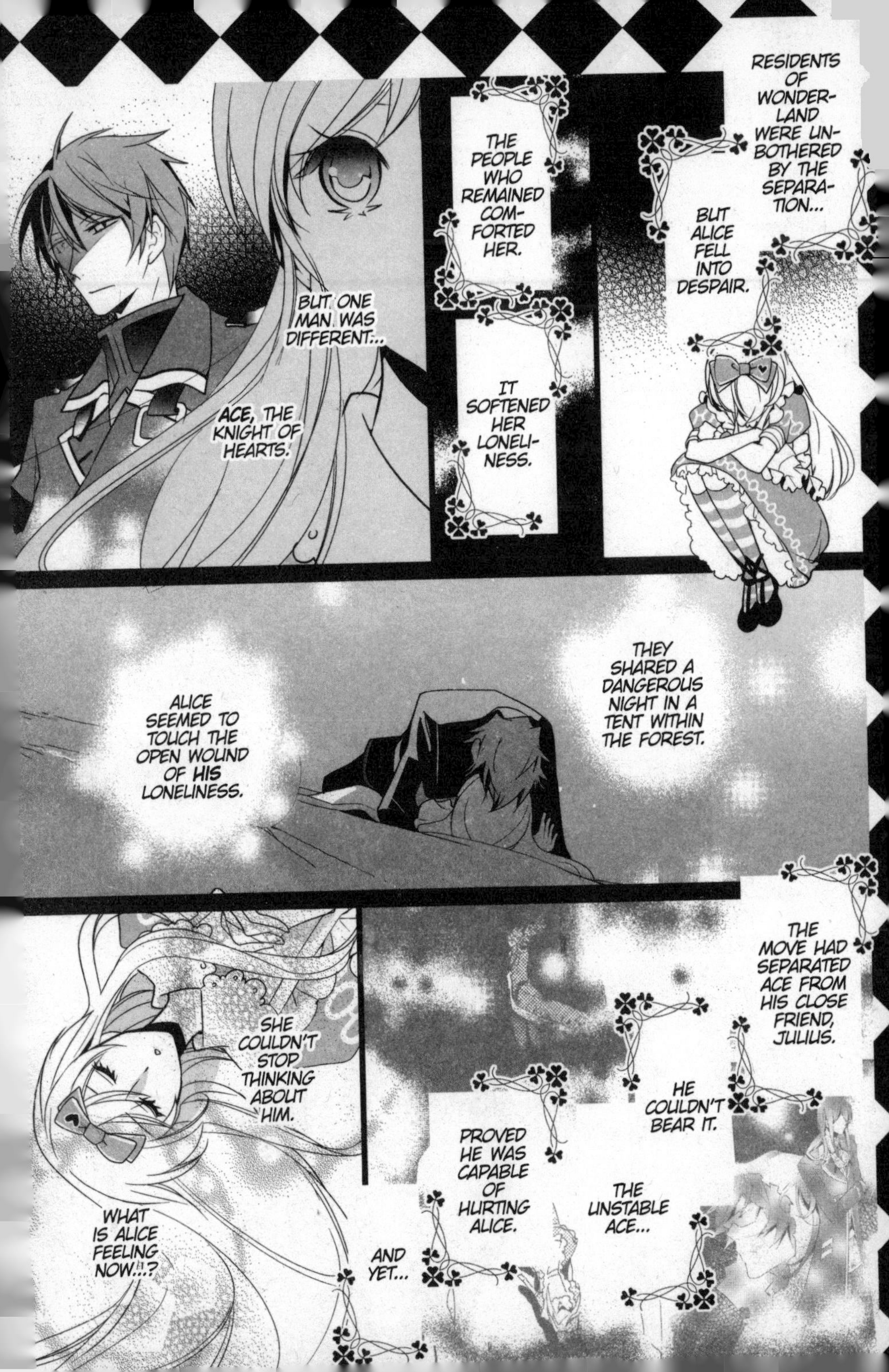
RESIDENTS OF WONDERLAND WERE UNBOTHERED BY THE SEPARATION...
BUT ALICE FELL INTO DESPAIR.
THE PEOPLE WHO REMAINED COMFORTED HER.
IT SOFTENED HER LONELINESS.
BUT ONE MAN WAS DIFFERENT...
ACE, THE KNIGHT OF HEARTS.
THEY SHARED A DANGEROUS NIGHT IN A TENT WITHIN THE FOREST.
ALICE SEEMED TO TOUCH THE OPEN WOUND OF HIS LONELINESS.
THE MOVE HAD SEPARATED ACE FROM HIS CLOSE FRIEND, JULIUS.
HE COULDN'T BEAR IT.
THE UNSTABLE ACE...
PROVED HE WAS CAPABLE OF HURTING ALICE.
AND YET...
SHE COULDN'T STOP THINKING ABOUT HIM.
WHAT IS ALICE FEELING NOW...?

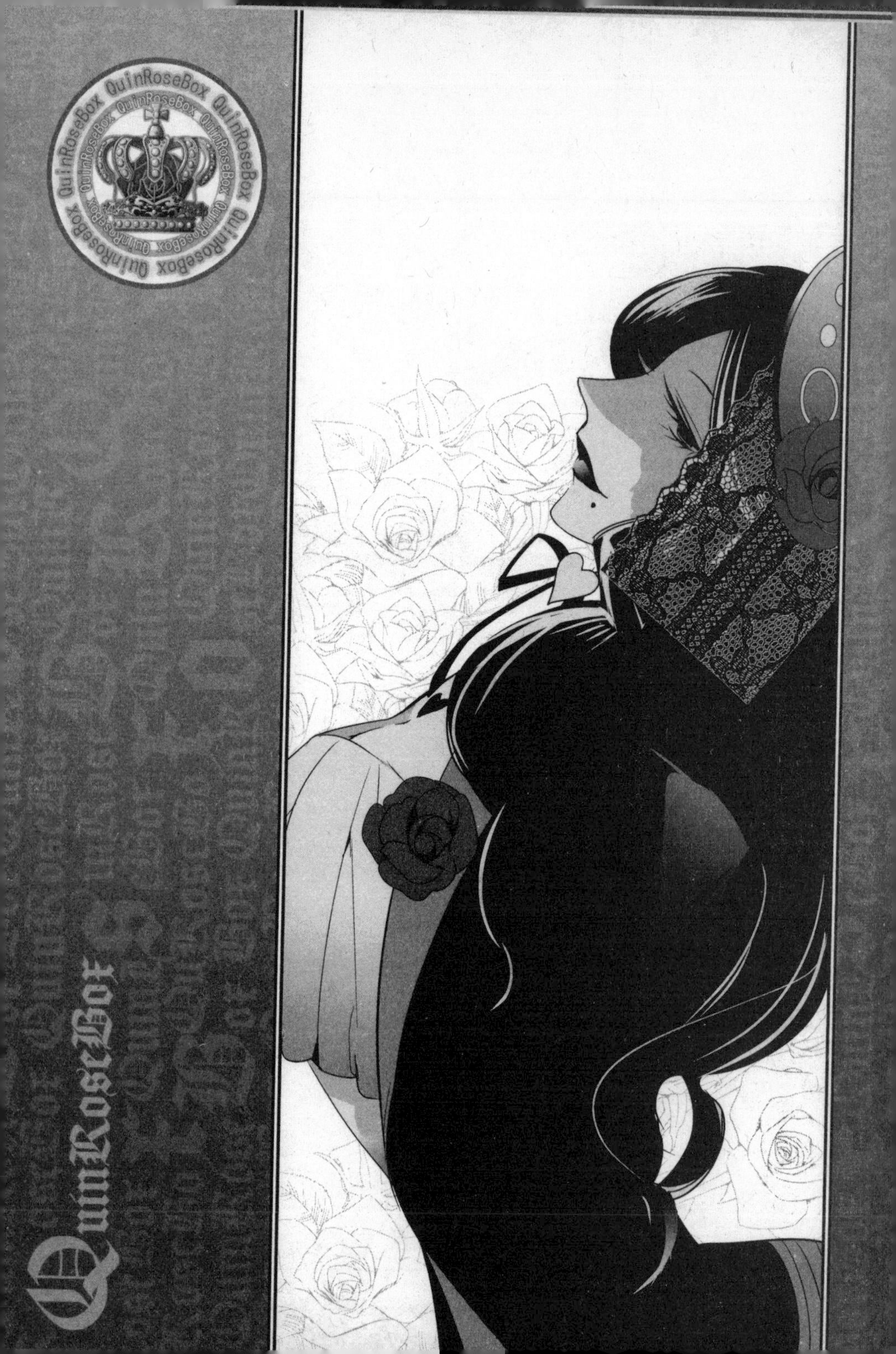
QuinRoseBox

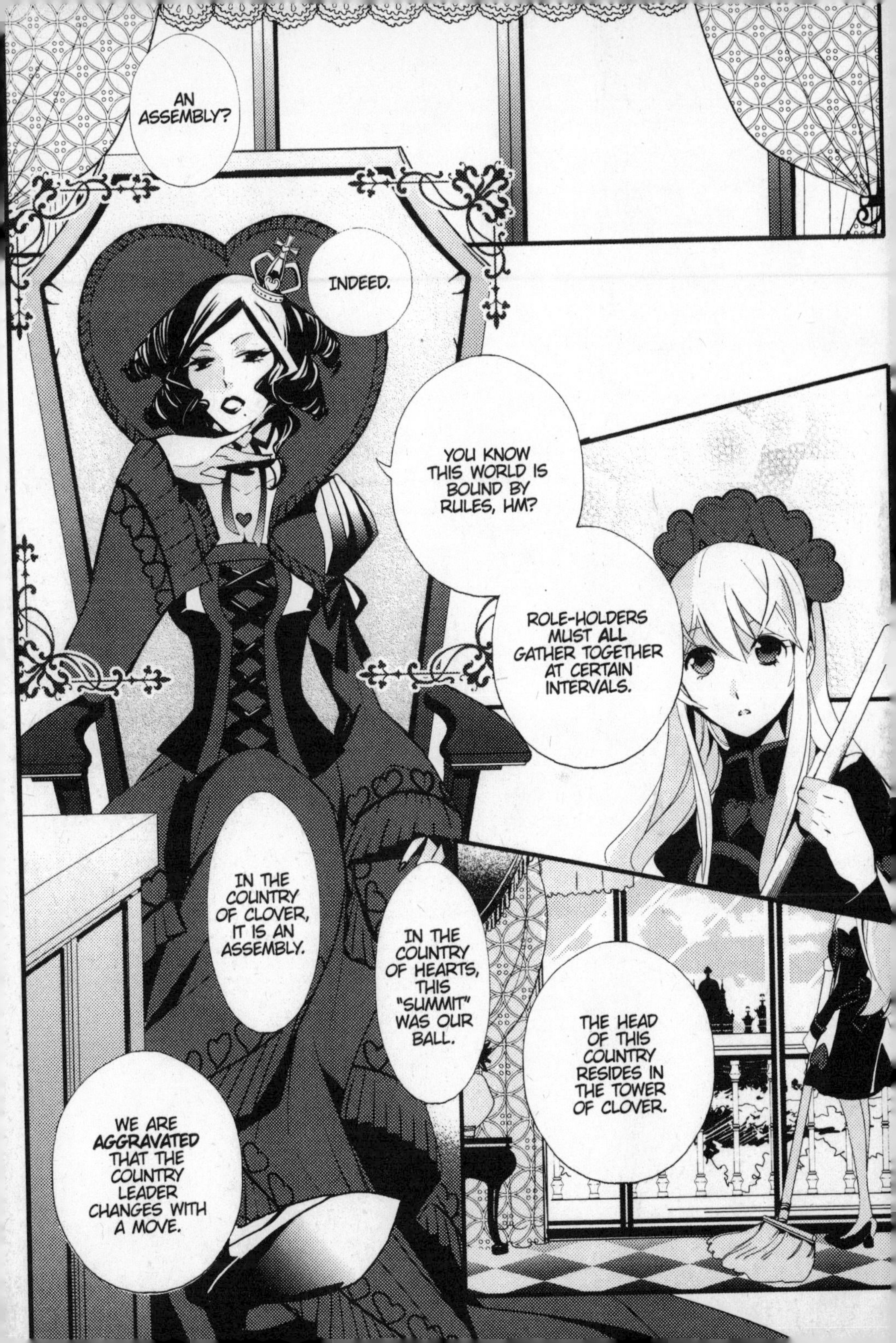
AN ASSEMBLY?
INDEED.
YOU KNOW THIS WORLD IS BOUND BY RULES, HM?
ROLE-HOLDERS MUST ALL GATHER TOGETHER AT CERTAIN INTERVALS.
IN THE COUNTRY OF HEARTS, THIS "SUMMIT" WAS OUR BALL.
IN THE COUNTRY OF CLOVER, IT IS AN ASSEMBLY.
THE HEAD OF THIS COUNTRY RESIDES IN THE TOWER OF CLOVER.
WE ARE **AGGRAVATED** THAT THE COUNTRY LEADER CHANGES WITH A MOVE.

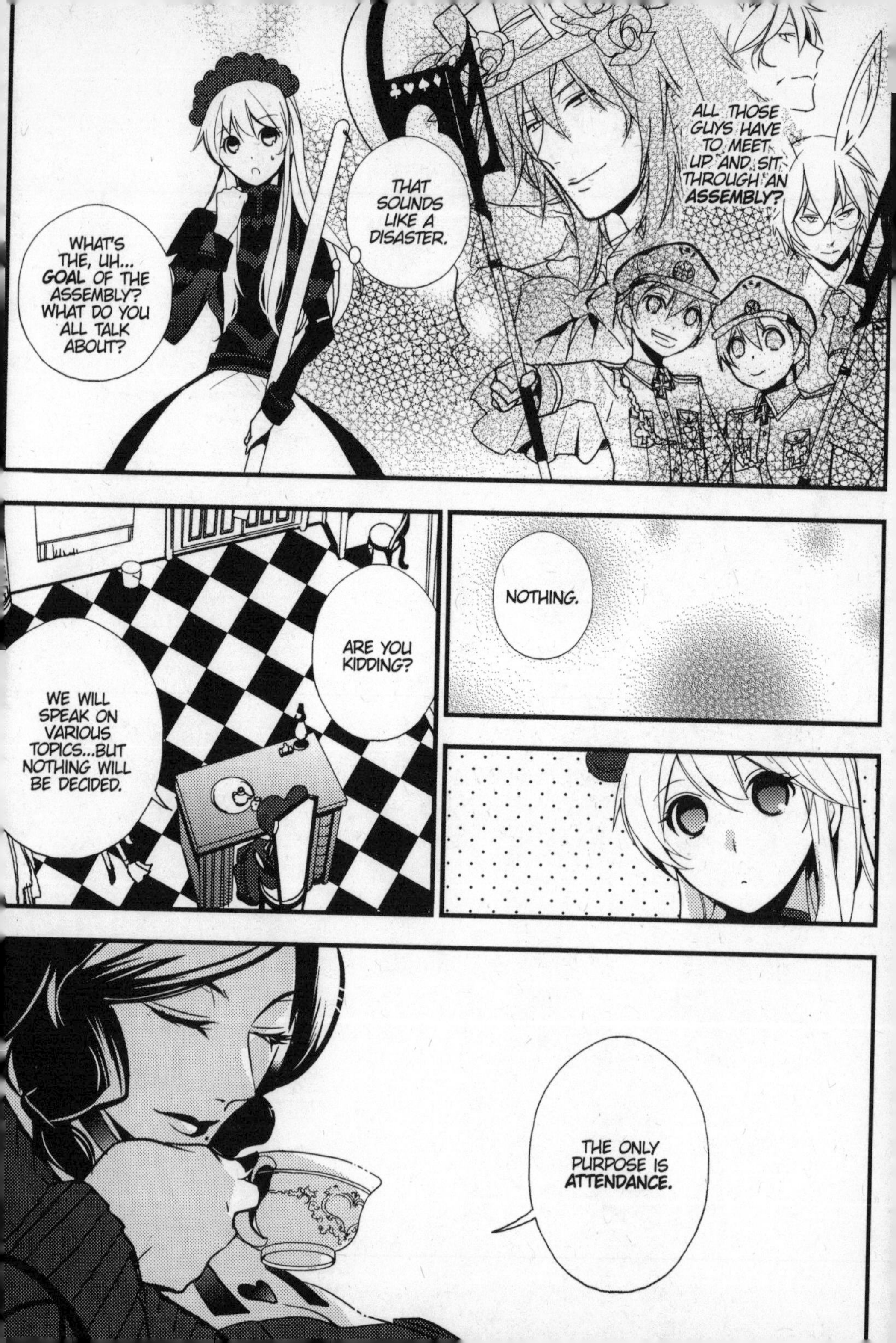
ALL THOSE GUYS HAVE TO MEET UP AND SIT THROUGH AN ASSEMBLY?
THAT SOUNDS LIKE A DISASTER.
WHAT'S THE, UH... GOAL OF THE ASSEMBLY? WHAT DO YOU ALL TALK ABOUT?
NOTHING.
ARE YOU KIDDING?
WE WILL SPEAK ON VARIOUS TOPICS...BUT NOTHING WILL BE DECIDED.
THE ONLY PURPOSE IS ATTENDANCE.

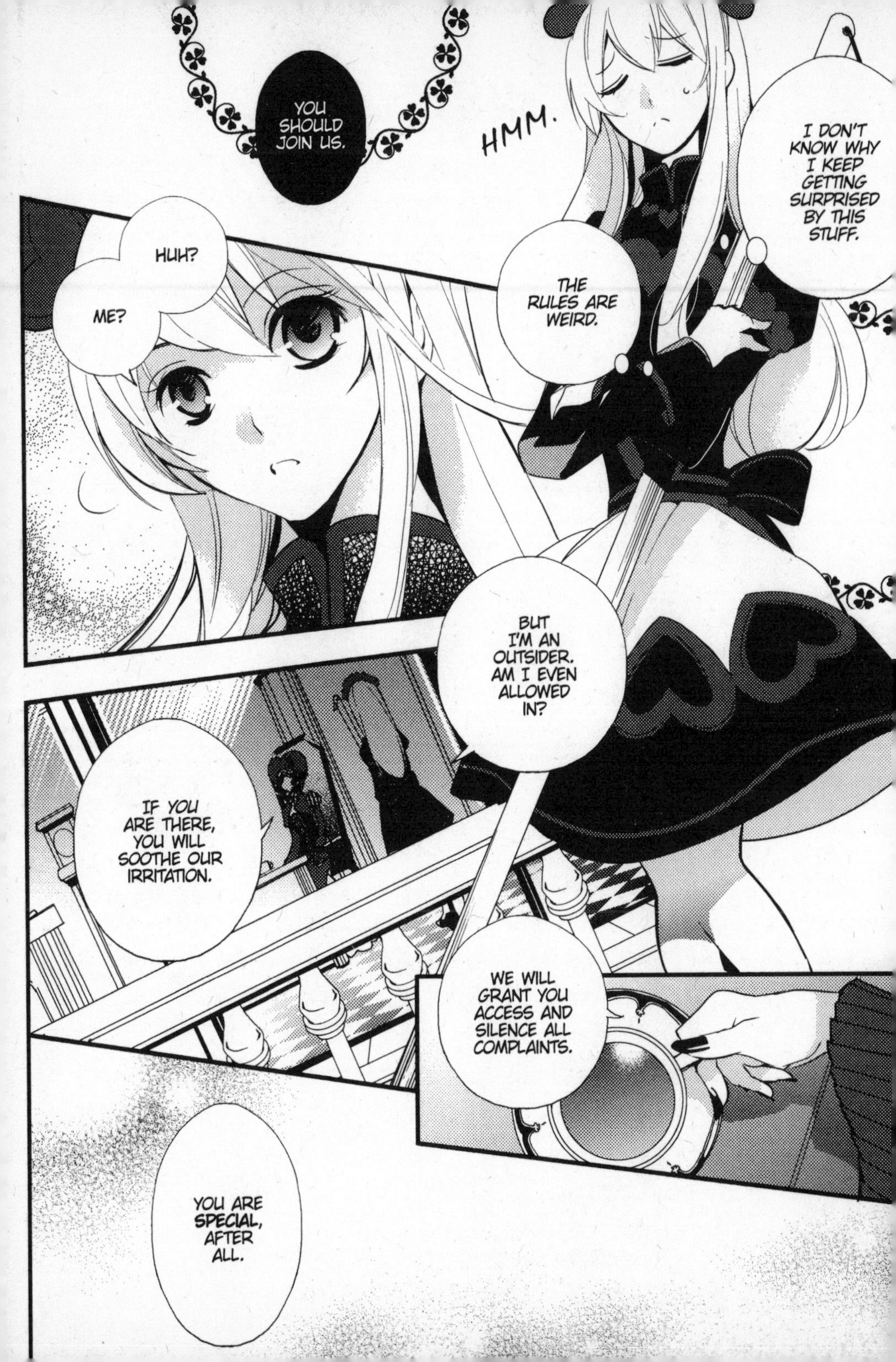
I DON'T KNOW WHY I KEEP GETTING SURPRISED BY THIS STUFF.
HMM.
YOU SHOULD JOIN US.
HUH?
ME?
THE RULES ARE WEIRD.
BUT I'M AN OUTSIDER. AM I EVEN ALLOWED IN?
IF YOU ARE THERE, YOU WILL SOOTHE OUR IRRITATION.
WE WILL GRANT YOU ACCESS AND SILENCE ALL COMPLAINTS.
YOU ARE **SPECIAL**, AFTER ALL.

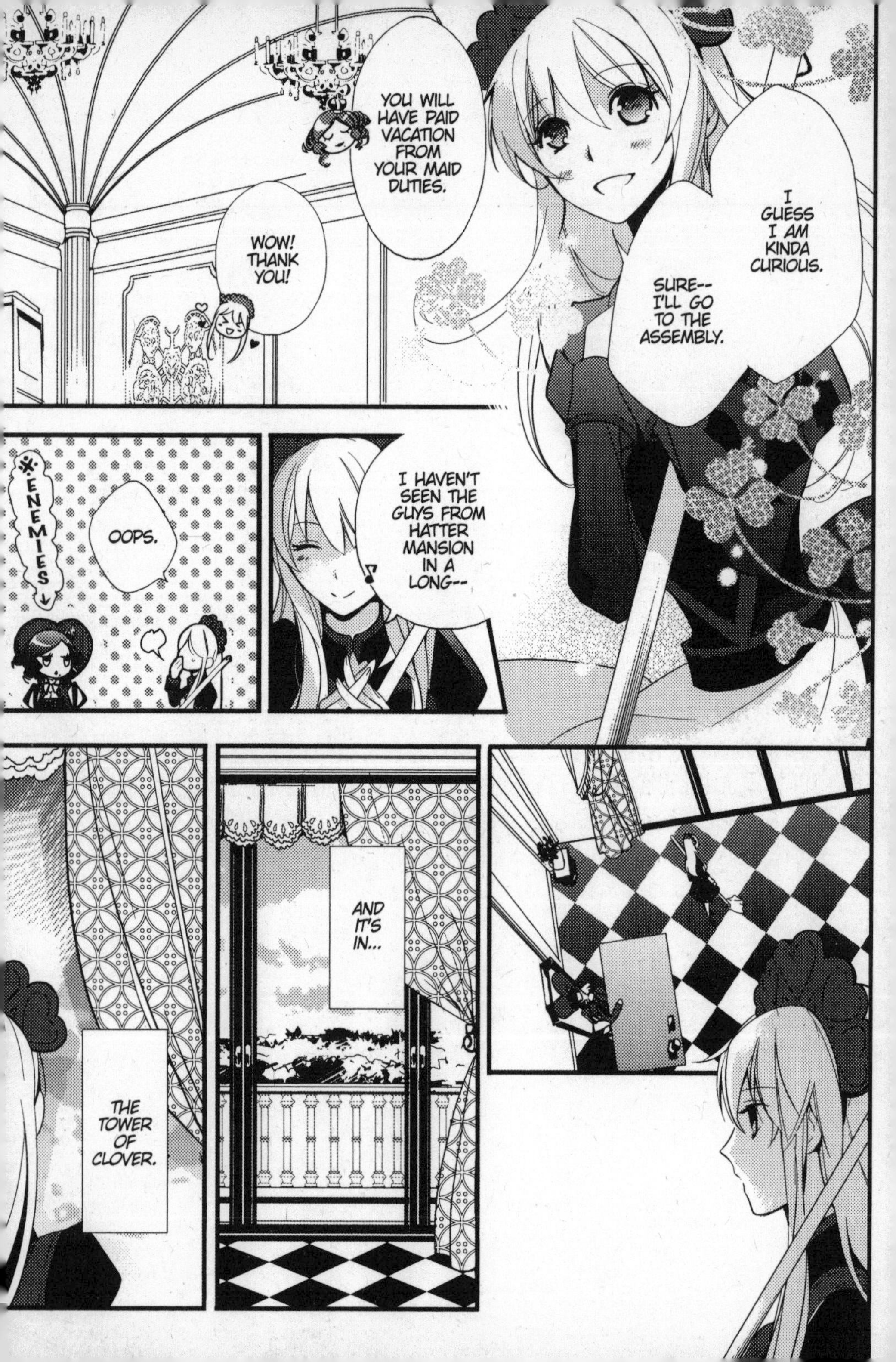
I GUESS I AM KINDA CURIOUS.
SURE-- I'LL GO TO THE ASSEMBLY.
YOU WILL HAVE PAID VACATION FROM YOUR MAID DUTIES.
WOW! THANK YOU!
I HAVEN'T SEEN THE GUYS FROM HATTER MANSION IN A LONG--
※ENEMIES
OOPS.
AND IT'S IN...
THE TOWER OF CLOVER.

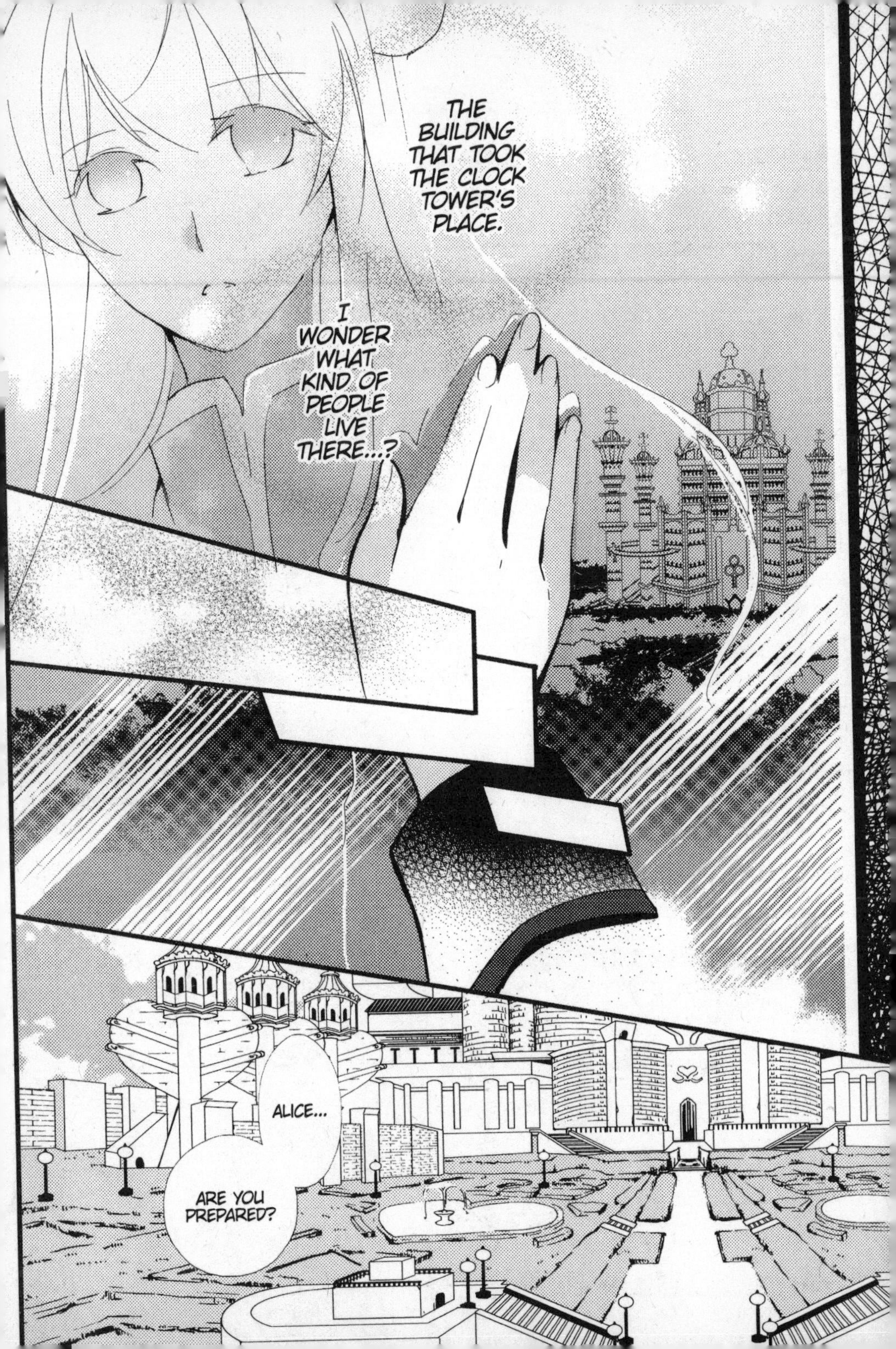
THE BUILDING THAT TOOK THE CLOCK TOWER'S PLACE.
I WONDER WHAT KIND OF PEOPLE LIVE THERE...?
ALICE...
ARE YOU PREPARED?

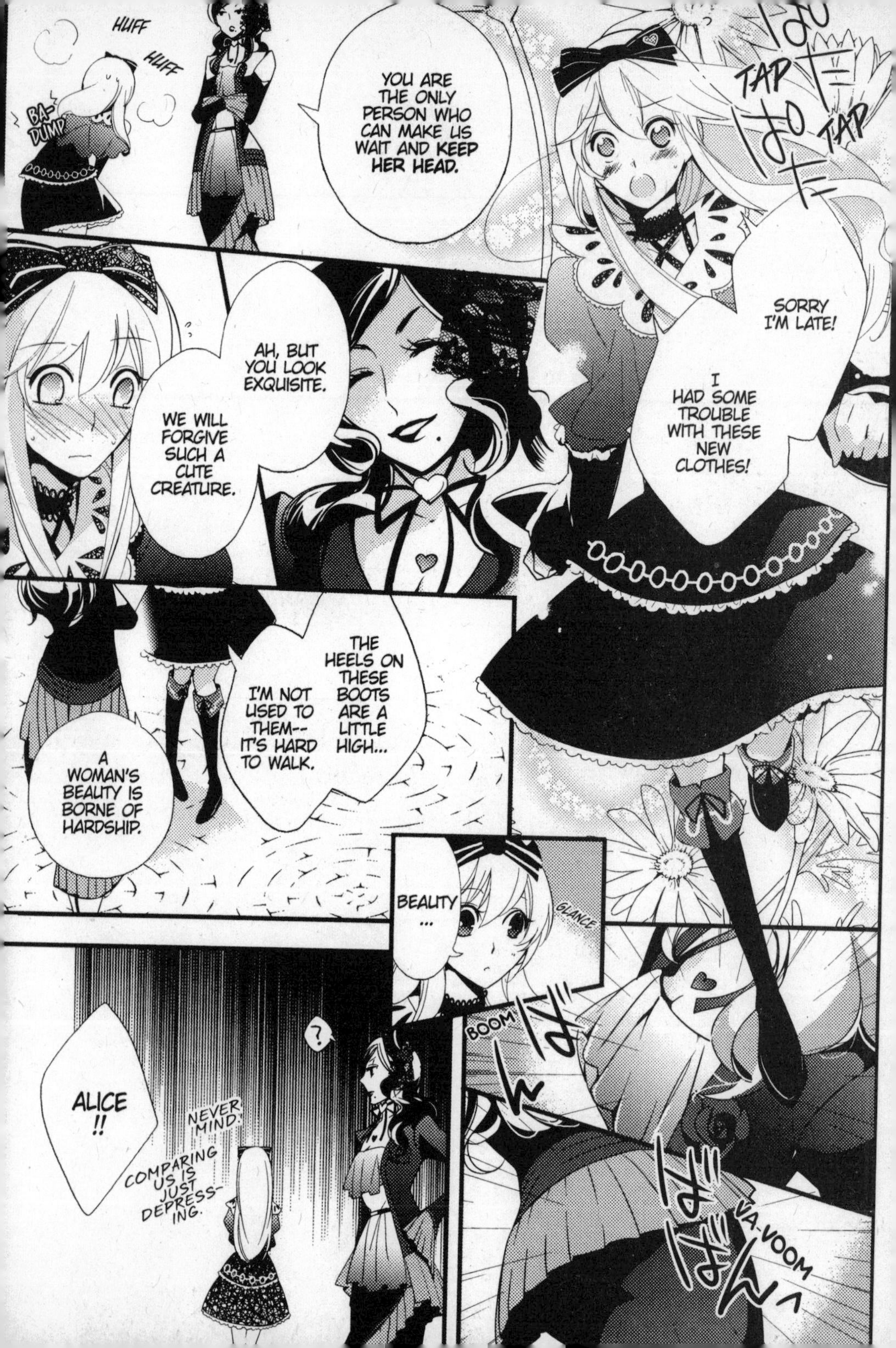

TAP
TAP
SORRY I'M LATE!
I HAD SOME TROUBLE WITH THESE NEW CLOTHES!
HUFF
HUFF
BA-DUMP
YOU ARE THE ONLY PERSON WHO CAN MAKE US WAIT AND KEEP HER HEAD.
AH, BUT YOU LOOK EXQUISITE.
WE WILL FORGIVE SUCH A CUTE CREATURE.
THE HEELS ON THESE BOOTS ARE A LITTLE HIGH...
I'M NOT USED TO THEM-- IT'S HARD TO WALK.
A WOMAN'S BEAUTY IS BORNE OF HARDSHIP.
BEAUTY ...
GLANCE
BOOM
VA-VOOM
ALICE !!
?
NEVER MIND.
COMPARING US IS JUST DEPRESSING.

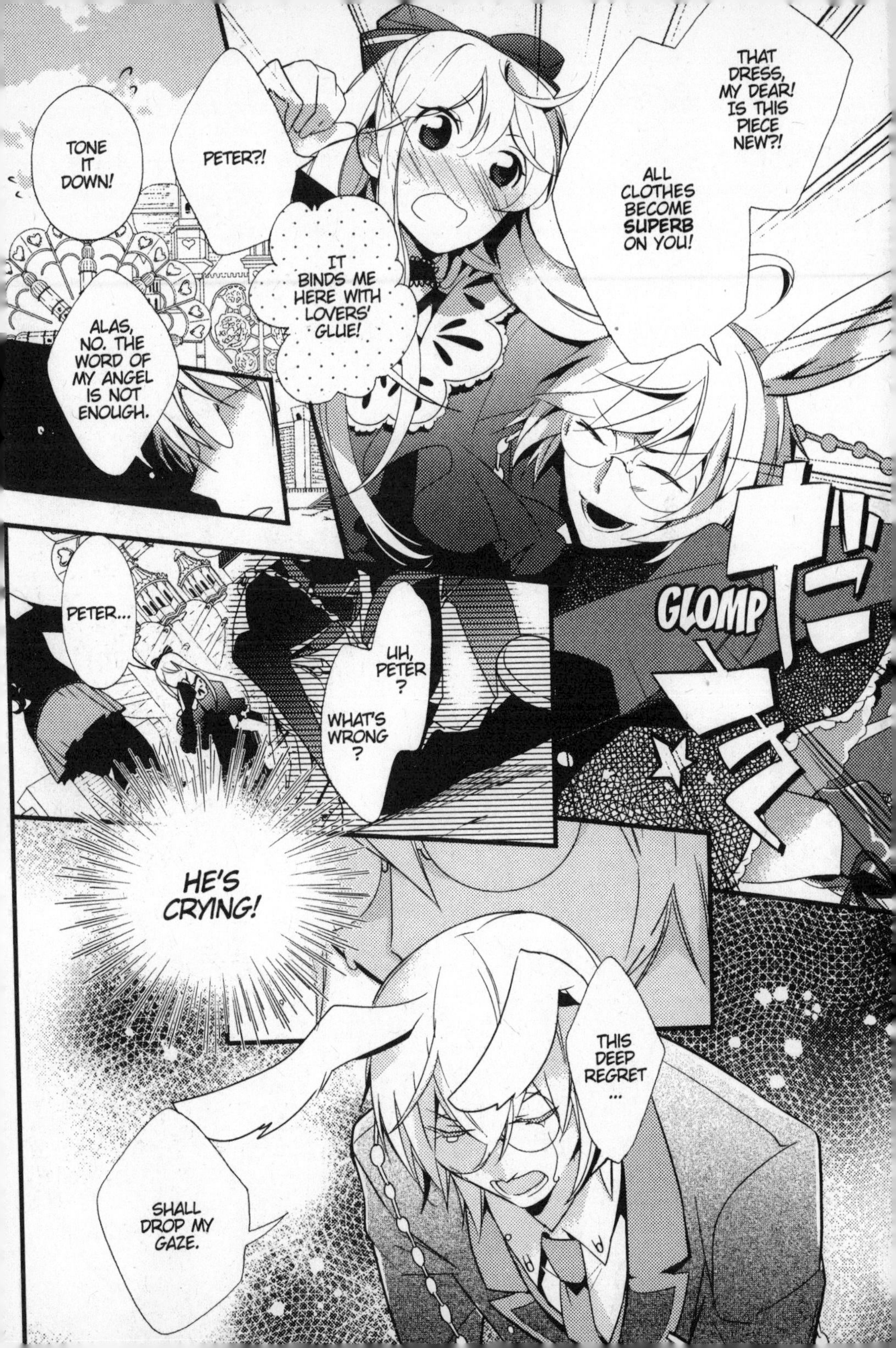
THAT DRESS, MY DEAR! IS THIS PIECE NEW?!
ALL CLOTHES BECOME SUPERB ON YOU!
PETER?!
TONE IT DOWN!
IT BINDS ME HERE WITH LOVERS' GLUE!
GLOMP
ALAS, NO. THE WORD OF MY ANGEL IS NOT ENOUGH.
UH, PETER?
WHAT'S WRONG?
PETER...
HE'S CRYING!
THIS DEEP REGRET...
SHALL DROP MY GAZE.

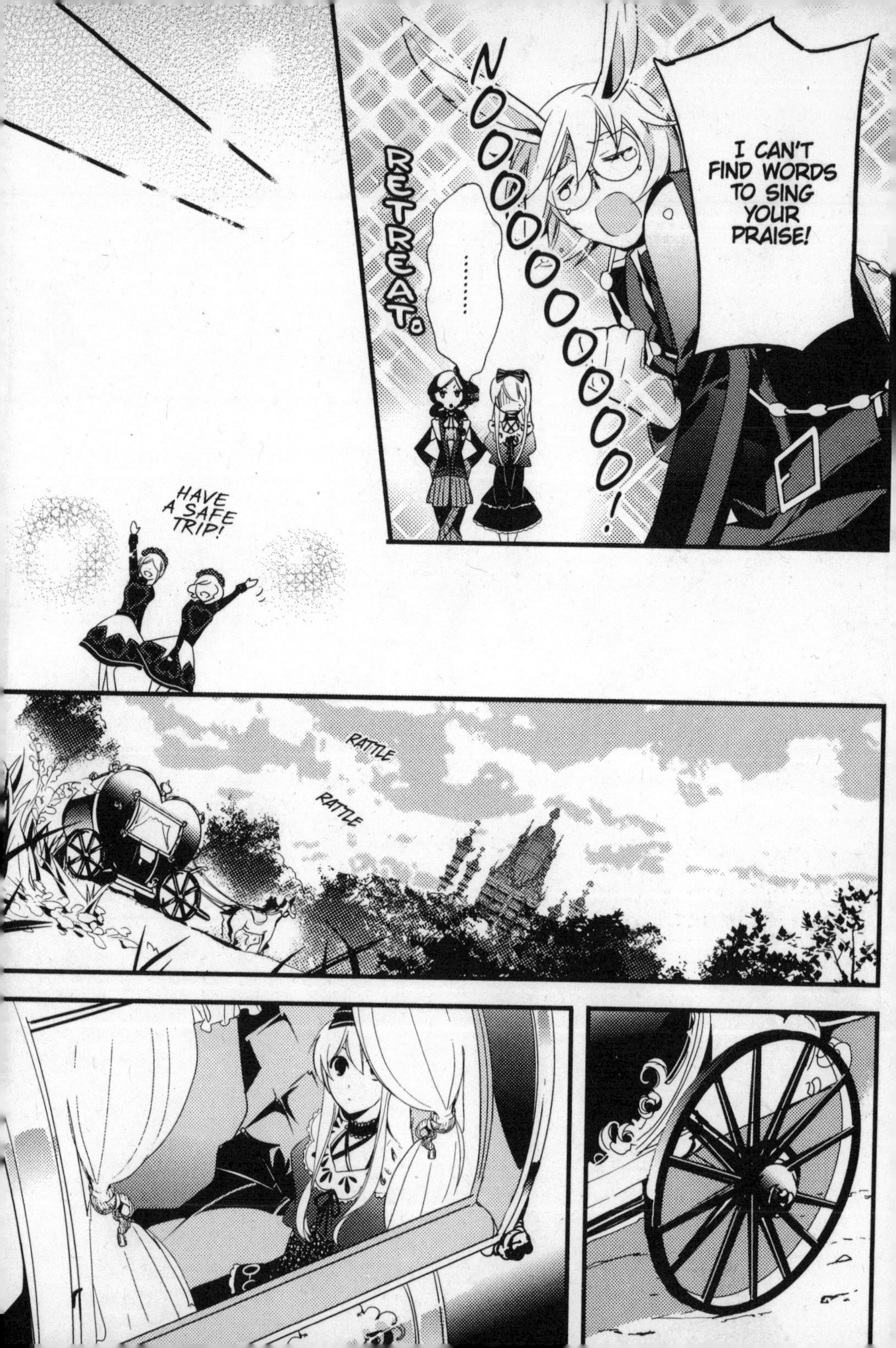
I CAN'T FIND WORDS TO SING YOUR PRAISE!
NOOOOOOOOOOOO!
RETREAT.
......
HAVE A SAFE TRIP!
RATTLE
RATTLE

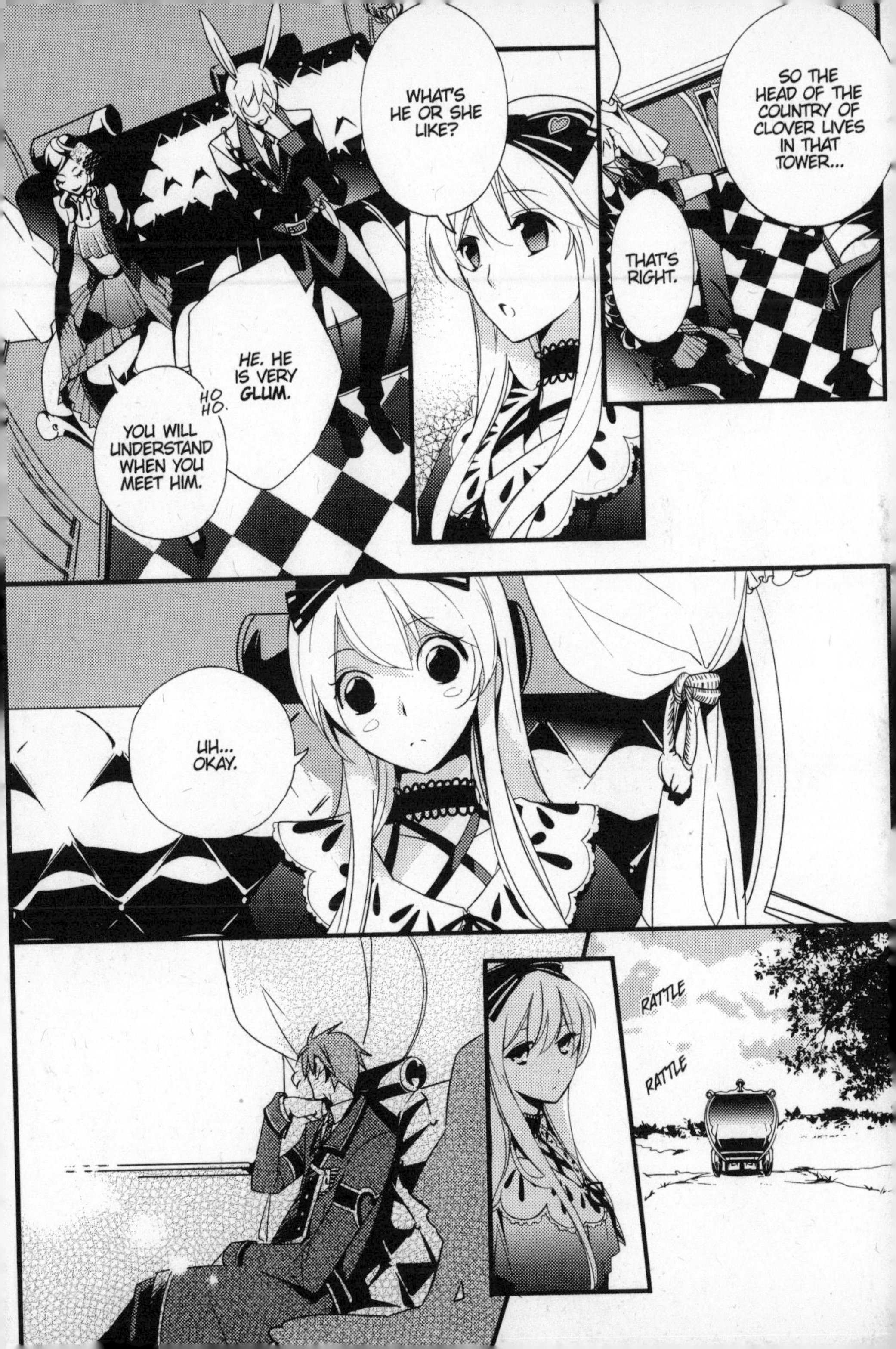
SO THE HEAD OF THE COUNTRY OF CLOVER LIVES IN THAT TOWER...
THAT'S RIGHT.
WHAT'S HE OR SHE LIKE?
HE, HE IS VERY GLUM.
HO HO.
YOU WILL UNDERSTAND WHEN YOU MEET HIM.
UH... OKAY.
RATTLE
RATTLE

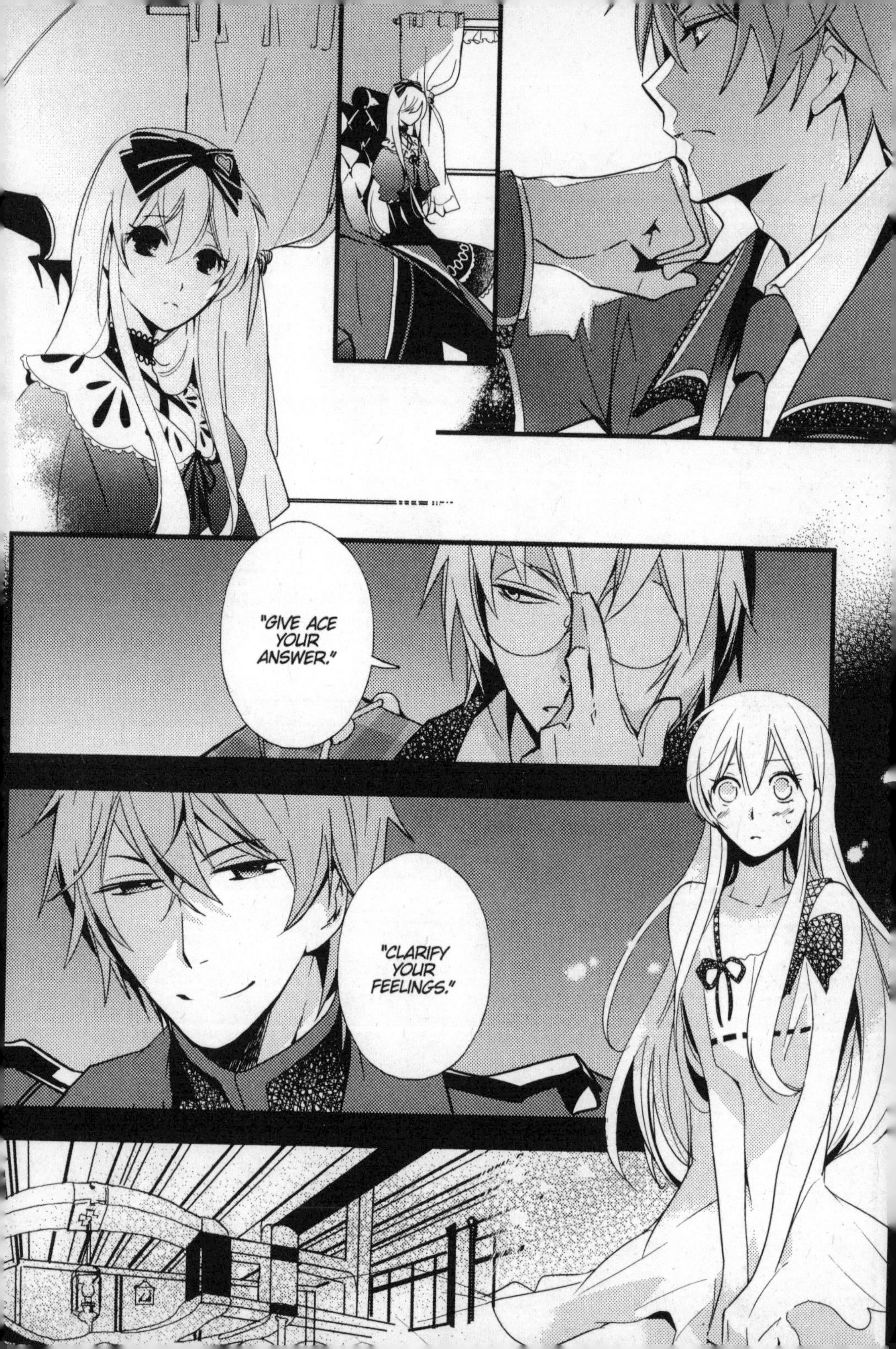
"GIVE ACE YOUR ANSWER."
"CLARIFY YOUR FEELINGS."

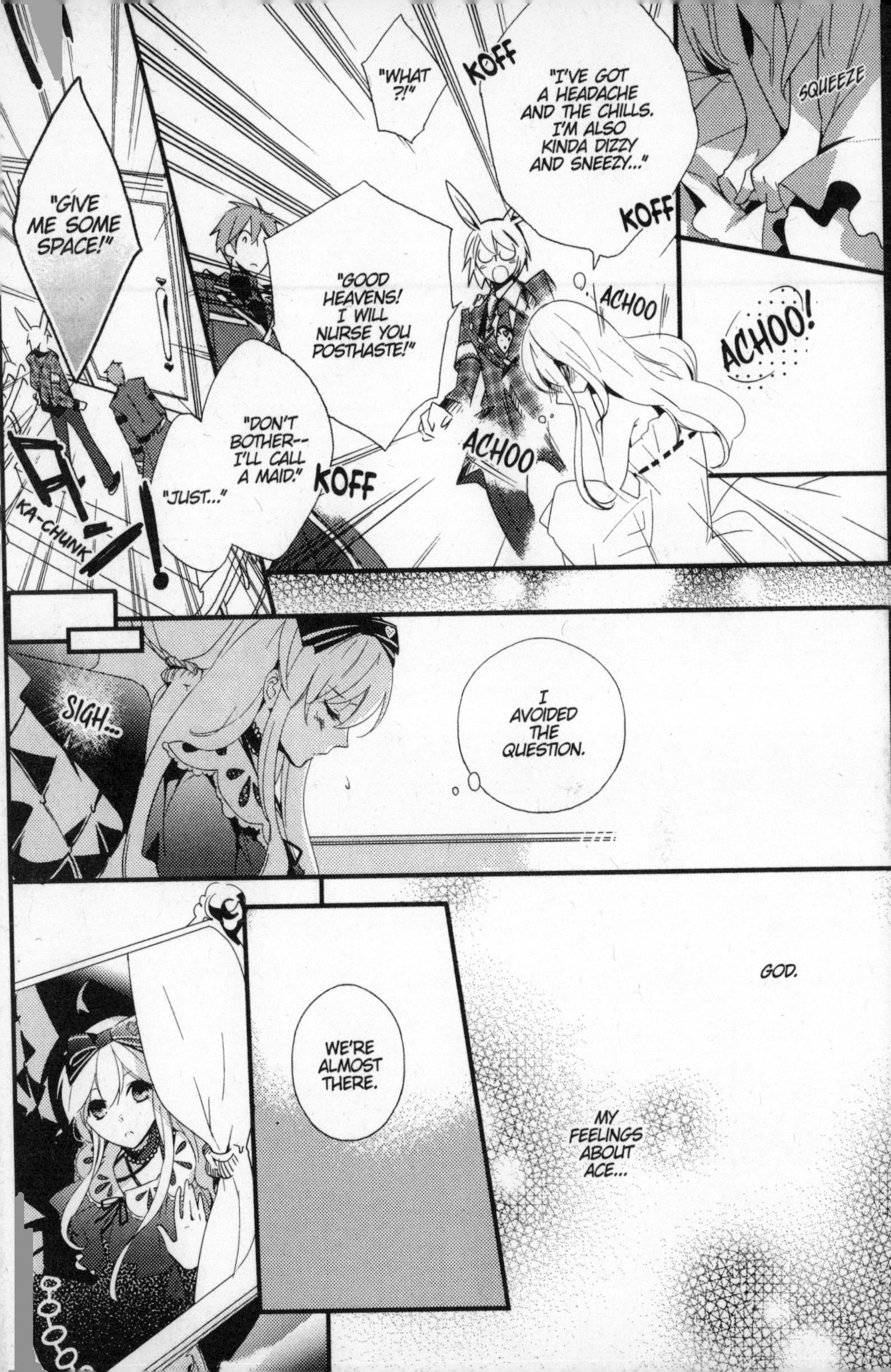
SQUEEZE
ACHOO!
"I'VE GOT A HEADACHE AND THE CHILLS. I'M ALSO KINDA DIZZY AND SNEEZY..."
KOFF
KOFF
ACHOO
"WHAT ?!"
"GOOD HEAVENS! I WILL NURSE YOU POSTHASTE!"
"DON'T BOTHER-- I'LL CALL A MAID."
KOFF
ACHOO
"JUST..."
"GIVE ME SOME SPACE!"
KA-CHUNK
I AVOIDED THE QUESTION.
SIGH...
GOD.
MY FEELINGS ABOUT ACE...
WE'RE ALMOST THERE.

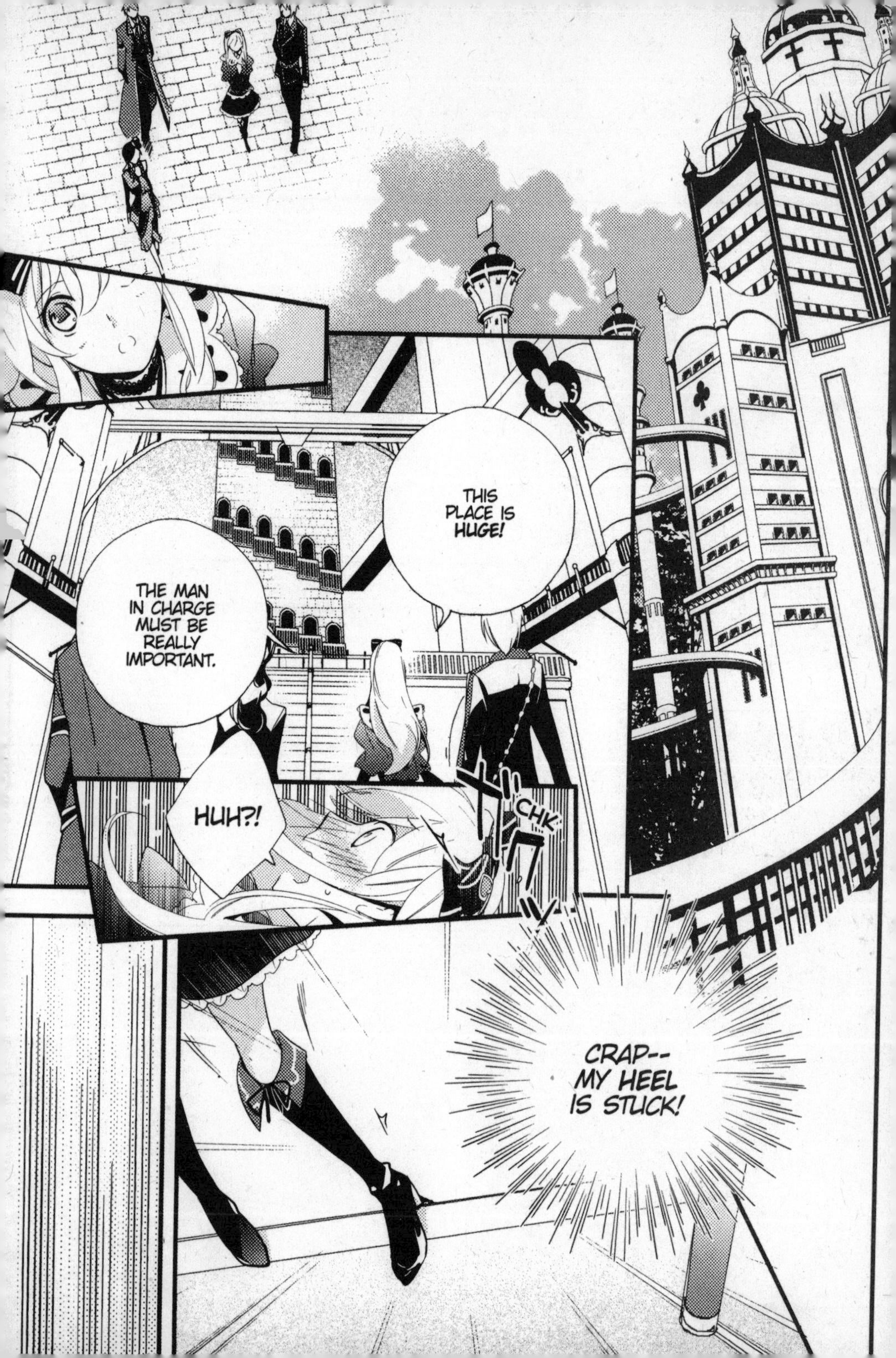
THIS PLACE IS HUGE!
THE MAN IN CHARGE MUST BE REALLY IMPORTANT.
CHK
HUH?!
CRAP-- MY HEEL IS STUCK!

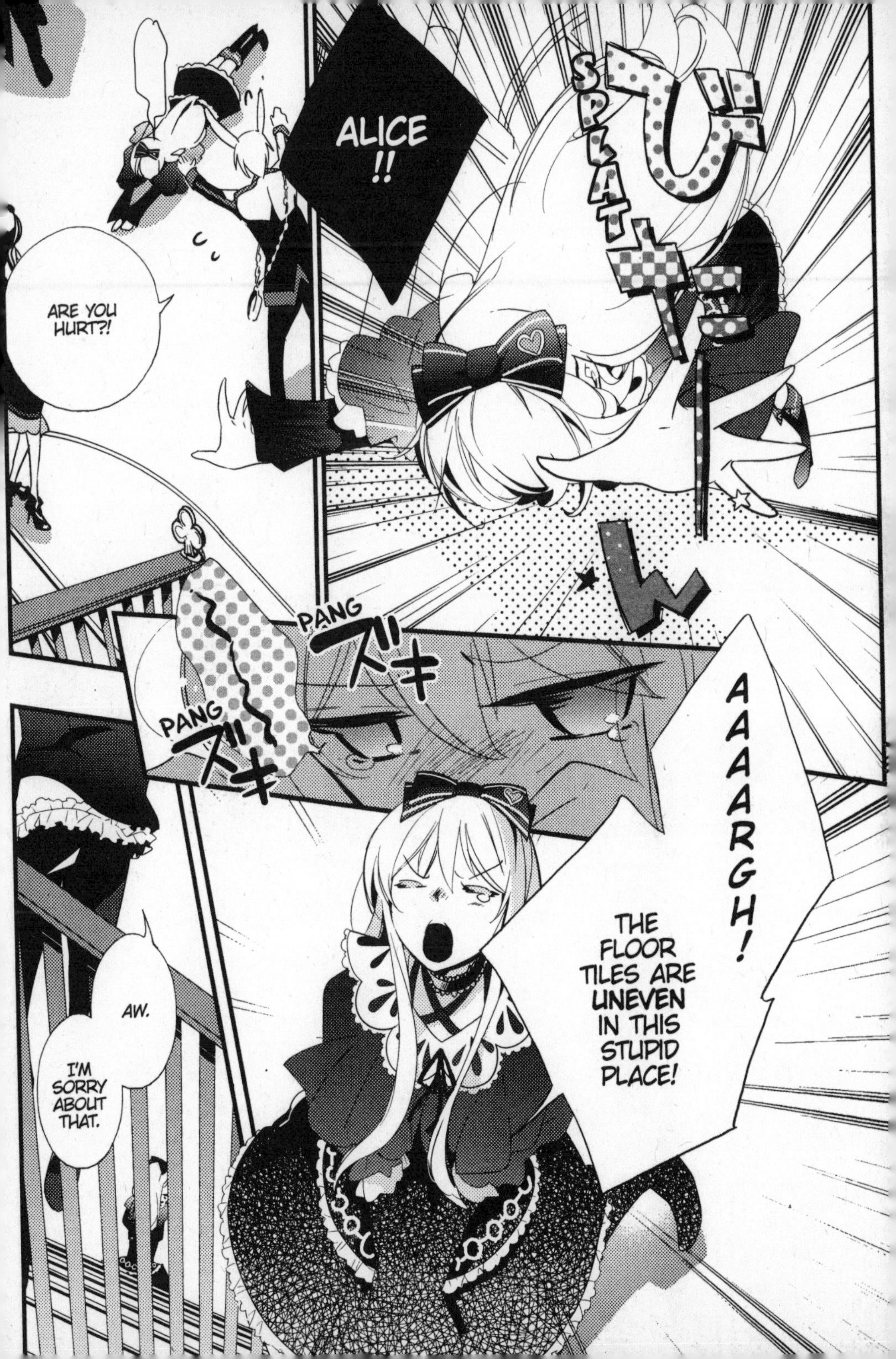
SPLAT
ALICE !!
ARE YOU HURT?!
PANG
PANG
AAAARGH!
THE FLOOR TILES ARE UNEVEN IN THIS STUPID PLACE!
AW.
I'M SORRY ABOUT THAT.

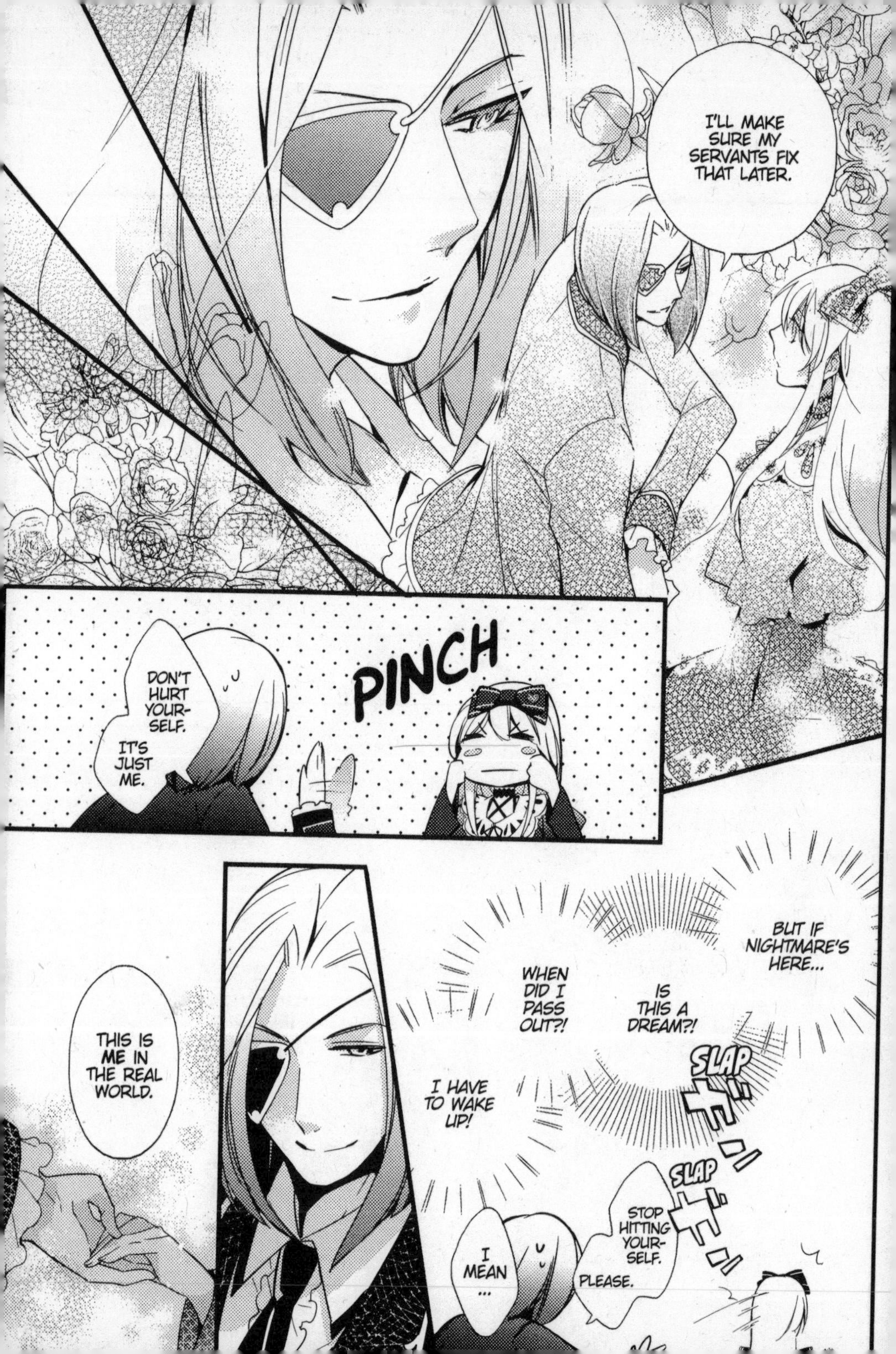
I'LL MAKE SURE MY SERVANTS FIX THAT LATER.
PINCH
DON'T HURT YOUR-SELF.
IT'S JUST ME.
BUT IF NIGHTMARE'S HERE...
IS THIS A DREAM?!
WHEN DID I PASS OUT?!
SLAP
I HAVE TO WAKE UP!
SLAP
STOP HITTING YOUR-SELF.
PLEASE.
I MEAN ...
THIS IS ME IN THE REAL WORLD.

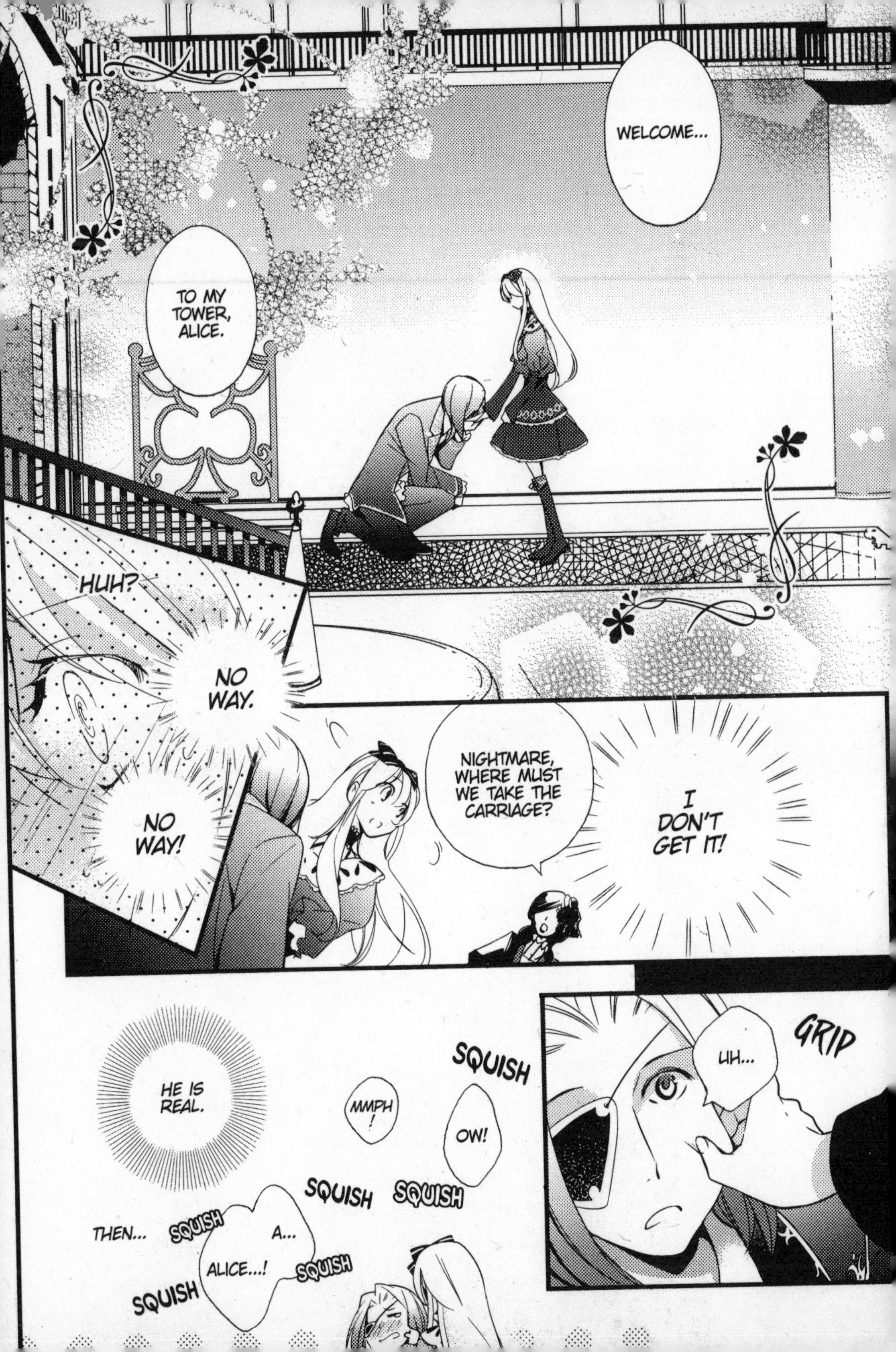
WELCOME...
TO MY TOWER, ALICE.
NIGHTMARE, WHERE MUST WE TAKE THE CARRIAGE?
I DON'T GET IT!
HUH?
NO WAY.
NO WAY!
GRIP
UH...
SQUISH
OW!
MMPH!
HE IS REAL.
SQUISH
SQUISH
A...
ALICE...!
SQUISH
THEN...
SQUISH
SQUISH

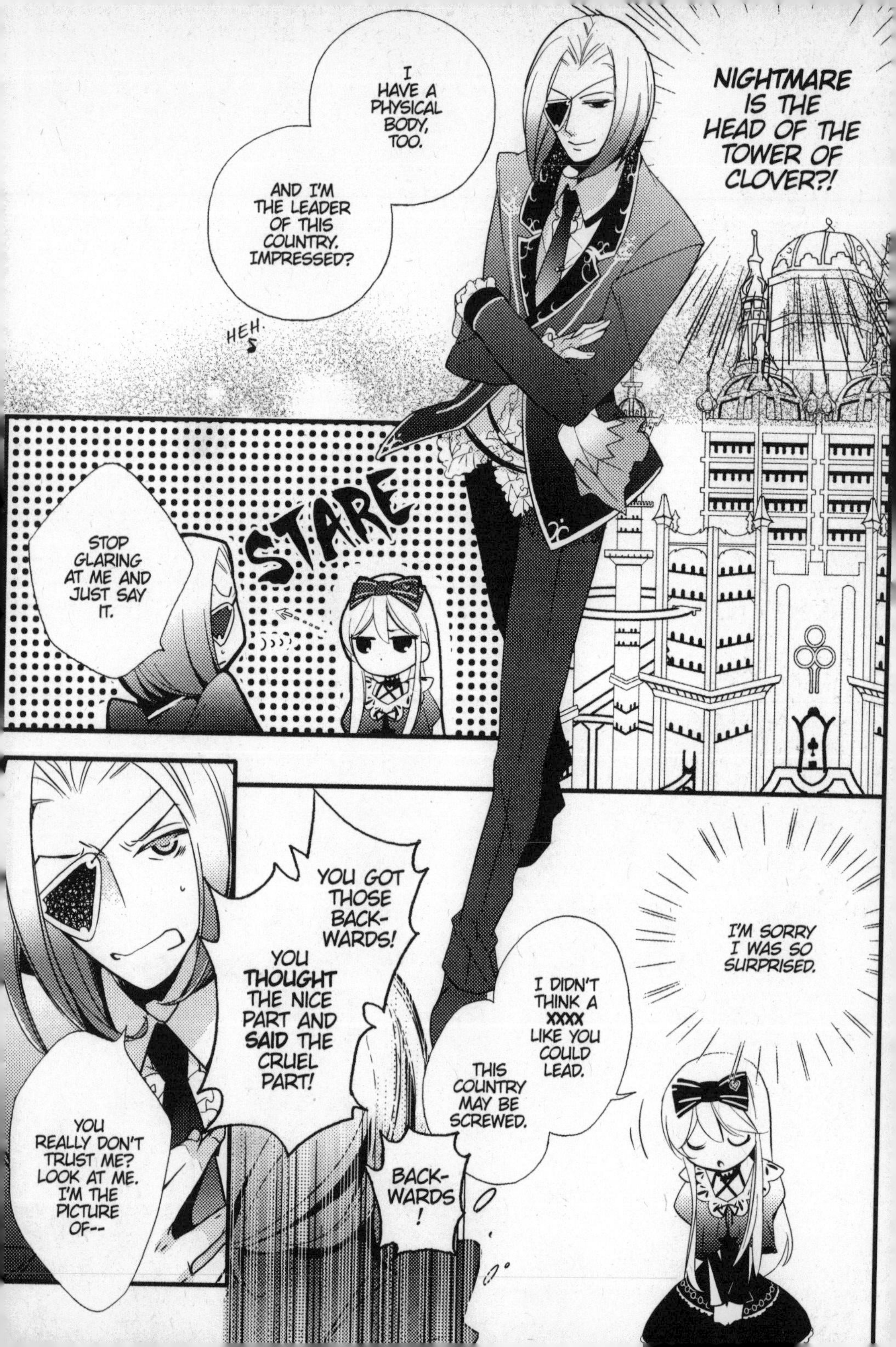
NIGHTMARE IS THE HEAD OF THE TOWER OF CLOVER?!
I HAVE A PHYSICAL BODY, TOO.
AND I'M THE LEADER OF THIS COUNTRY. IMPRESSED?
HEH.
STARE
STOP GLARING AT ME AND JUST SAY IT.
I'M SORRY I WAS SO SURPRISED.
I DIDN'T THINK A XXXX LIKE YOU COULD LEAD.
THIS COUNTRY MAY BE SCREWED.
YOU GOT THOSE BACKWARDS!
YOU THOUGHT THE NICE PART AND SAID THE CRUEL PART!
BACKWARDS!
YOU REALLY DON'T TRUST ME? LOOK AT ME. I'M THE PICTURE OF--

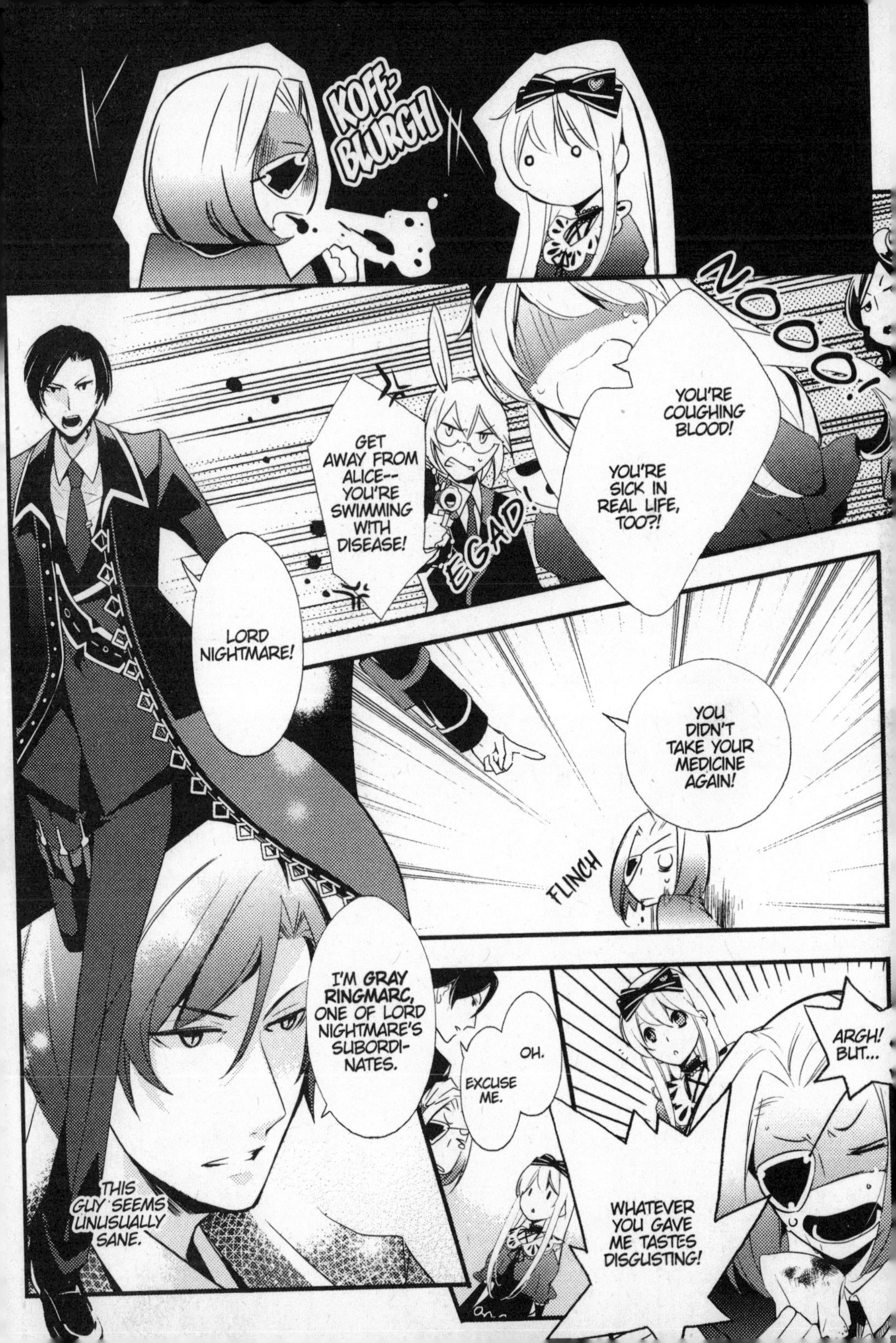
KOFF-BLURGH
NOOOO!
YOU'RE COUGHING BLOOD!
YOU'RE SICK IN REAL LIFE, TOO?!
GET AWAY FROM ALICE-- YOU'RE SWIMMING WITH DISEASE!
EGAD!
LORD NIGHTMARE!
YOU DIDN'T TAKE YOUR MEDICINE AGAIN!
FLINCH
ARGH! BUT...
WHATEVER YOU GAVE ME TASTES DISGUSTING!
OH.
EXCUSE ME.
I'M GRAY RINGMARC, ONE OF LORD NIGHTMARE'S SUBORDI-NATES.
THIS GUY SEEMS UNUSUALLY SANE.

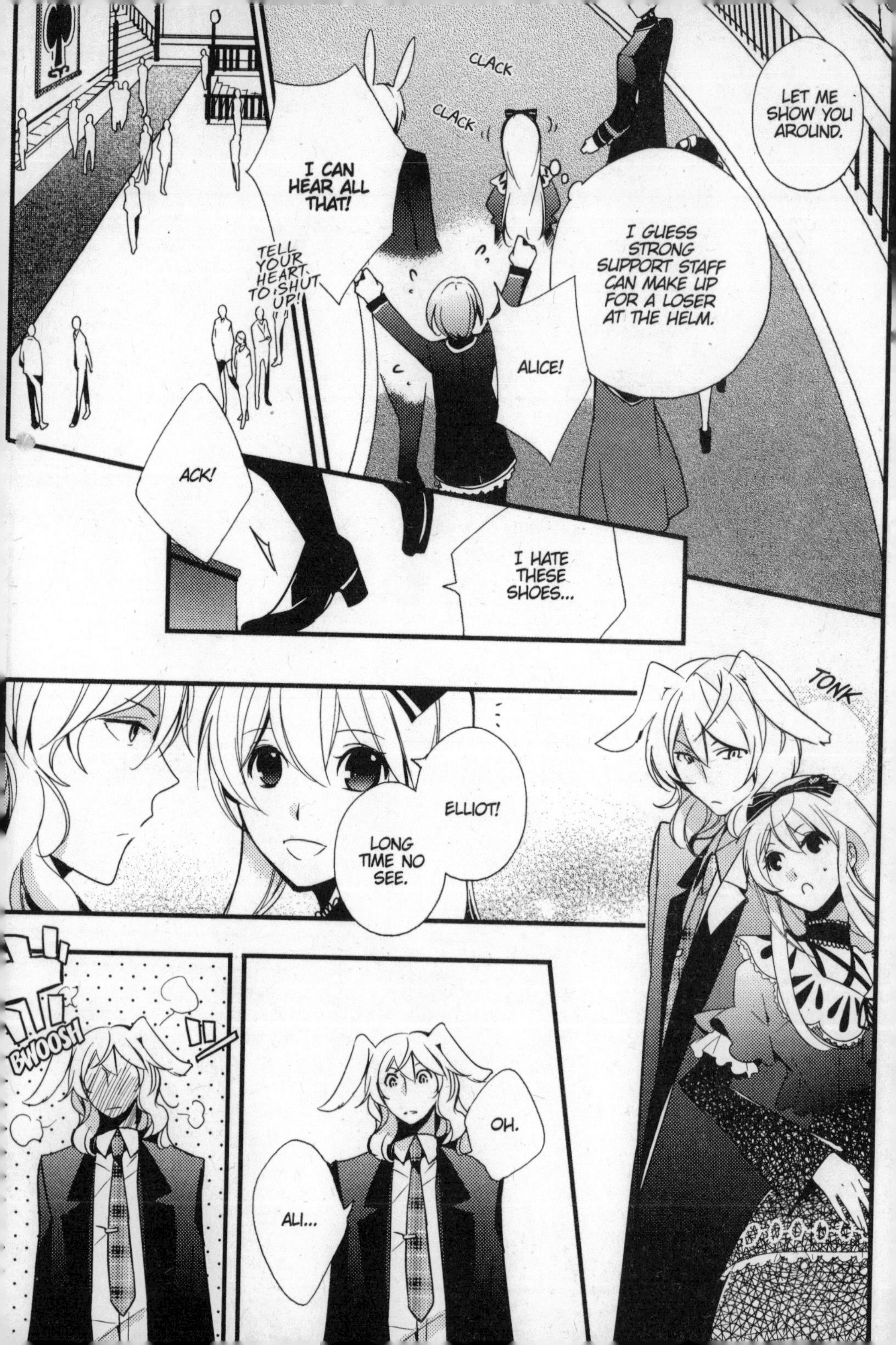
LET ME SHOW YOU AROUND.
CLACK
CLACK
I GUESS STRONG SUPPORT STAFF CAN MAKE UP FOR A LOSER AT THE HELM.
I CAN HEAR ALL THAT!
TELL YOUR HEART TO SHUT UP!
ALICE!
ACK!
I HATE THESE SHOES...
TONK
ELLIOT!
LONG TIME NO SEE.
OH.
ALI...
BWOOSH

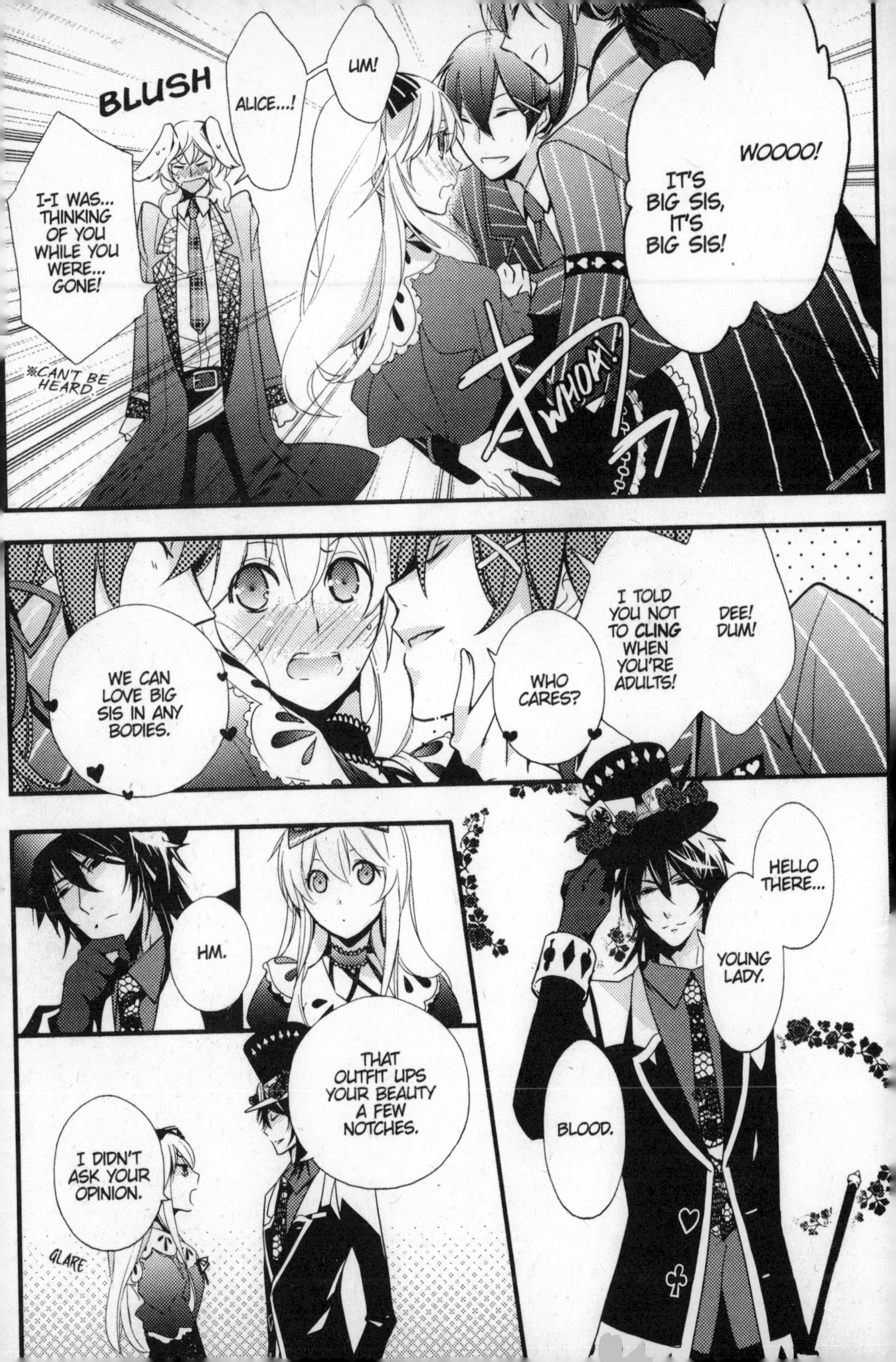
WOOOO!
IT'S BIG SIS, IT'S BIG SIS!
WHOA!
UM!
ALICE...!
BLUSH
I-I WAS... THINKING OF YOU WHILE YOU WERE... GONE!
※CAN'T BE HEARD.
DEE! DUM!
I TOLD YOU NOT TO CLING WHEN YOU'RE ADULTS!
WHO CARES?
WE CAN LOVE BIG SIS IN ANY BODIES.
HELLO THERE...
YOUNG LADY.
BLOOD.
HM.
THAT OUTFIT UPS YOUR BEAUTY A FEW NOTCHES.
I DIDN'T ASK YOUR OPINION.
GLARE

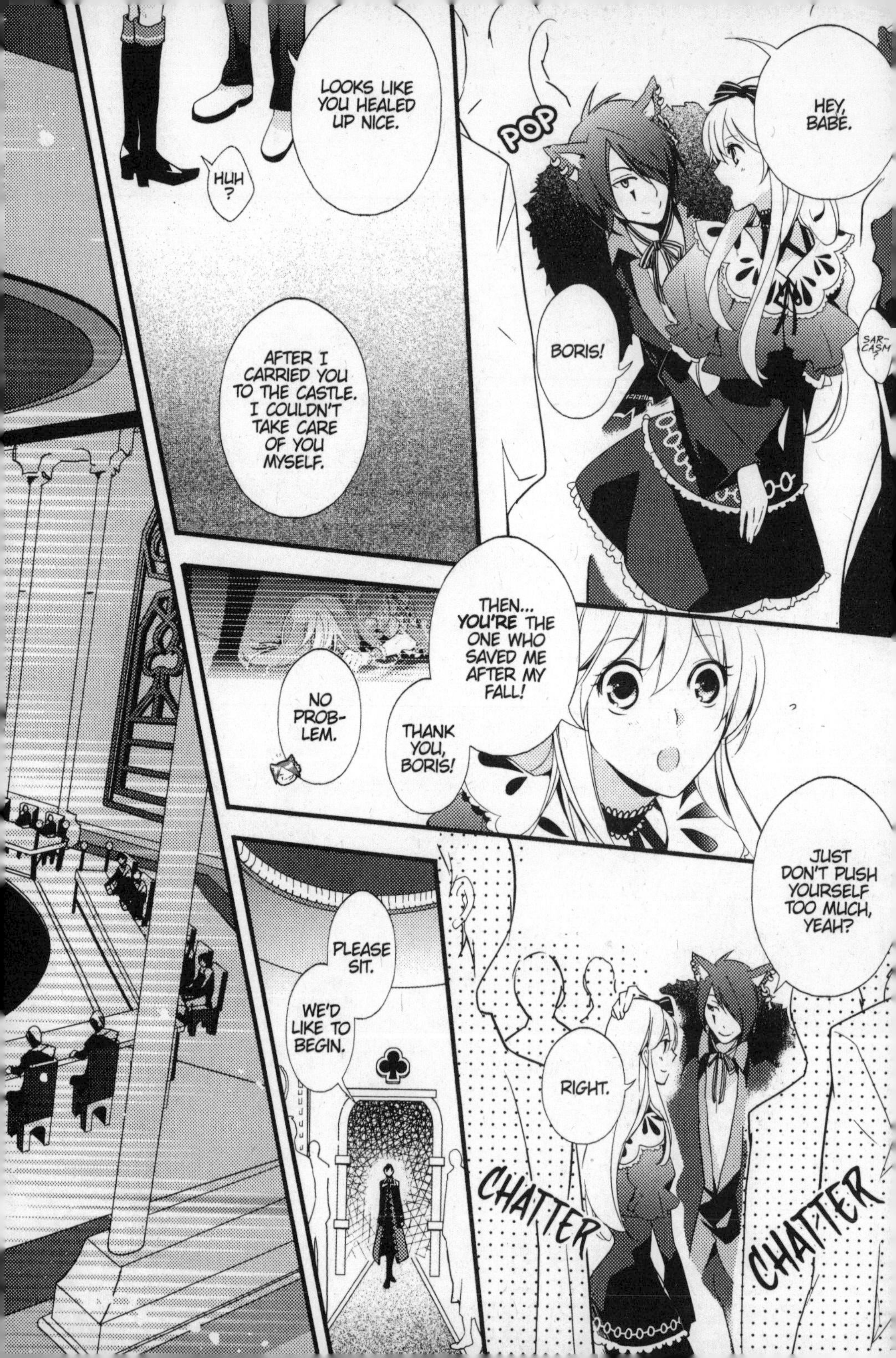
HEY, BABE.
POP
BORIS!
SARCASM?
LOOKS LIKE YOU HEALED UP NICE.
HUH?
AFTER I CARRIED YOU TO THE CASTLE. I COULDN'T TAKE CARE OF YOU MYSELF.
THEN... **YOU'RE** THE ONE WHO SAVED ME AFTER MY FALL!
THANK YOU, BORIS!
NO PROBLEM.
JUST DON'T PUSH YOURSELF TOO MUCH, YEAH?
RIGHT.
CHATTER
CHATTER
PLEASE SIT.
WE'D LIKE TO BEGIN.

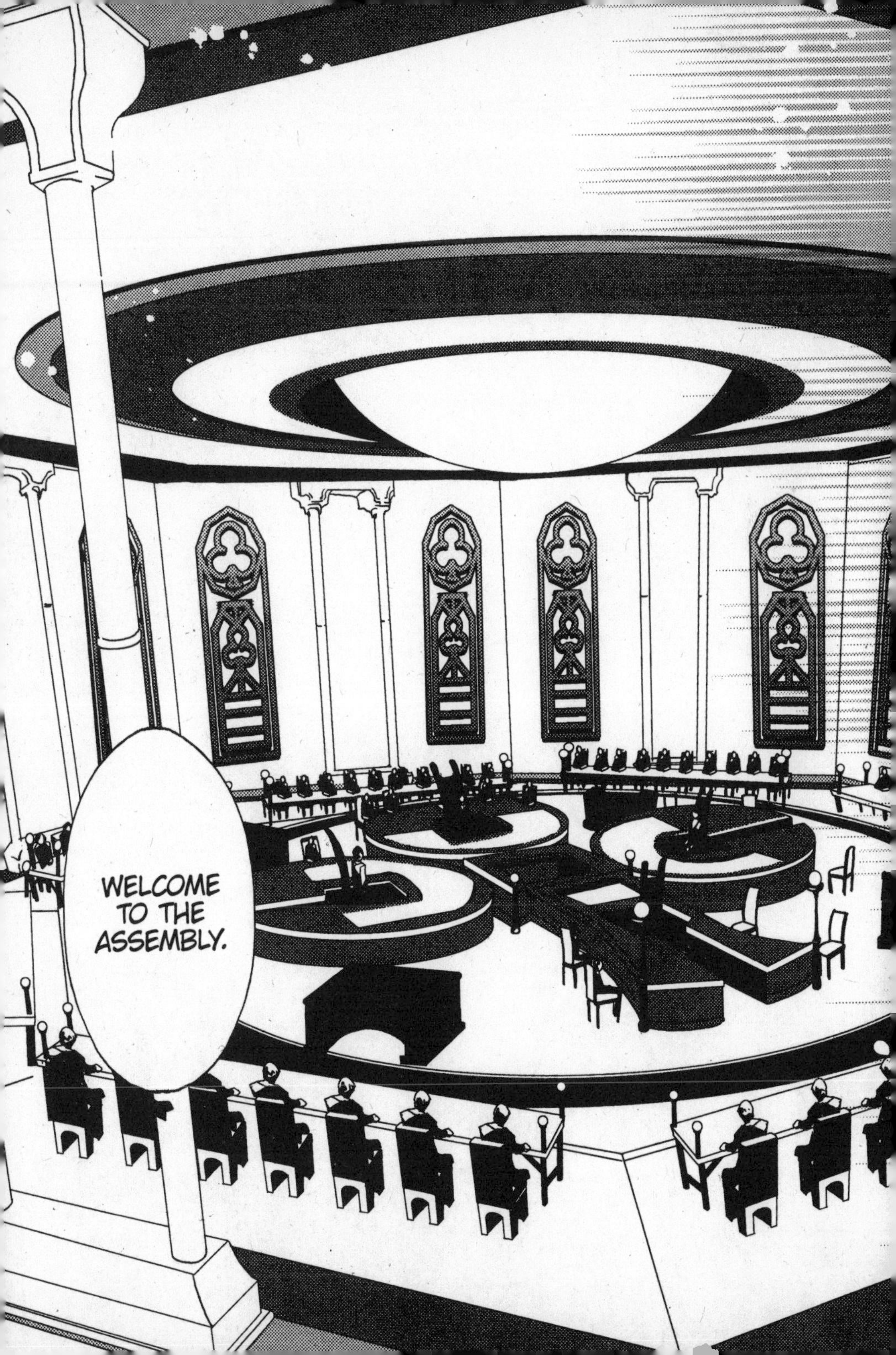
WELCOME TO THE ASSEMBLY.

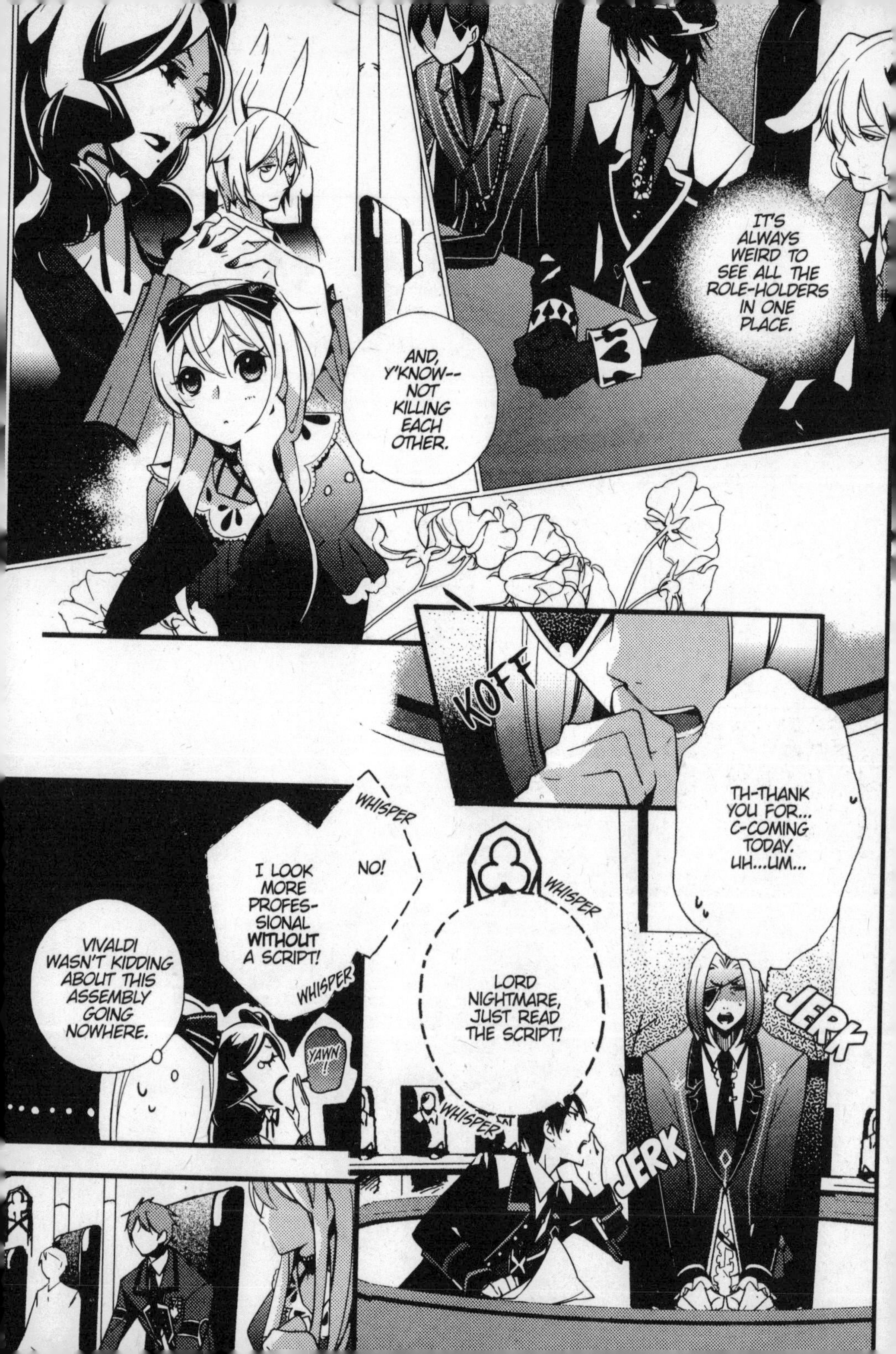
IT'S ALWAYS WEIRD TO SEE ALL THE ROLE-HOLDERS IN ONE PLACE.
AND, Y'KNOW-- NOT KILLING EACH OTHER.
KOFF
TH-THANK YOU FOR... C-COMING TODAY. UH...UM...
JERK
JERK
WHISPER
LORD NIGHTMARE, JUST READ THE SCRIPT!
WHISPER
WHISPER
NO!
I LOOK MORE PROFES-SIONAL WITHOUT A SCRIPT!
WHISPER
VIVALDI WASN'T KIDDING ABOUT THIS ASSEMBLY GOING NOWHERE.
YAWN!

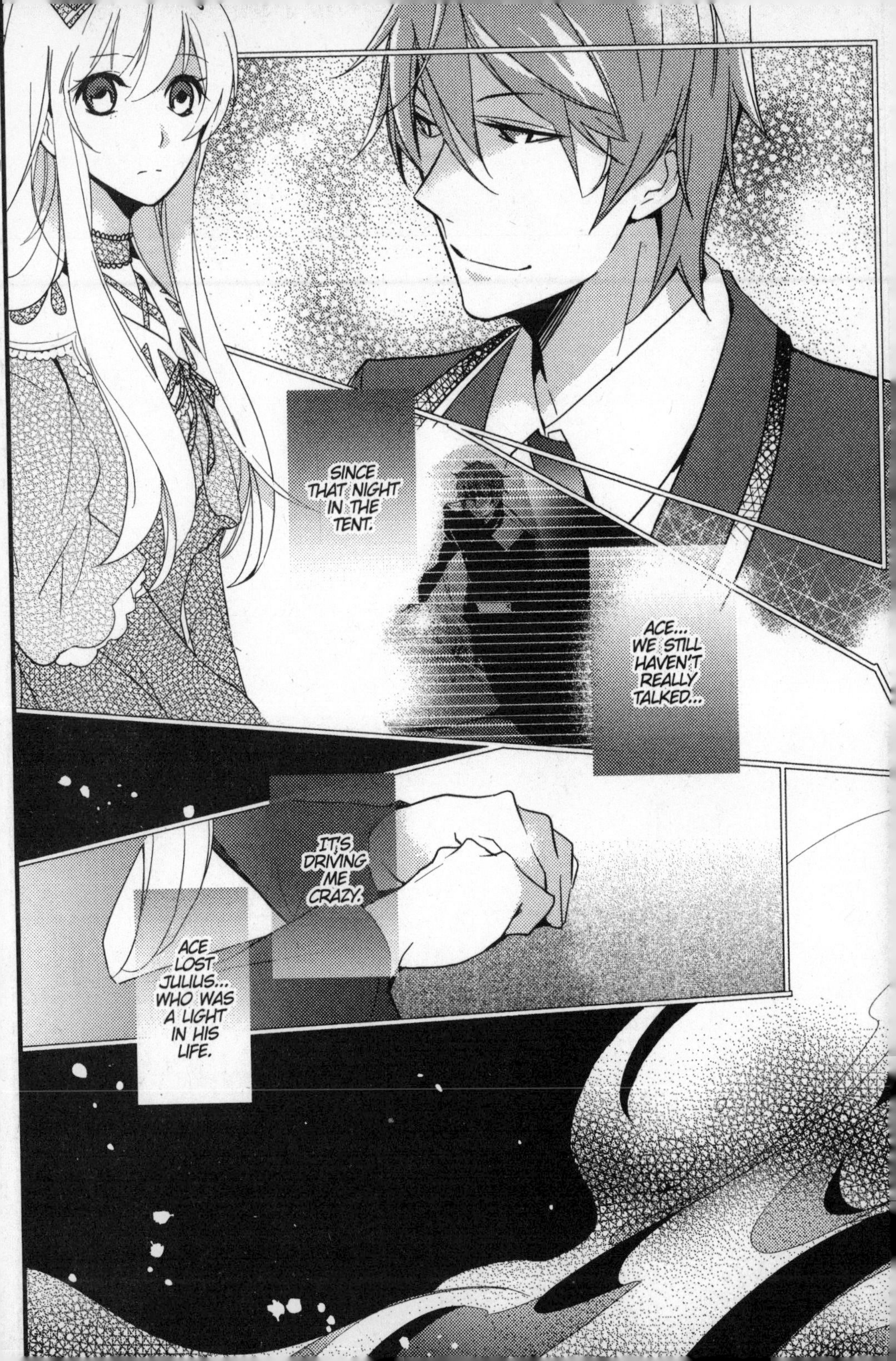
ACE... WE STILL HAVEN'T REALLY TALKED...
SINCE THAT NIGHT IN THE TENT.
IT'S DRIVING ME CRAZY.
ACE LOST JULIUS... WHO WAS A LIGHT IN HIS LIFE.

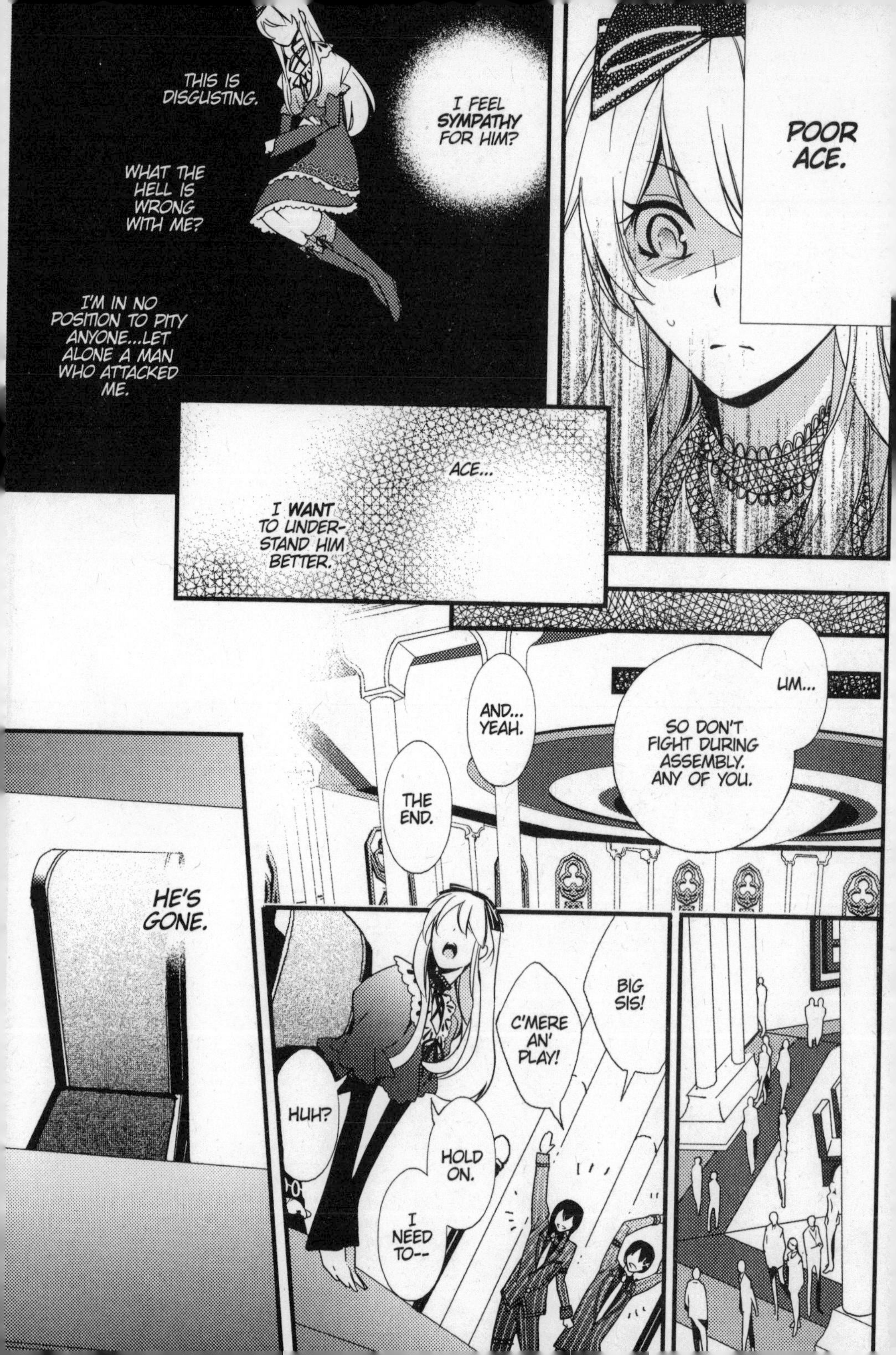
POOR ACE.
I FEEL SYMPATHY FOR HIM?
THIS IS DISGUSTING.
WHAT THE HELL IS WRONG WITH ME?
I'M IN NO POSITION TO PITY ANYONE...LET ALONE A MAN WHO ATTACKED ME.
ACE...
I WANT TO UNDER-STAND HIM BETTER.
UM...
SO DON'T FIGHT DURING ASSEMBLY. ANY OF YOU.
AND... YEAH.
THE END.
HE'S GONE.
BIG SIS!
C'MERE AN' PLAY!
HUH?
HOLD ON.
I NEED TO--

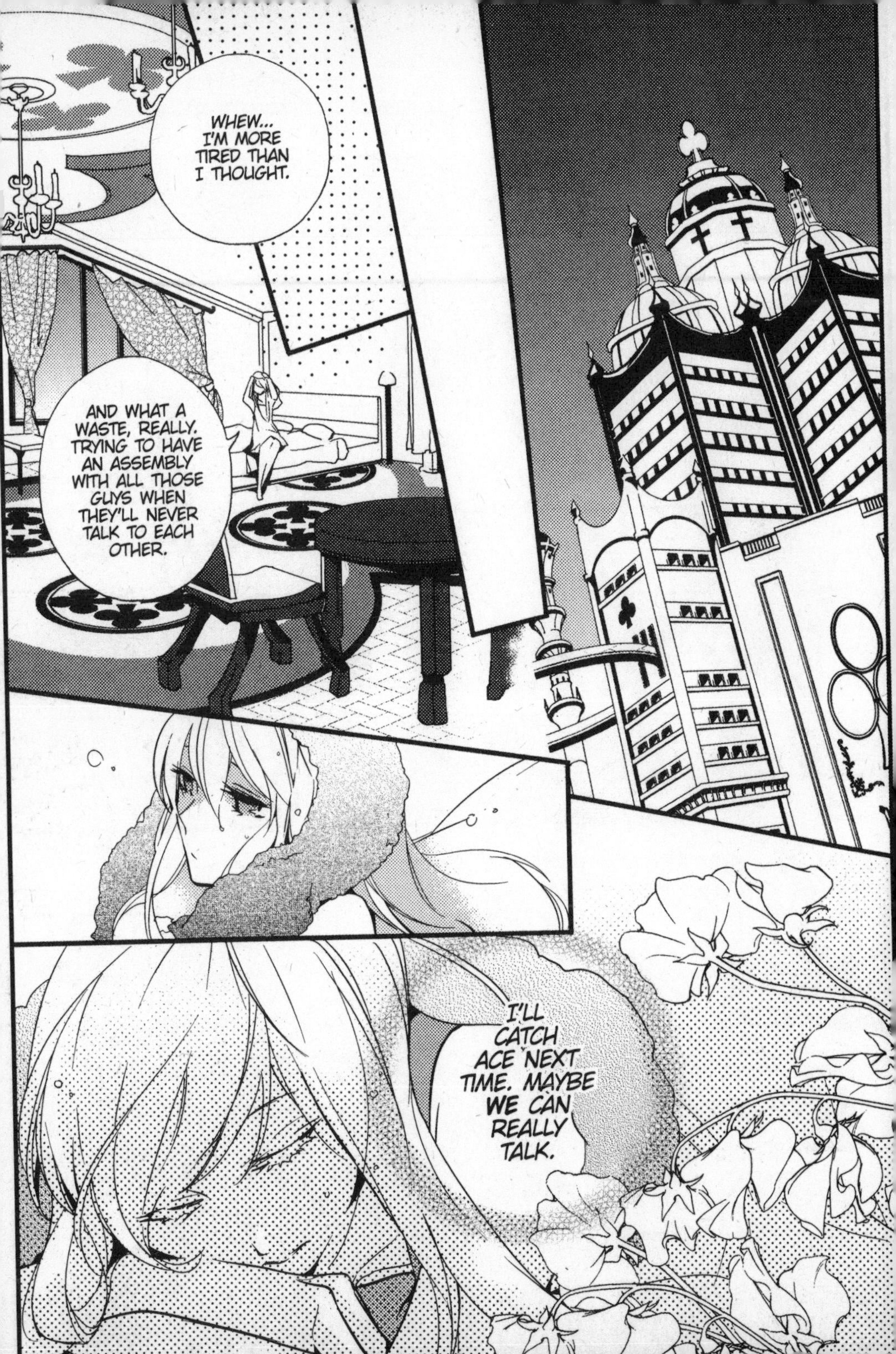
WHEW... I'M MORE TIRED THAN I THOUGHT.
AND WHAT A WASTE, REALLY. TRYING TO HAVE AN ASSEMBLY WITH ALL THOSE GUYS WHEN THEY'LL NEVER TALK TO EACH OTHER.
I'LL CATCH ACE NEXT TIME. MAYBE WE CAN REALLY TALK.

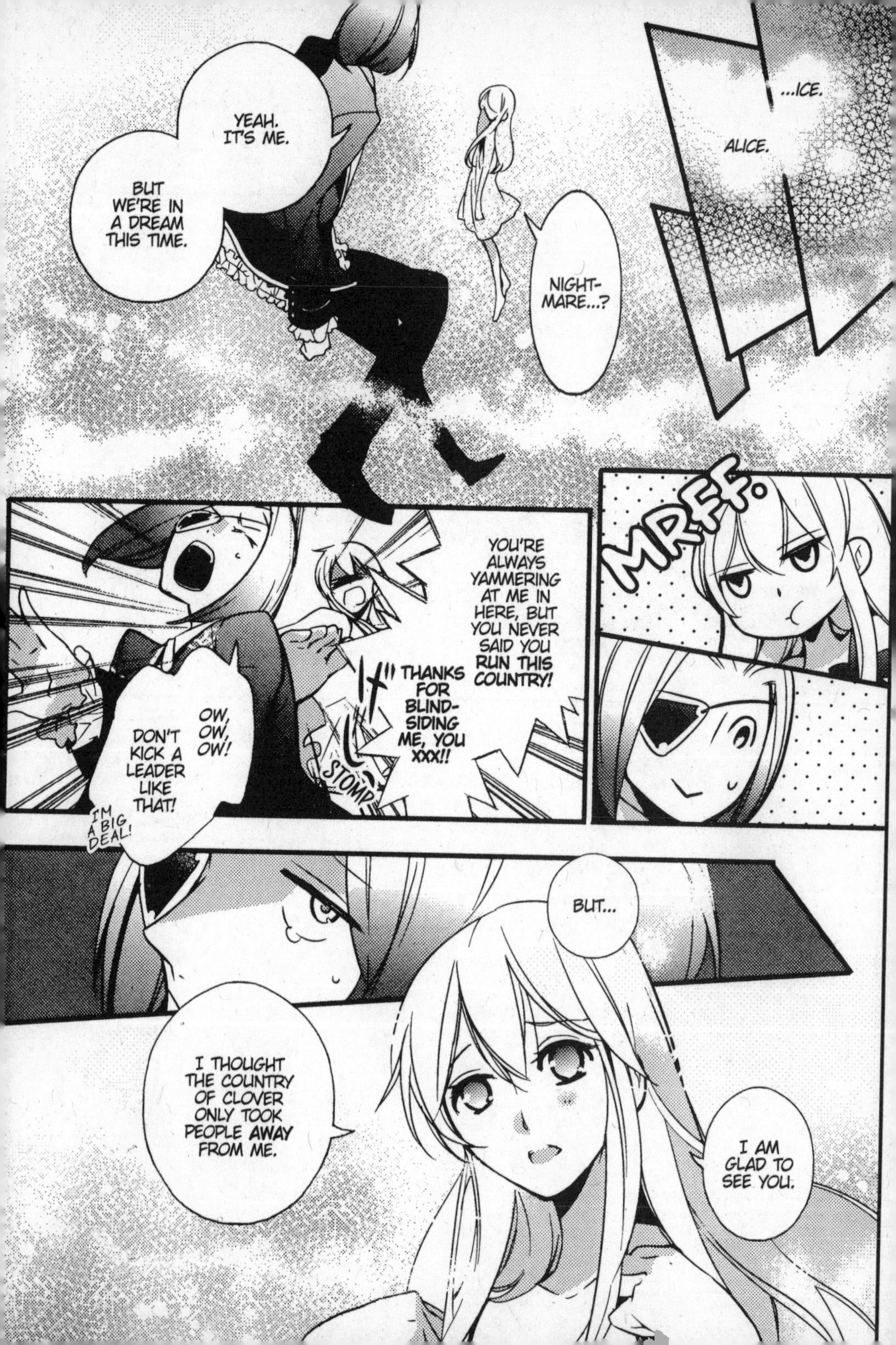

...ICE.
ALICE.
NIGHT-MARE...?
YEAH. IT'S ME.
BUT WE'RE IN A DREAM THIS TIME.
MRFF.
YOU'RE ALWAYS YAMMERING AT ME IN HERE, BUT YOU NEVER SAID YOU RUN THIS COUNTRY!
THANKS FOR BLIND-SIDING ME, YOU XXX!!
STOMP
OW, OW, OW!
DON'T KICK A LEADER LIKE THAT!
I'M A BIG DEAL!
BUT...
I THOUGHT THE COUNTRY OF CLOVER ONLY TOOK PEOPLE AWAY FROM ME.
I AM GLAD TO SEE YOU.

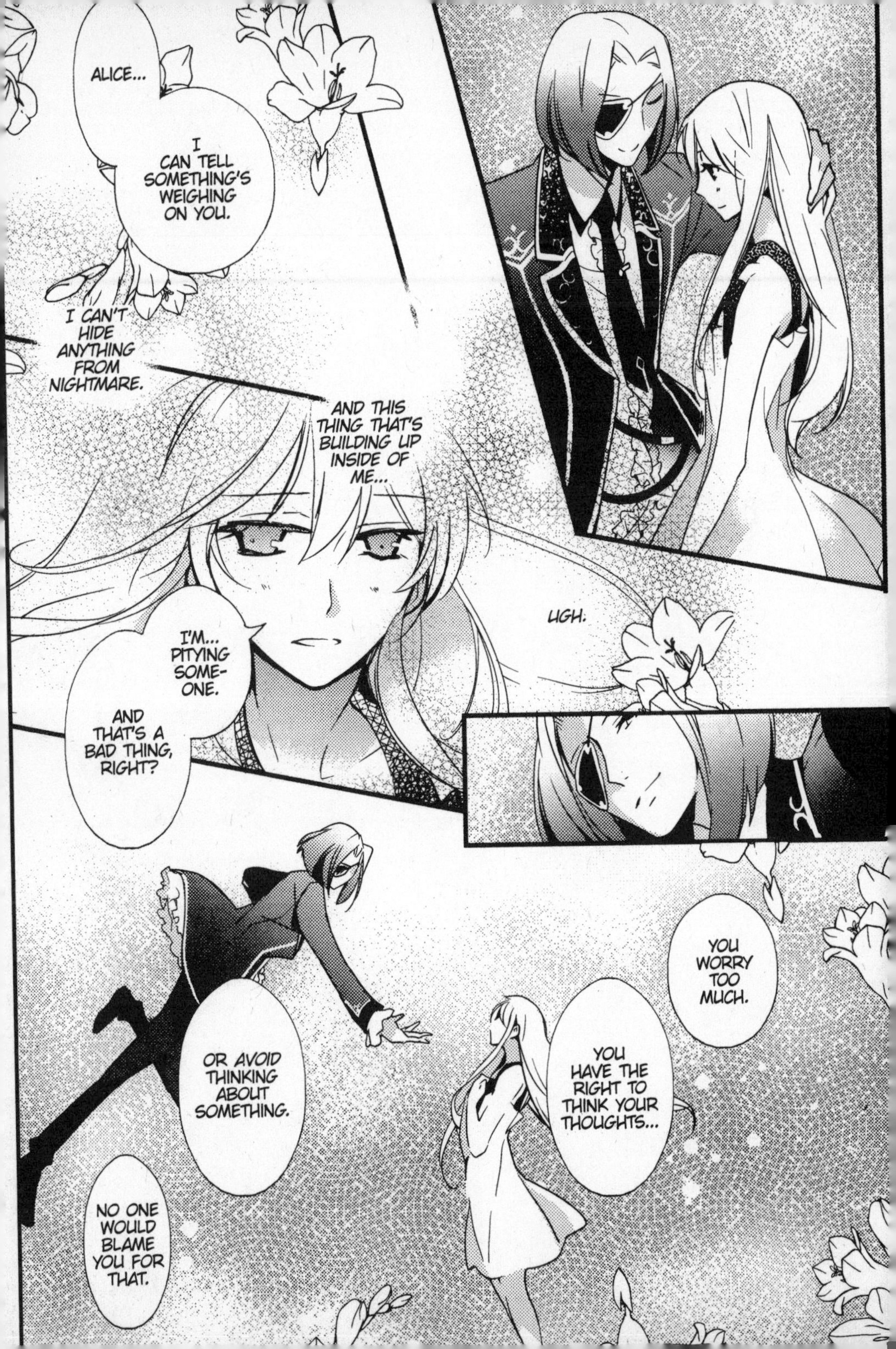
ALICE...
I CAN TELL SOMETHING'S WEIGHING ON YOU.
I CAN'T HIDE ANYTHING FROM NIGHTMARE.
AND THIS THING THAT'S BUILDING UP INSIDE OF ME...
UGH.
I'M... PITYING SOME-ONE.
AND THAT'S A BAD THING, RIGHT?
YOU WORRY TOO MUCH.
YOU HAVE THE RIGHT TO THINK YOUR THOUGHTS...
OR AVOID THINKING ABOUT SOMETHING.
NO ONE WOULD BLAME YOU FOR THAT.

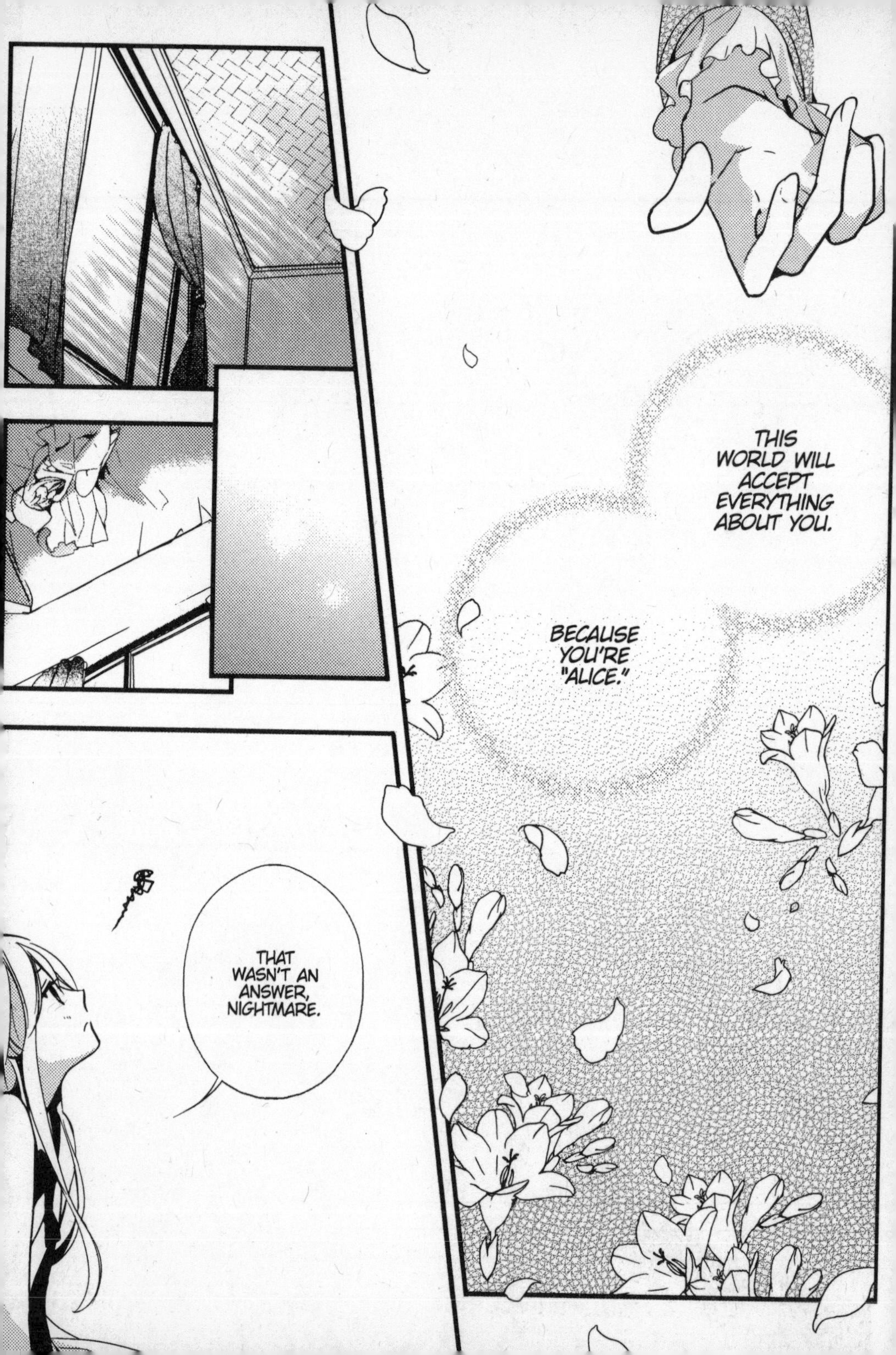
THIS WORLD WILL ACCEPT EVERYTHING ABOUT YOU.
BECAUSE YOU'RE "ALICE."
THAT WASN'T AN ANSWER, NIGHTMARE.

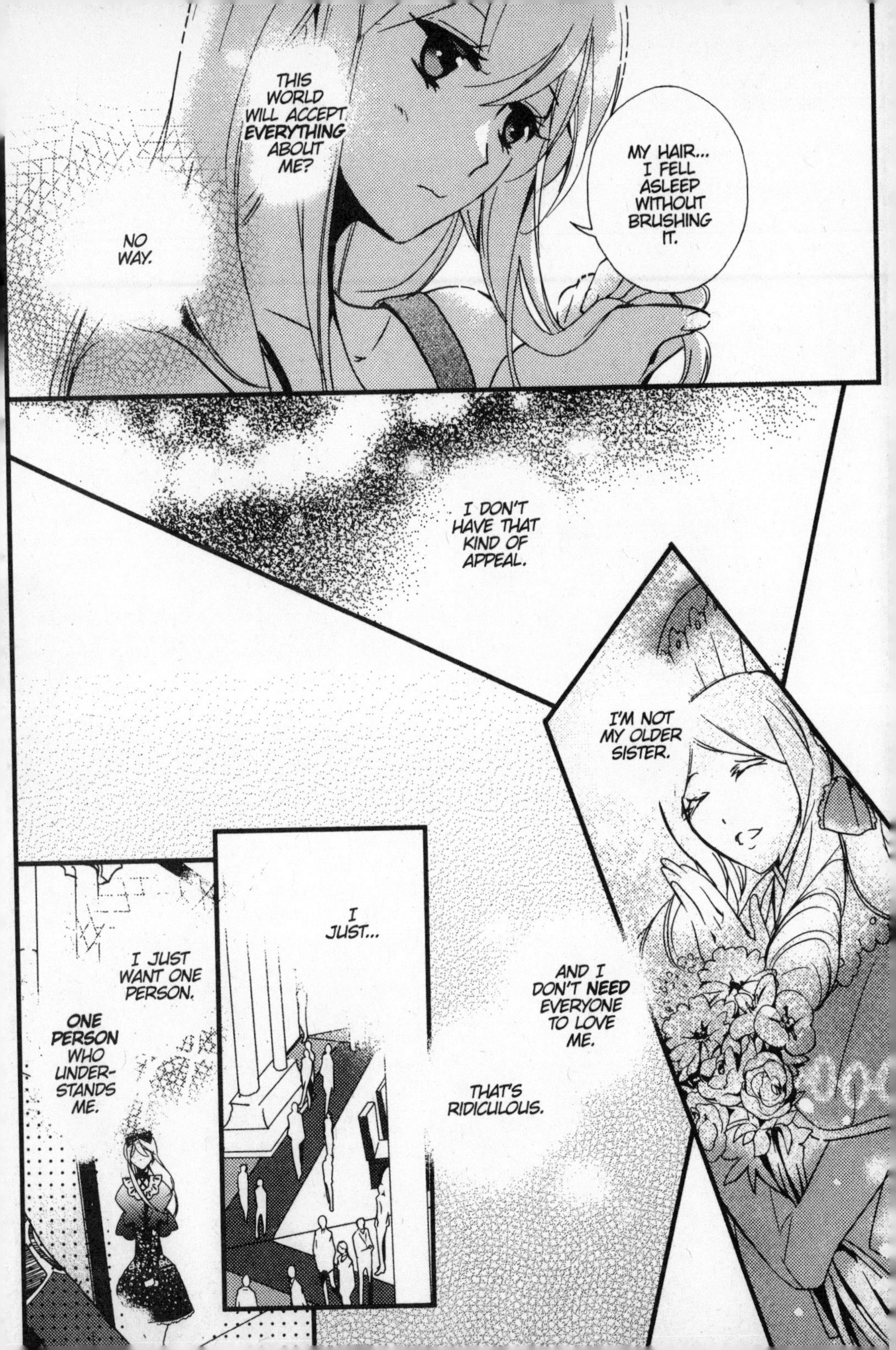
MY HAIR... I FELL ASLEEP WITHOUT BRUSHING IT.
THIS WORLD WILL ACCEPT EVERYTHING ABOUT ME?
NO WAY.
I DON'T HAVE THAT KIND OF APPEAL.
I'M NOT MY OLDER SISTER.
AND I DON'T NEED EVERYONE TO LOVE ME.
THAT'S RIDICULOUS.
I JUST...
I JUST WANT ONE PERSON.
ONE PERSON WHO UNDER-STANDS ME.

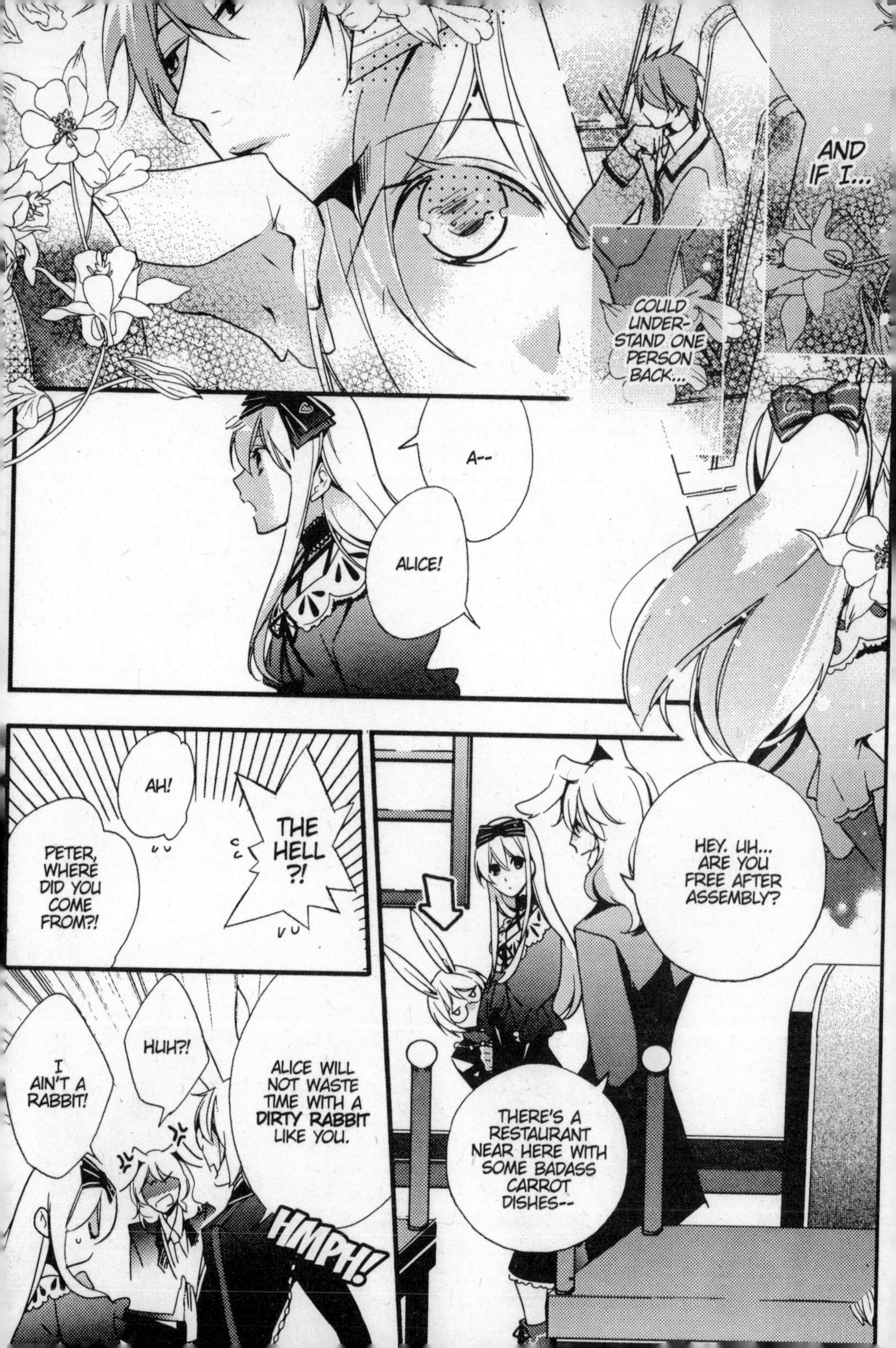
AND IF I...
COULD UNDER-STAND ONE PERSON BACK...
A--
ALICE!
HEY. UH... ARE YOU FREE AFTER ASSEMBLY?
THERE'S A RESTAURANT NEAR HERE WITH SOME BADASS CARROT DISHES--
AH!
THE HELL ?!
PETER, WHERE DID YOU COME FROM?!
ALICE WILL NOT WASTE TIME WITH A DIRTY RABBIT LIKE YOU.
HMPH!
HUH?!
I AIN'T A RABBIT!

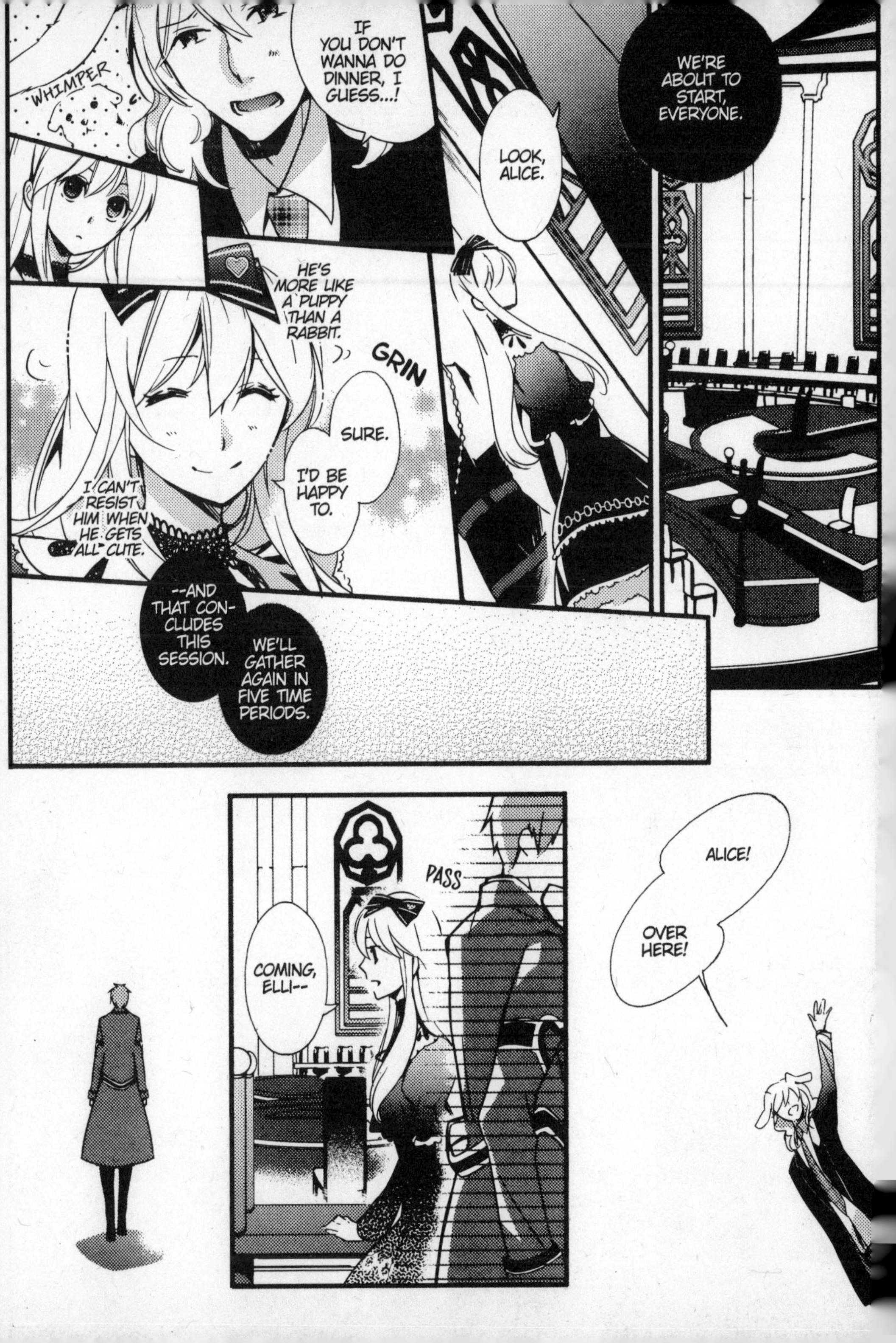
WE'RE ABOUT TO START, EVERYONE.
LOOK, ALICE.
IF YOU DON'T WANNA DO DINNER, I GUESS...!
WHIMPER
HE'S MORE LIKE A PUPPY THAN A RABBIT.
GRIN
SURE.
I'D BE HAPPY TO.
I CAN'T RESIST HIM WHEN HE GETS ALL CUTE.
--AND THAT CON-CLUDES THIS SESSION.
WE'LL GATHER AGAIN IN FIVE TIME PERIODS.
ALICE!
OVER HERE!
PASS
COMING, ELLI--

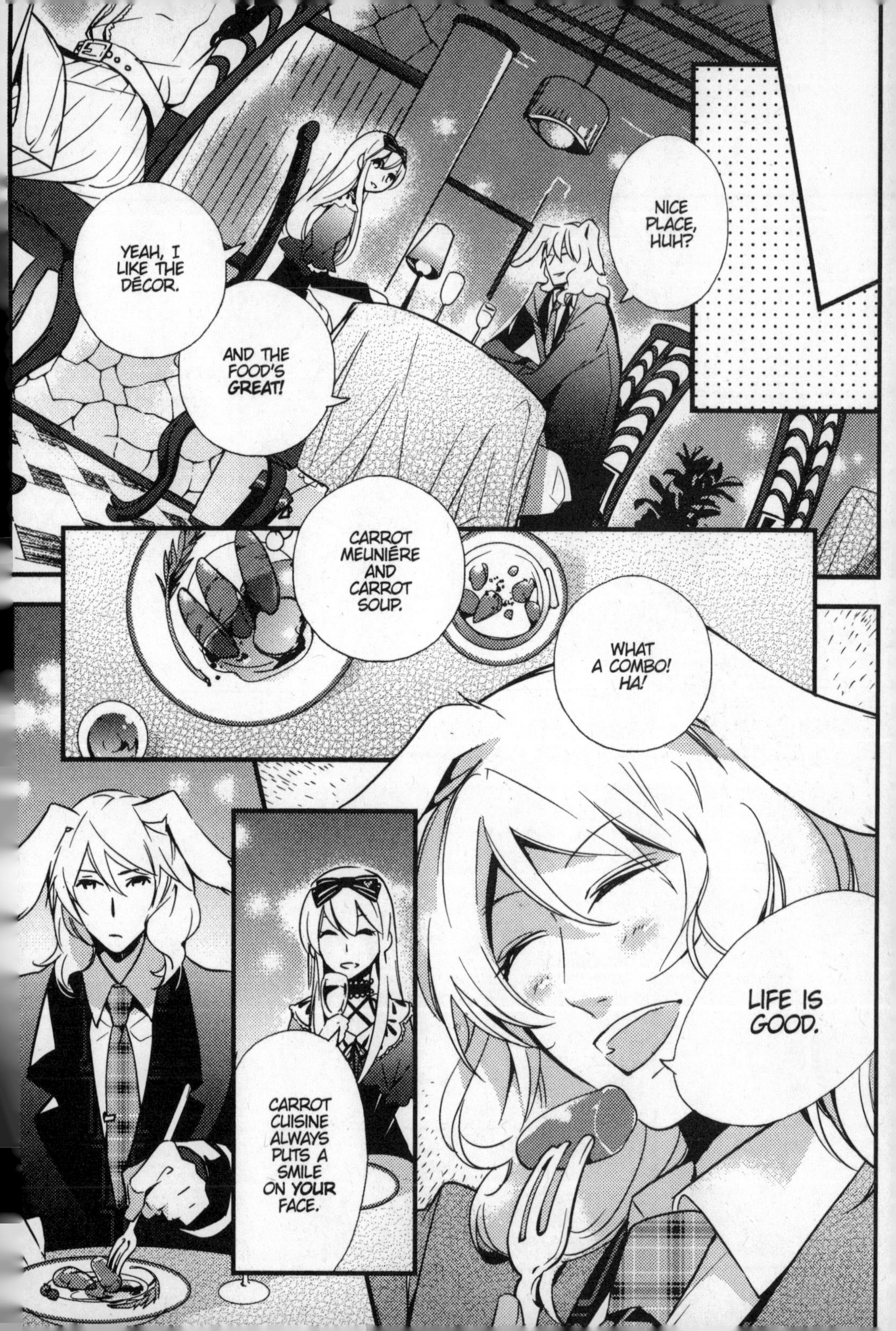
NICE PLACE, HUH?
YEAH, I LIKE THE DÉCOR.
AND THE FOOD'S GREAT!
CARROT MEUNIÉRE AND CARROT SOUP.
WHAT A COMBO! HA!
LIFE IS GOOD.
CARROT CUISINE ALWAYS PUTS A SMILE ON YOUR FACE.

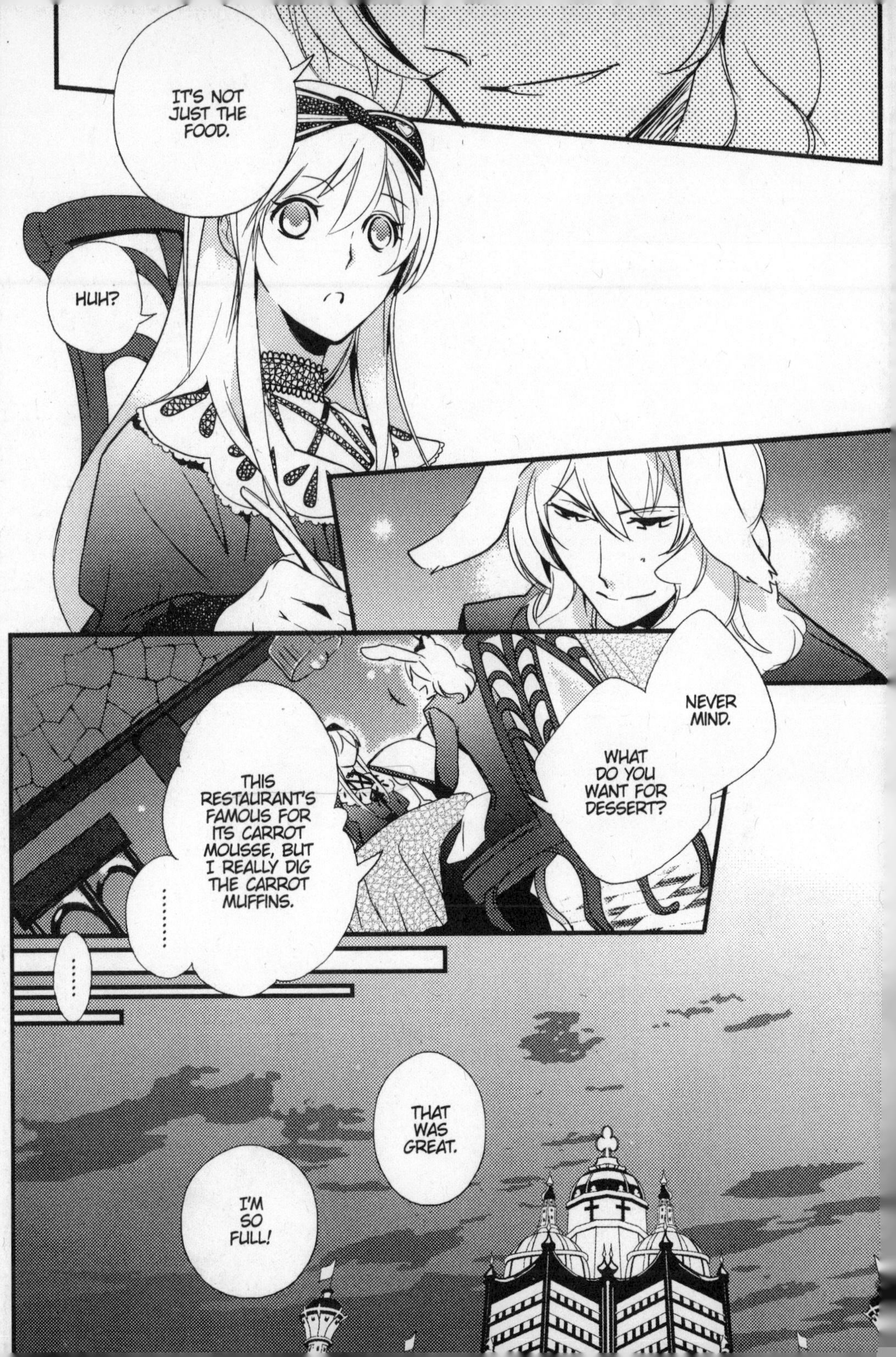
IT'S NOT JUST THE FOOD.
HUH?
NEVER MIND.
WHAT DO YOU WANT FOR DESSERT?
THIS RESTAURANT'S FAMOUS FOR ITS CARROT MOUSSE, BUT I REALLY DIG THE CARROT MUFFINS.
......
......
THAT WAS GREAT.
I'M SO FULL!

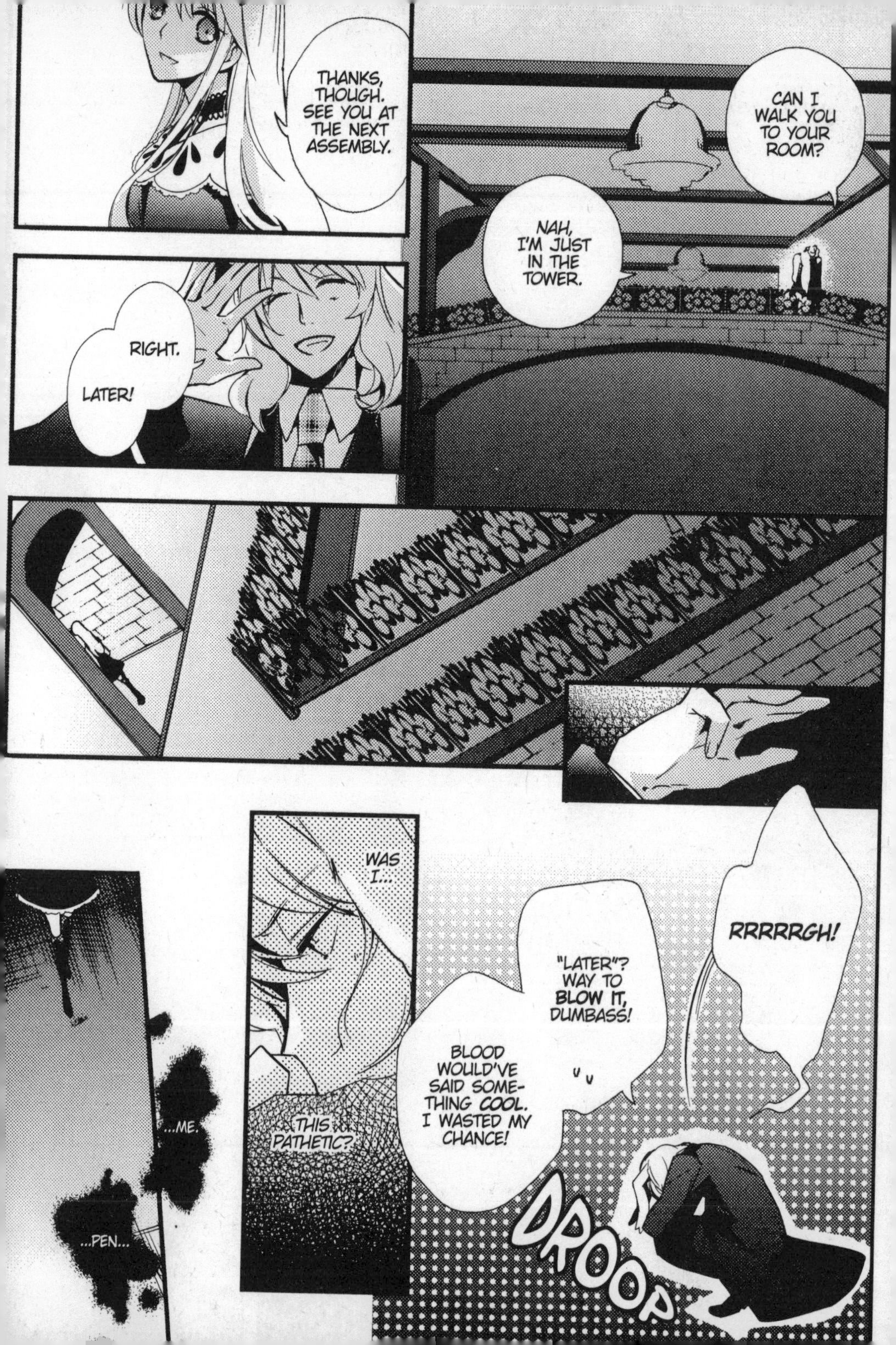
CAN I WALK YOU TO YOUR ROOM?
NAH, I'M JUST IN THE TOWER.
THANKS, THOUGH. SEE YOU AT THE NEXT ASSEMBLY.
RIGHT.
LATER!
RRRRRGH!
"LATER"? WAY TO BLOW IT, DUMBASS!
BLOOD WOULD'VE SAID SOME-THING COOL. I WASTED MY CHANCE!
DROOP
WAS I...
THIS PATHETIC?
...ME.
...PEN...

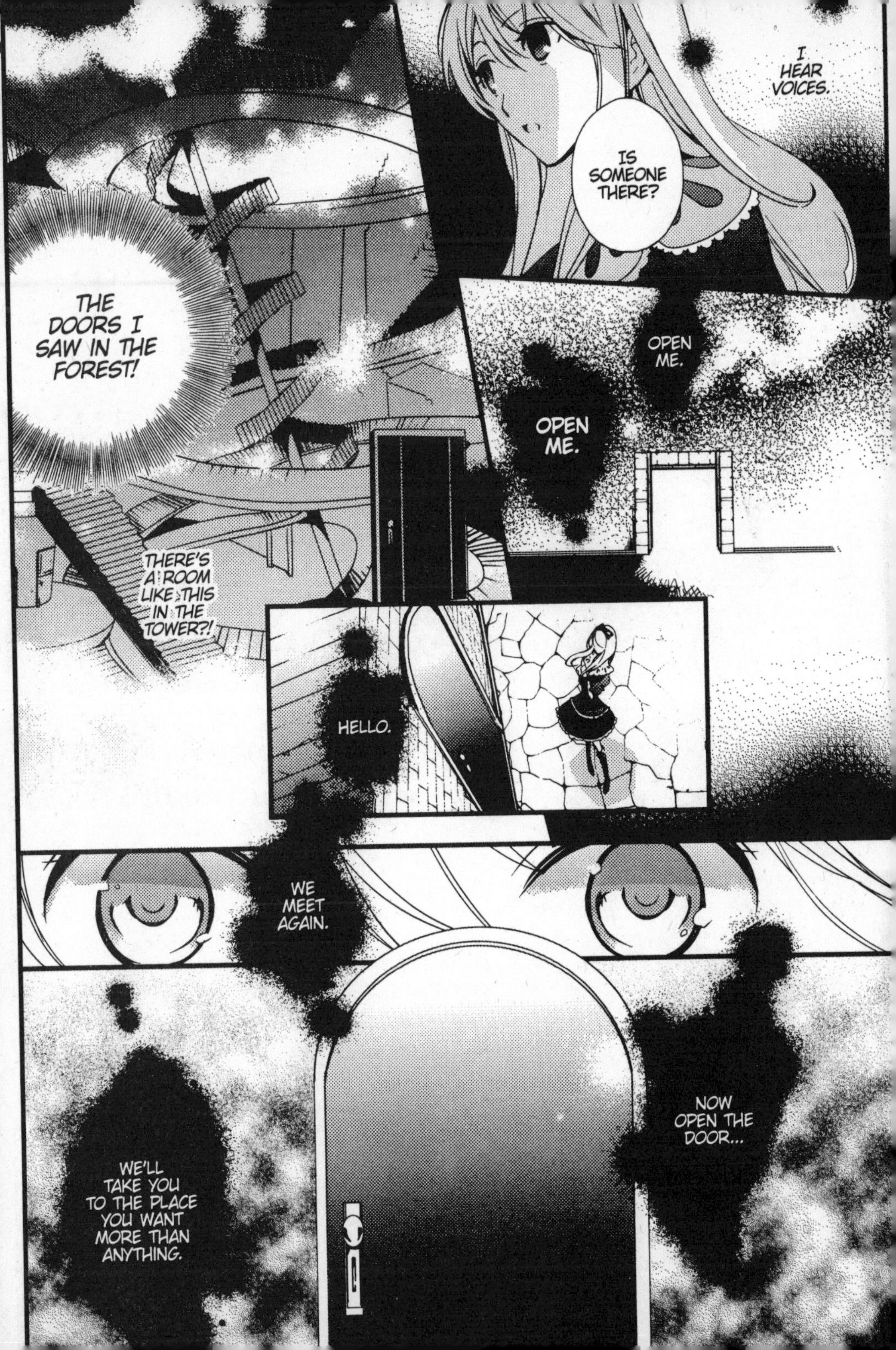
I HEAR VOICES.
IS SOMEONE THERE?
OPEN ME.
OPEN ME.
HELLO.
THE DOORS I SAW IN THE FOREST!
THERE'S A ROOM LIKE THIS IN THE TOWER?!
WE MEET AGAIN.
NOW OPEN THE DOOR...
WE'LL TAKE YOU TO THE PLACE YOU WANT MORE THAN ANYTHING.

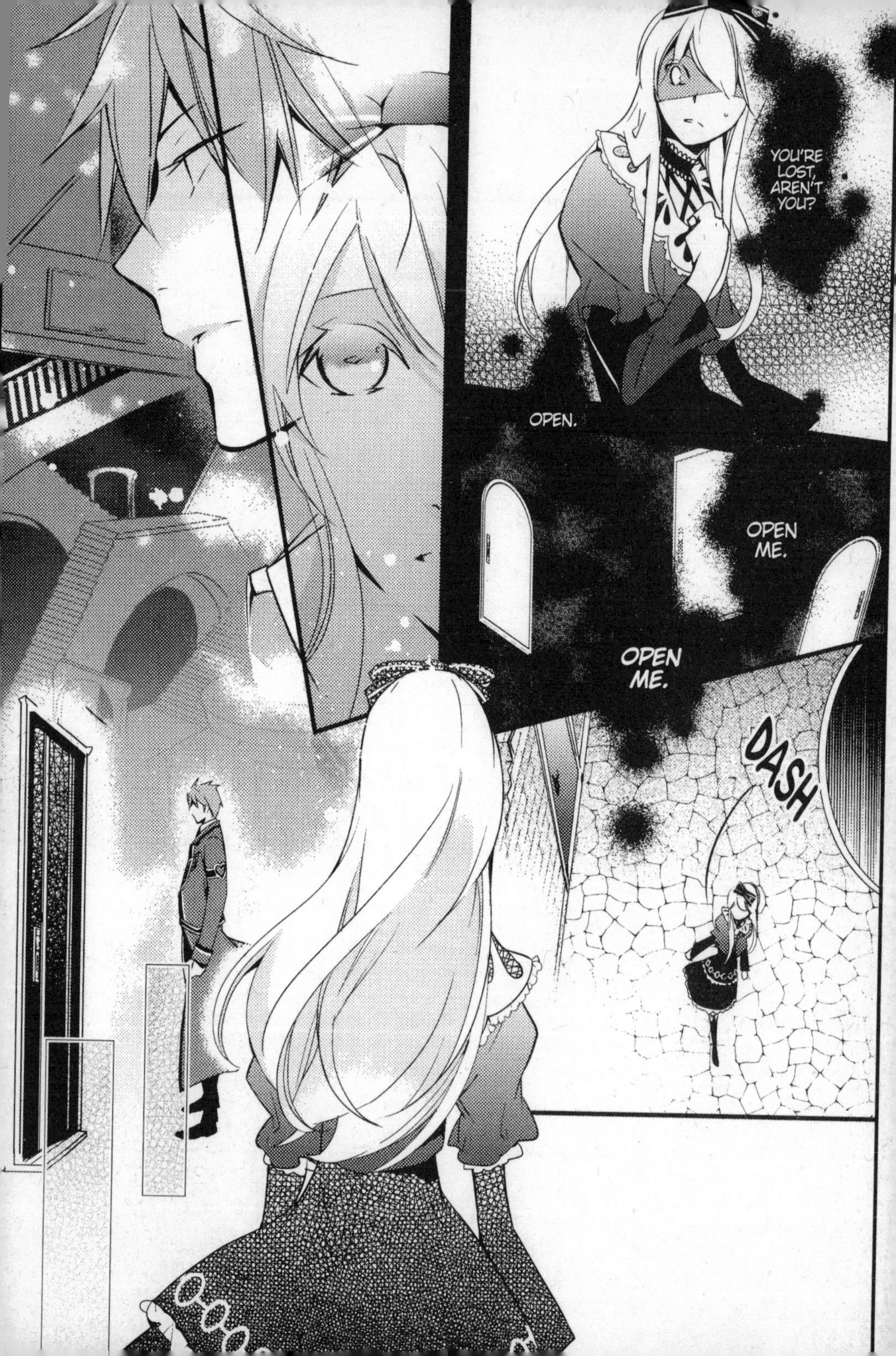
YOU'RE LOST, AREN'T YOU?
OPEN.
OPEN ME.
OPEN ME.
DASH

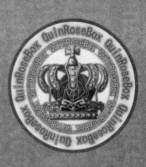

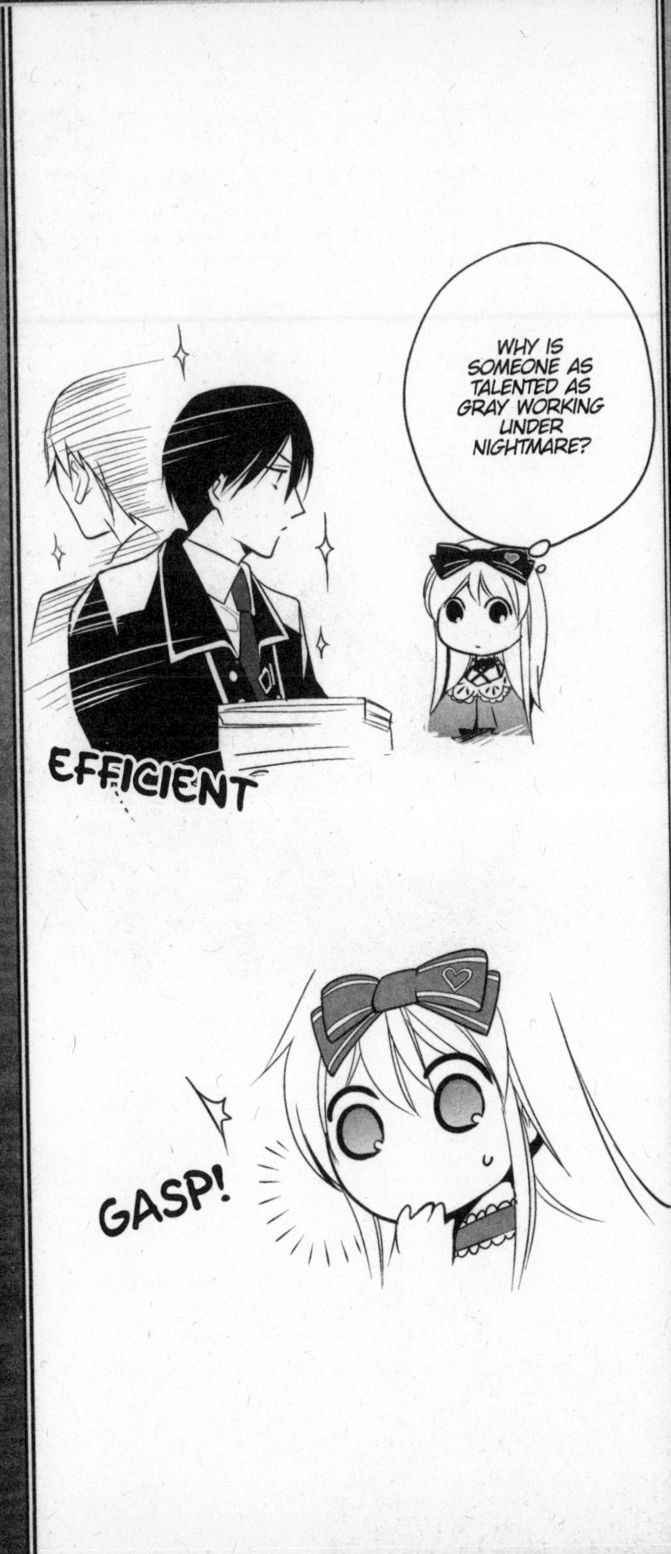
WHY IS SOMEONE AS TALENTED AS GRAY WORKING UNDER NIGHTMARE?
EFFICIENT
GASP!

YOU'LL GET THROUGH THIS, GRAY! JUST KEEP SAVING WHAT YOU CAN!

I DON'T GET PAID A LOT, BUT MAYBE I CAN CHIP IN--

YOU MISUNDER-STAND.

I WORK UNDER LORD NIGHTMARE BECAUSE HE HAS SOME GOOD POINTS. SOME.

DON'T SAY "SOME"!

GRAB

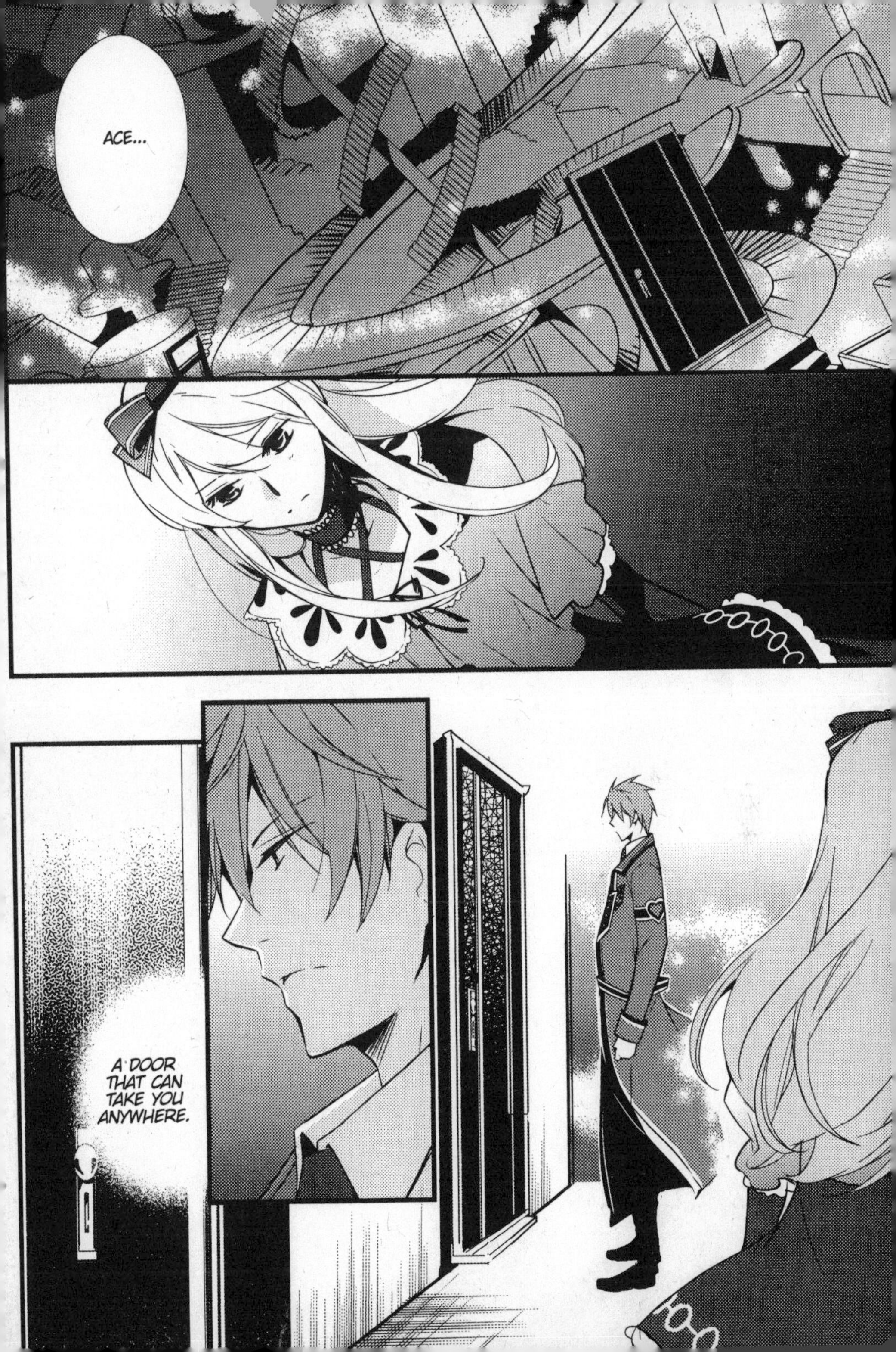
ACE...
A DOOR THAT CAN TAKE YOU ANYWHERE.

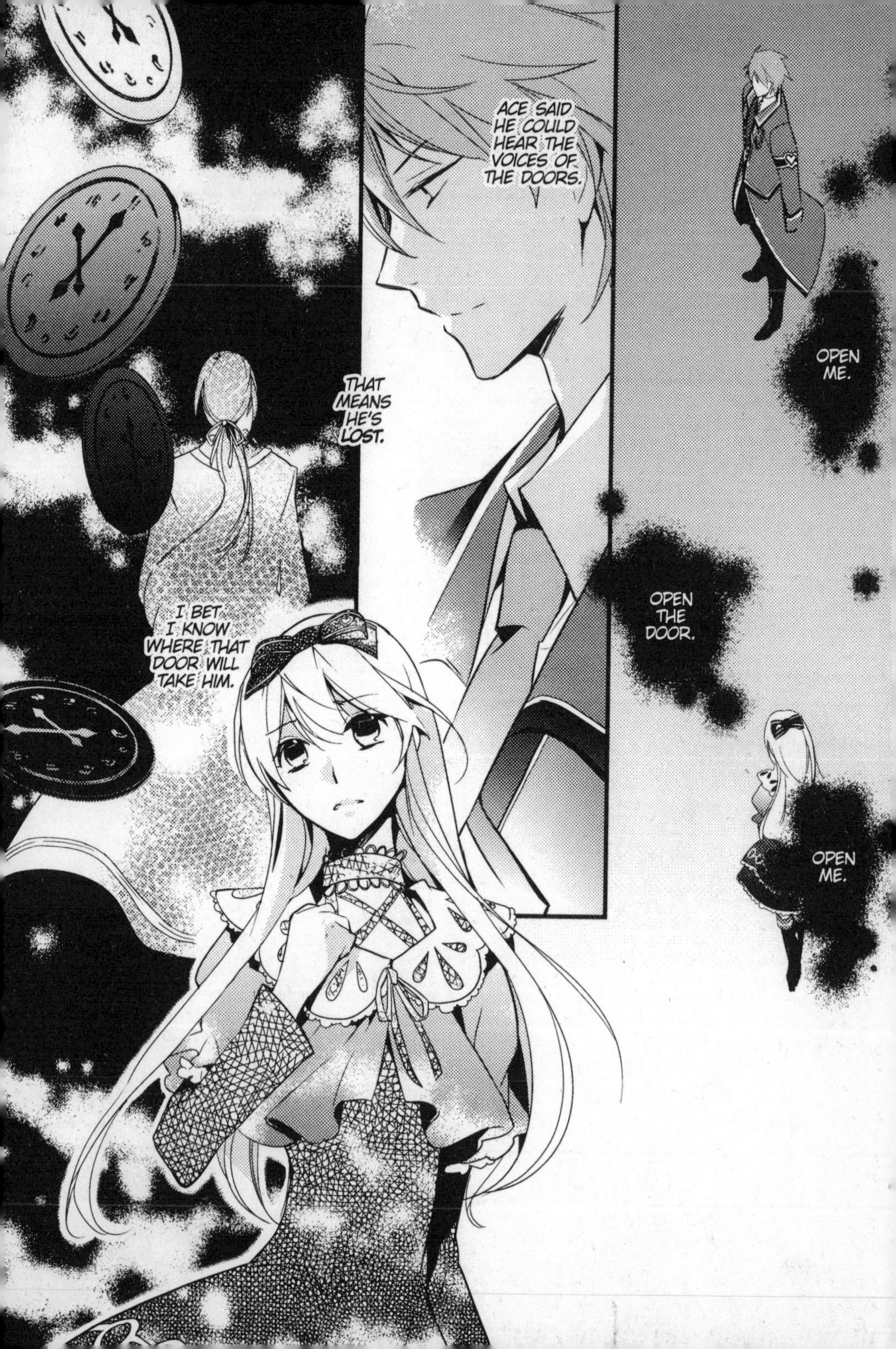
OPEN ME.
OPEN THE DOOR.
OPEN ME.
ACE SAID HE COULD HEAR THE VOICES OF THE DOORS.
THAT MEANS HE'S LOST.
I BET I KNOW WHERE THAT DOOR WILL TAKE HIM.

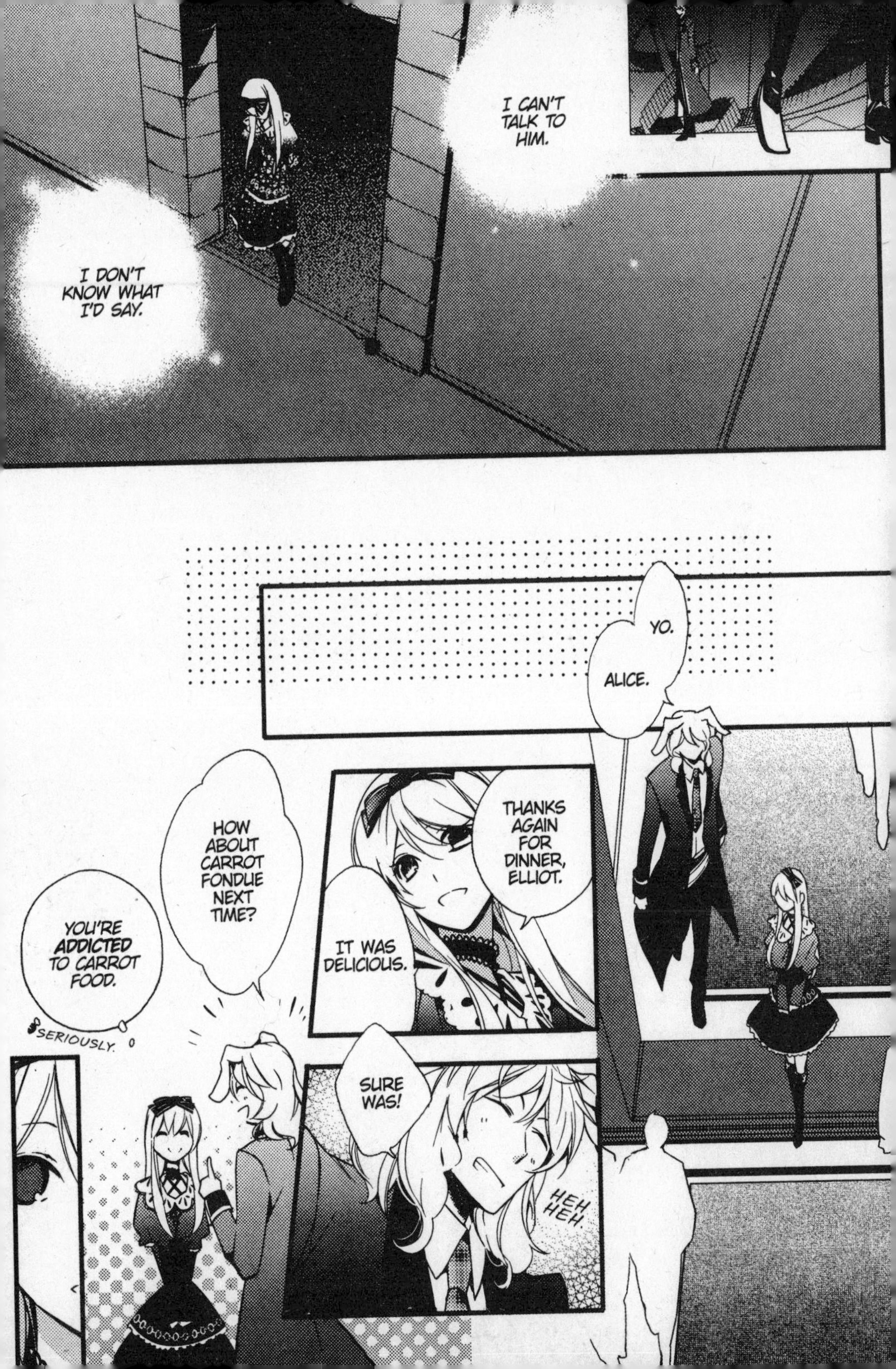

I CAN'T TALK TO HIM.
I DON'T KNOW WHAT I'D SAY.
YO.
ALICE.
THANKS AGAIN FOR DINNER, ELLIOT.
IT WAS DELICIOUS.
SURE WAS!
HEH HEH.
HOW ABOUT CARROT FONDUE NEXT TIME?
YOU'RE ADDICTED TO CARROT FOOD.
SERIOUSLY.

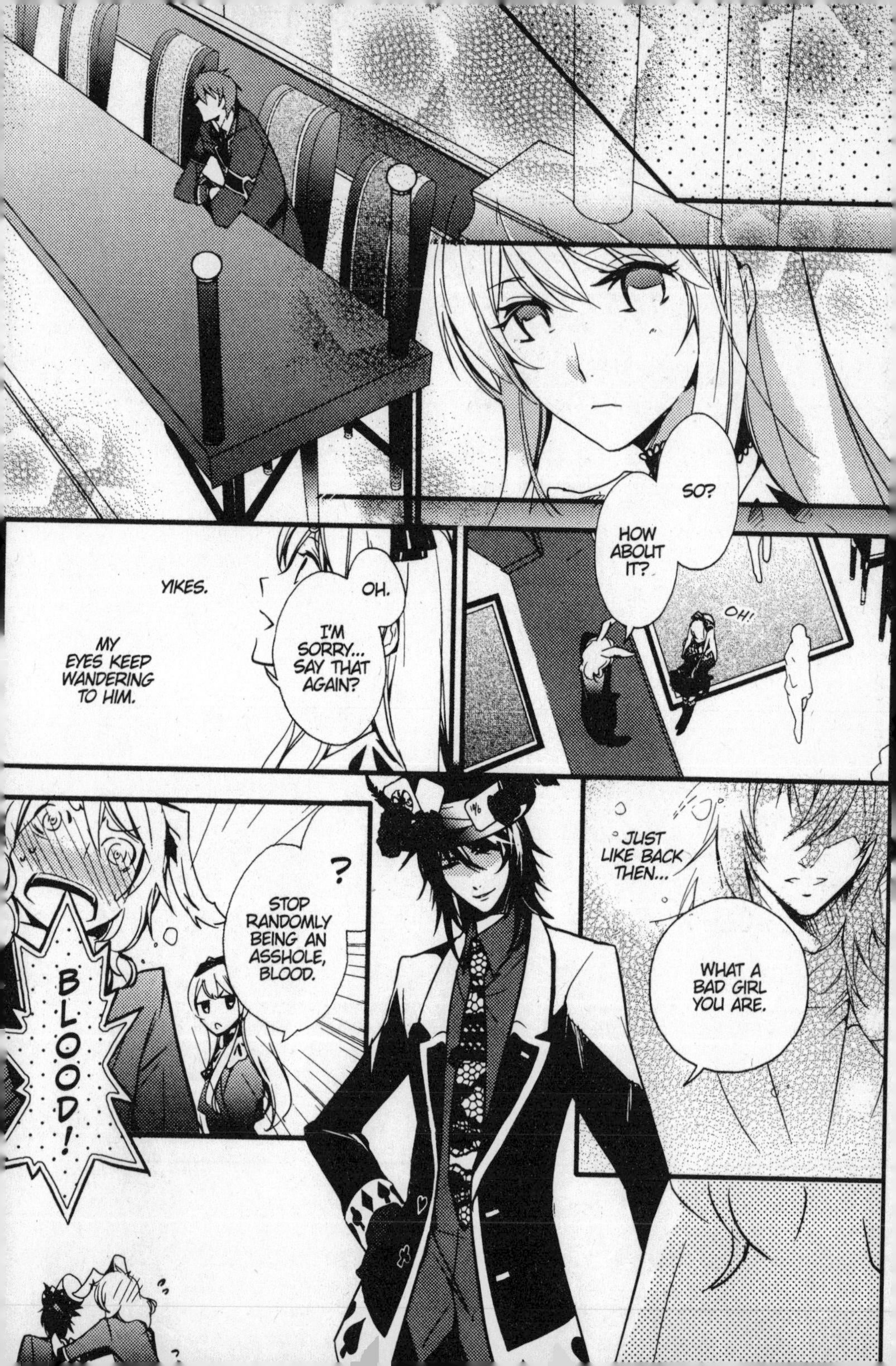
SO?
HOW ABOUT IT?
OH!
OH.
I'M SORRY... SAY THAT AGAIN?
YIKES.
MY EYES KEEP WANDERING TO HIM.
JUST LIKE BACK THEN...
WHAT A BAD GIRL YOU ARE.
?
STOP RANDOMLY BEING AN ASSHOLE, BLOOD.
BLOOD!

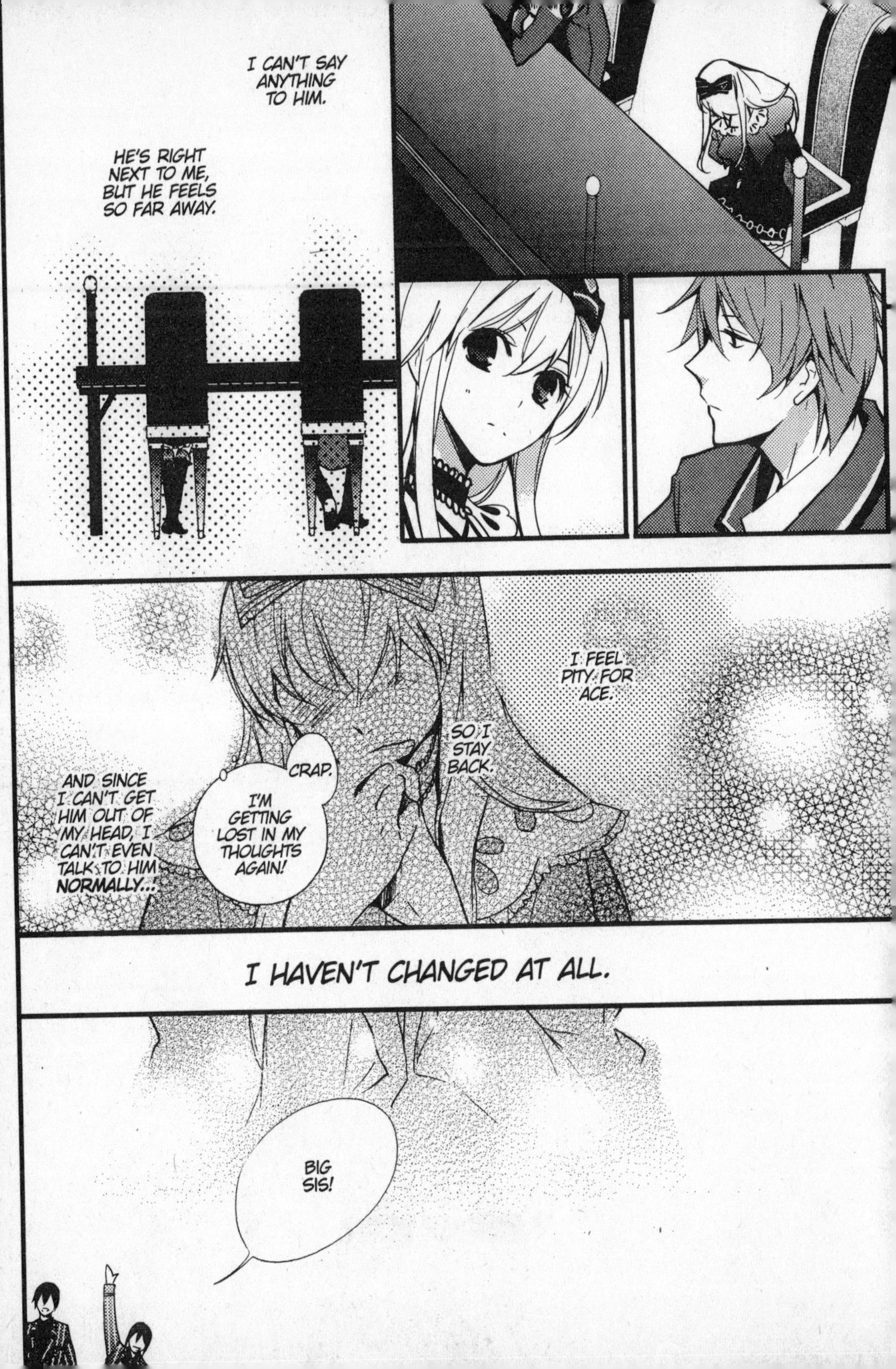
I CAN'T SAY ANYTHING TO HIM.
HE'S RIGHT NEXT TO ME, BUT HE FEELS SO FAR AWAY.
I FEEL PITY FOR ACE.
SO I STAY BACK.
CRAP.
I'M GETTING LOST IN MY THOUGHTS AGAIN!
AND SINCE I CAN'T GET HIM OUT OF MY HEAD, I CAN'T EVEN TALK TO HIM NORMALLY...
I HAVEN'T CHANGED AT ALL.
BIG SIS!

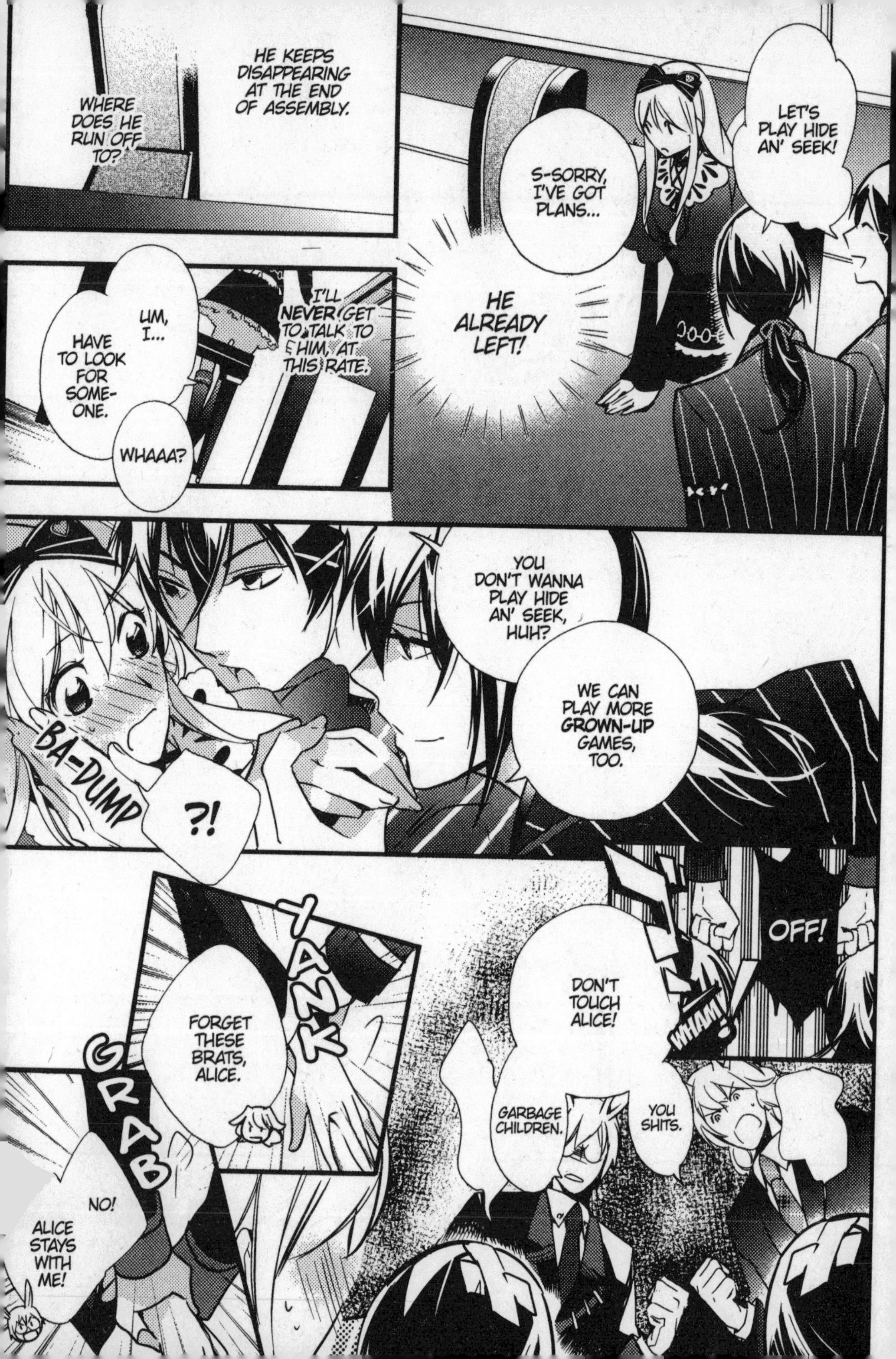
LET'S PLAY HIDE AN' SEEK!
S-SORRY, I'VE GOT PLANS...
HE ALREADY LEFT!
HE KEEPS DISAPPEARING AT THE END OF ASSEMBLY.
WHERE DOES HE RUN OFF TO?
I'LL NEVER GET TO TALK TO HIM, AT THIS RATE.
UM, I... HAVE TO LOOK FOR SOMEONE.
WHAAA?
YOU DON'T WANNA PLAY HIDE AN' SEEK, HUH?
WE CAN PLAY MORE GROWN-UP GAMES, TOO.
BA-DUMP
?!
OFF!
DON'T TOUCH ALICE!
WHAM
YOU SHITS.
GARBAGE CHILDREN.
YANK
FORGET THESE BRATS, ALICE.
GRAB
NO! ALICE STAYS WITH ME!

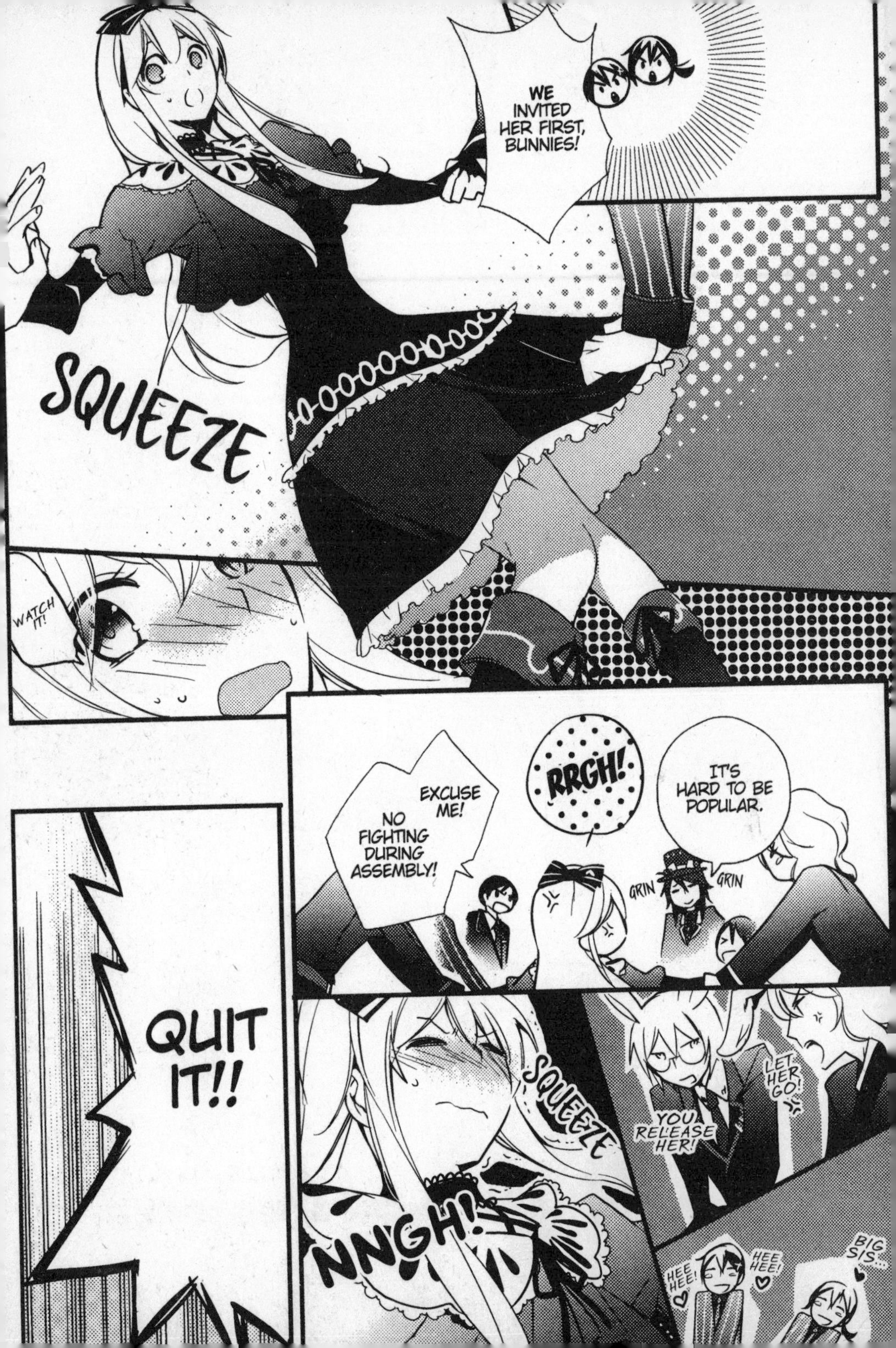
WE INVITED HER FIRST, BUNNIES!
SQUEEZE
WATCH IT!
IT'S HARD TO BE POPULAR.
GRIN
GRIN
RRGH!
EXCUSE ME!
NO FIGHTING DURING ASSEMBLY!
LET HER GO!
YOU RELEASE HER!
SQUEEZE
NNGH!
BIG SIS...
HEE HEE!
HEE HEE!
QUIT IT!!

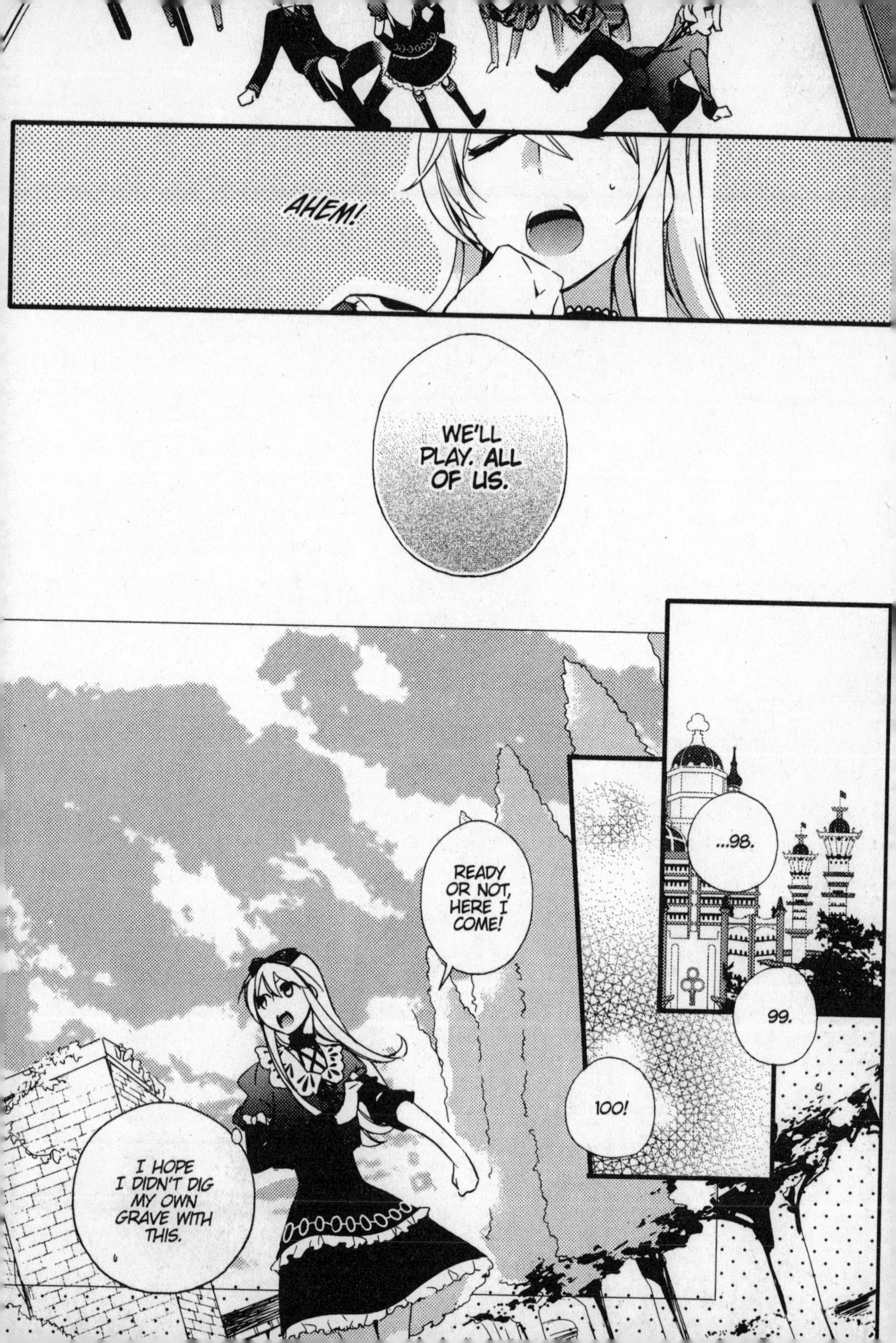
AHEM!
WE'LL PLAY. ALL OF US.
...98.
99.
100!
READY OR NOT, HERE I COME!
I HOPE I DIDN'T DIG MY OWN GRAVE WITH THIS.

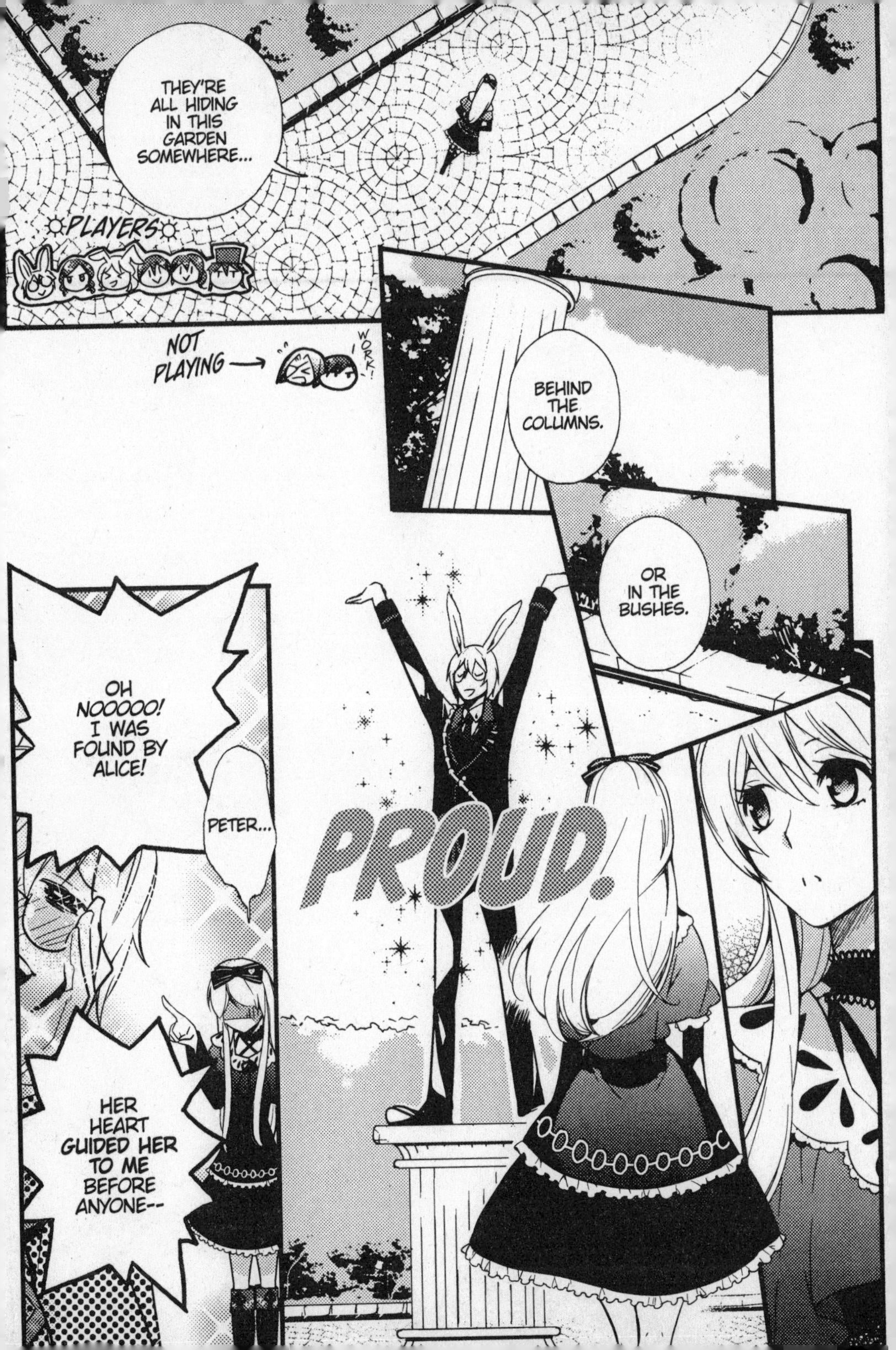
THEY'RE ALL HIDING IN THIS GARDEN SOMEWHERE...
PLAYERS
NOT PLAYING
WORK!
BEHIND THE COLUMNS.
OR IN THE BUSHES.
PROUD.
OH NOOOOO! I WAS FOUND BY ALICE!
PETER...
HER HEART GUIDED HER TO ME BEFORE ANYONE--

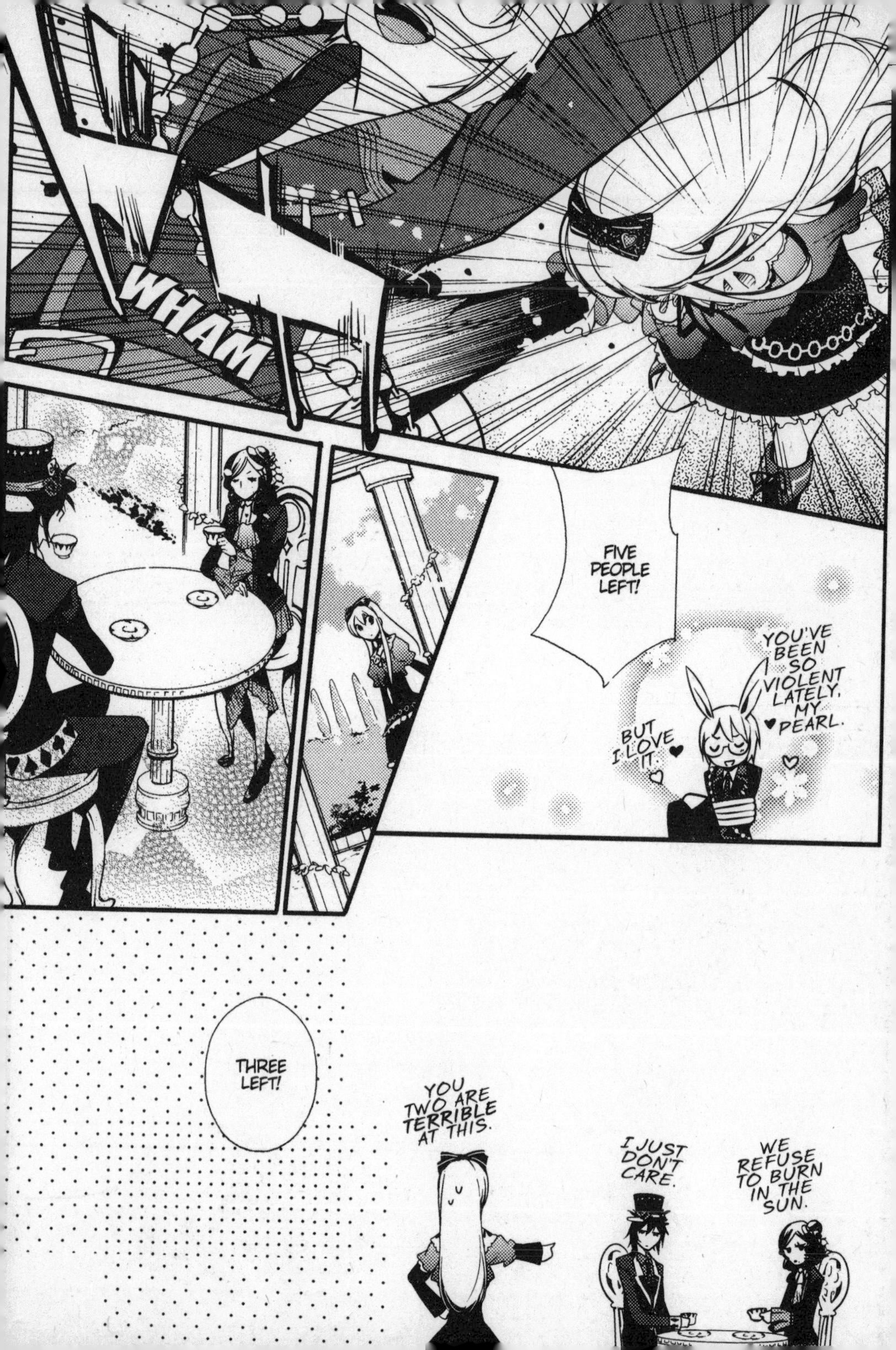
WHAM
FIVE PEOPLE LEFT!
YOU'VE BEEN SO VIOLENT LATELY, MY PEARL.
BUT I LOVE IT.
THREE LEFT!
YOU TWO ARE TERRIBLE AT THIS.
I JUST DON'T CARE.
WE REFUSE TO BURN IN THE SUN.

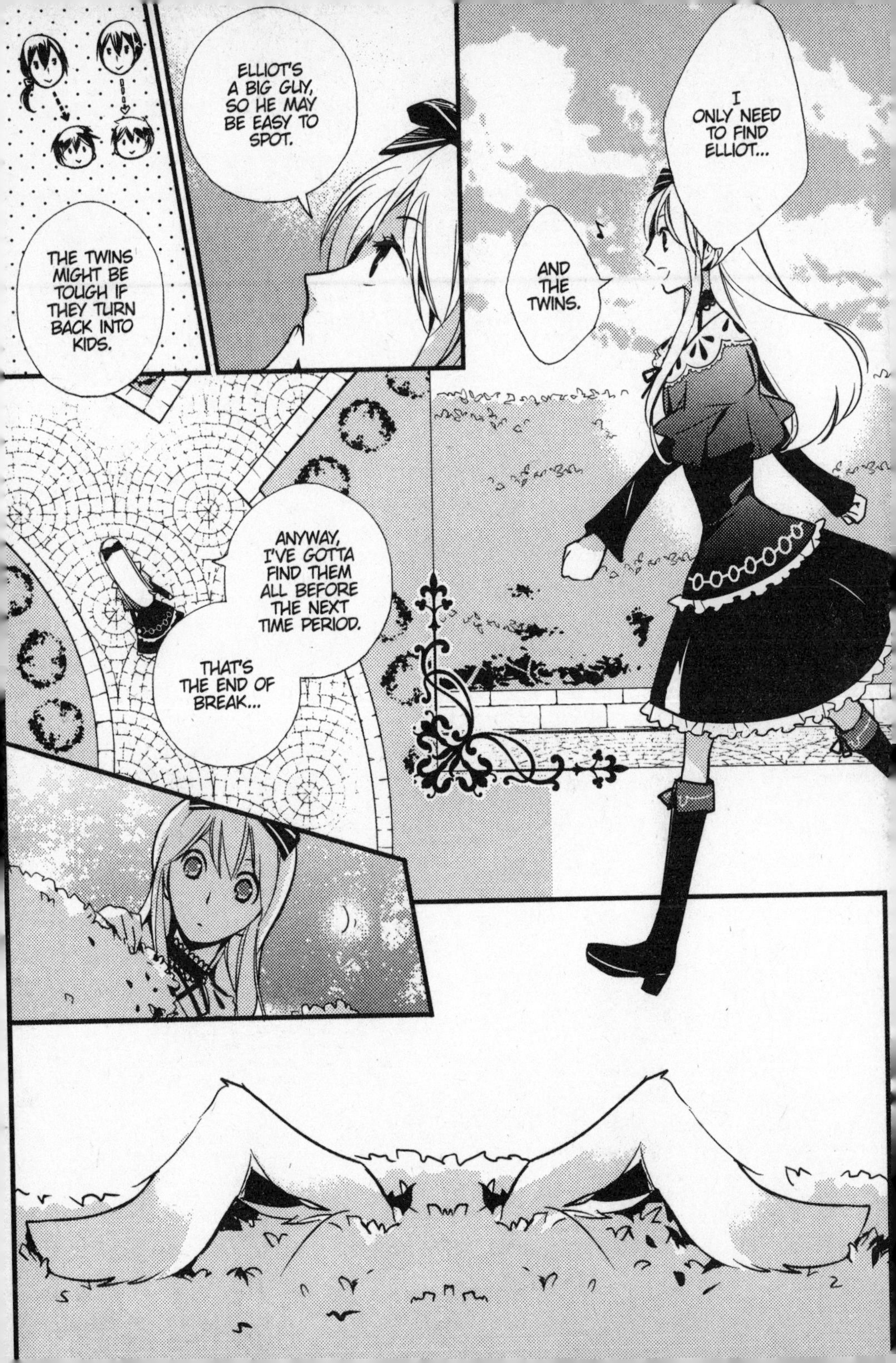
I ONLY NEED TO FIND ELLIOT...
AND THE TWINS.
ELLIOT'S A BIG GUY, SO HE MAY BE EASY TO SPOT.
THE TWINS MIGHT BE TOUGH IF THEY TURN BACK INTO KIDS.
ANYWAY, I'VE GOTTA FIND THEM ALL BEFORE THE NEXT TIME PERIOD.
THAT'S THE END OF BREAK...

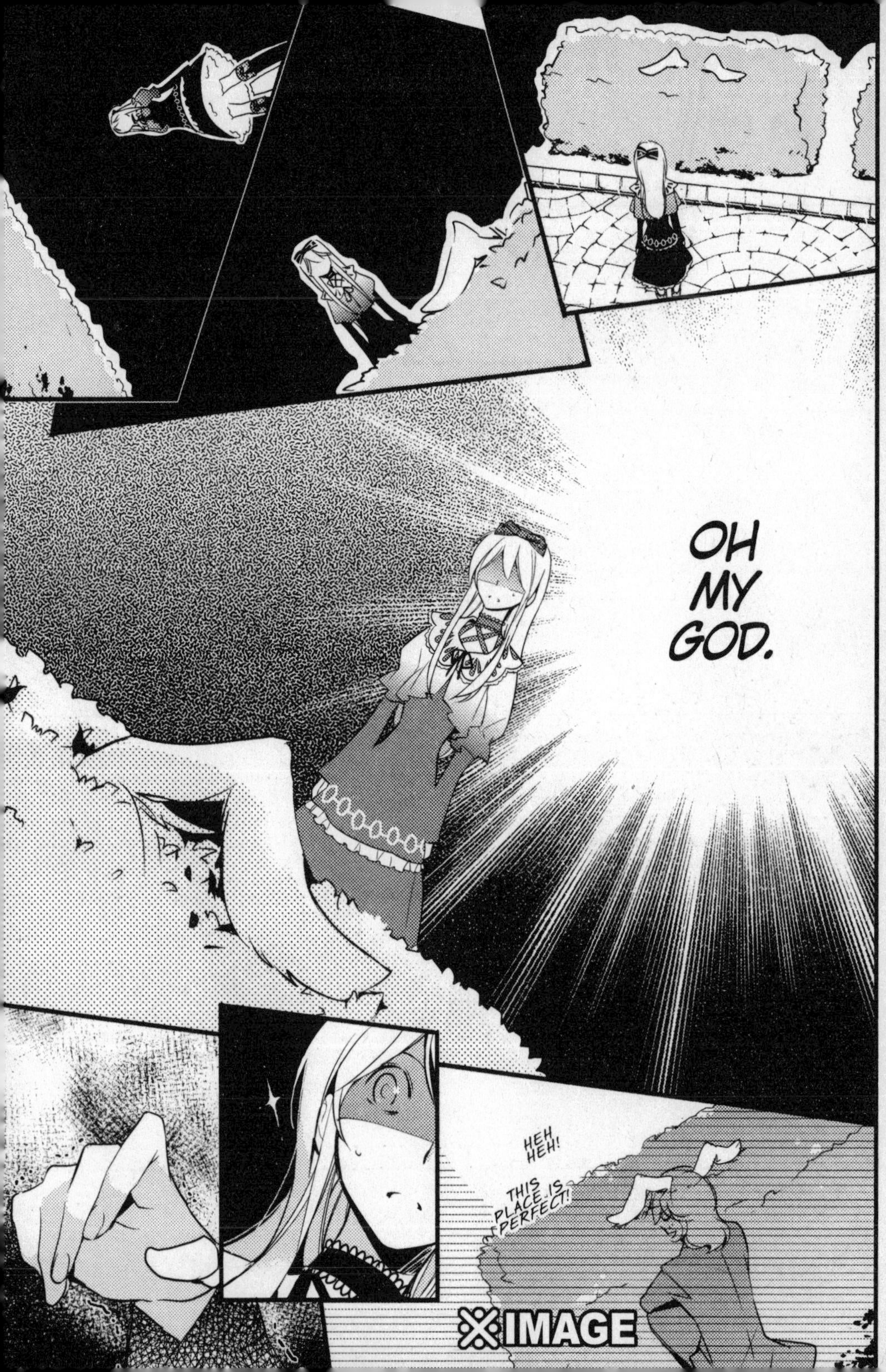
OH MY GOD.
HEH HEH!
THIS PLACE IS PERFECT!
※IMAGE

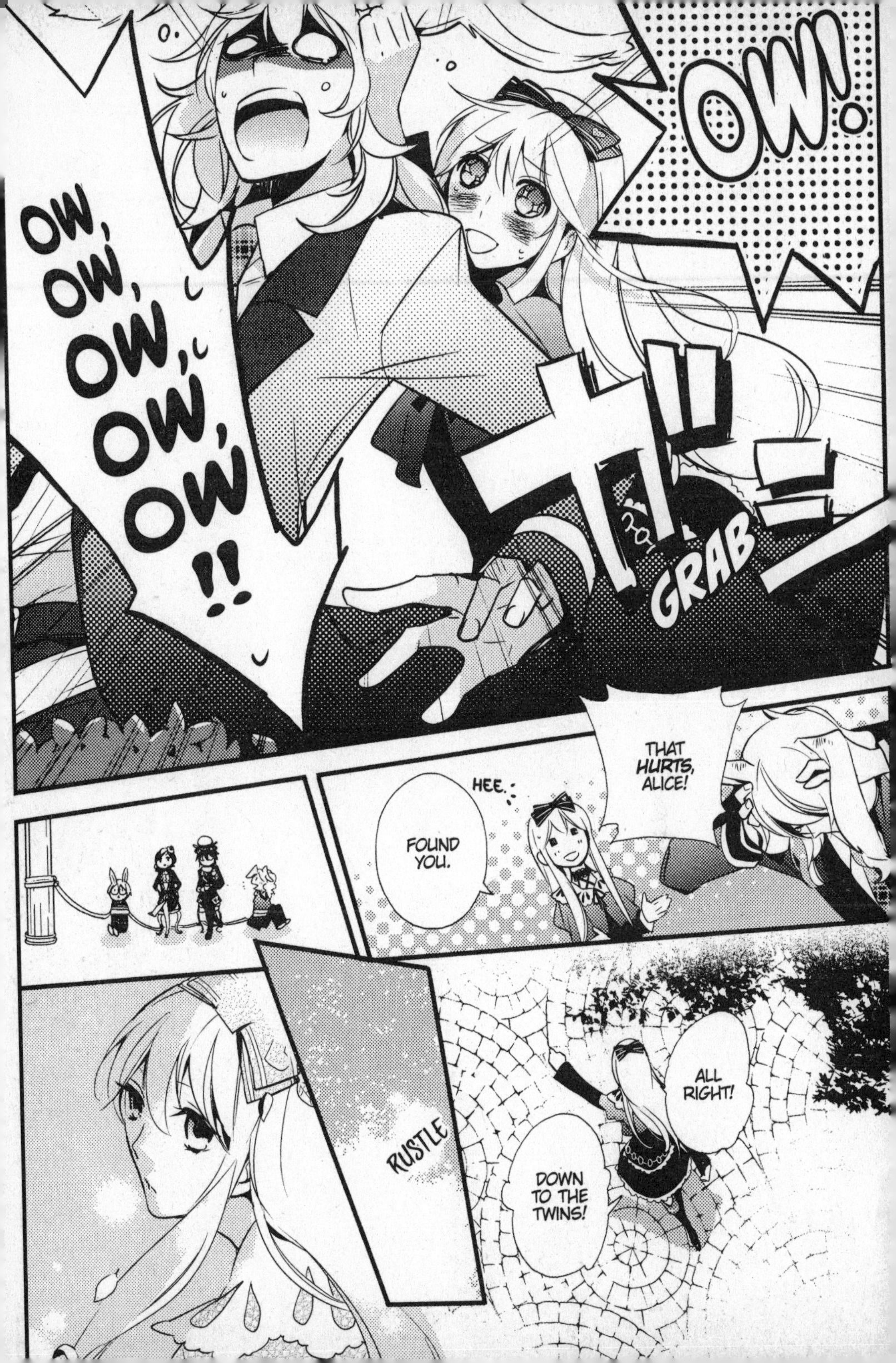
OW!
OW, OW, OW, OW, OW!!
GRAB
THAT HURTS, ALICE!
HEE.
FOUND YOU.
ALL RIGHT!
DOWN TO THE TWINS!
RUSTLE

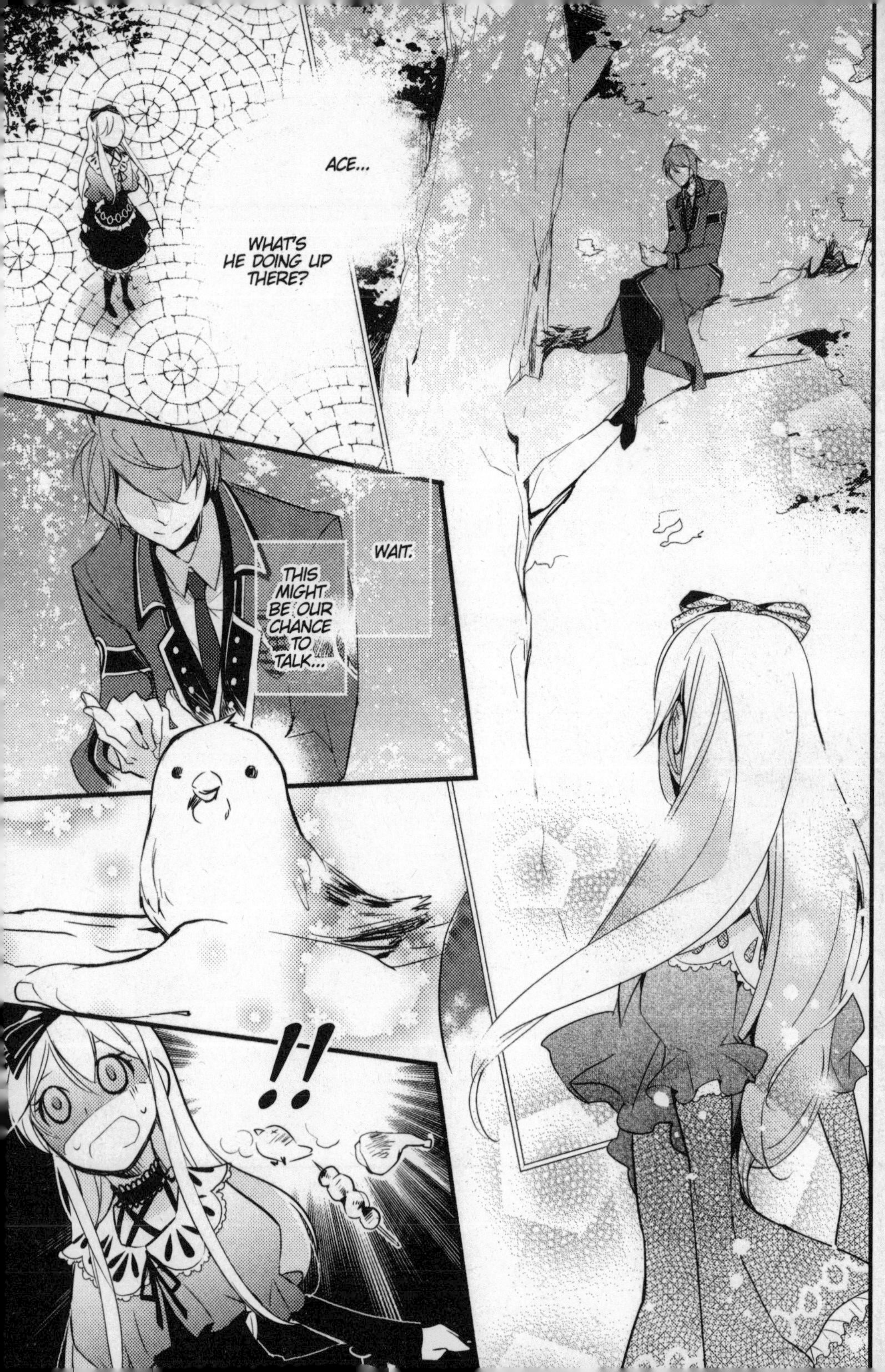
ACE...
WHAT'S HE DOING UP THERE?
WAIT.
THIS MIGHT BE OUR CHANCE TO TALK...
!!

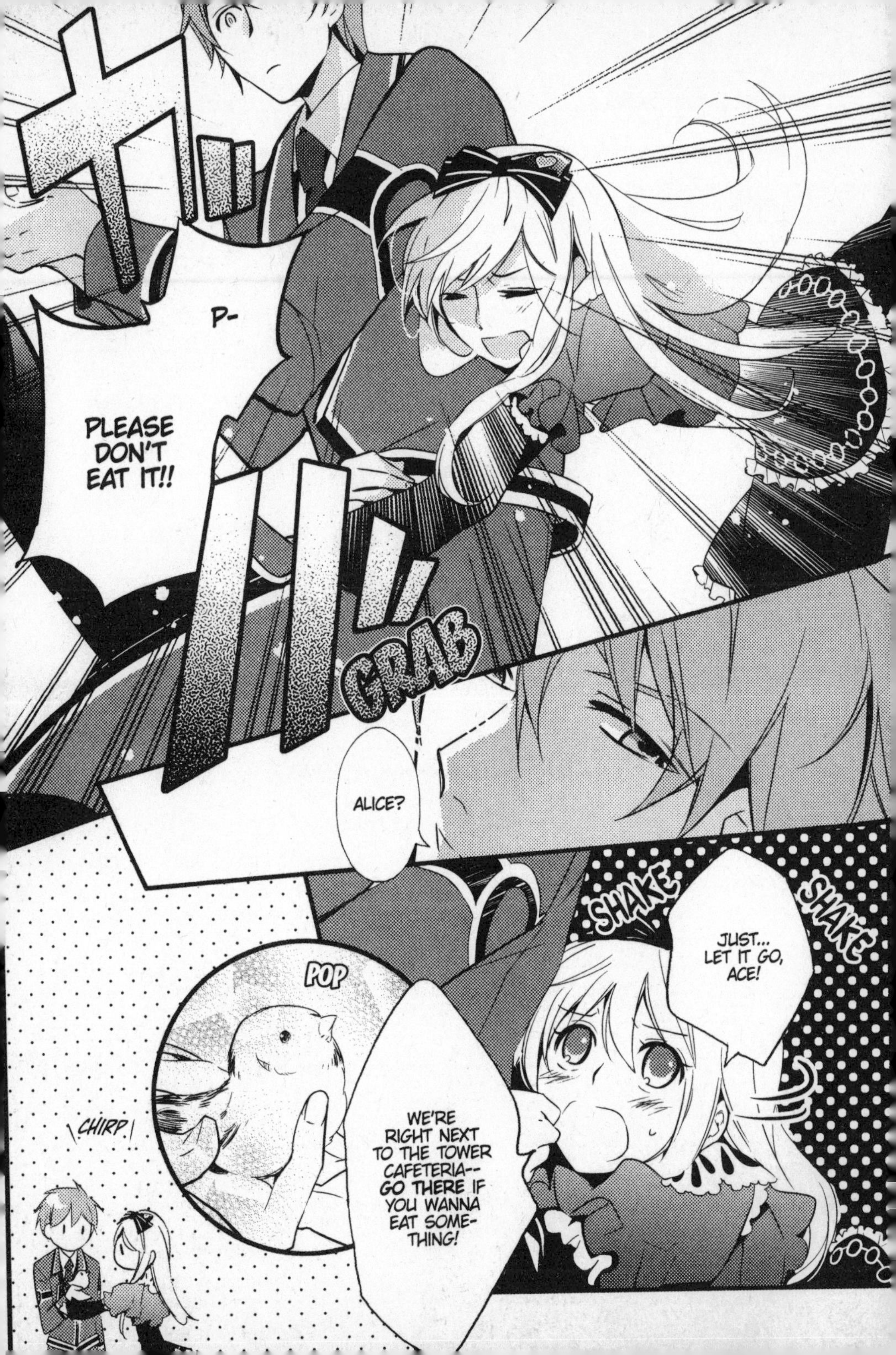

P-
PLEASE DON'T EAT IT!!
GRAB
ALICE?
SHAKE SHAKE
JUST... LET IT GO, ACE!
WE'RE RIGHT NEXT TO THE TOWER CAFETERIA-- GO THERE IF YOU WANNA EAT SOME-THING!
POP
CHIRP!

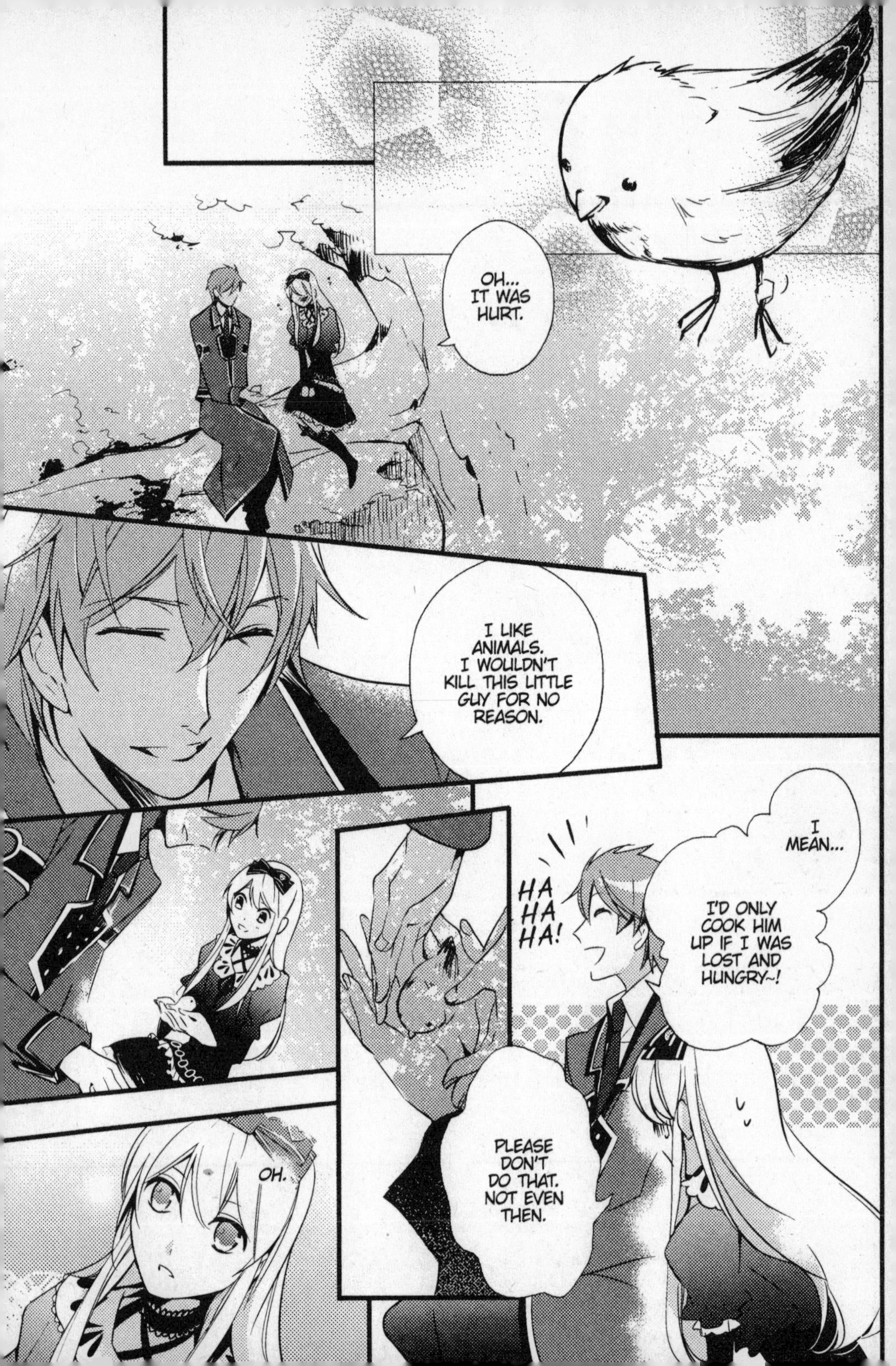
OH... IT WAS HURT.
I LIKE ANIMALS. I WOULDN'T KILL THIS LITTLE GUY FOR NO REASON.
I MEAN...
I'D ONLY COOK HIM UP IF I WAS LOST AND HUNGRY~!
HA HA HA HA!
PLEASE DON'T DO THAT. NOT EVEN THEN.
OH.

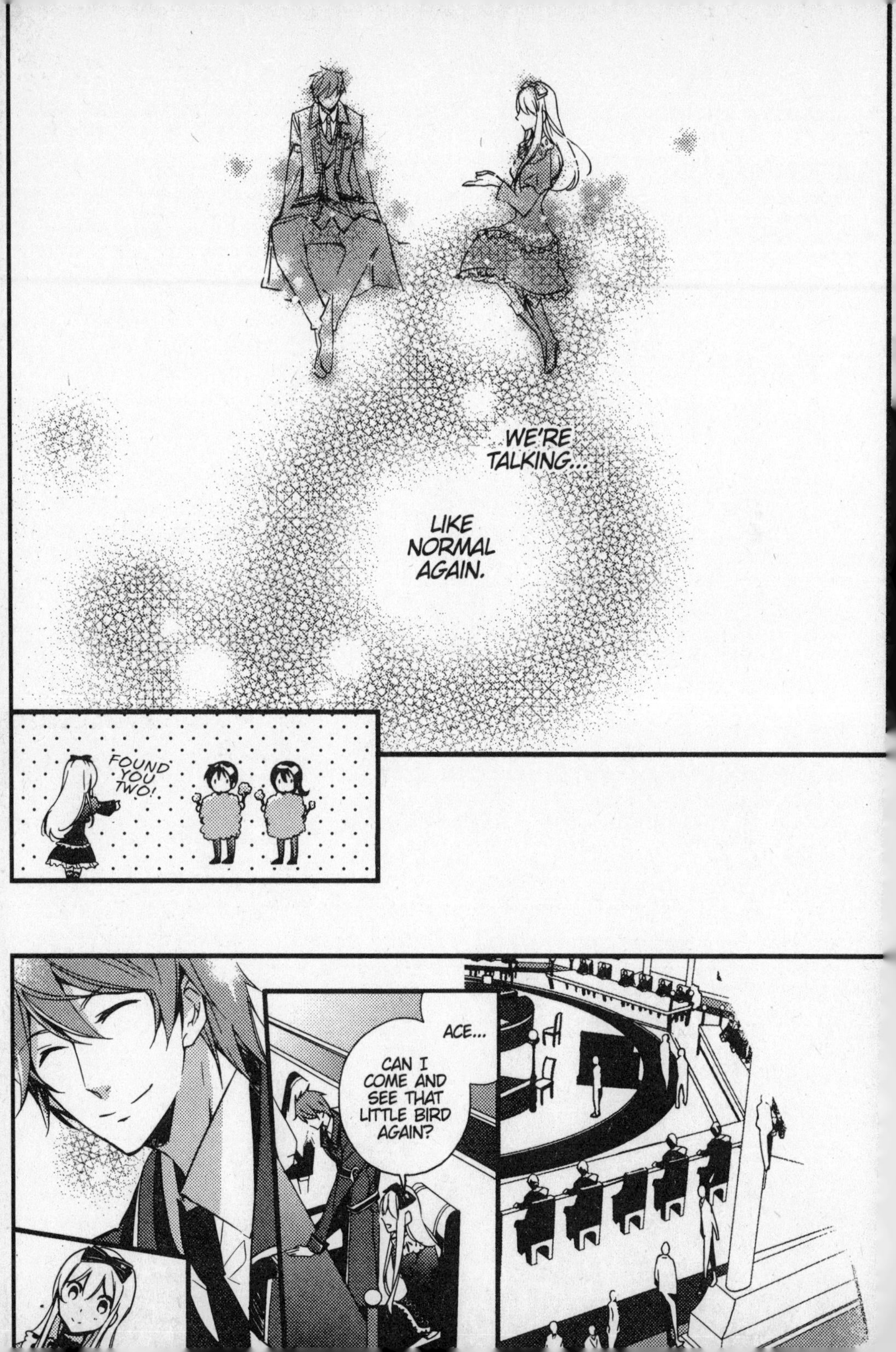
WE'RE TALKING...
LIKE NORMAL AGAIN.
FOUND YOU TWO!
ACE...
CAN I COME AND SEE THAT LITTLE BIRD AGAIN?

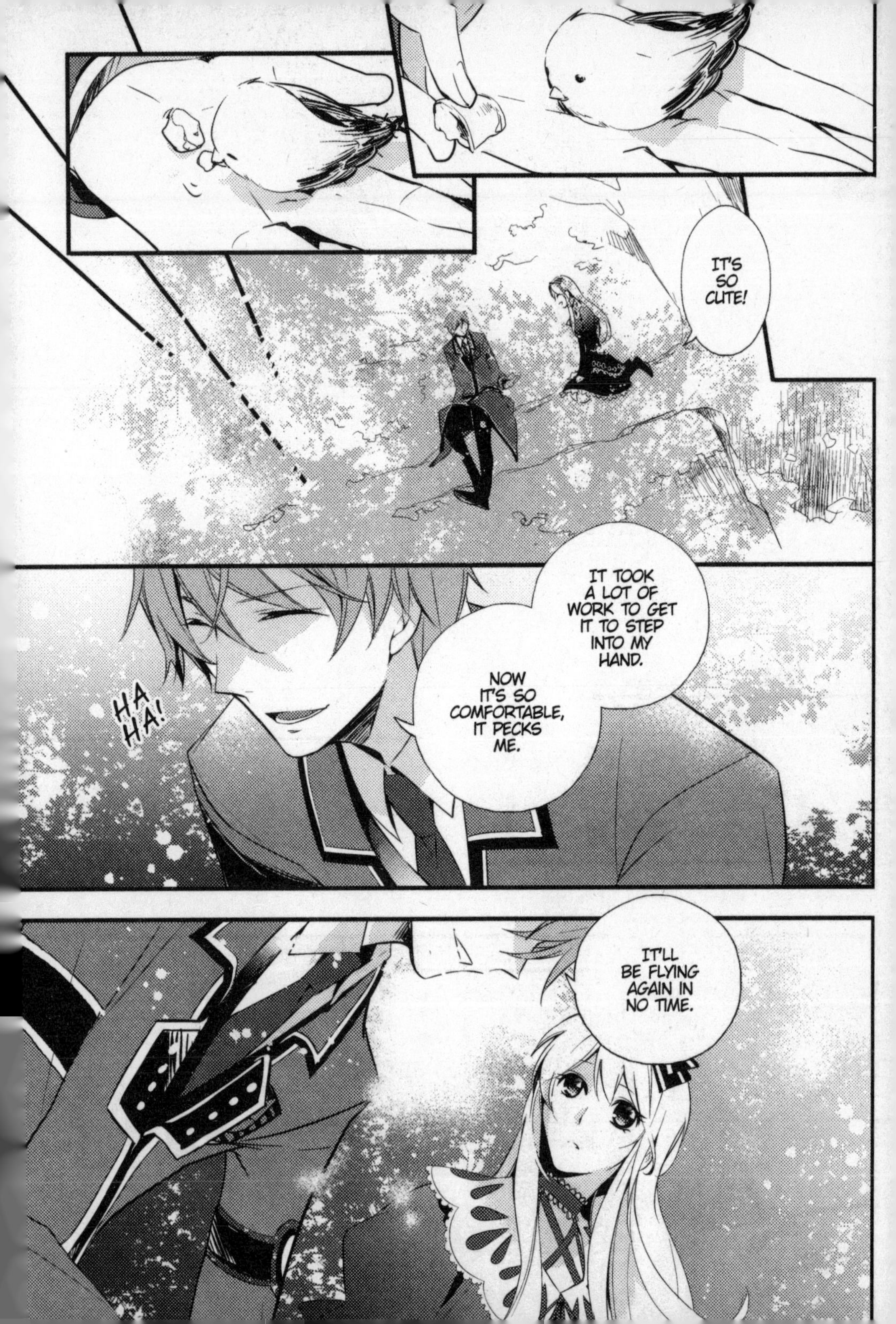
IT'S SO CUTE!
IT TOOK A LOT OF WORK TO GET IT TO STEP INTO MY HAND.
NOW IT'S SO COMFORTABLE, IT PECKS ME.
HA HA!
IT'LL BE FLYING AGAIN IN NO TIME.

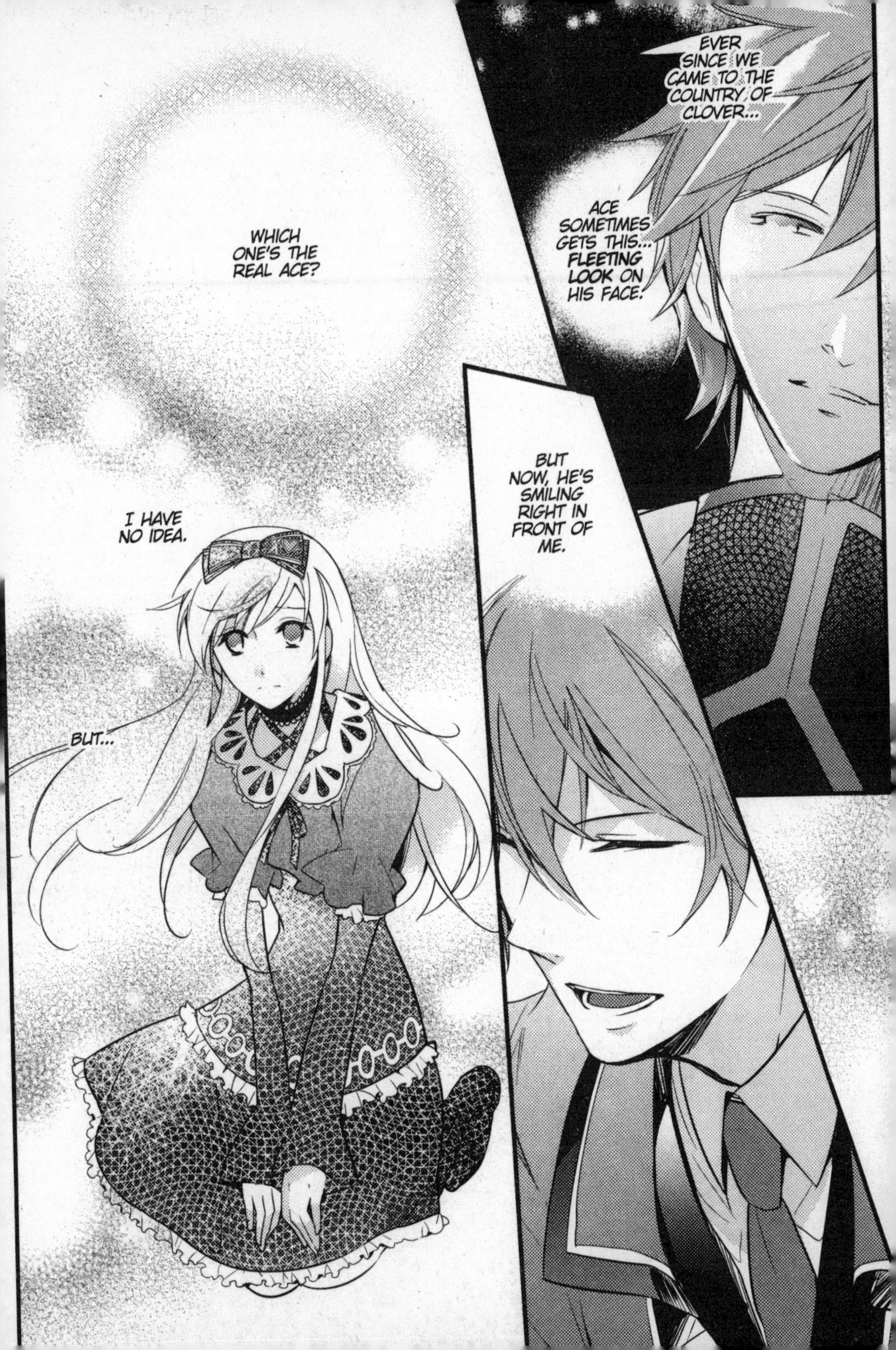

EVER SINCE WE CAME TO THE COUNTRY OF CLOVER...
ACE SOMETIMES GETS THIS... FLEETING LOOK ON HIS FACE.
BUT NOW, HE'S SMILING RIGHT IN FRONT OF ME.
WHICH ONE'S THE REAL ACE?
I HAVE NO IDEA.
BUT...

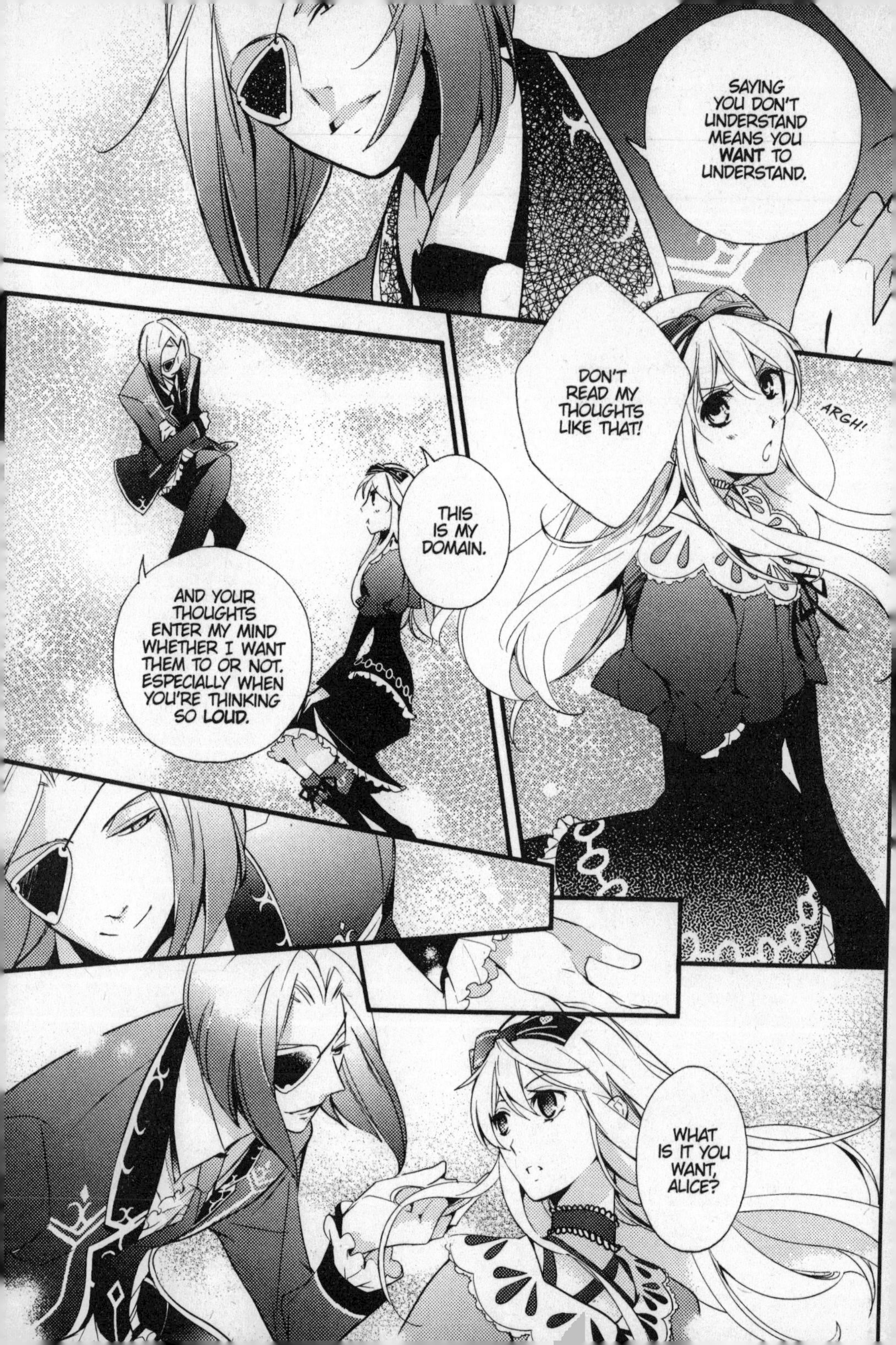
SAYING YOU DON'T UNDERSTAND MEANS YOU WANT TO UNDERSTAND.
DON'T READ MY THOUGHTS LIKE THAT!
ARGH!
THIS IS MY DOMAIN.
AND YOUR THOUGHTS ENTER MY MIND WHETHER I WANT THEM TO OR NOT. ESPECIALLY WHEN YOU'RE THINKING SO LOUD.
WHAT IS IT YOU WANT, ALICE?

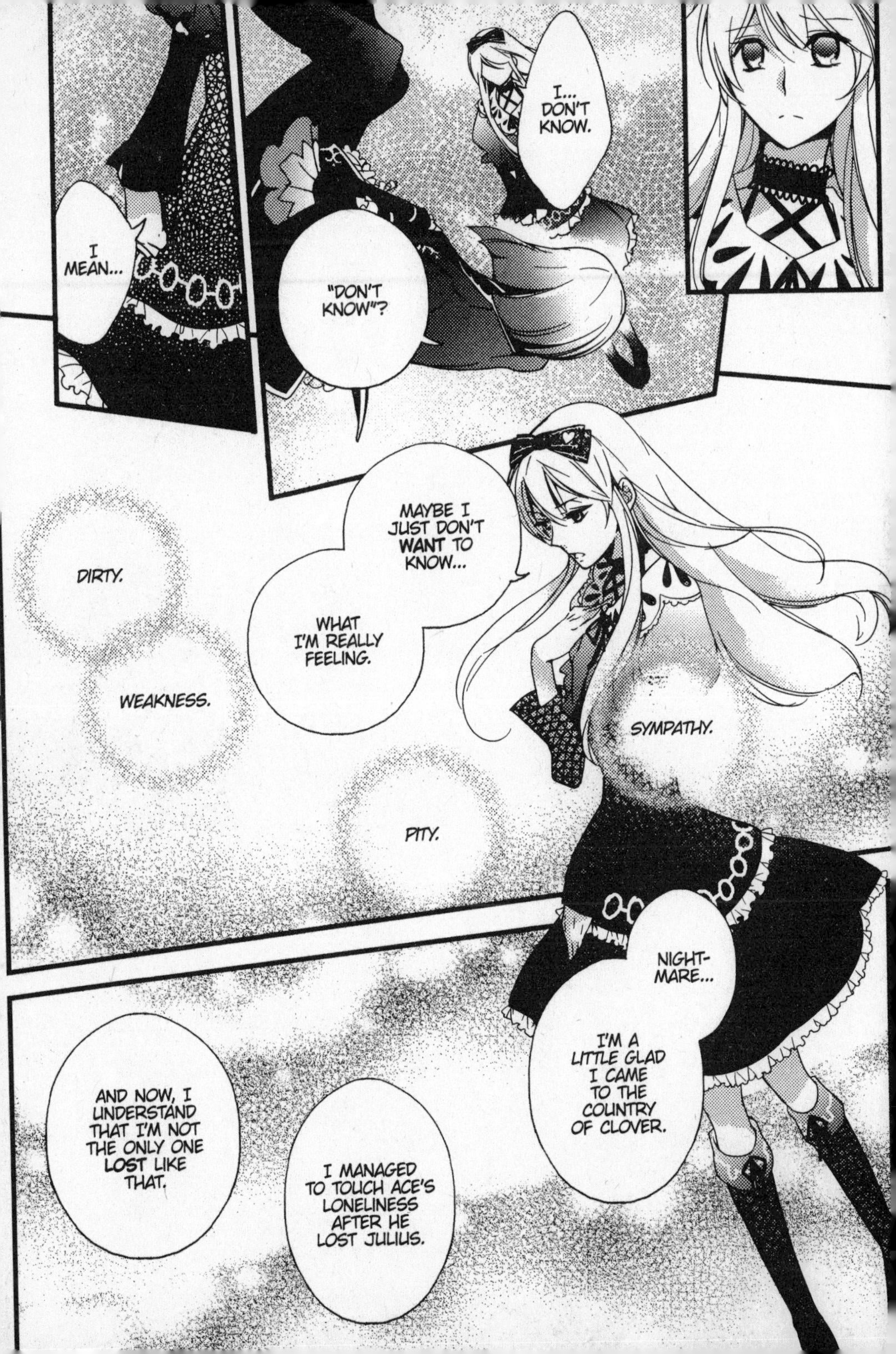
I... DON'T KNOW.
"DON'T KNOW"?
I MEAN...
MAYBE I JUST DON'T WANT TO KNOW...
WHAT I'M REALLY FEELING.
SYMPATHY.
DIRTY.
WEAKNESS.
PITY.
NIGHT-MARE...
I'M A LITTLE GLAD I CAME TO THE COUNTRY OF CLOVER.
I MANAGED TO TOUCH ACE'S LONELINESS AFTER HE LOST JULIUS.
AND NOW, I UNDERSTAND THAT I'M NOT THE ONLY ONE LOST LIKE THAT.

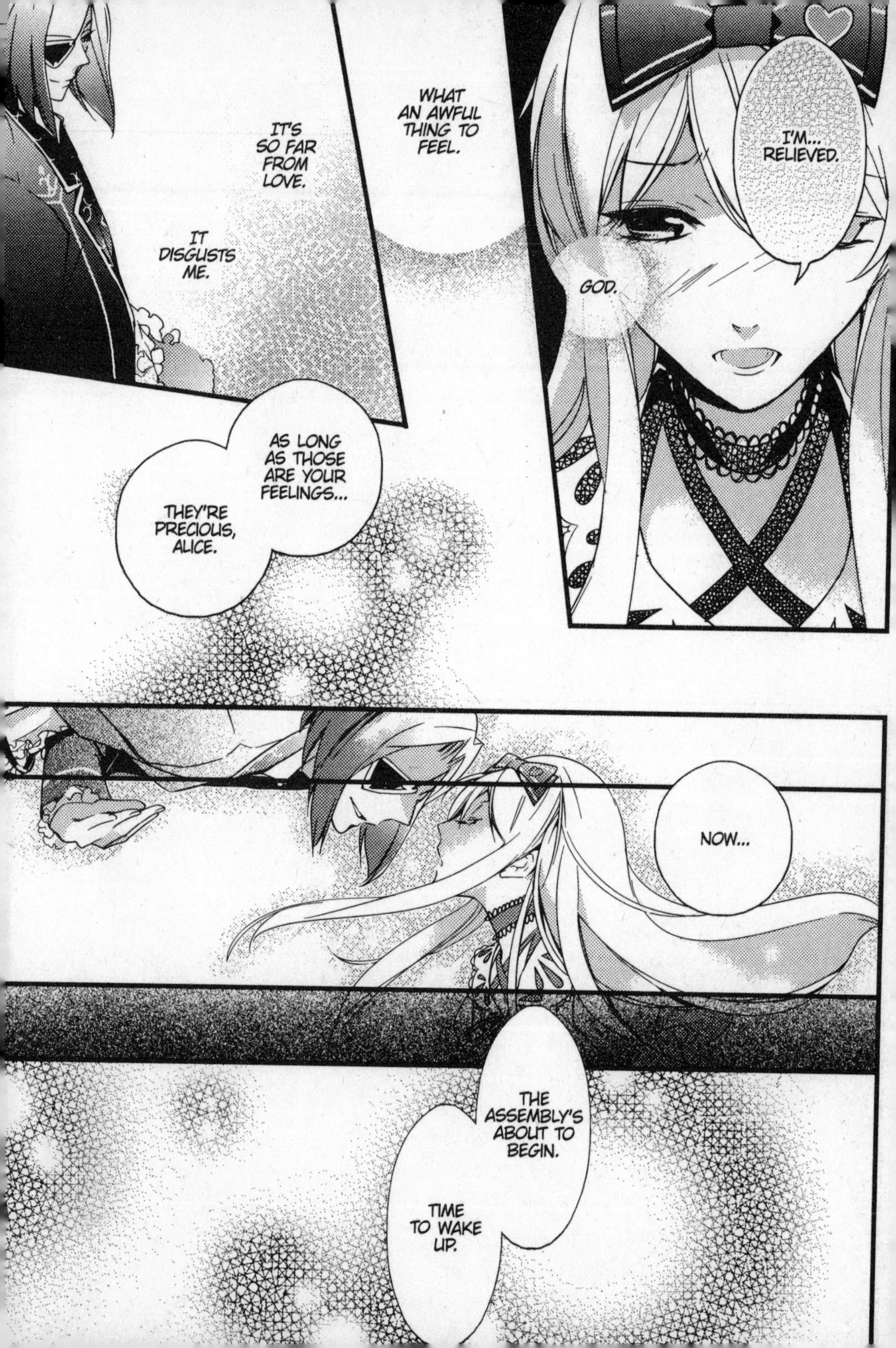
I'M... RELIEVED.
GOD.
WHAT AN AWFUL THING TO FEEL.
IT'S SO FAR FROM LOVE.
IT DISGUSTS ME.
AS LONG AS THOSE ARE YOUR FEELINGS...
THEY'RE PRECIOUS, ALICE.
NOW...
THE ASSEMBLY'S ABOUT TO BEGIN.
TIME TO WAKE UP.

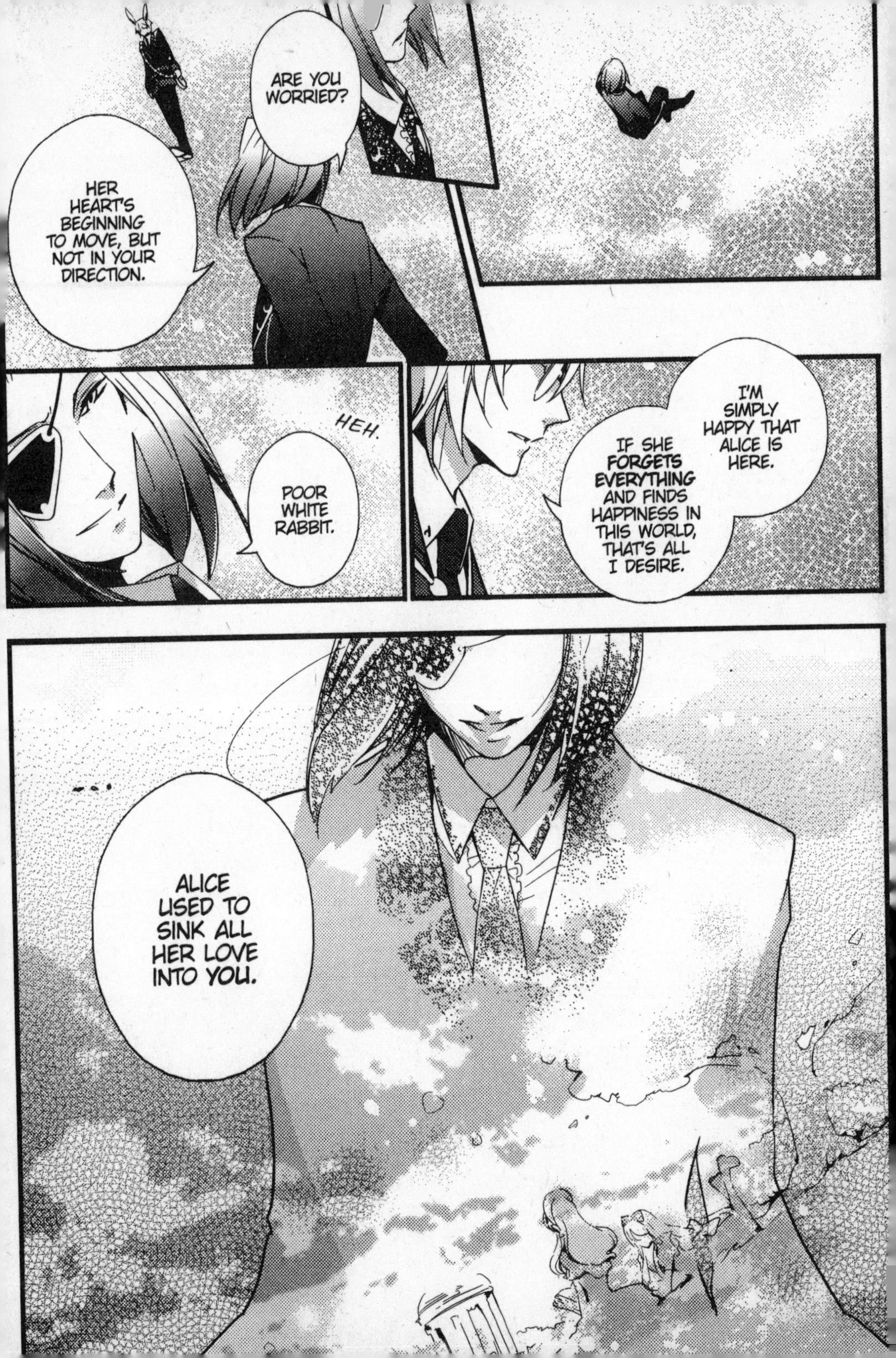
ARE YOU WORRIED?
HER HEART'S BEGINNING TO MOVE, BUT NOT IN YOUR DIRECTION.
I'M SIMPLY HAPPY THAT ALICE IS HERE.
IF SHE FORGETS EVERYTHING AND FINDS HAPPINESS IN THIS WORLD, THAT'S ALL I DESIRE.
HEH.
POOR WHITE RABBIT.
ALICE USED TO SINK ALL HER LOVE INTO YOU.

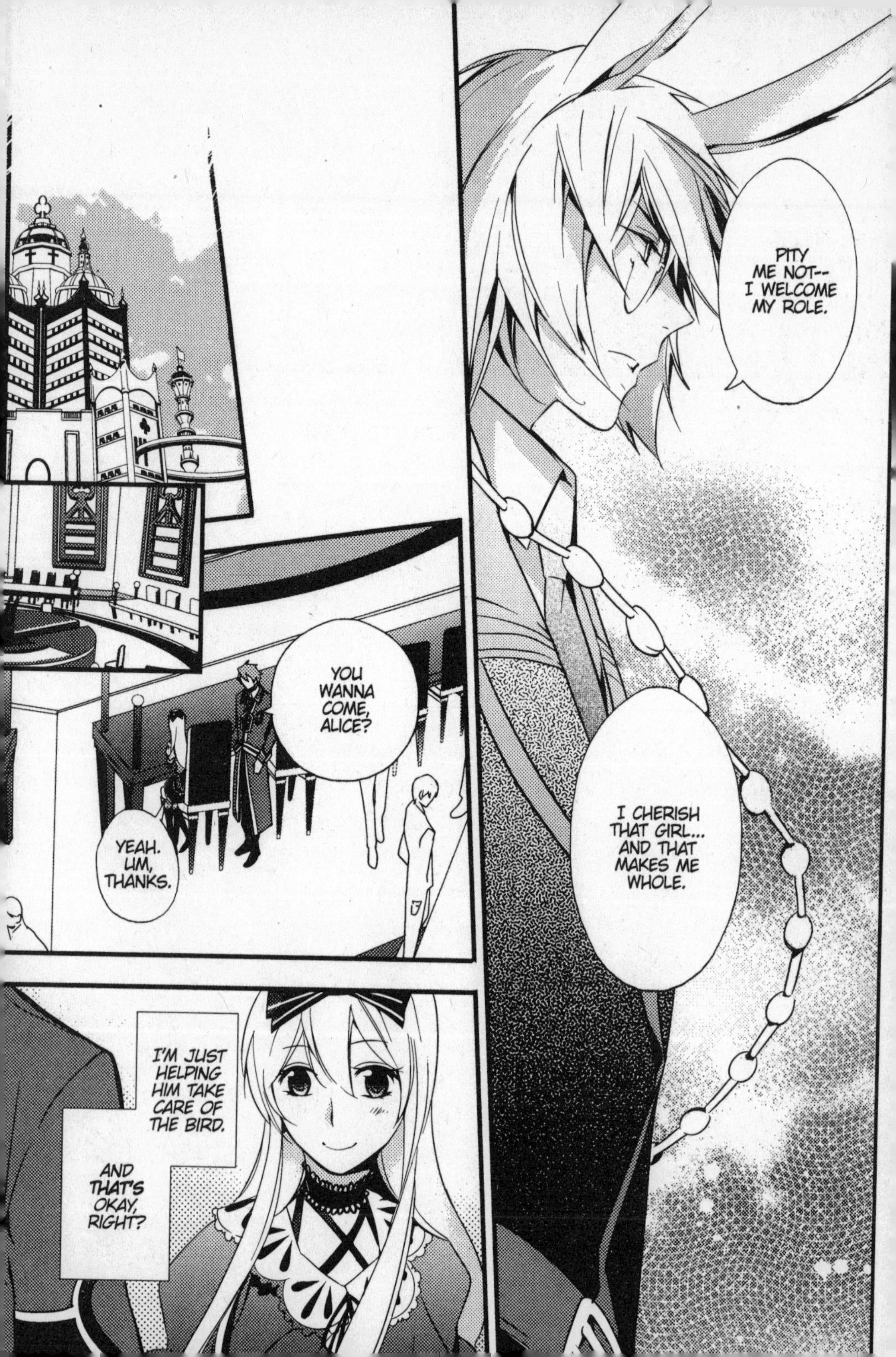
PITY ME NOT-- I WELCOME MY ROLE.
I CHERISH THAT GIRL... AND THAT MAKES ME WHOLE.
YOU WANNA COME, ALICE?
YEAH. UM, THANKS.
I'M JUST HELPING HIM TAKE CARE OF THE BIRD.
AND THAT'S OKAY, RIGHT?

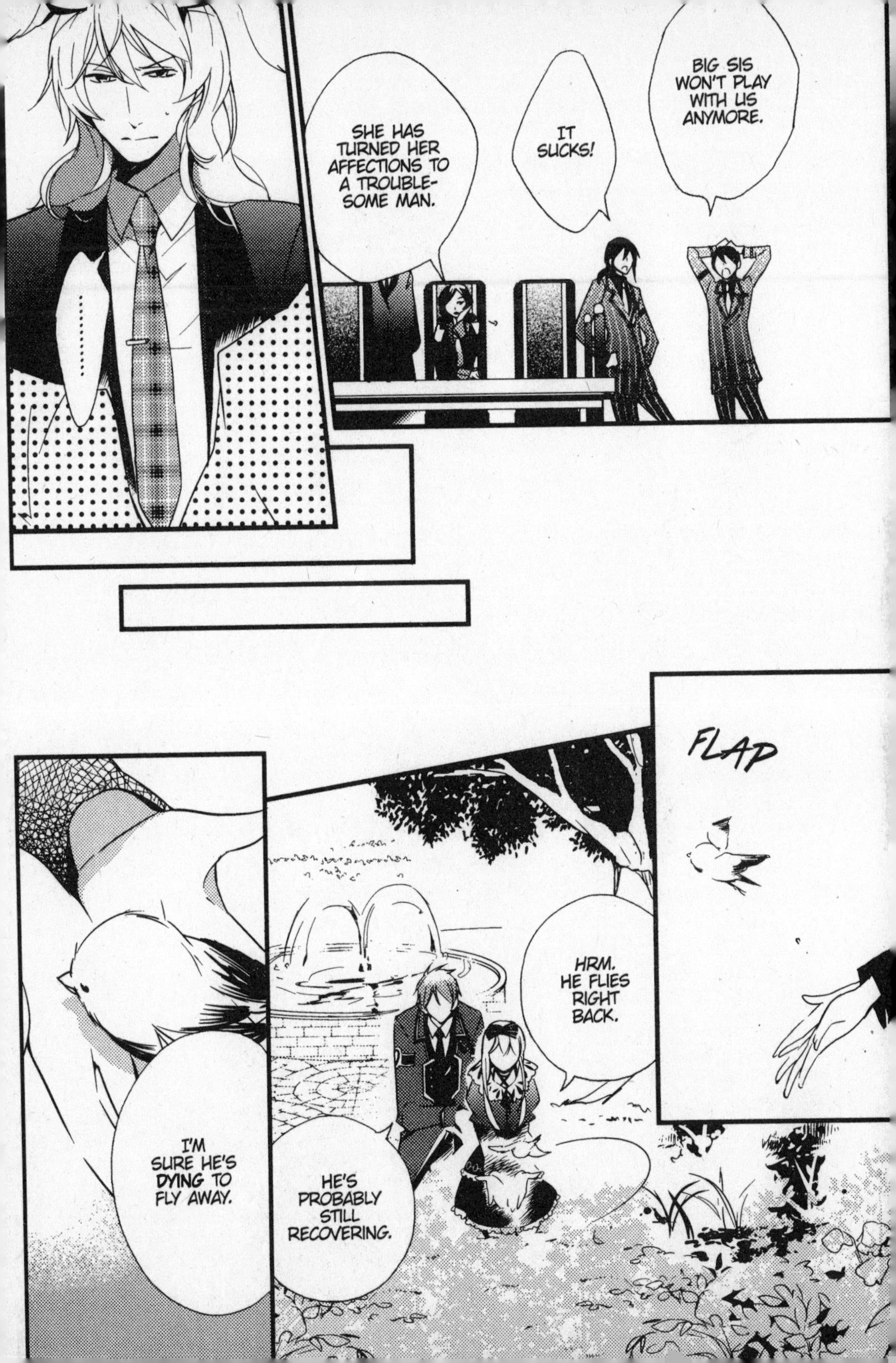
BIG SIS WON'T PLAY WITH US ANYMORE.
IT SUCKS!
SHE HAS TURNED HER AFFECTIONS TO A TROUBLE-SOME MAN.
FLAP
HRM. HE FLIES RIGHT BACK.
HE'S PROBABLY STILL RECOVERING.
I'M SURE HE'S DYING TO FLY AWAY.

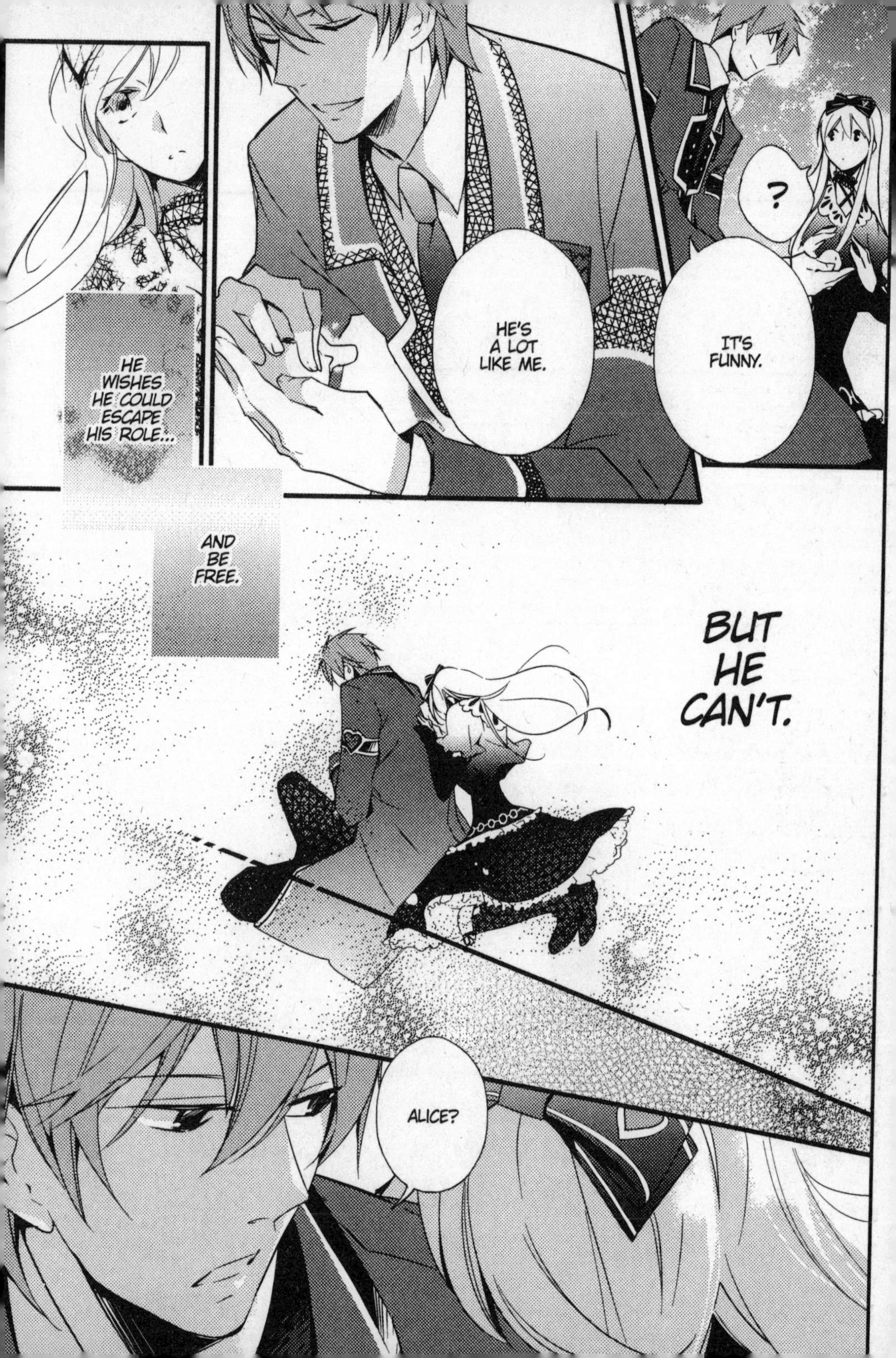
?
IT'S FUNNY.
HE'S A LOT LIKE ME.
HE WISHES HE COULD ESCAPE HIS ROLE...
AND BE FREE.
BUT HE CAN'T.
ALICE?

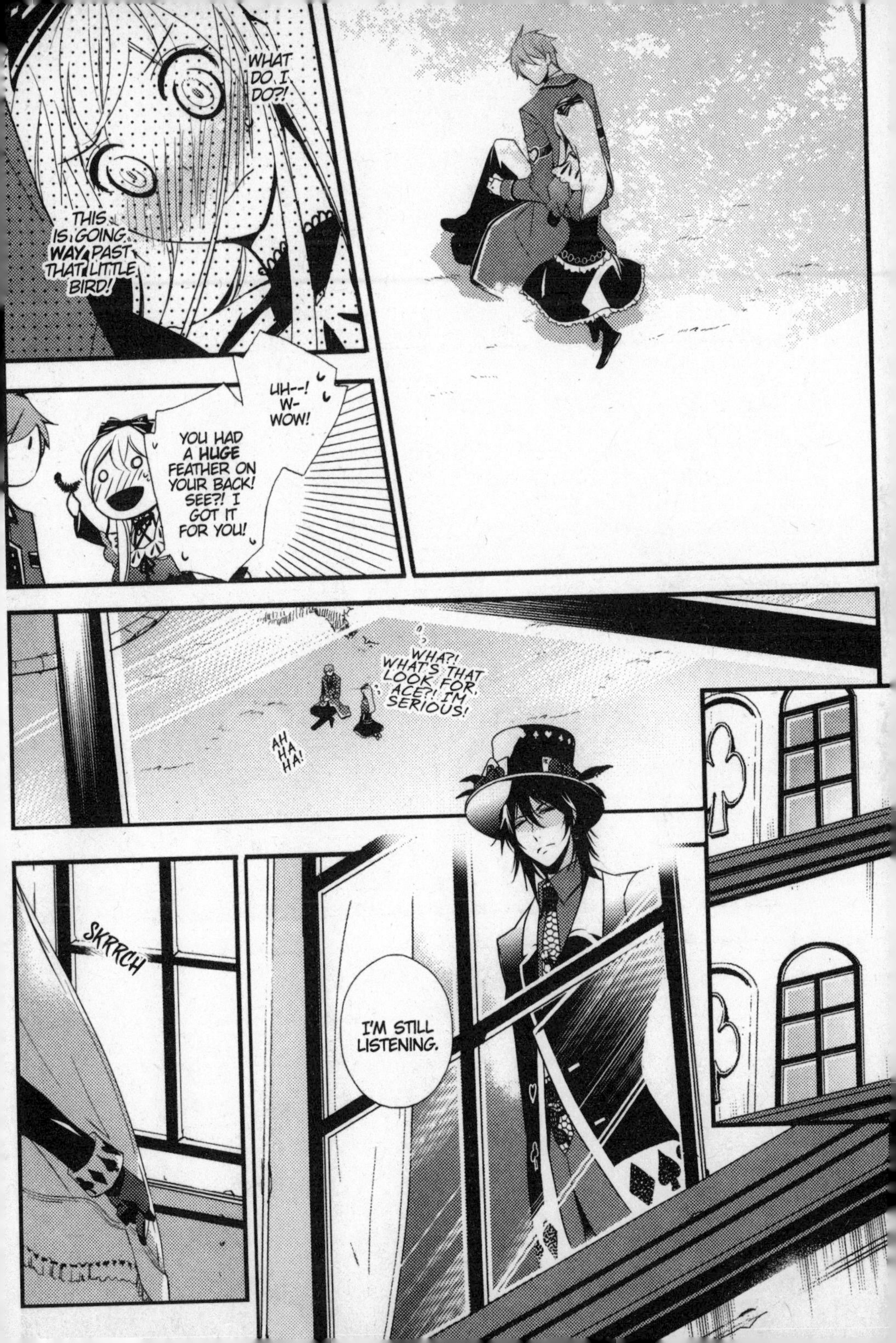
WHAT DO I DO?!
THIS IS GOING WAY PAST THAT LITTLE BIRD!
UH--! W-WOW!
YOU HAD A HUGE FEATHER ON YOUR BACK! SEE?! I GOT IT FOR YOU!
WHA?! WHAT'S THAT LOOK FOR, ACE?! I'M SERIOUS!
AH HA HA!
I'M STILL LISTENING.
SKRRCH

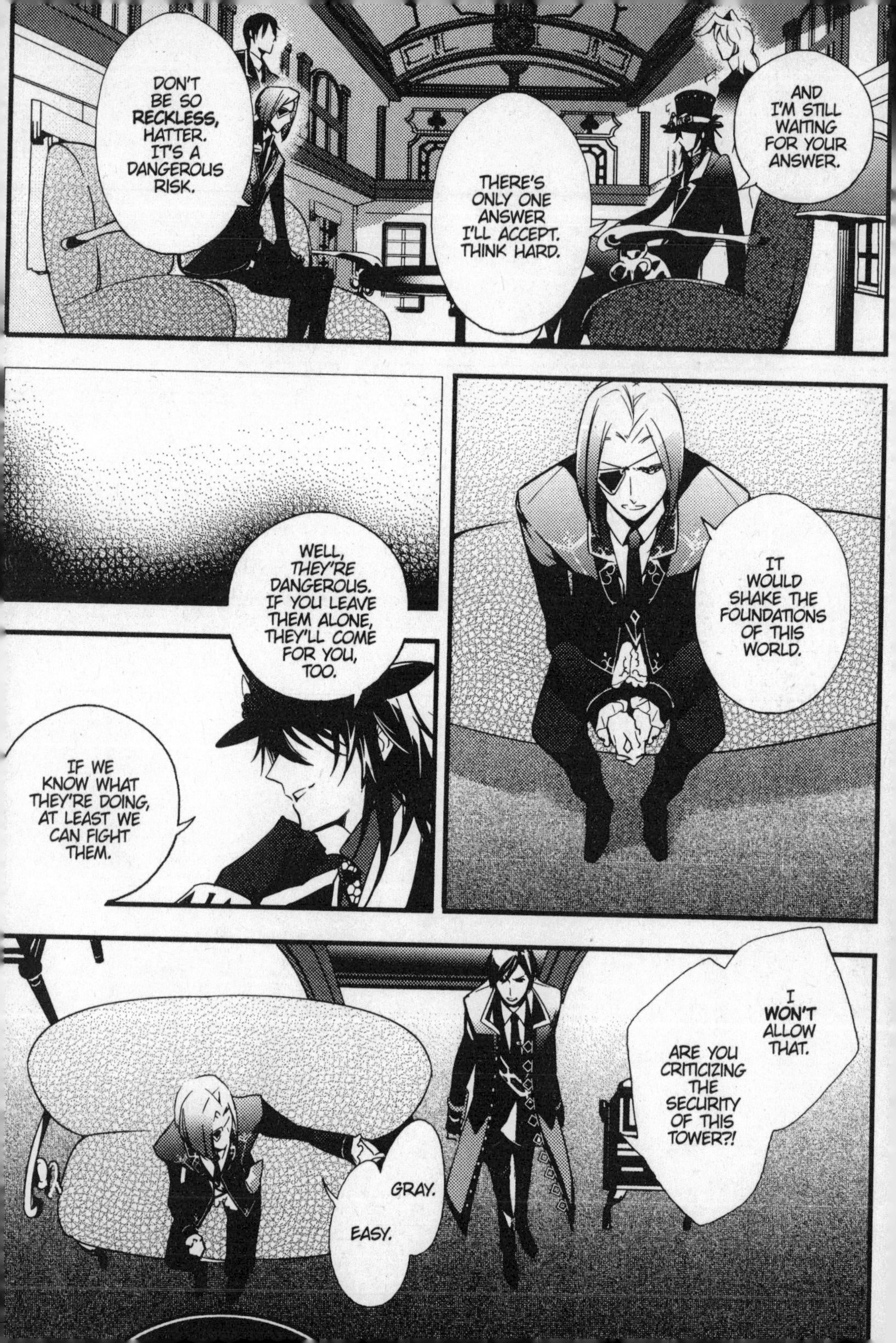
AND I'M STILL WAITING FOR YOUR ANSWER.
THERE'S ONLY ONE ANSWER I'LL ACCEPT. THINK HARD.
DON'T BE SO RECKLESS, HATTER. IT'S A DANGEROUS RISK.
IT WOULD SHAKE THE FOUNDATIONS OF THIS WORLD.
WELL, THEY'RE DANGEROUS. IF YOU LEAVE THEM ALONE, THEY'LL COME FOR YOU, TOO.
IF WE KNOW WHAT THEY'RE DOING, AT LEAST WE CAN FIGHT THEM.
I WON'T ALLOW THAT.
ARE YOU CRITICIZING THE SECURITY OF THIS TOWER?!
GRAY.
EASY.

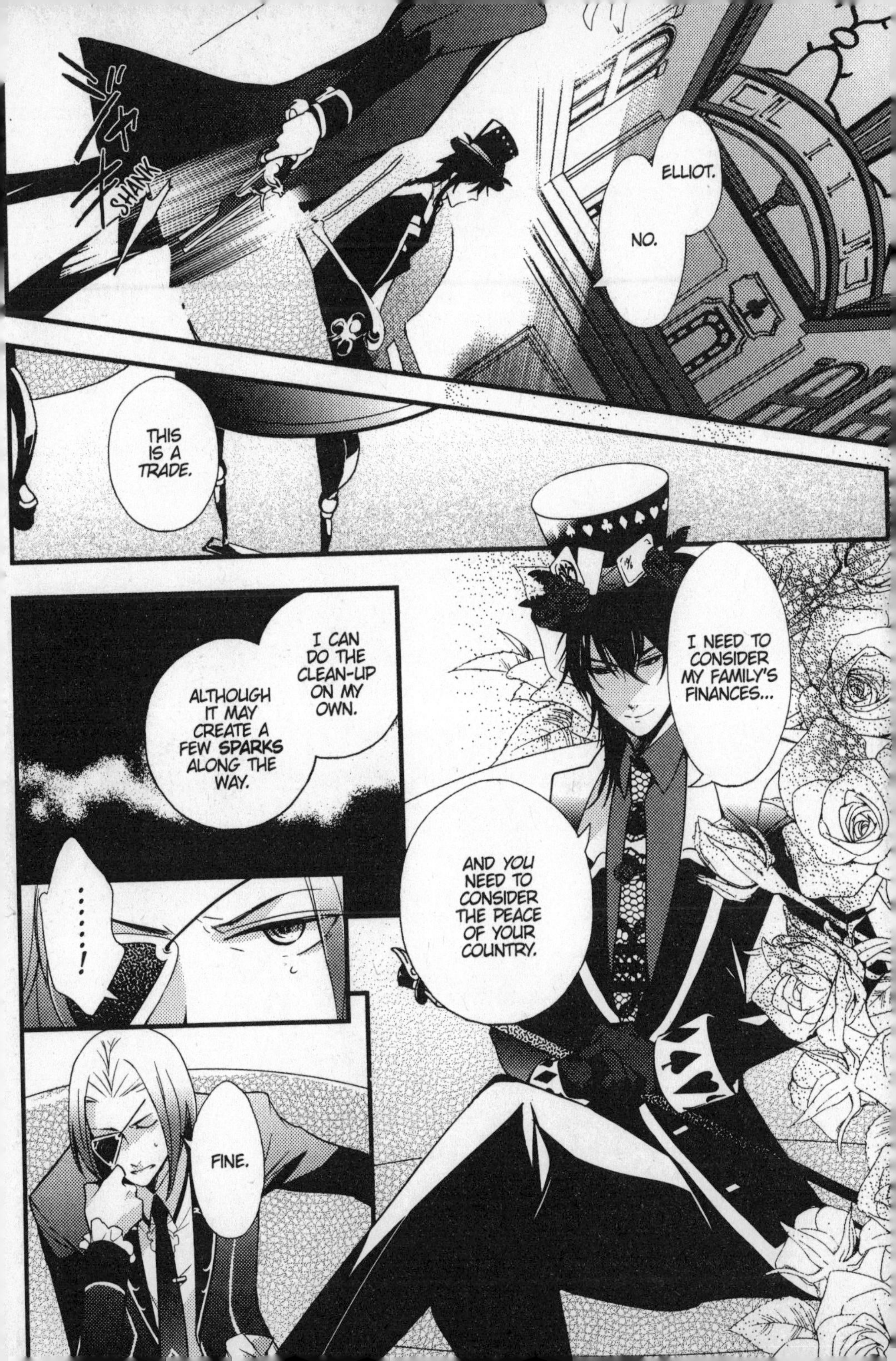
ELLIOT.
NO.
SHANK
THIS IS A TRADE.
I NEED TO CONSIDER MY FAMILY'S FINANCES...
AND YOU NEED TO CONSIDER THE PEACE OF YOUR COUNTRY.
I CAN DO THE CLEAN-UP ON MY OWN.
ALTHOUGH IT MAY CREATE A FEW SPARKS ALONG THE WAY.
......!
FINE.

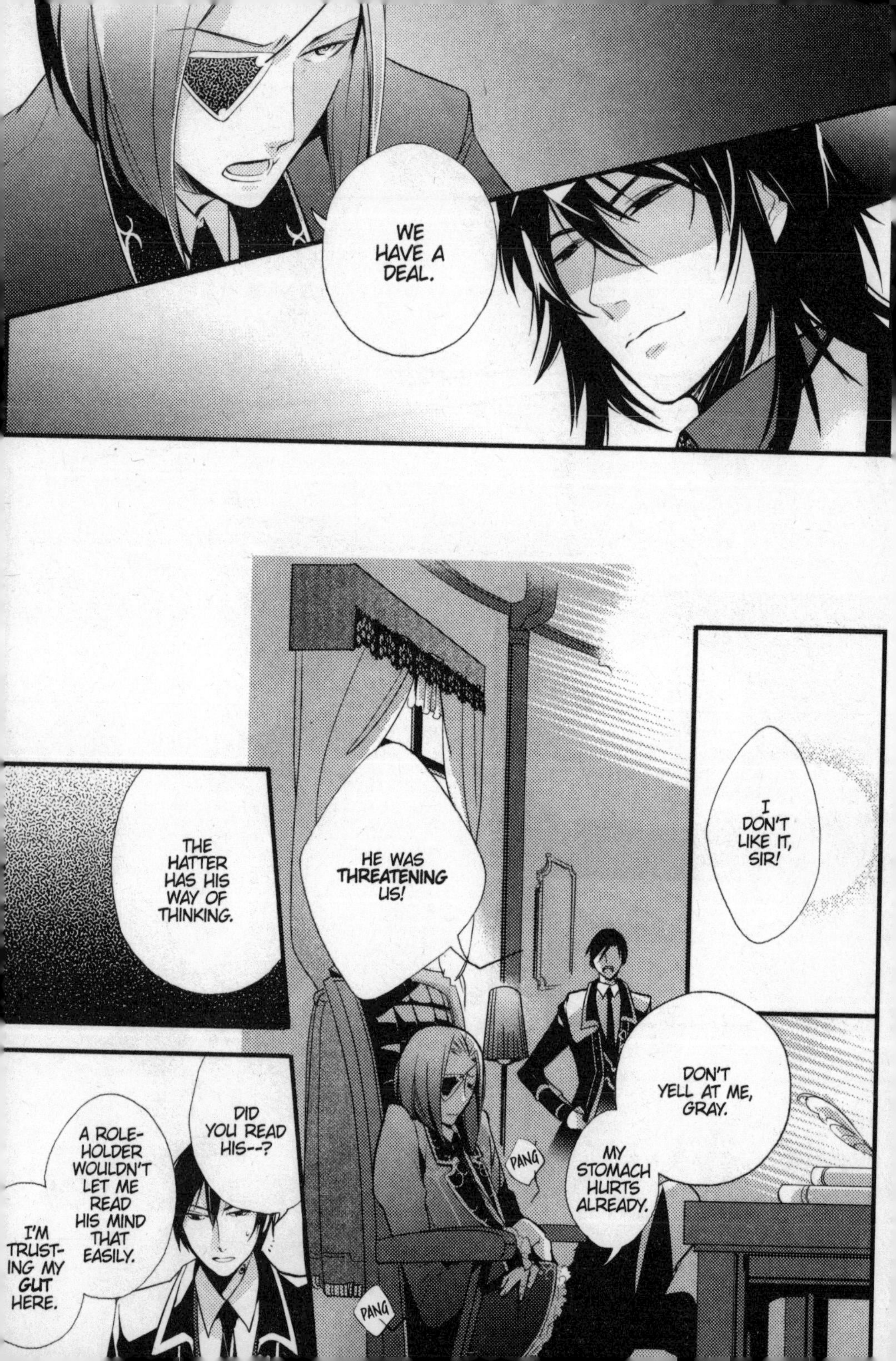
WE HAVE A DEAL.
I DON'T LIKE IT, SIR!
HE WAS THREATENING US!
DON'T YELL AT ME, GRAY.
PANG
MY STOMACH HURTS ALREADY.
PANG
THE HATTER HAS HIS WAY OF THINKING.
DID YOU READ HIS--?
A ROLE-HOLDER WOULDN'T LET ME READ HIS MIND THAT EASILY.
I'M TRUSTING MY GUT HERE.

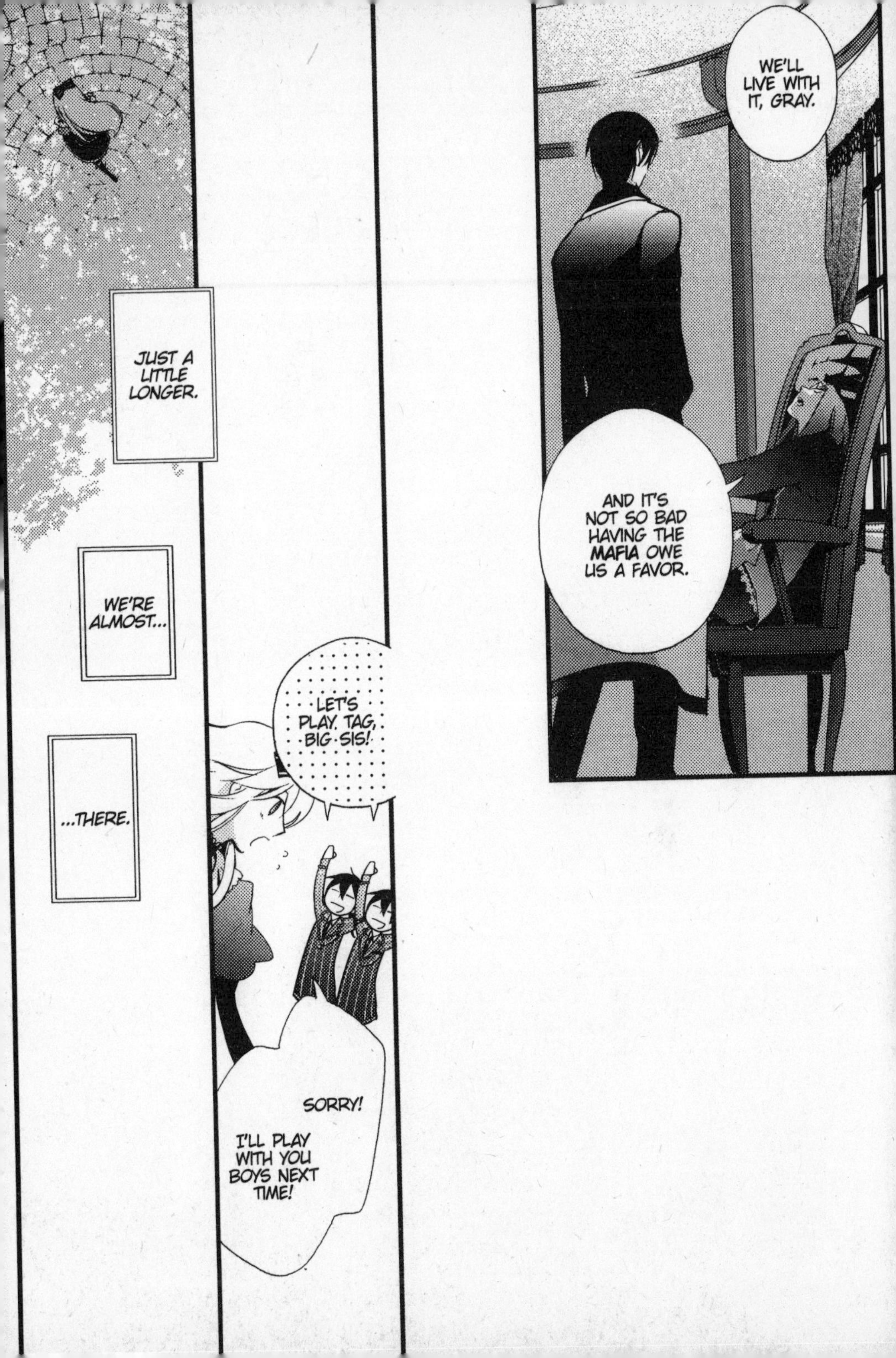
WE'LL LIVE WITH IT, GRAY.
AND IT'S NOT SO BAD HAVING THE MAFIA OWE US A FAVOR.
LET'S PLAY. TAG, BIG SIS!
SORRY!
I'LL PLAY WITH YOU BOYS NEXT TIME!
JUST A LITTLE LONGER.
WE'RE ALMOST...
...THERE.

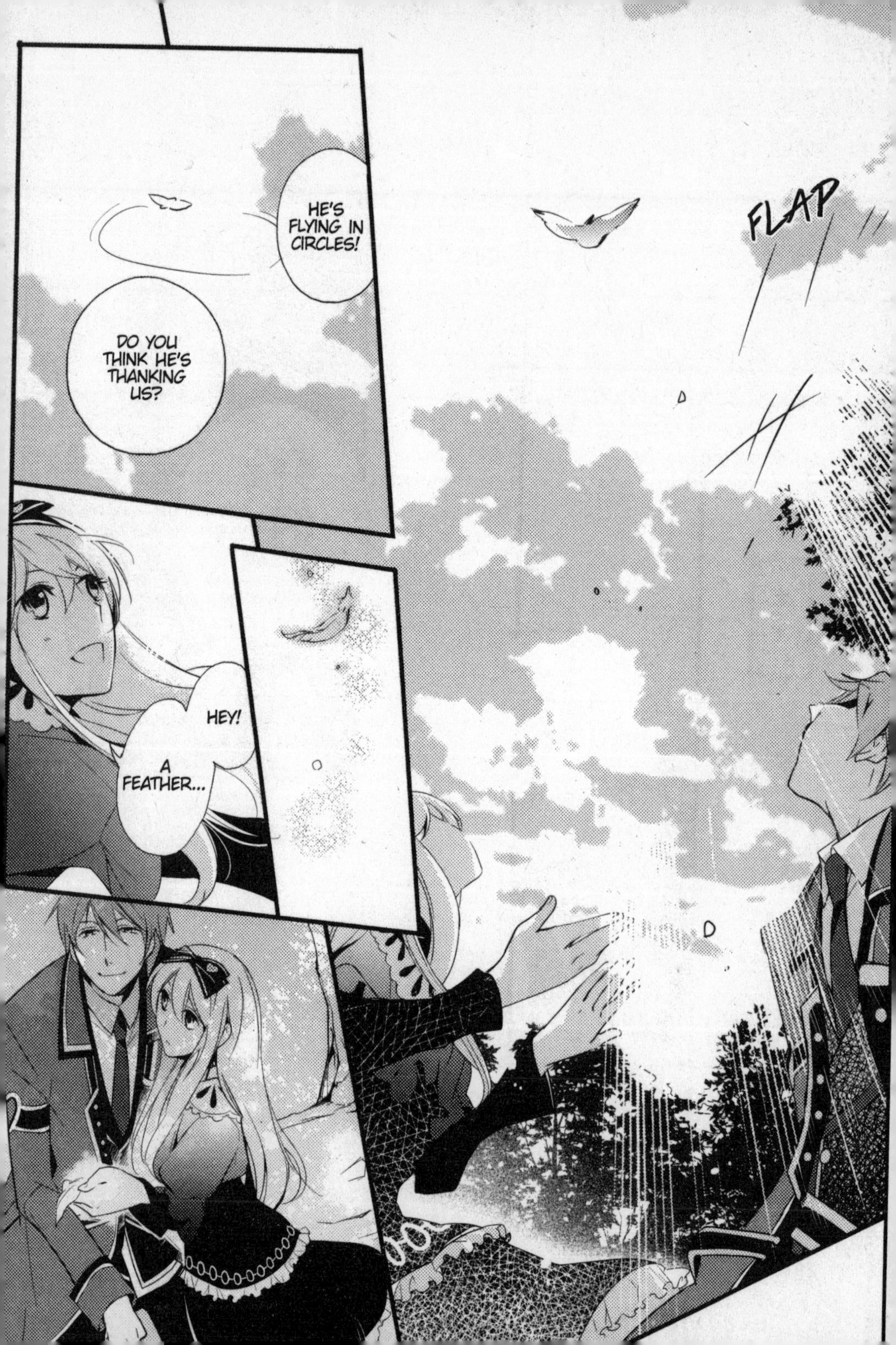
FLAP
HE'S FLYING IN CIRCLES!
DO YOU THINK HE'S THANKING US?
HEY!
A FEATHER...

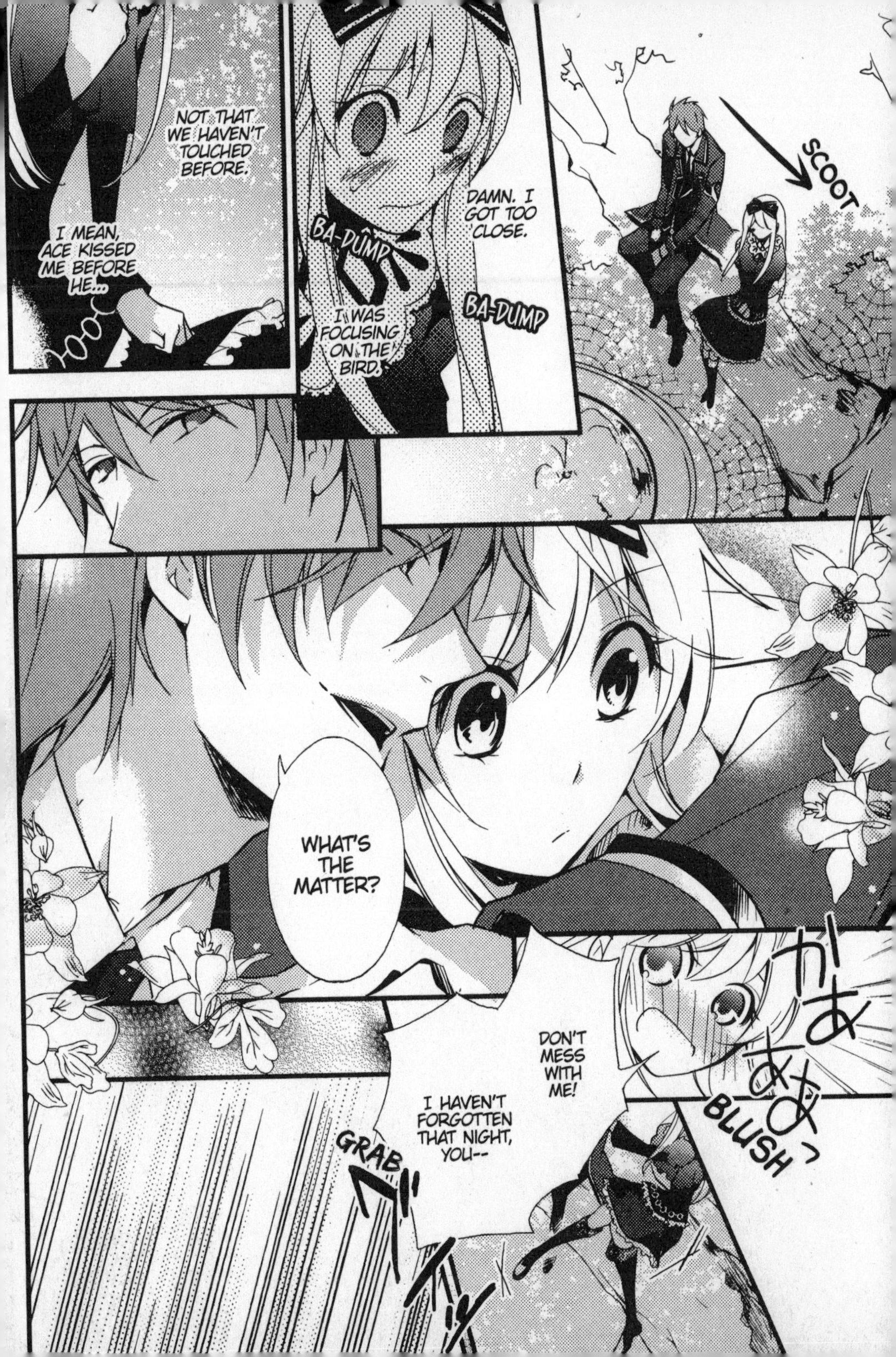
SCOOT
DAMN. I GOT TOO CLOSE.
BA-DUMP
BA-DUMP
I WAS FOCUSING ON THE BIRD.
NOT THAT WE HAVEN'T TOUCHED BEFORE.
I MEAN, ACE KISSED ME BEFORE HE...
WHAT'S THE MATTER?
かああっ
BLUSH
DON'T MESS WITH ME!
I HAVEN'T FORGOTTEN THAT NIGHT, YOU--
GRAB

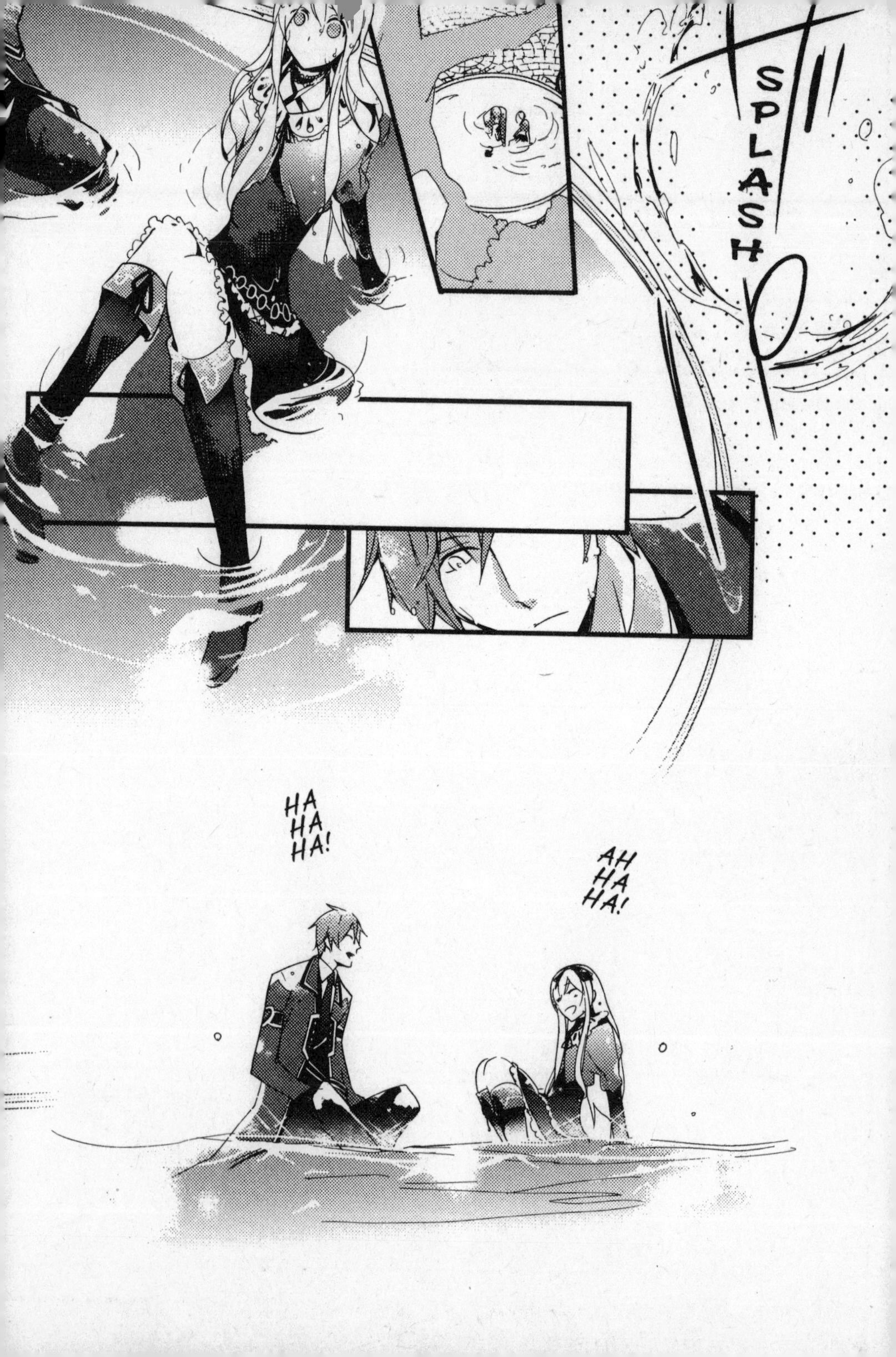
SPLASH
AH HA HA!
HA HA HA!

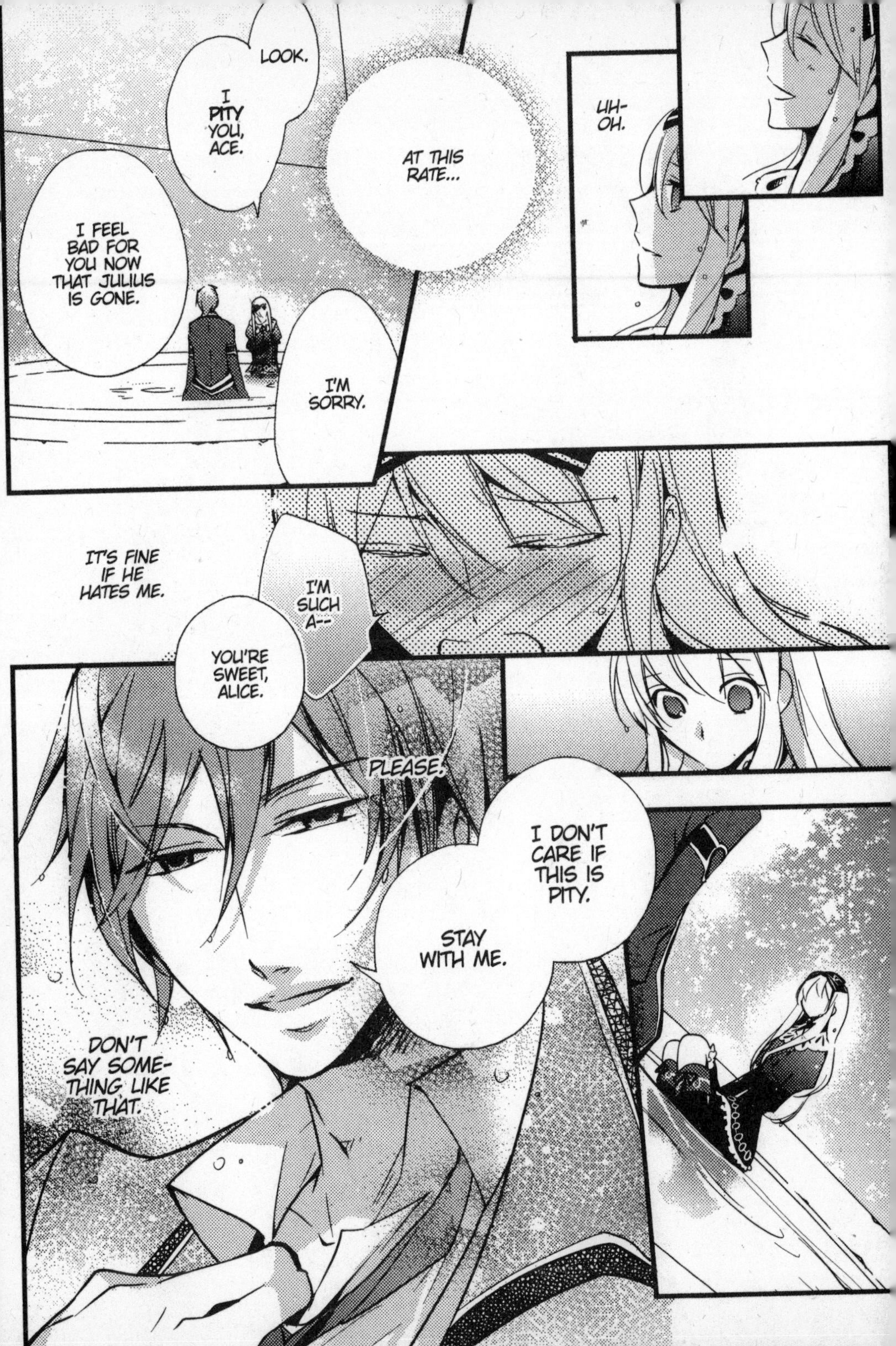
UH-OH.
AT THIS RATE...
LOOK.
I PITY YOU, ACE.
I FEEL BAD FOR YOU NOW THAT JULIUS IS GONE.
I'M SORRY.
I'M SUCH A--
IT'S FINE IF HE HATES ME.
YOU'RE SWEET, ALICE.
I DON'T CARE IF THIS IS PITY.
STAY WITH ME.
PLEASE.
DON'T SAY SOMETHING LIKE THAT.

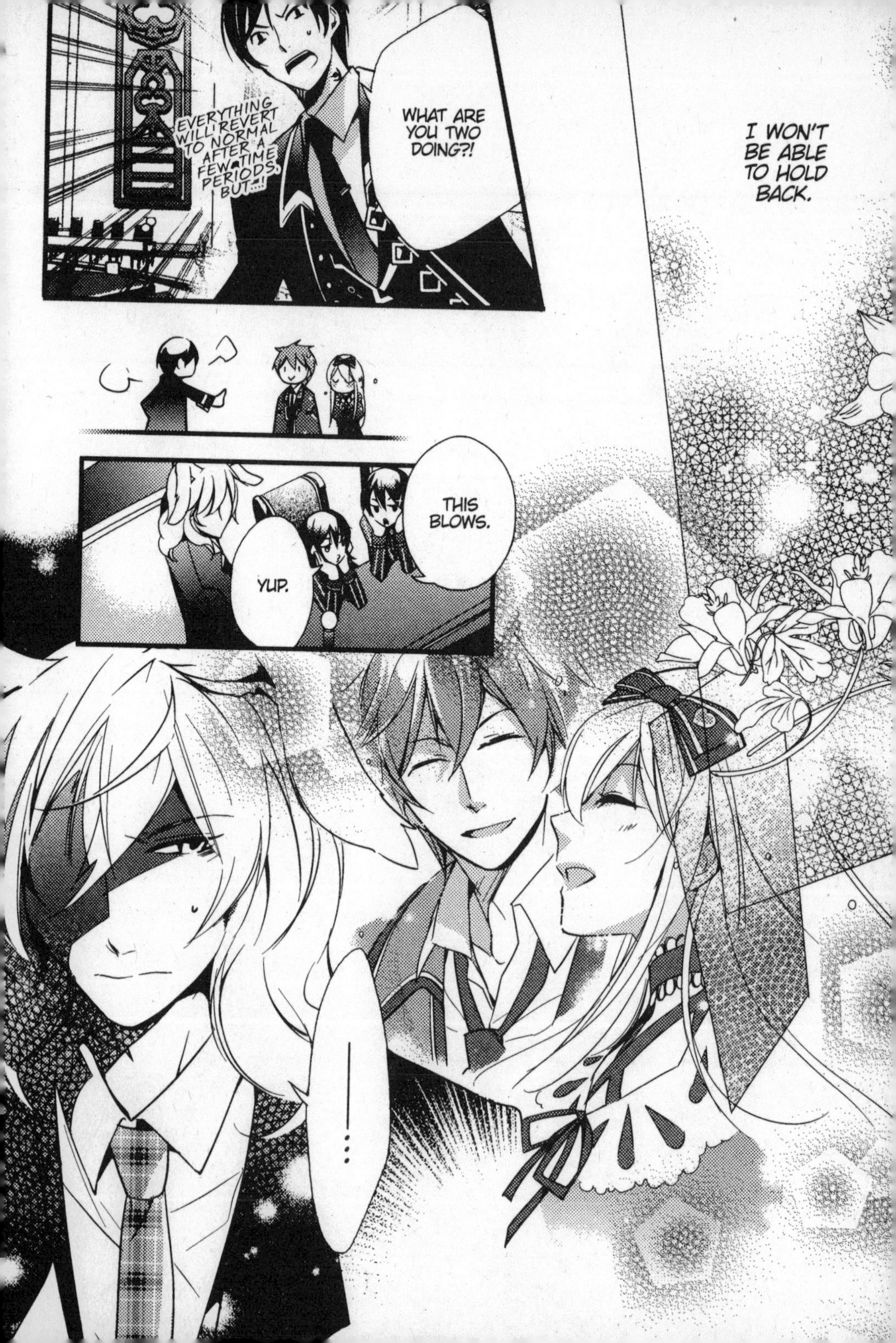
I WON'T BE ABLE TO HOLD BACK.
WHAT ARE YOU TWO DOING?!
EVERYTHING WILL REVERT TO NORMAL AFTER A FEW TIME PERIODS, BUT...!
THIS BLOWS.
YUP.
......

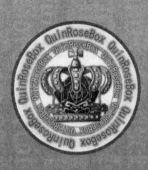

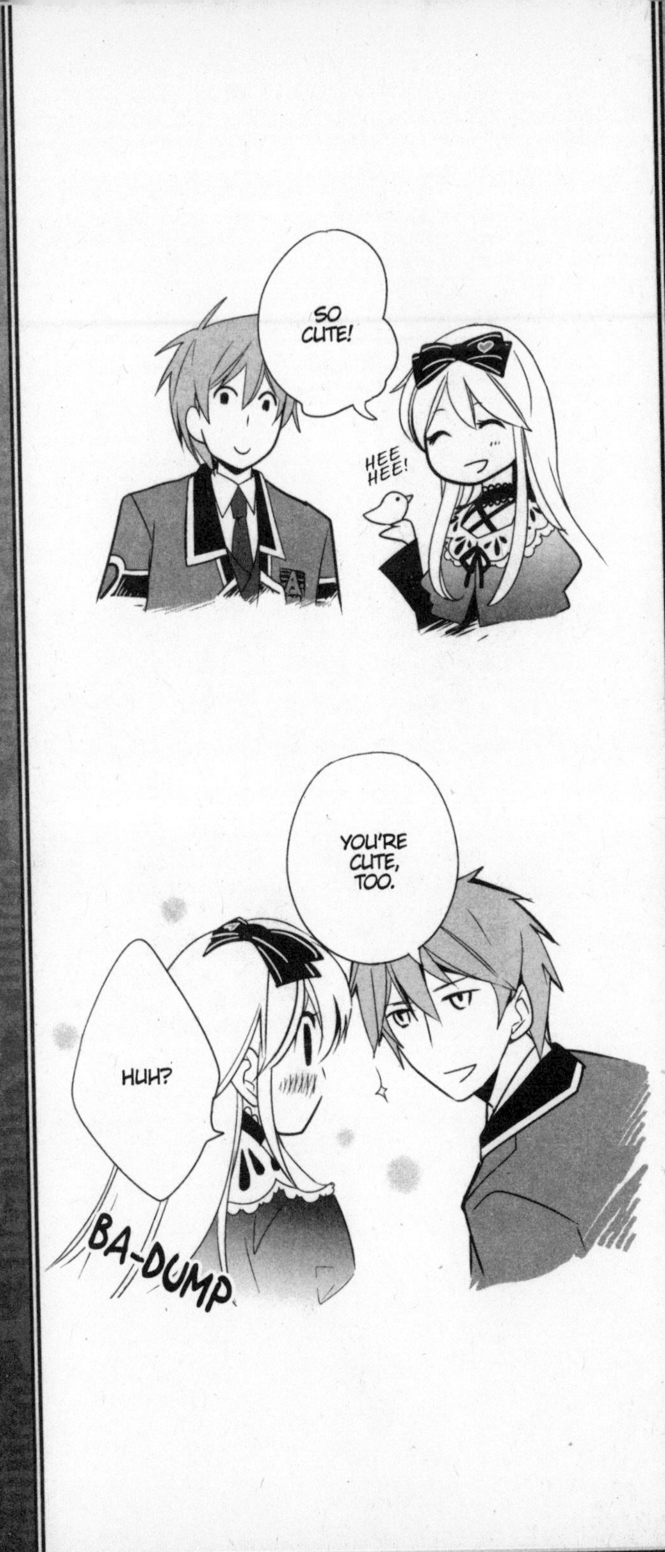
SO CUTE!
HEE HEE!
YOU'RE CUTE, TOO.
HUH?
BA-DUMP

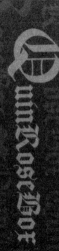

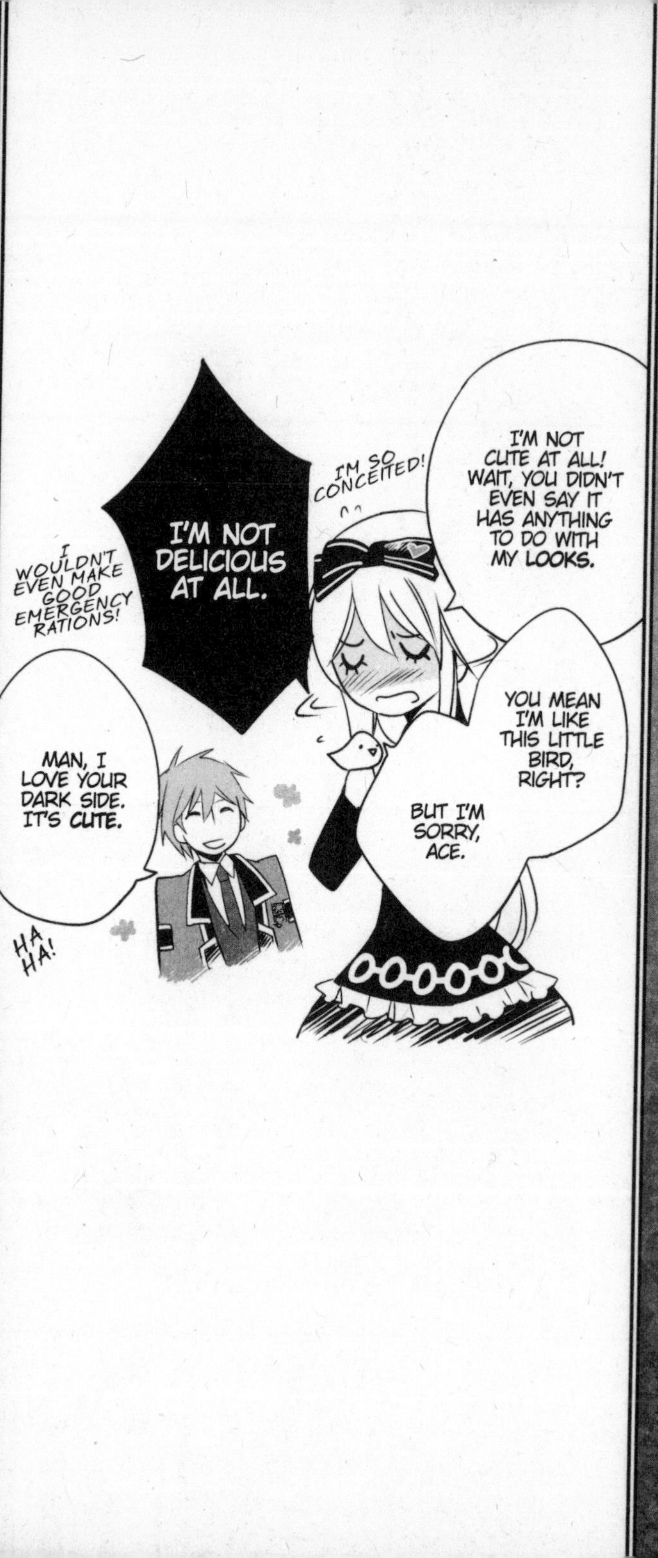
I'M NOT CUTE AT ALL! WAIT, YOU DIDN'T EVEN SAY IT HAS ANYTHING TO DO WITH MY LOOKS.
I'M SO CONCEITED!
I'M NOT DELICIOUS AT ALL.
I WOULDN'T EVEN MAKE GOOD EMERGENCY RATIONS!
YOU MEAN I'M LIKE THIS LITTLE BIRD, RIGHT?
BUT I'M SORRY, ACE.
MAN, I LOVE YOUR DARK SIDE. IT'S CUTE.
HA HA!

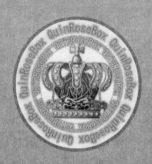

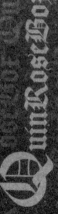

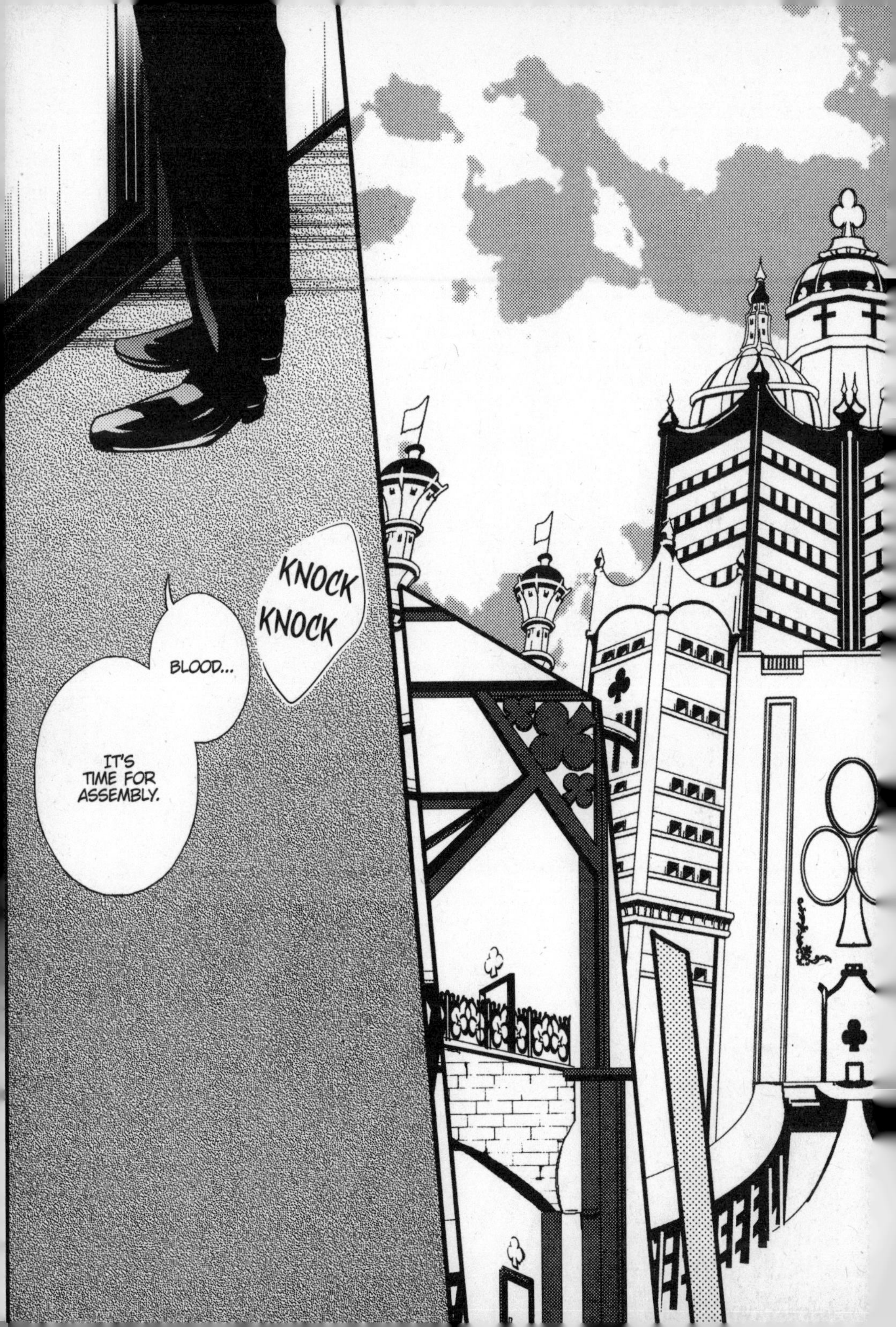
KNOCK KNOCK
BLOOD...
IT'S TIME FOR ASSEMBLY.

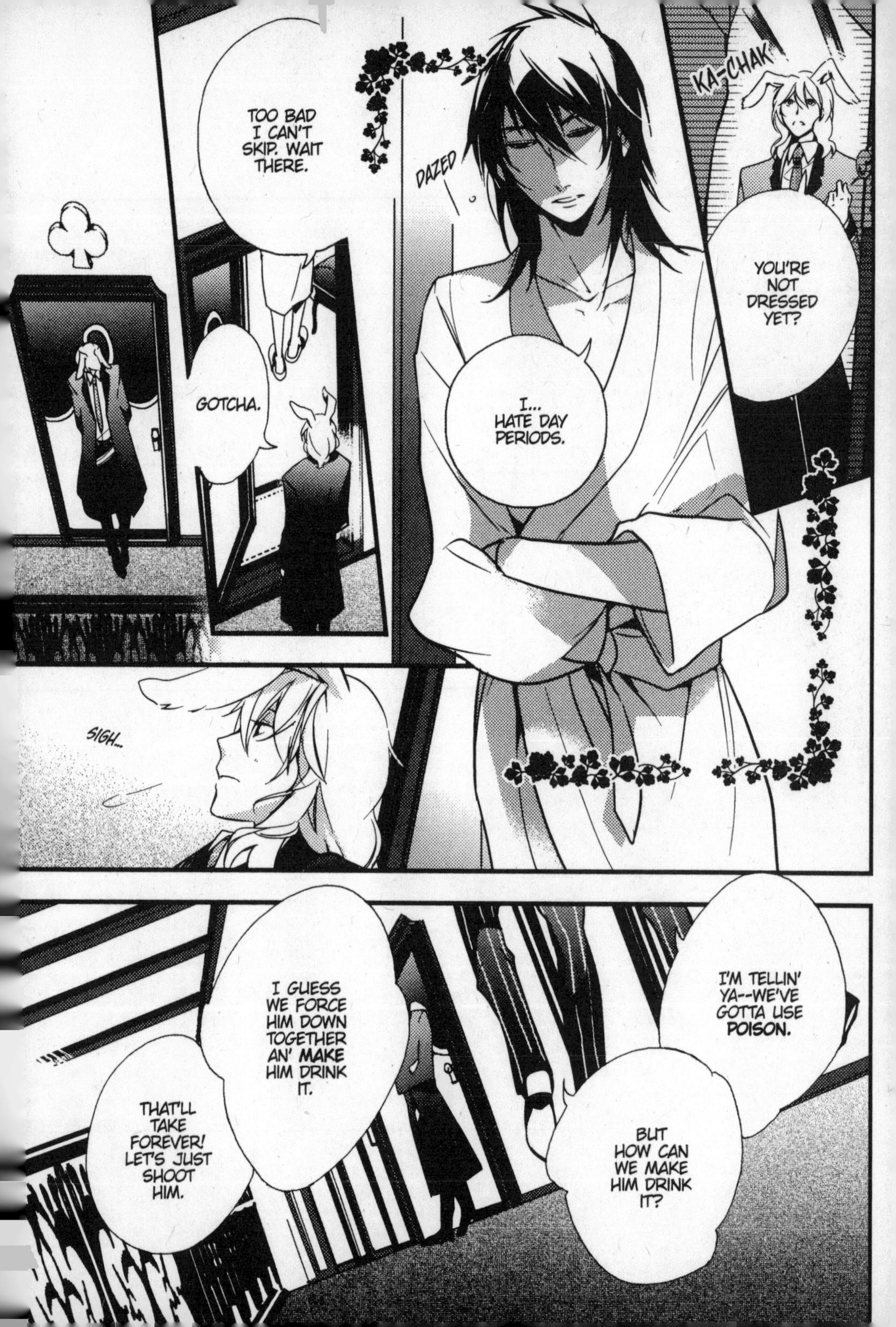
KA-CHAK
YOU'RE NOT DRESSED YET?
DAZED
I... HATE DAY PERIODS.
TOO BAD I CAN'T SKIP. WAIT THERE.
GOTCHA.
SIGH...
I'M TELLIN' YA--WE'VE GOTTA USE POISON.
BUT HOW CAN WE MAKE HIM DRINK IT?
I GUESS WE FORCE HIM DOWN TOGETHER AN' MAKE HIM DRINK IT.
THAT'LL TAKE FOREVER! LET'S JUST SHOOT HIM.

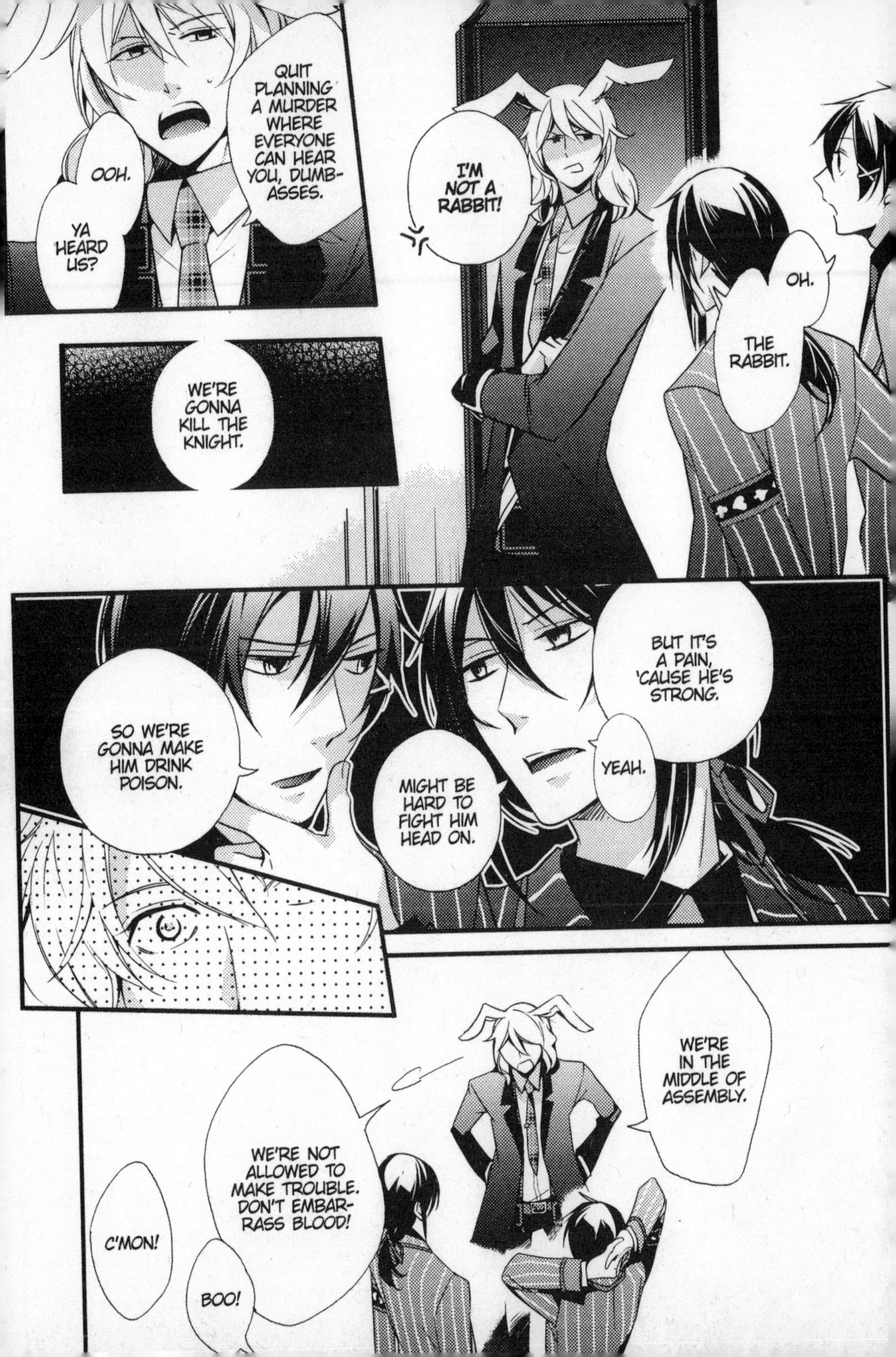
OH.
THE RABBIT.
I'M NOT A RABBIT!
QUIT PLANNING A MURDER WHERE EVERYONE CAN HEAR YOU, DUMBASSES.
OOH.
YA HEARD US?
WE'RE GONNA KILL THE KNIGHT.
BUT IT'S A PAIN, 'CAUSE HE'S STRONG.
YEAH.
MIGHT BE HARD TO FIGHT HIM HEAD ON.
SO WE'RE GONNA MAKE HIM DRINK POISON.
WE'RE IN THE MIDDLE OF ASSEMBLY.
WE'RE NOT ALLOWED TO MAKE TROUBLE. DON'T EMBARRASS BLOOD!
C'MON!
BOO!

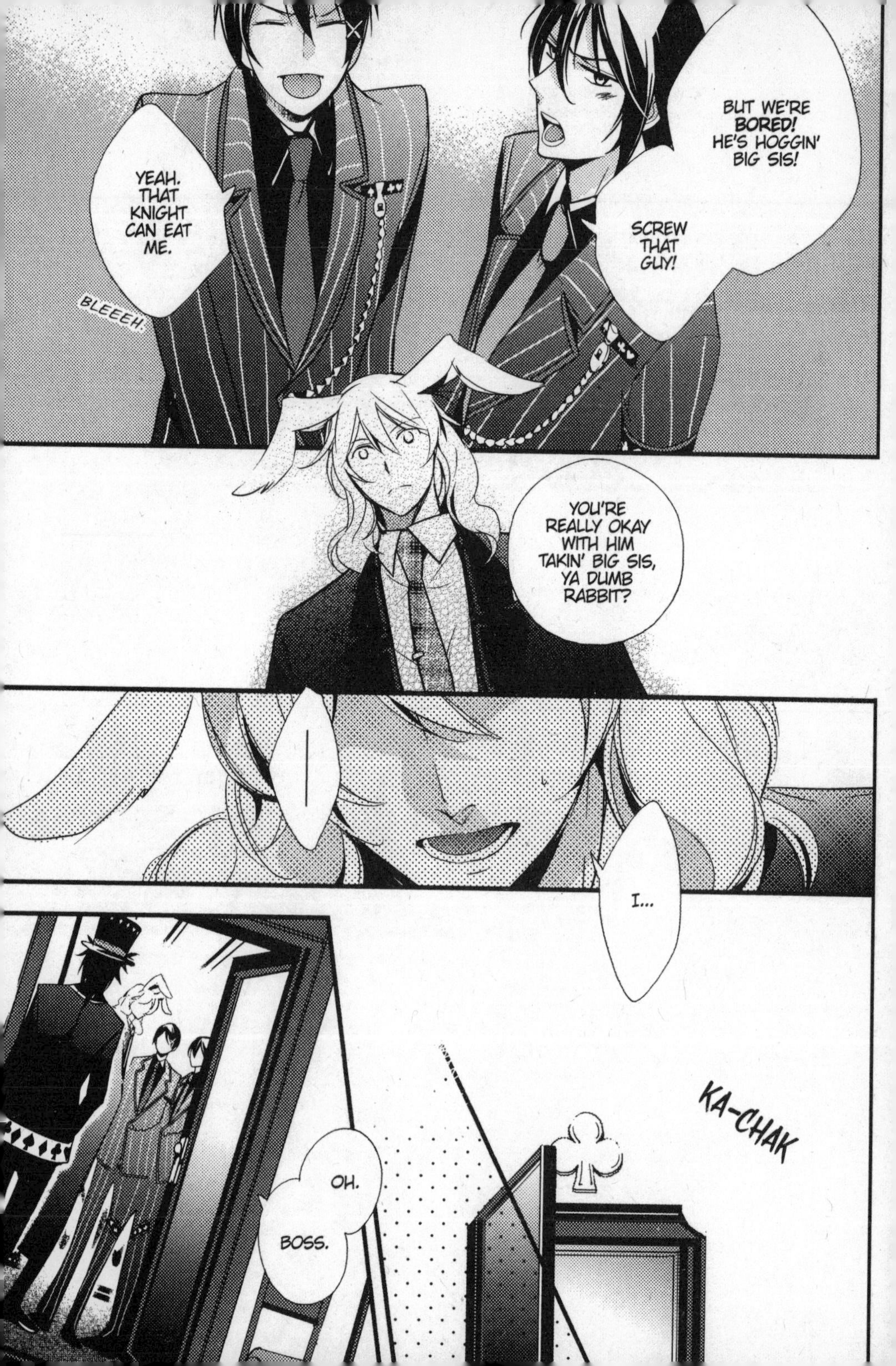
BUT WE'RE BORED! HE'S HOGGIN' BIG SIS!
SCREW THAT GUY!
YEAH. THAT KNIGHT CAN EAT ME.
BLEEEH.
YOU'RE REALLY OKAY WITH HIM TAKIN' BIG SIS, YA DUMB RABBIT?
—
I...
KA-CHAK
OH.
BOSS.

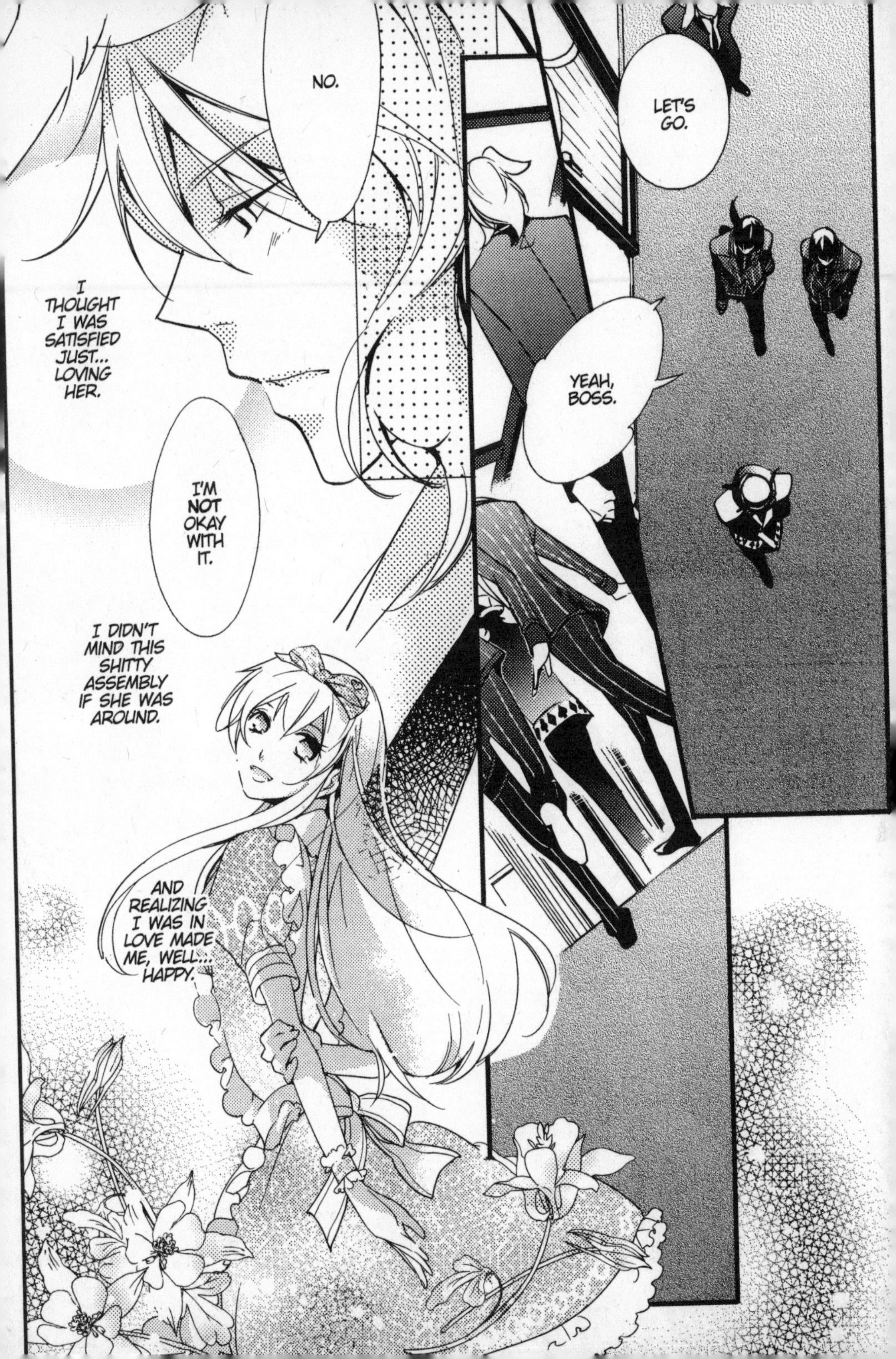
LET'S GO.
YEAH, BOSS.
NO.
I THOUGHT I WAS SATISFIED JUST... LOVING HER.
I'M NOT OKAY WITH IT.
I DIDN'T MIND THIS SHITTY ASSEMBLY IF SHE WAS AROUND.
AND REALIZING I WAS IN LOVE MADE ME, WELL... HAPPY.

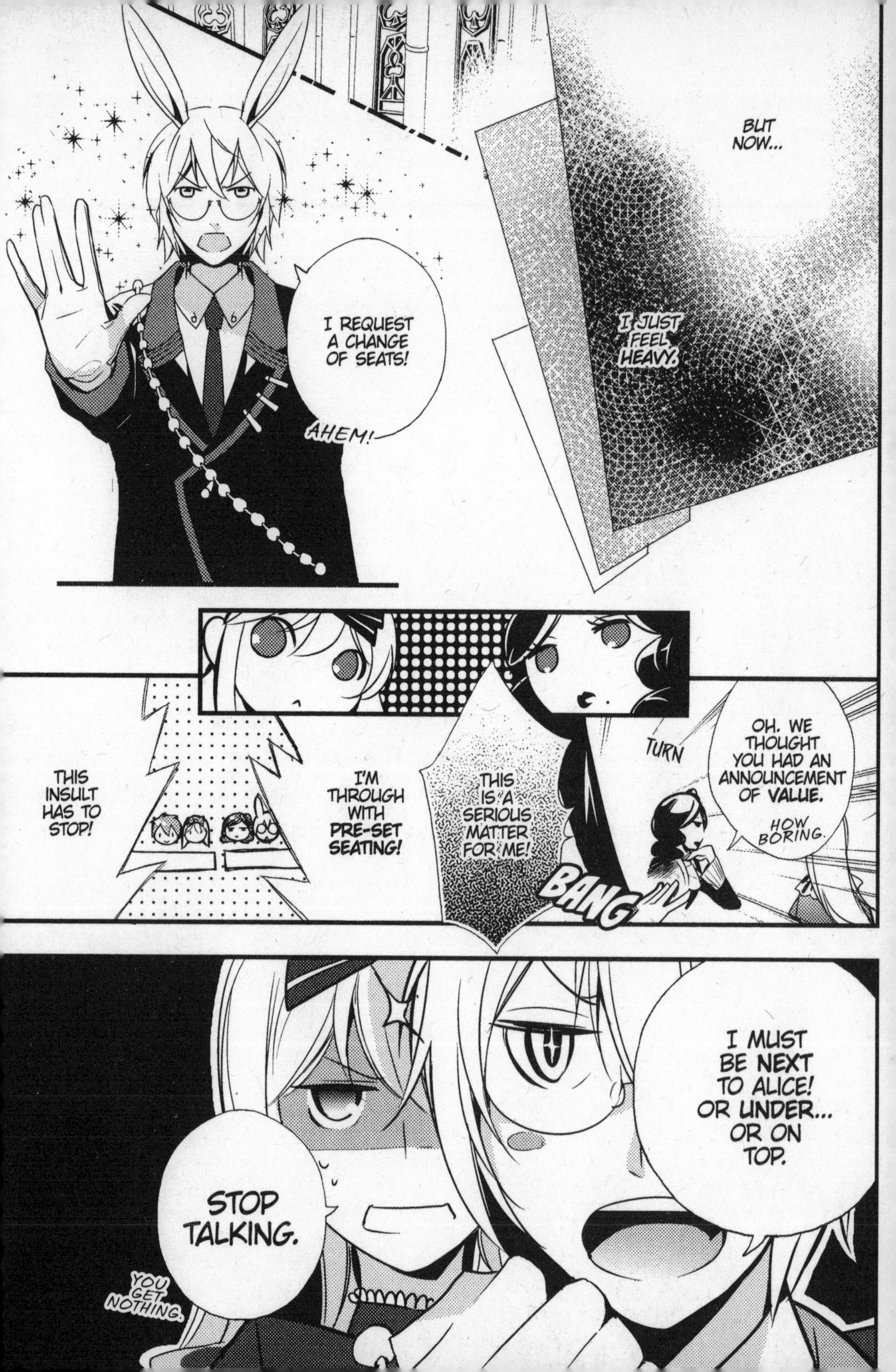
BUT NOW...
I JUST FEEL HEAVY.
I REQUEST A CHANGE OF SEATS!
AHEM!
OH. WE THOUGHT YOU HAD AN ANNOUNCEMENT OF VALUE.
HOW BORING.
TURN
THIS IS A SERIOUS MATTER FOR ME!
BANG
I'M THROUGH WITH PRE-SET SEATING!
THIS INSULT HAS TO STOP!
I MUST BE NEXT TO ALICE! OR UNDER... OR ON TOP.
STOP TALKING.
YOU GET NOTHING.

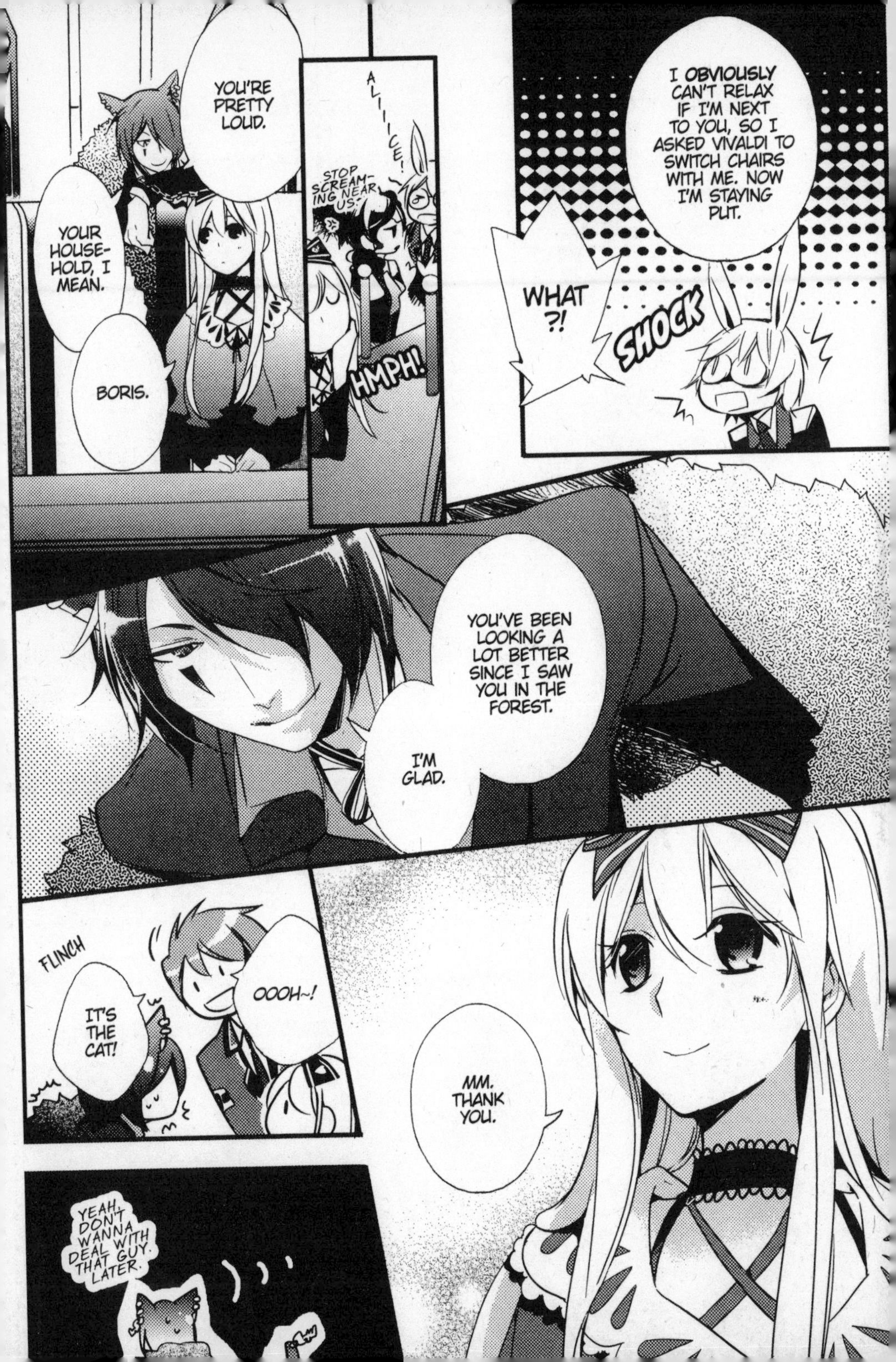
I OBVIOUSLY CAN'T RELAX IF I'M NEXT TO YOU, SO I ASKED VIVALDI TO SWITCH CHAIRS WITH ME. NOW I'M STAYING PUT.
WHAT?!
SHOCK
A-LIIIICE!
STOP SCREAMING NEAR US.
HMPH!
YOU'RE PRETTY LOUD.
YOUR HOUSEHOLD, I MEAN.
BORIS.
YOU'VE BEEN LOOKING A LOT BETTER SINCE I SAW YOU IN THE FOREST.
I'M GLAD.
MM. THANK YOU.
OOOH~!
FLINCH
IT'S THE CAT!
YEAH, DON'T WANNA DEAL WITH THAT GUY LATER.

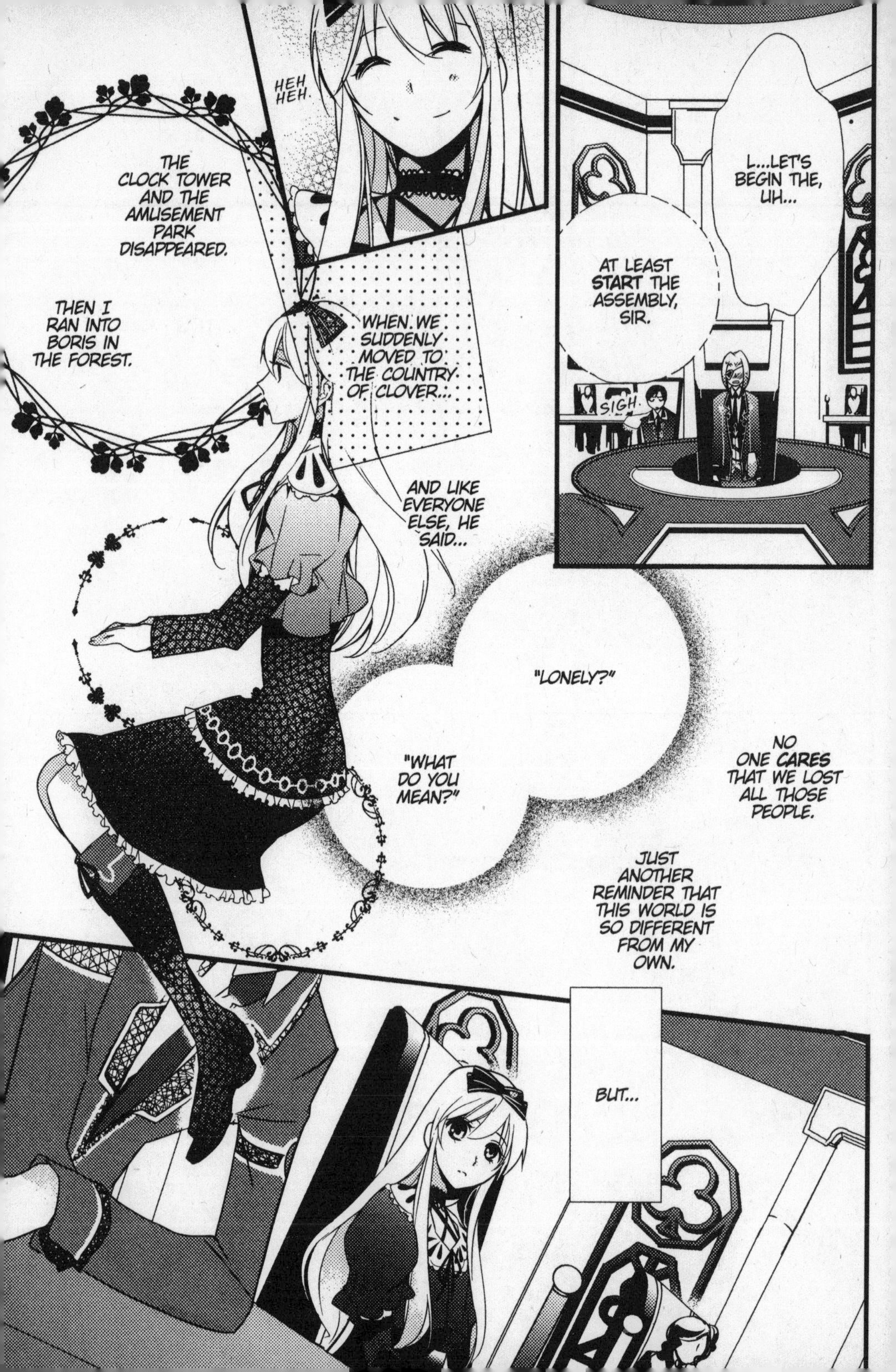
L...LET'S BEGIN THE, UH...
AT LEAST START THE ASSEMBLY, SIR.
SIGH.
HEH HEH.
WHEN WE SUDDENLY MOVED TO THE COUNTRY OF CLOVER...
THE CLOCK TOWER AND THE AMUSEMENT PARK DISAPPEARED.
THEN I RAN INTO BORIS IN THE FOREST.
AND LIKE EVERYONE ELSE, HE SAID...
"WHAT DO YOU MEAN?"
"LONELY?"
NO ONE CARES THAT WE LOST ALL THOSE PEOPLE.
JUST ANOTHER REMINDER THAT THIS WORLD IS SO DIFFERENT FROM MY OWN.
BUT...

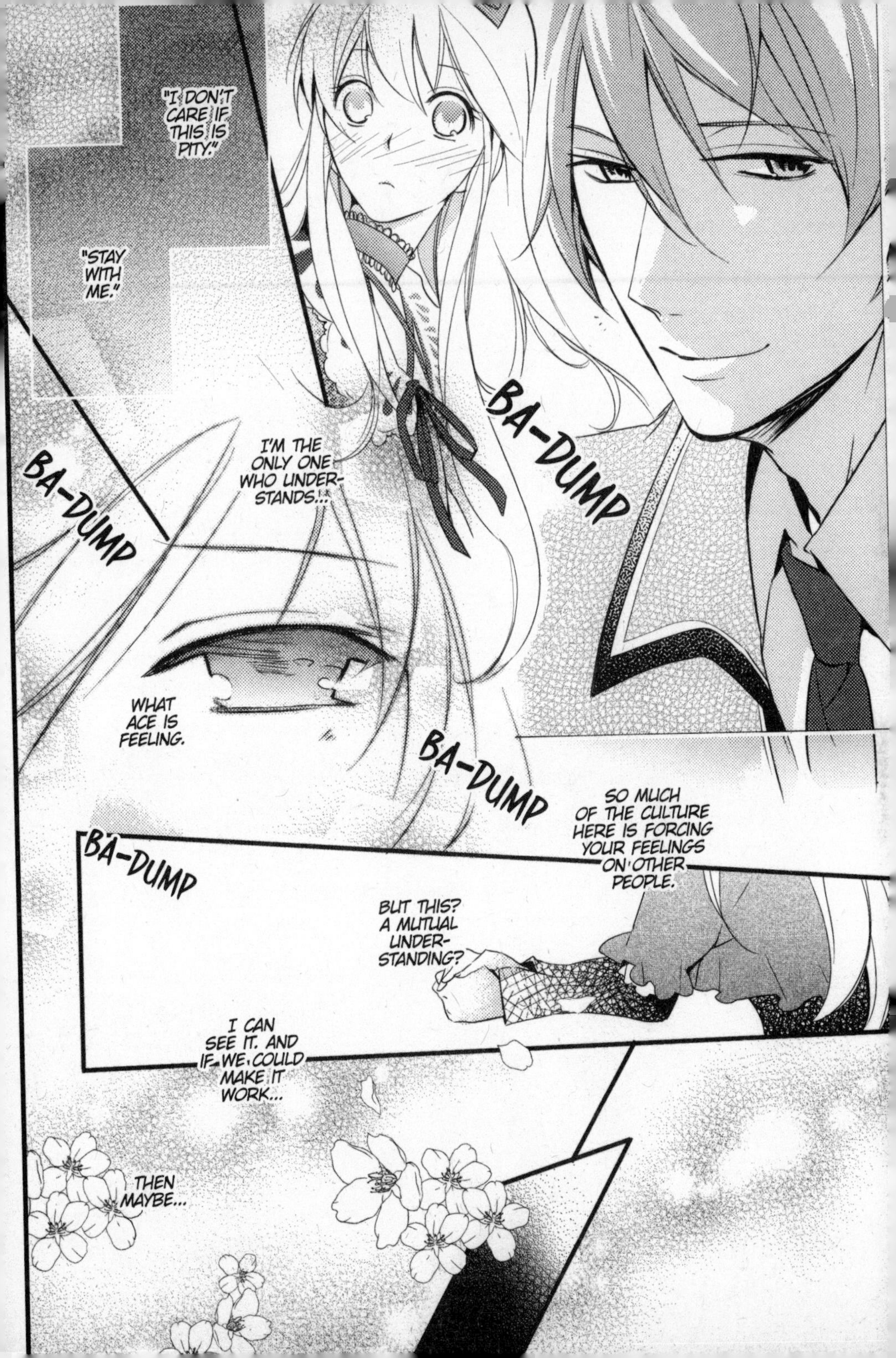
BA-DUMP
"I DON'T CARE IF THIS IS PITY."
"STAY WITH ME."
I'M THE ONLY ONE WHO UNDER-STANDS...
BA-DUMP
WHAT ACE IS FEELING.
BA-DUMP
SO MUCH OF THE CULTURE HERE IS FORCING YOUR FEELINGS ON OTHER PEOPLE.
BUT THIS? A MUTUAL UNDER-STANDING?
BA-DUMP
I CAN SEE IT. AND IF WE COULD MAKE IT WORK...
THEN MAYBE...

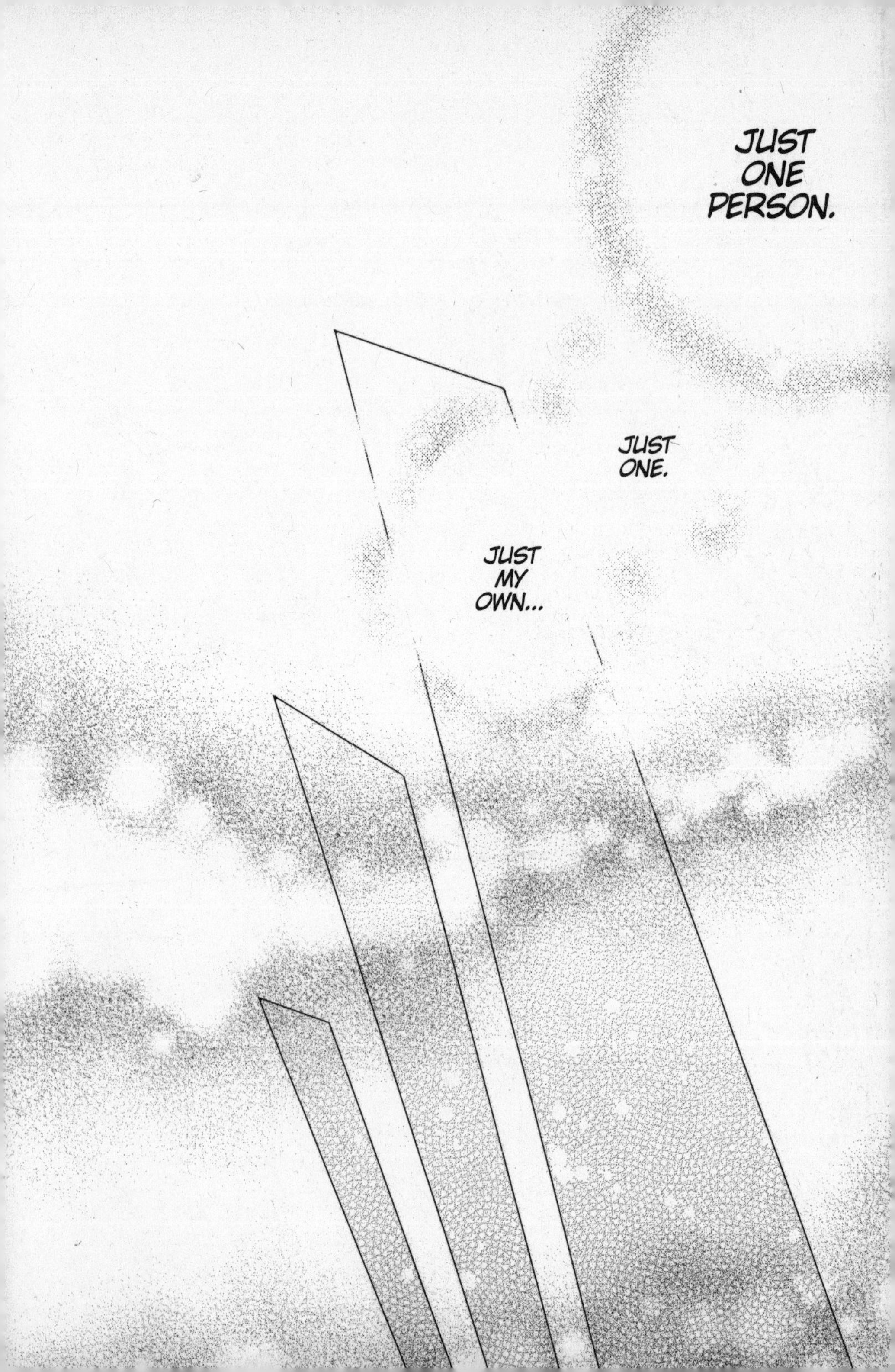
JUST ONE PERSON.
JUST ONE.
JUST MY OWN...

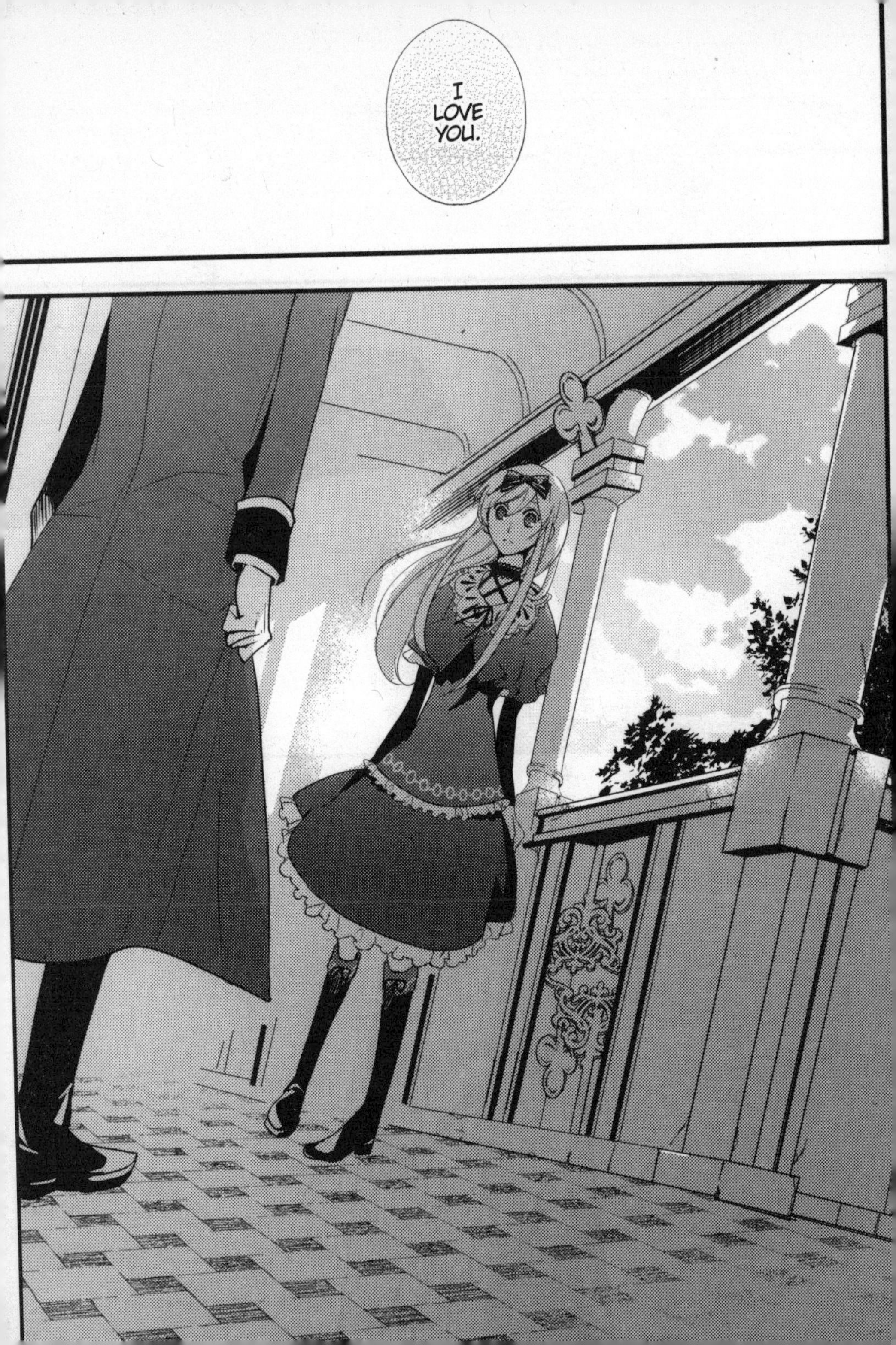
I LOVE YOU.

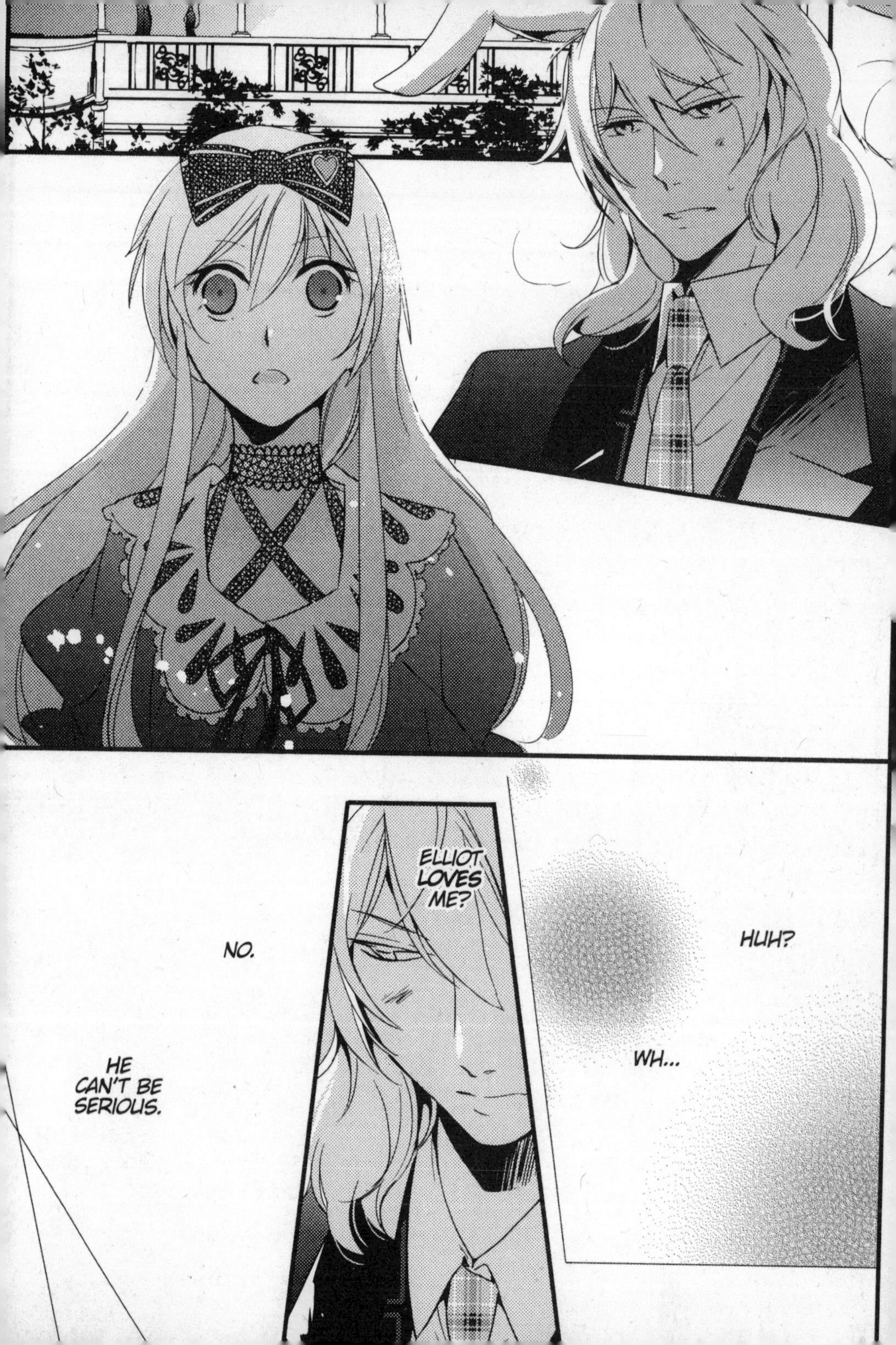
HUH?
WH...
ELLIOT LOVES ME?
NO.
HE CAN'T BE SERIOUS.

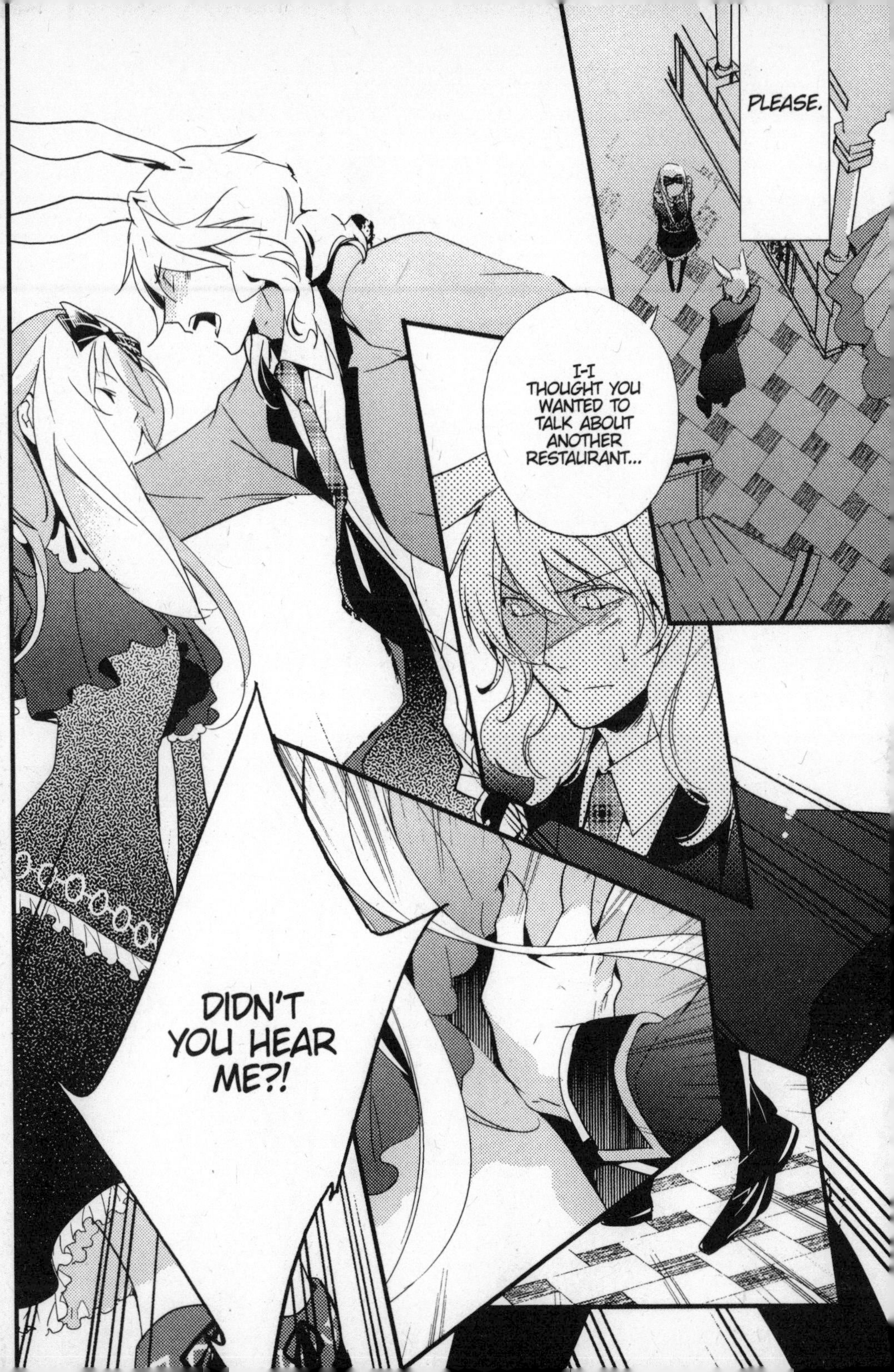
PLEASE.
I-I THOUGHT YOU WANTED TO TALK ABOUT ANOTHER RESTAURANT...
DIDN'T YOU HEAR ME?!

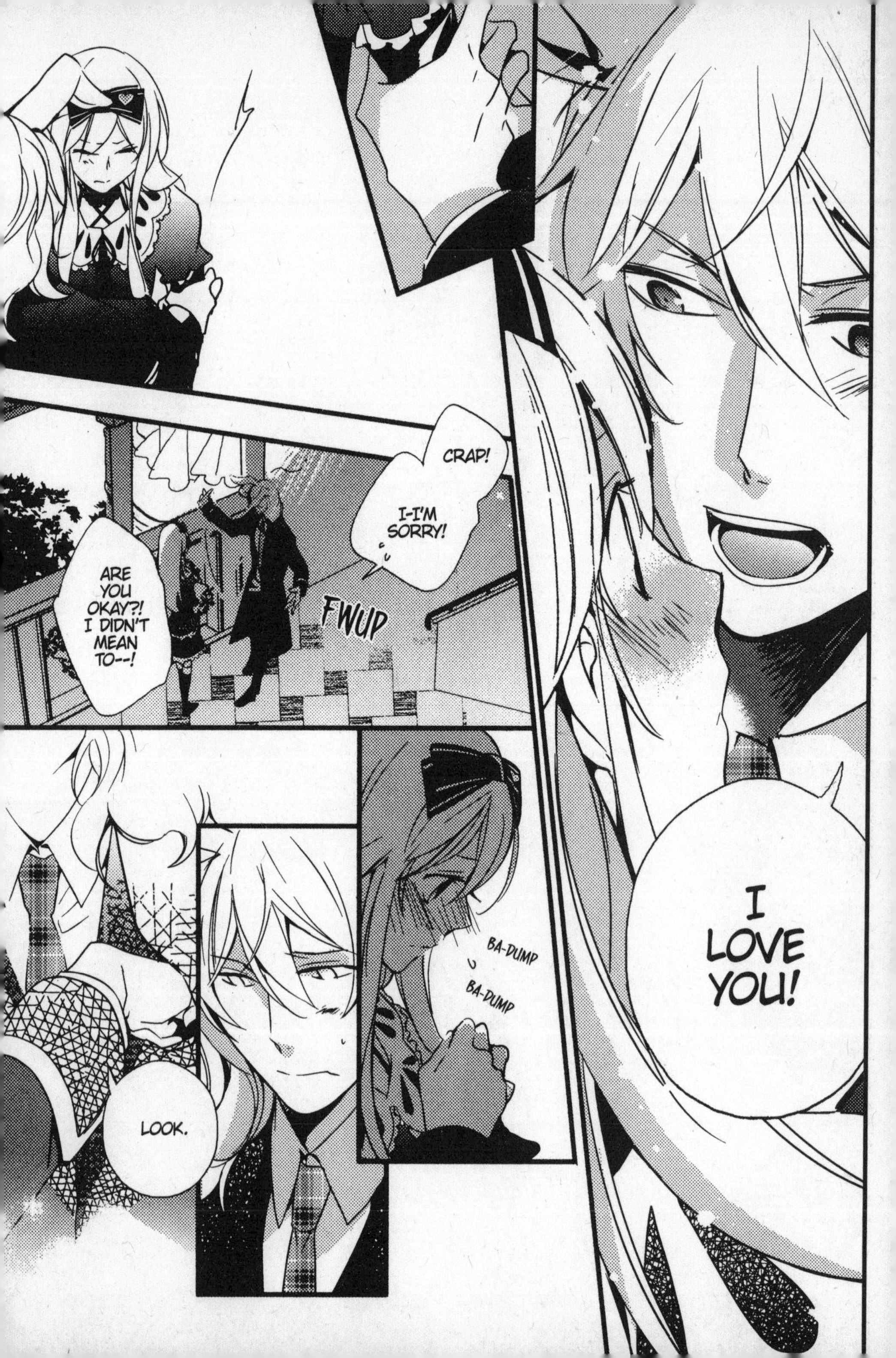
I LOVE YOU!
CRAP!
I-I'M SORRY!
FWUP
ARE YOU OKAY?! I DIDN'T MEAN TO--!
BA-DUMP
BA-DUMP
LOOK.

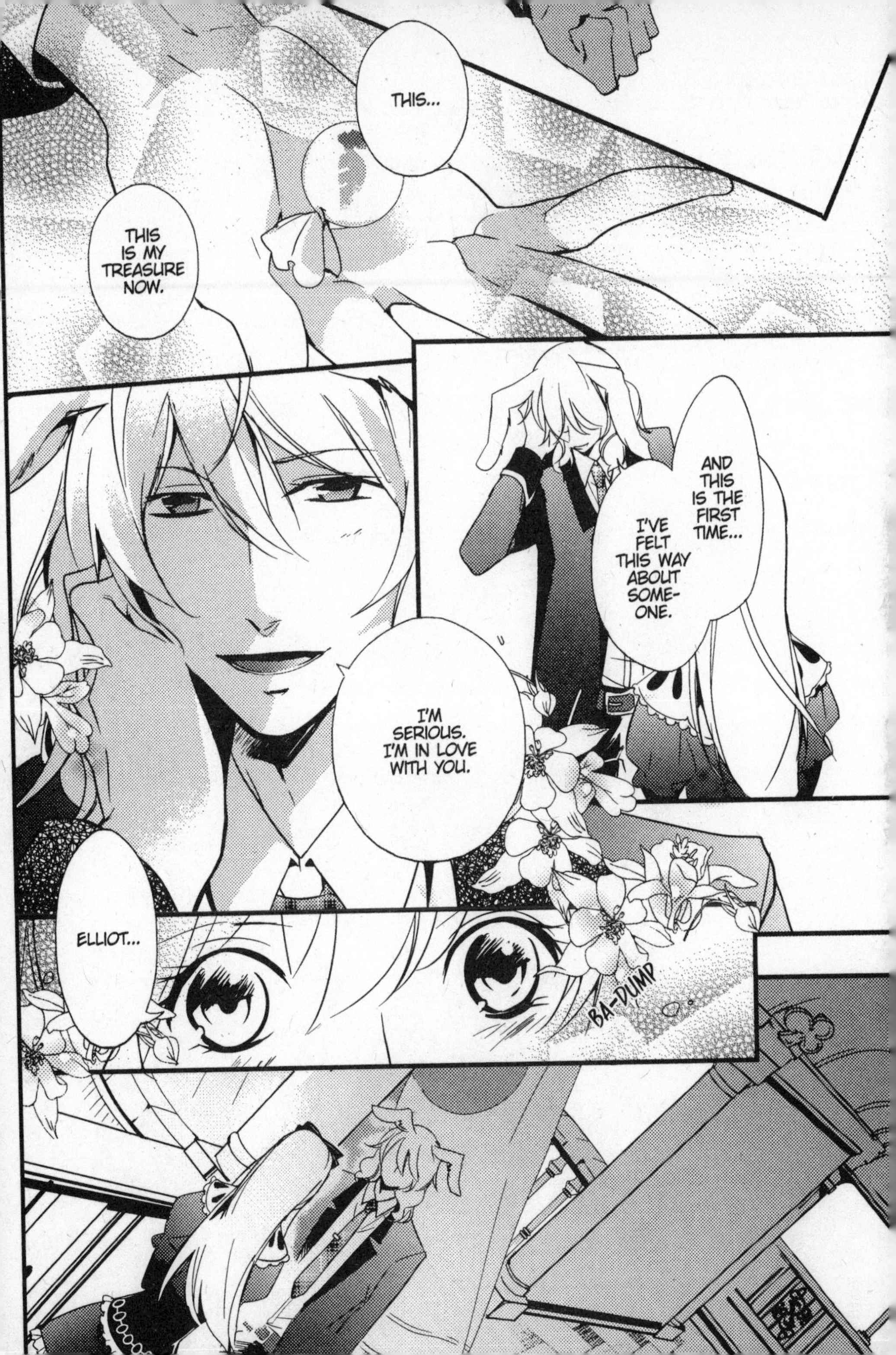
THIS...
THIS IS MY TREASURE NOW.
AND THIS IS THE FIRST TIME...
I'VE FELT THIS WAY ABOUT SOME-ONE.
I'M SERIOUS. I'M IN LOVE WITH YOU.
ELLIOT...
BA-DUMP

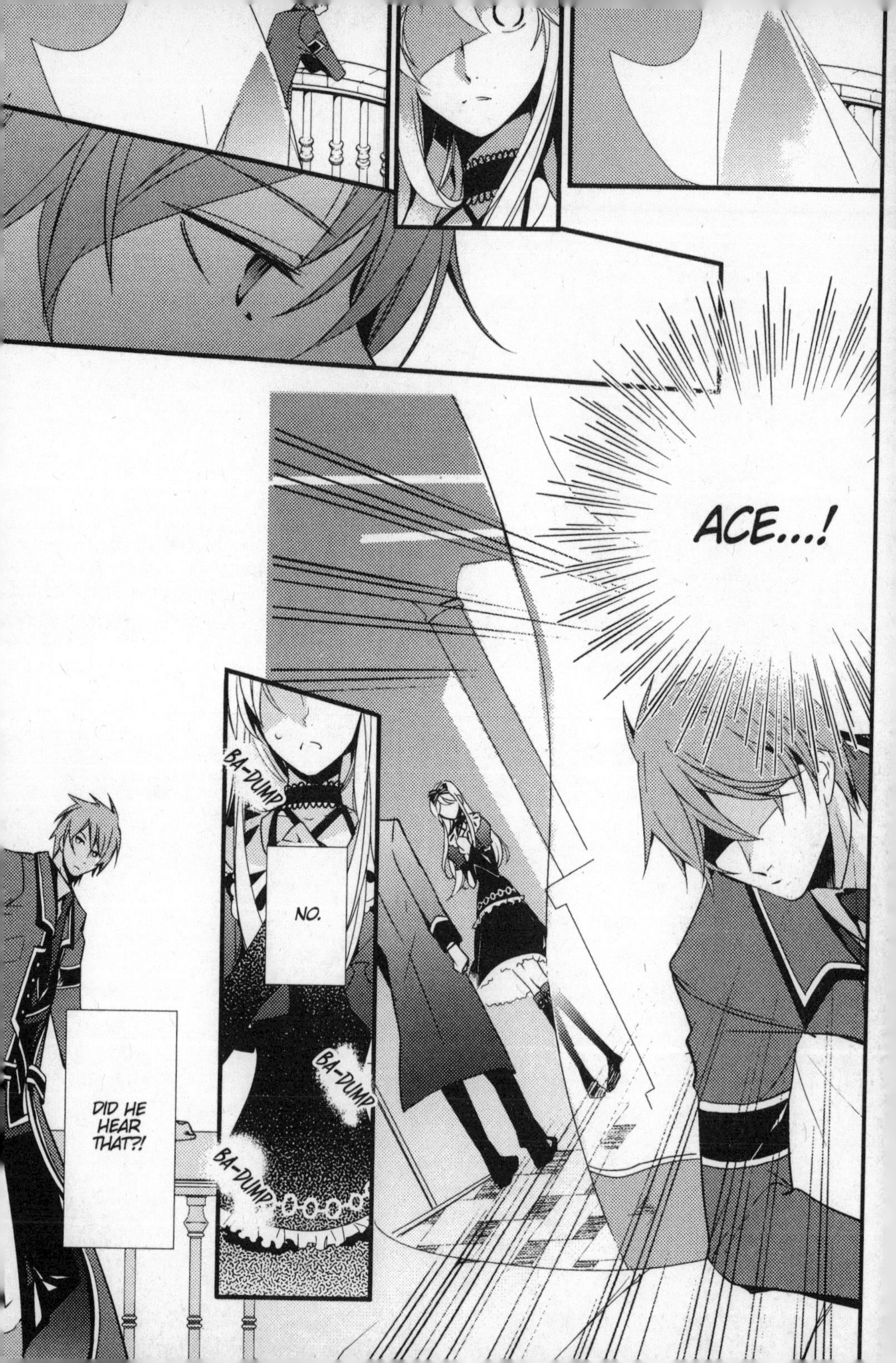
ACE...!
BA-DUMP
NO.
BA-DUMP
BA-DUMP
DID HE HEAR THAT?!

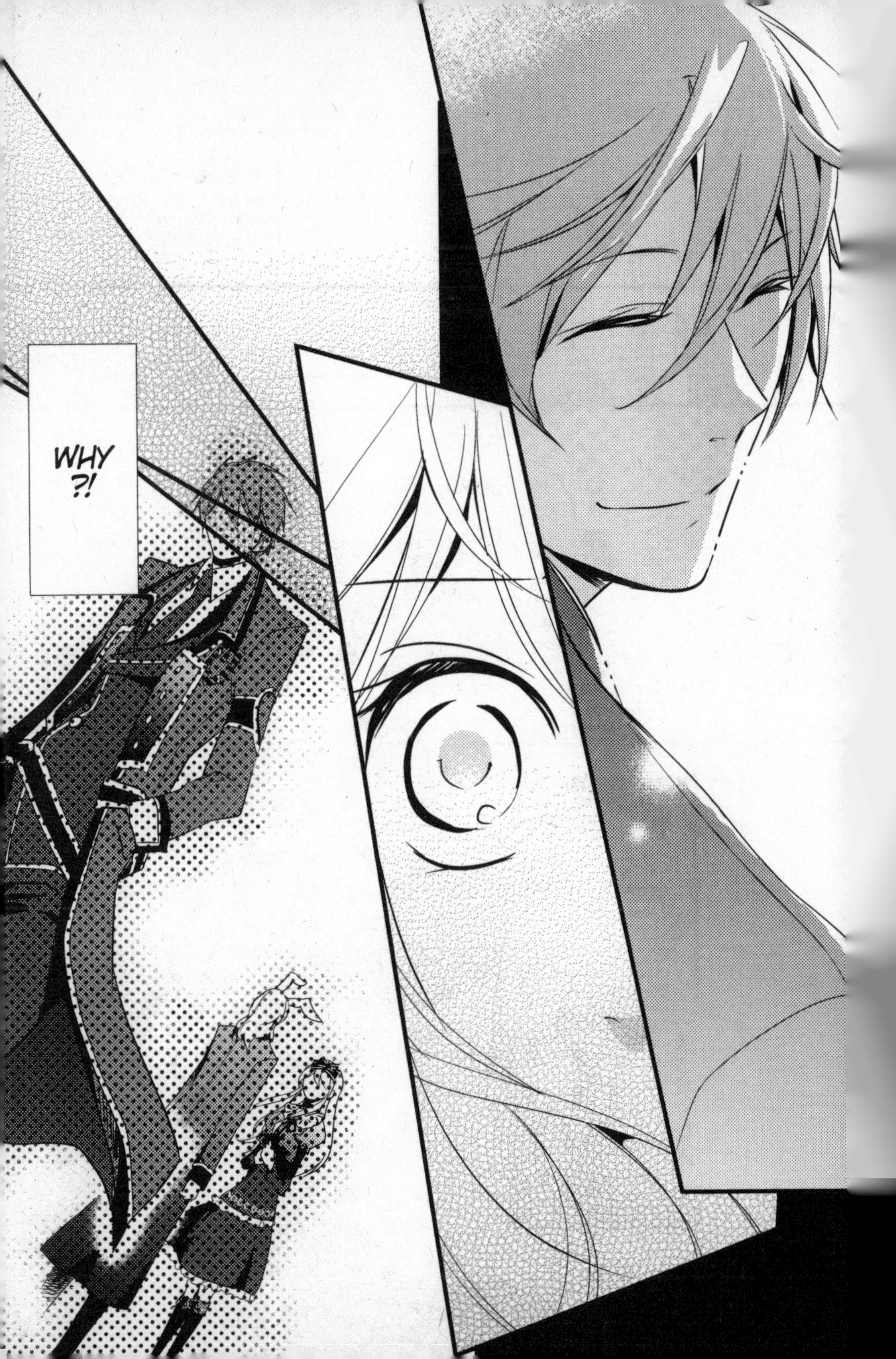
WHY ?!

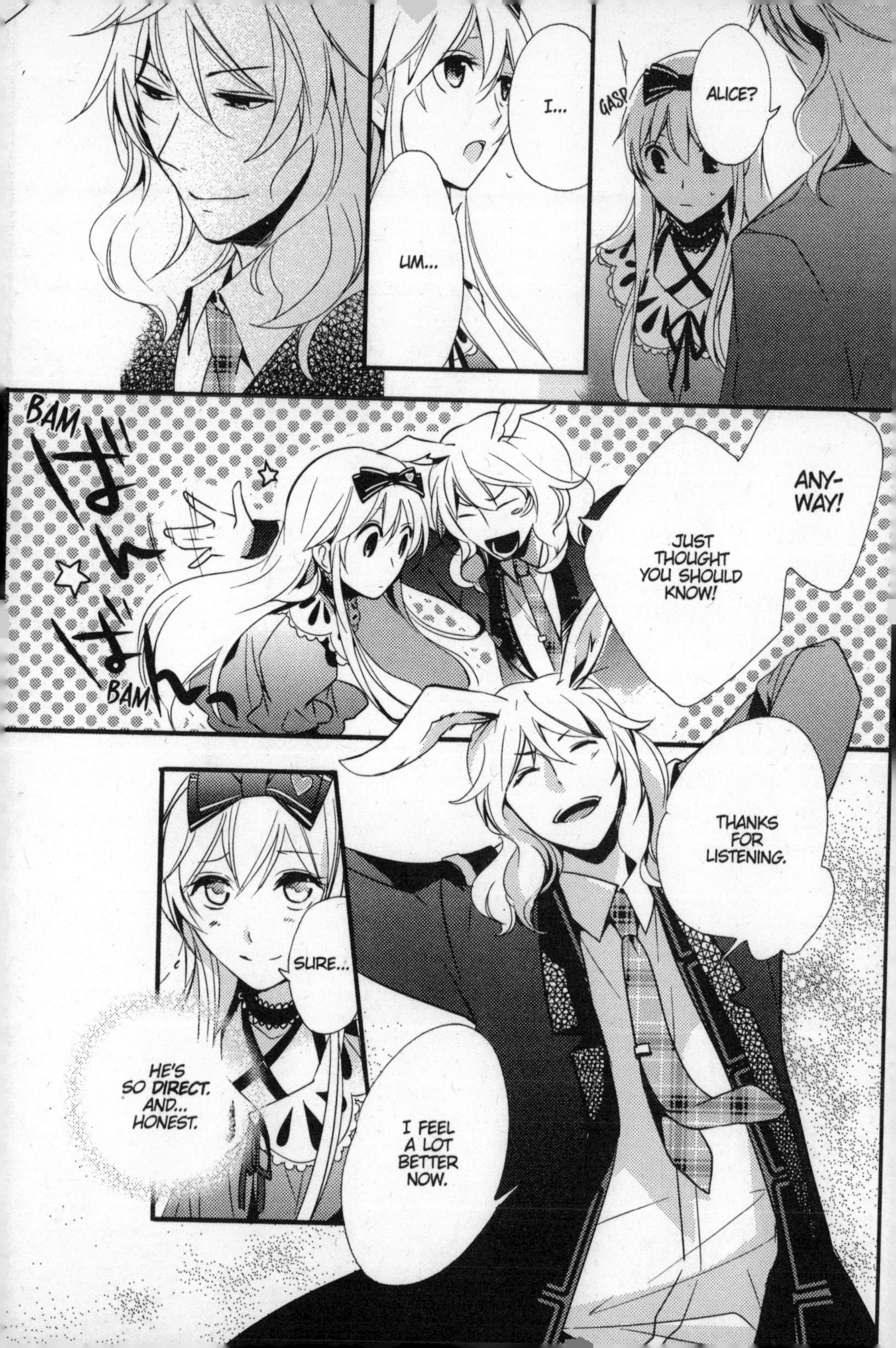
GASP
ALICE?
I...
UM...
ANY-WAY!
JUST THOUGHT YOU SHOULD KNOW!
BAM
ばん
ばん
BAM
THANKS FOR LISTENING.
SURE...
I FEEL A LOT BETTER NOW.
HE'S SO DIRECT. AND... HONEST.

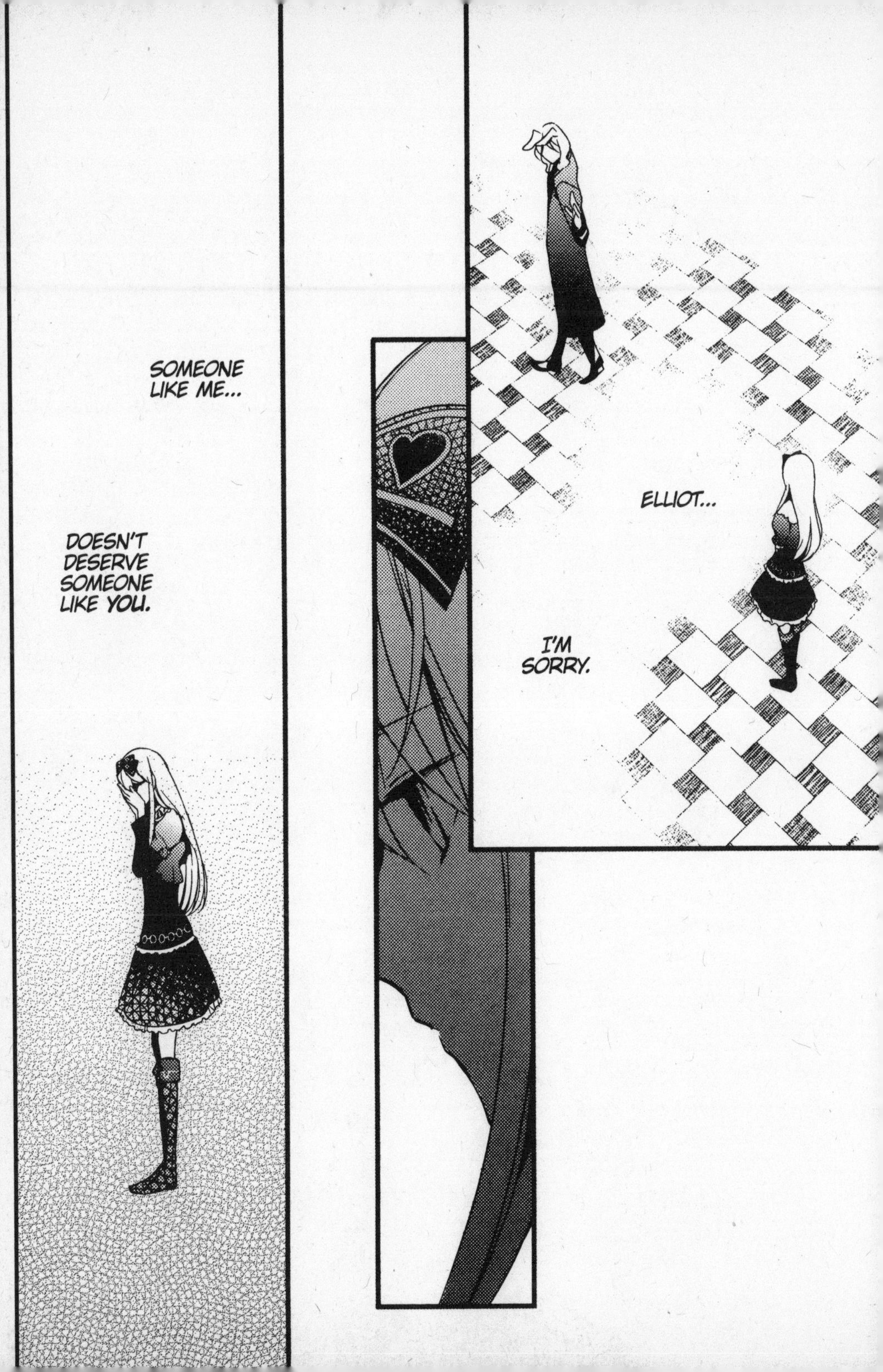
ELLIOT...
I'M SORRY.
SOMEONE LIKE ME...
DOESN'T DESERVE SOMEONE LIKE YOU.

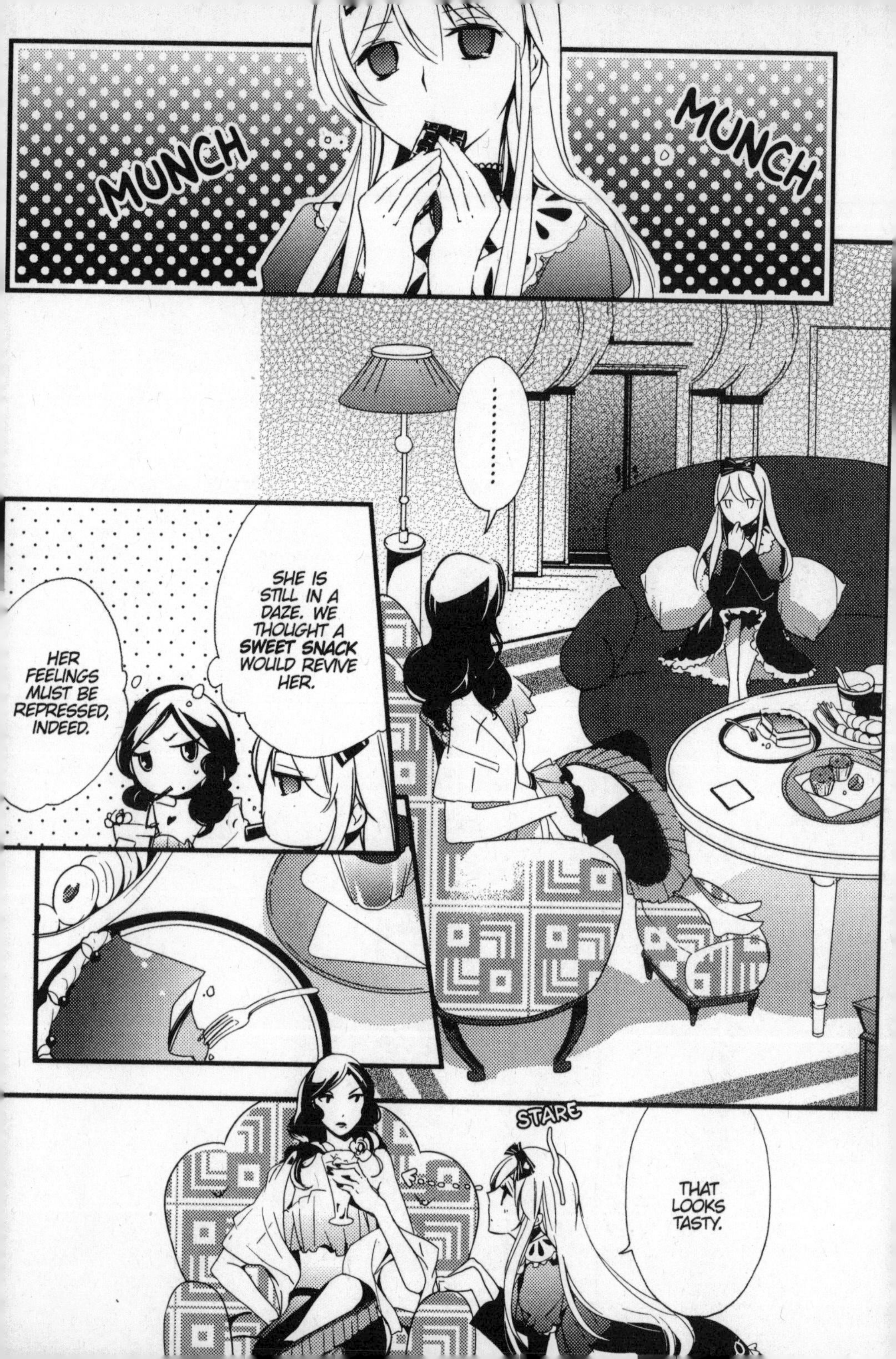
MUNCH
MUNCH
......
SHE IS STILL IN A DAZE. WE THOUGHT A **SWEET SNACK** WOULD REVIVE HER.
HER FEELINGS MUST BE REPRESSED, INDEED.
STARE
THAT LOOKS TASTY.

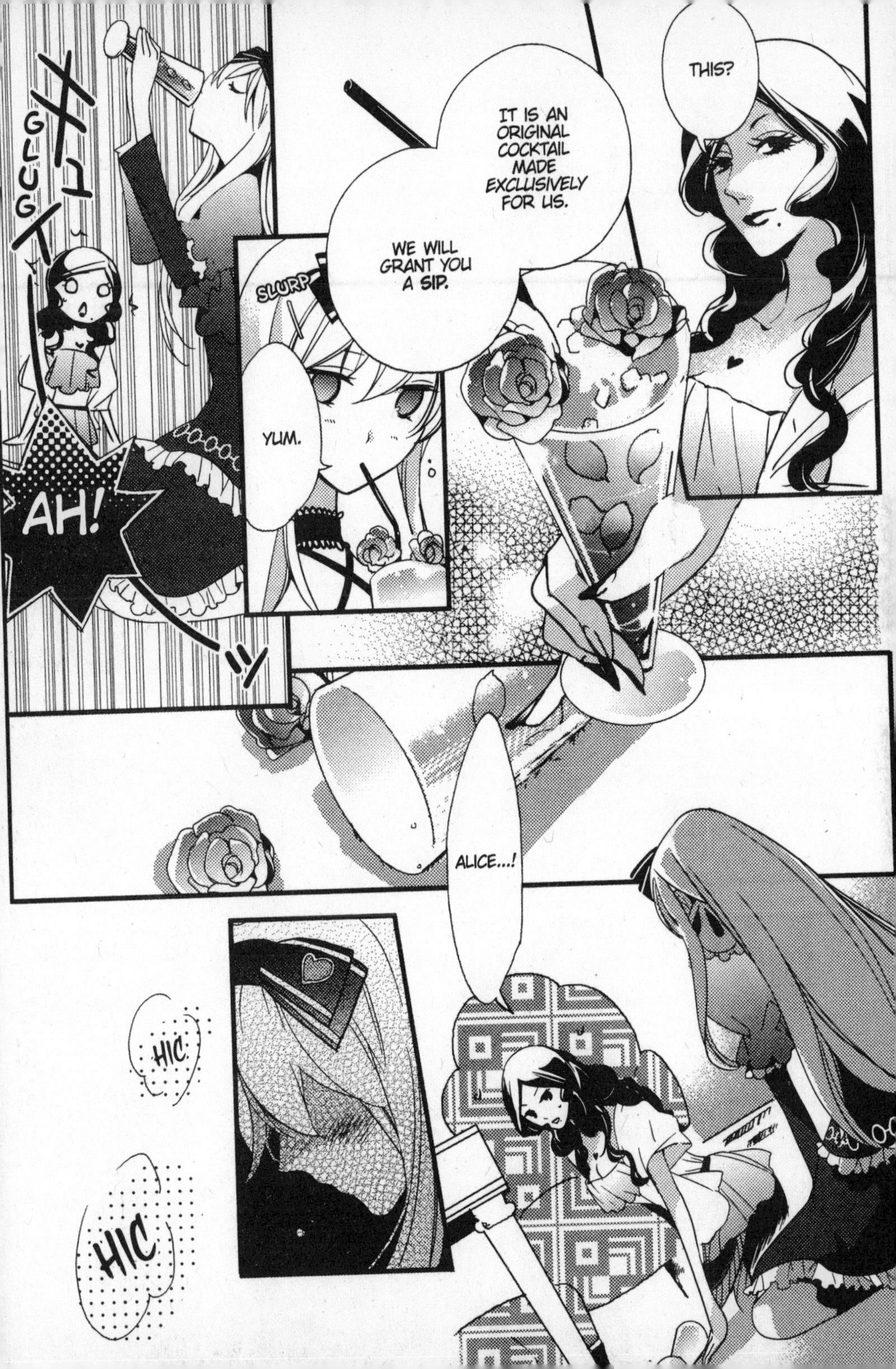
THIS?
IT IS AN ORIGINAL COCKTAIL MADE EXCLUSIVELY FOR US.
WE WILL GRANT YOU A SIP.
SLURP
YUM.
GLUG
AH!
ALICE...!
HIC
HIC

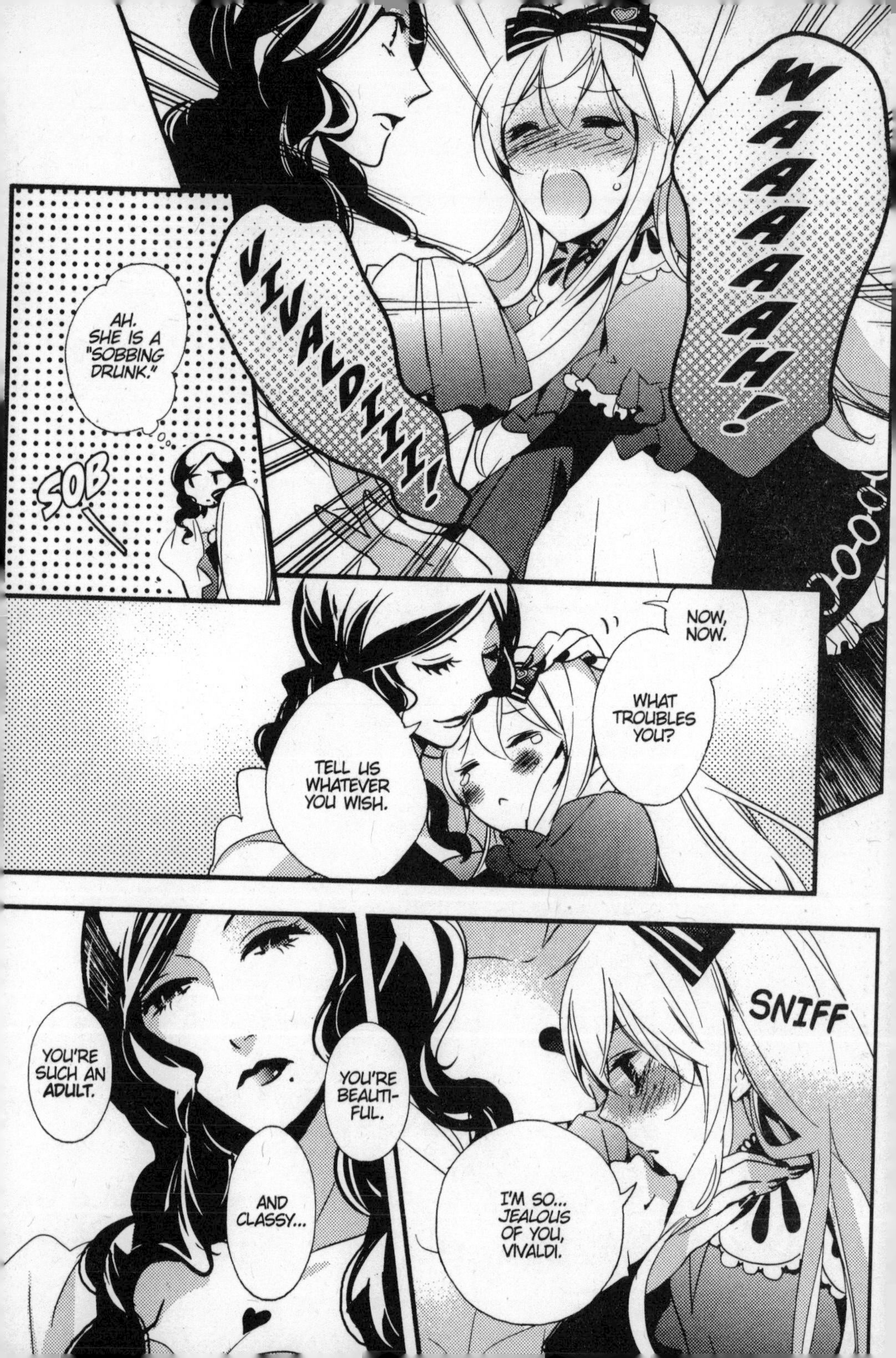
WAAAAAAH!
VIVALDIIII!
AH. SHE IS A "SOBBING DRUNK."
SOB
NOW, NOW.
WHAT TROUBLES YOU?
TELL US WHATEVER YOU WISH.
SNIFF
I'M SO... JEALOUS OF YOU, VIVALDI.
YOU'RE SUCH AN ADULT.
YOU'RE BEAUTI-FUL.
AND CLASSY...

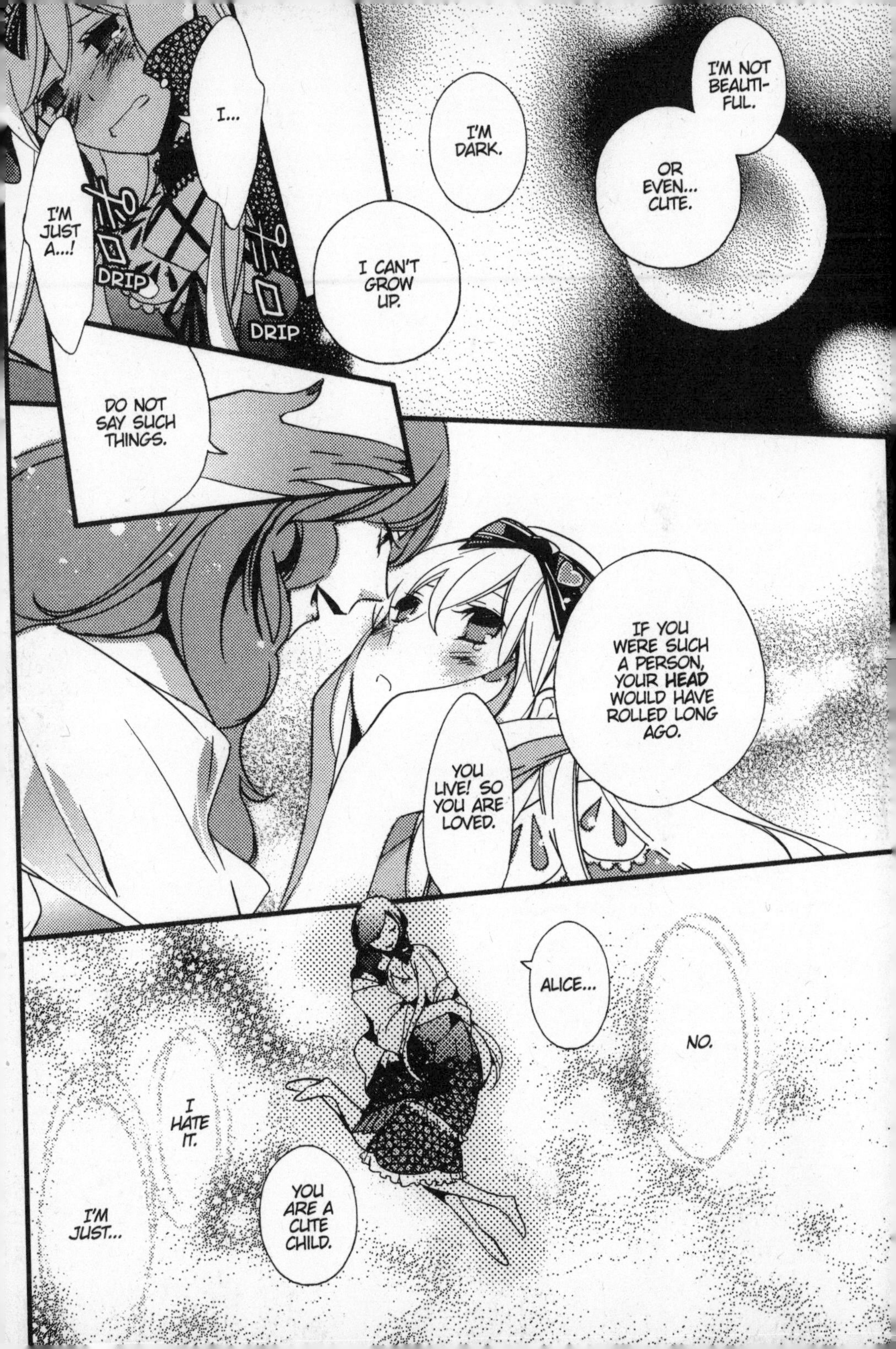
I'M NOT BEAUTI-FUL.
OR EVEN... CUTE.
I'M DARK.
I CAN'T GROW UP.
I...
I'M JUST A...!
DRIP
DRIP
DO NOT SAY SUCH THINGS.
IF YOU WERE SUCH A PERSON, YOUR HEAD WOULD HAVE ROLLED LONG AGO.
YOU LIVE! SO YOU ARE LOVED.
ALICE...
NO.
I HATE IT.
YOU ARE A CUTE CHILD.
I'M JUST...

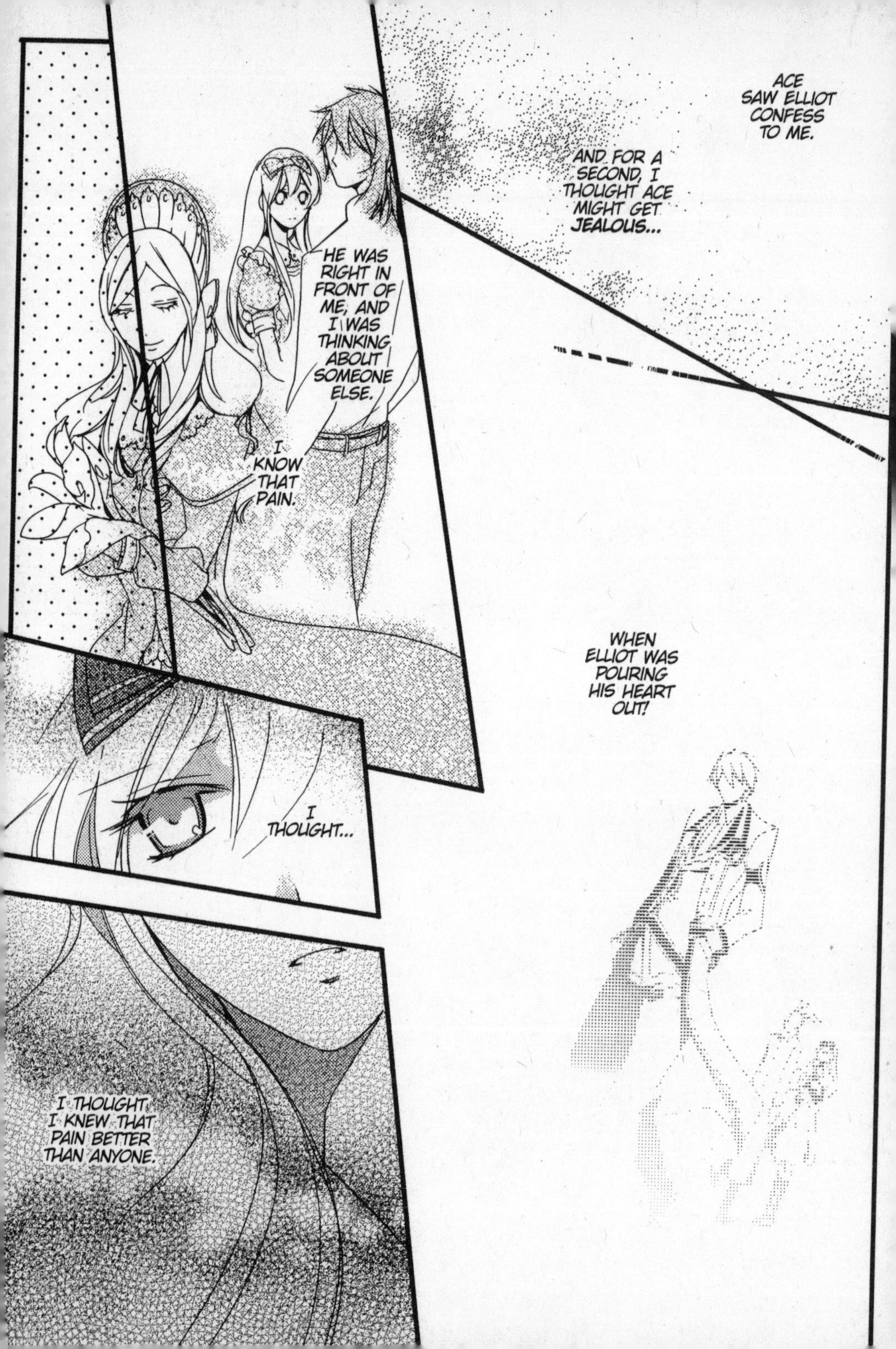
ACE SAW ELLIOT CONFESS TO ME.
AND FOR A SECOND, I THOUGHT ACE MIGHT GET JEALOUS...
WHEN ELLIOT WAS POURING HIS HEART OUT!
HE WAS RIGHT IN FRONT OF ME, AND I WAS THINKING ABOUT SOMEONE ELSE.
I KNOW THAT PAIN.
I THOUGHT...
I THOUGHT I KNEW THAT PAIN BETTER THAN ANYONE.

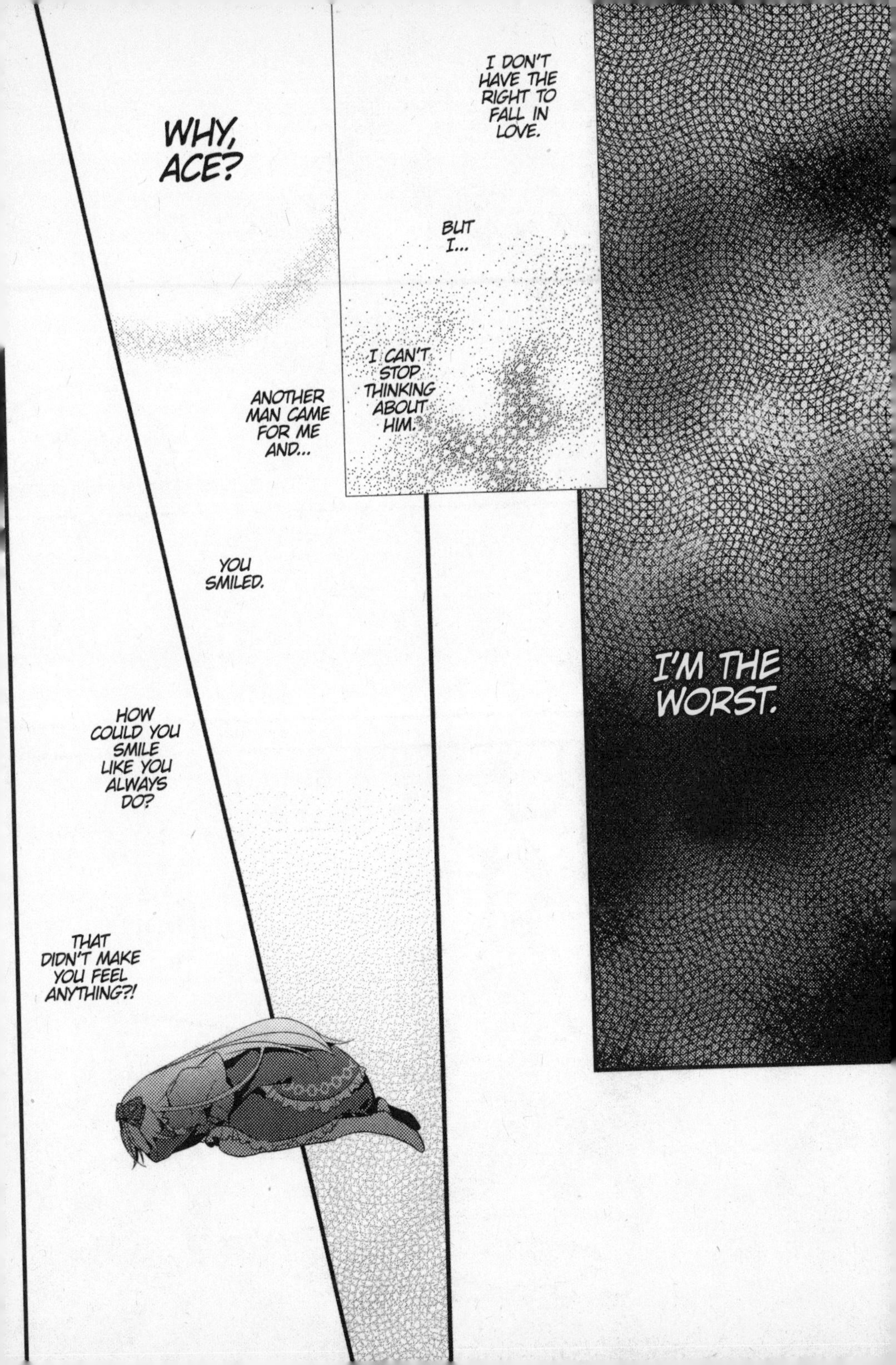
I'M THE WORST.
I DON'T HAVE THE RIGHT TO FALL IN LOVE.
BUT I...
I CAN'T STOP THINKING ABOUT HIM.
WHY, ACE?
ANOTHER MAN CAME FOR ME AND...
YOU SMILED.
HOW COULD YOU SMILE LIKE YOU ALWAYS DO?
THAT DIDN'T MAKE YOU FEEL ANYTHING?!

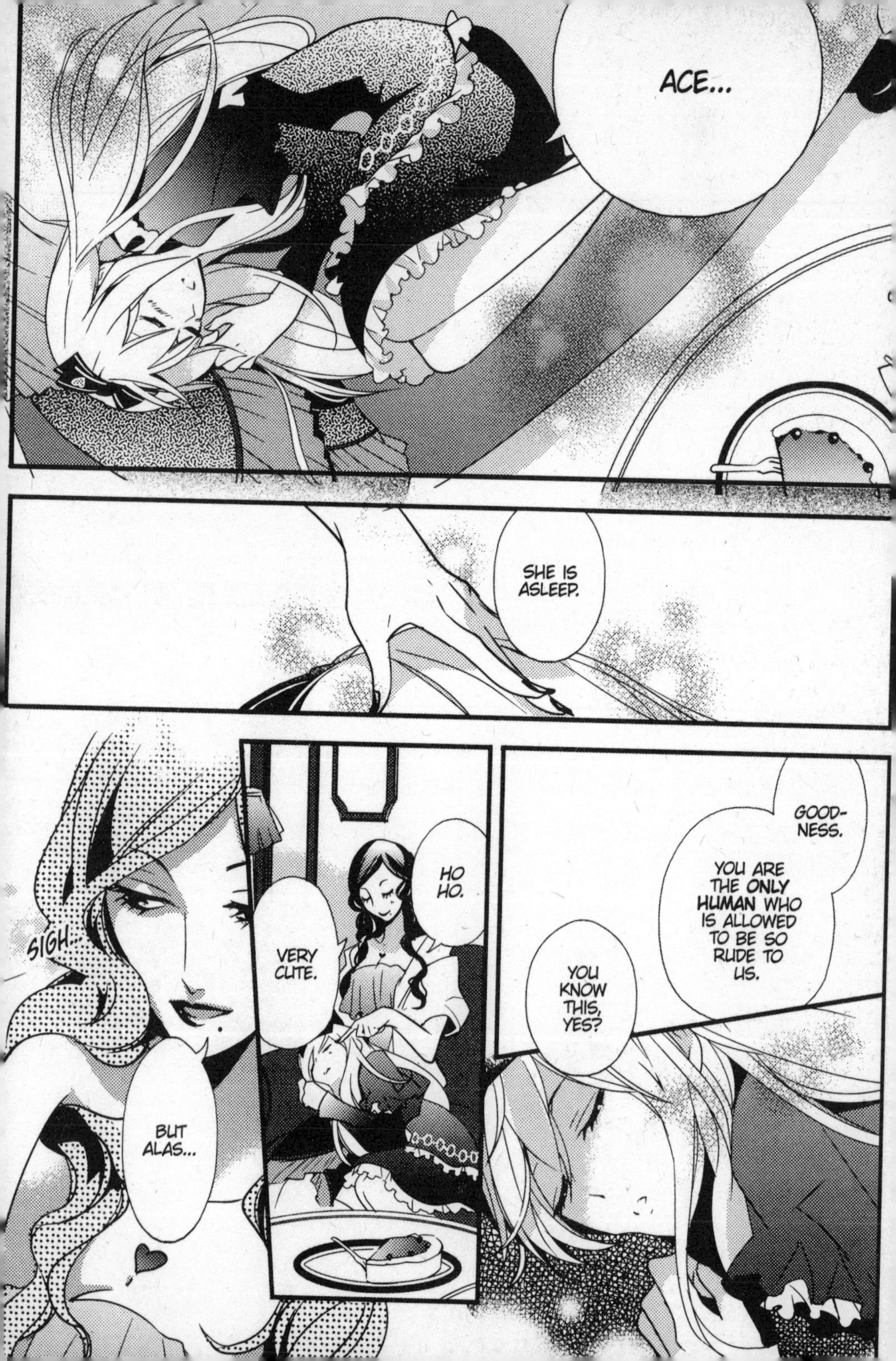
ACE...
SHE IS ASLEEP.
GOOD-NESS.
YOU ARE THE ONLY HUMAN WHO IS ALLOWED TO BE SO RUDE TO US.
YOU KNOW THIS, YES?
HO HO.
VERY CUTE.
SIGH...
BUT ALAS...

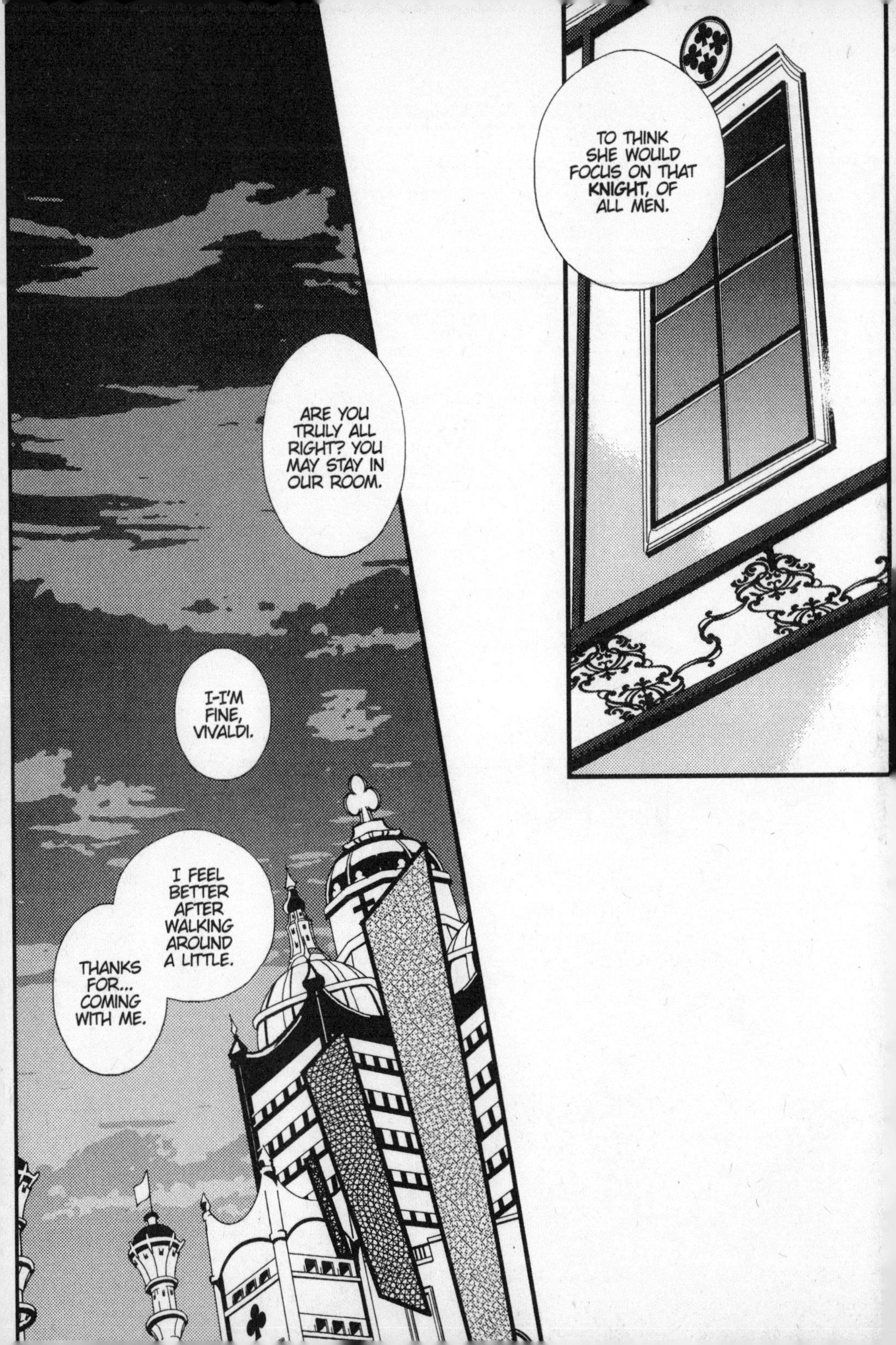
TO THINK SHE WOULD FOCUS ON THAT KNIGHT, OF ALL MEN.
ARE YOU TRULY ALL RIGHT? YOU MAY STAY IN OUR ROOM.
I-I'M FINE, VIVALDI.
I FEEL BETTER AFTER WALKING AROUND A LITTLE.
THANKS FOR... COMING WITH ME.

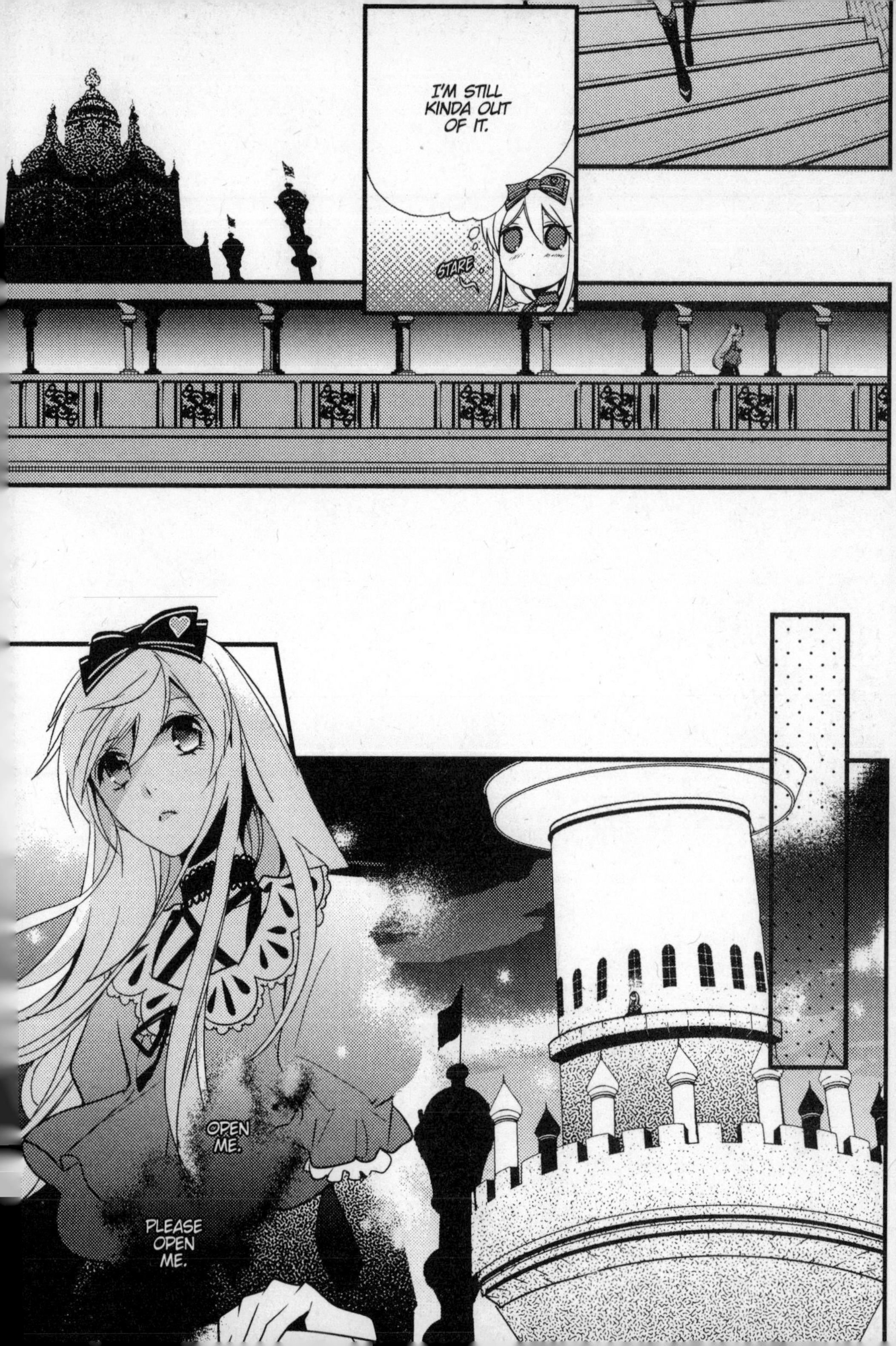
I'M STILL KINDA OUT OF IT.
STARE
OPEN ME.
PLEASE OPEN ME.

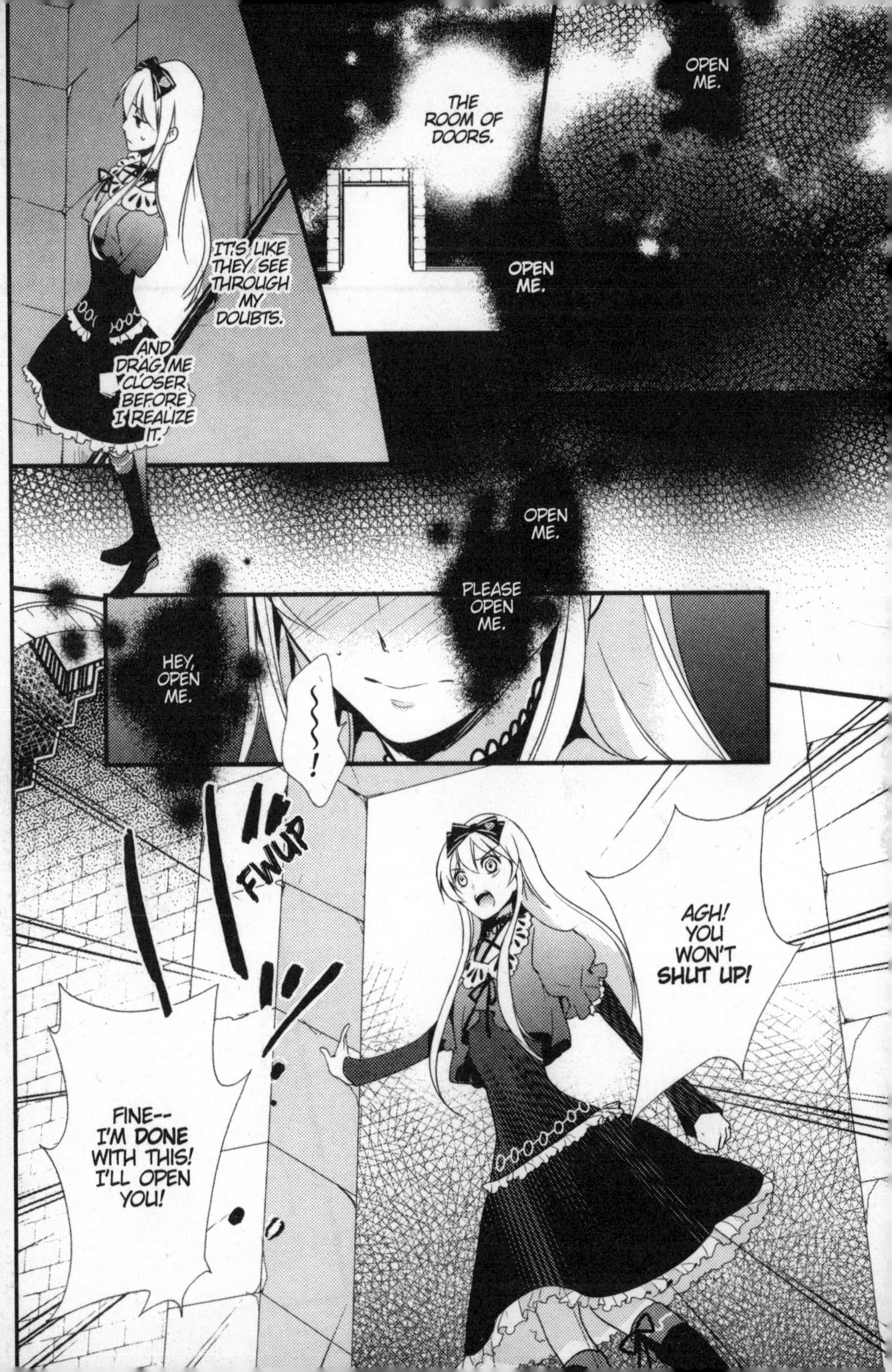
OPEN ME.
THE ROOM OF DOORS.
OPEN ME.
IT'S LIKE THEY SEE THROUGH MY DOUBTS.
AND DRAG ME CLOSER BEFORE I REALIZE IT.
OPEN ME.
PLEASE OPEN ME.
HEY, OPEN ME.
~~~!
FWUP
AGH! YOU WON'T SHUT UP!
FINE-- I'M DONE WITH THIS! I'LL OPEN YOU!
~~~

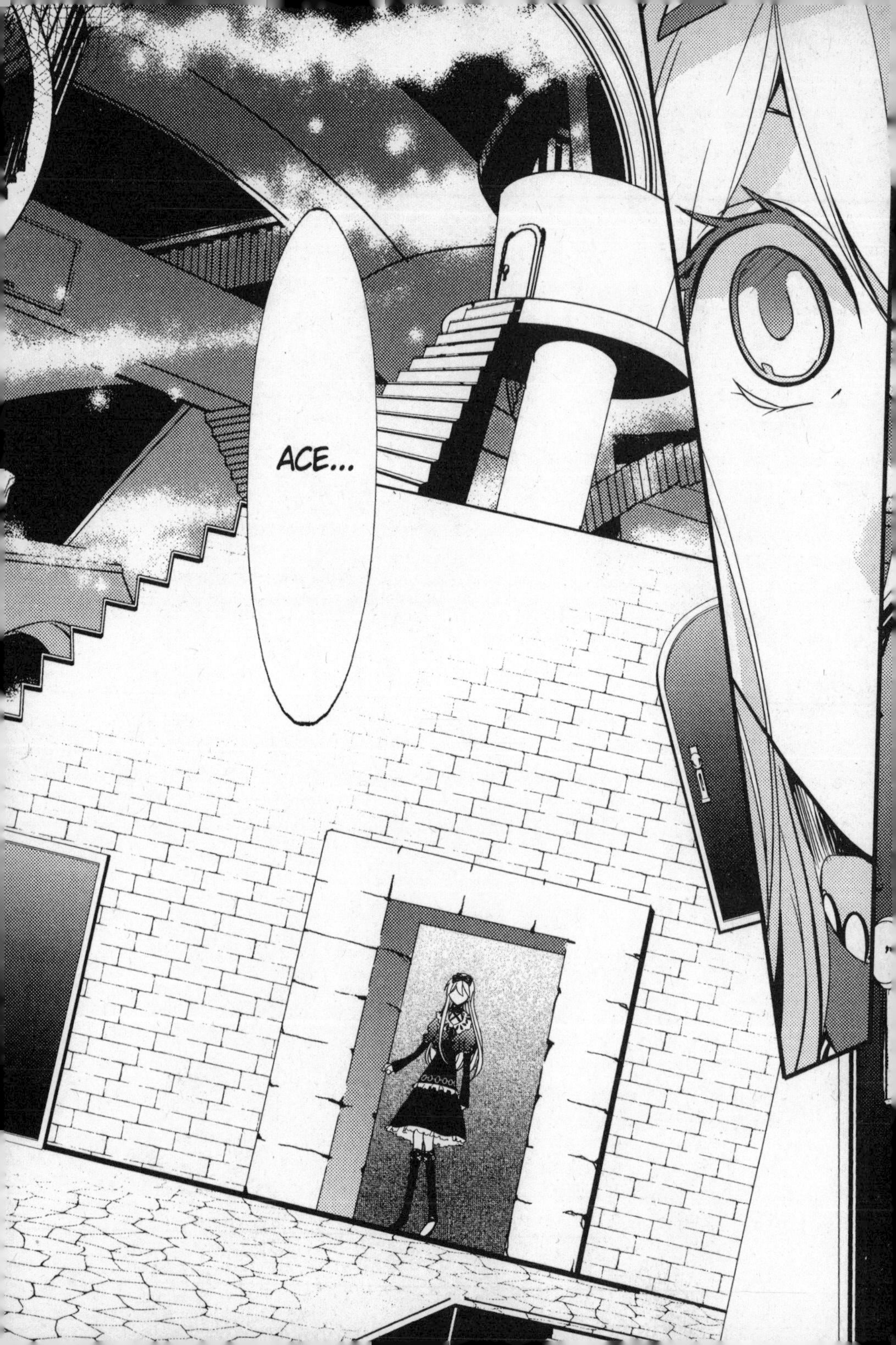
ACE...

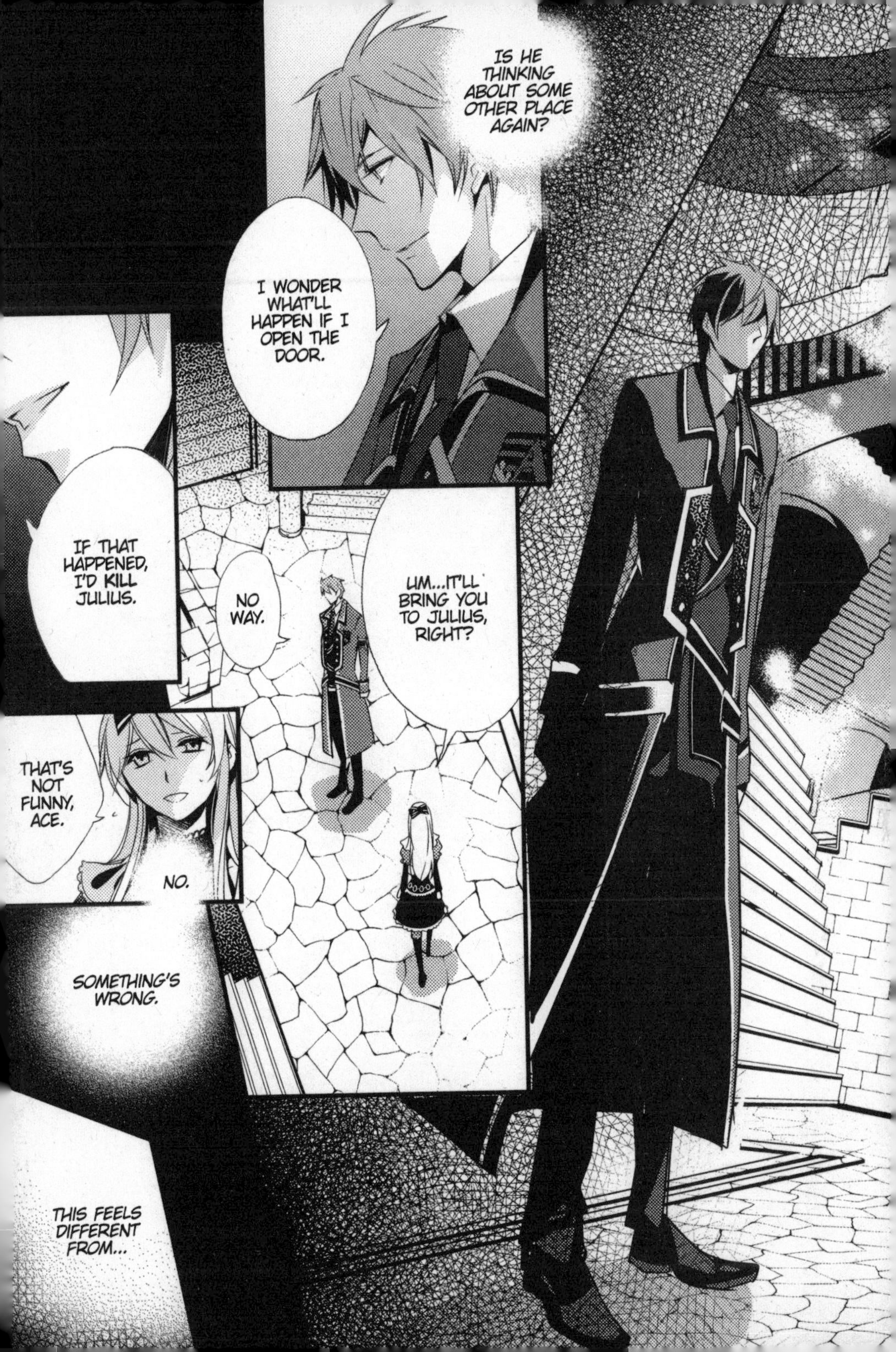
IS HE THINKING ABOUT SOME OTHER PLACE AGAIN?
I WONDER WHAT'LL HAPPEN IF I OPEN THE DOOR.
UM...IT'LL BRING YOU TO JULIUS, RIGHT?
NO WAY.
IF THAT HAPPENED, I'D KILL JULIUS.
THAT'S NOT FUNNY, ACE.
NO.
SOMETHING'S WRONG.
THIS FEELS DIFFERENT FROM...

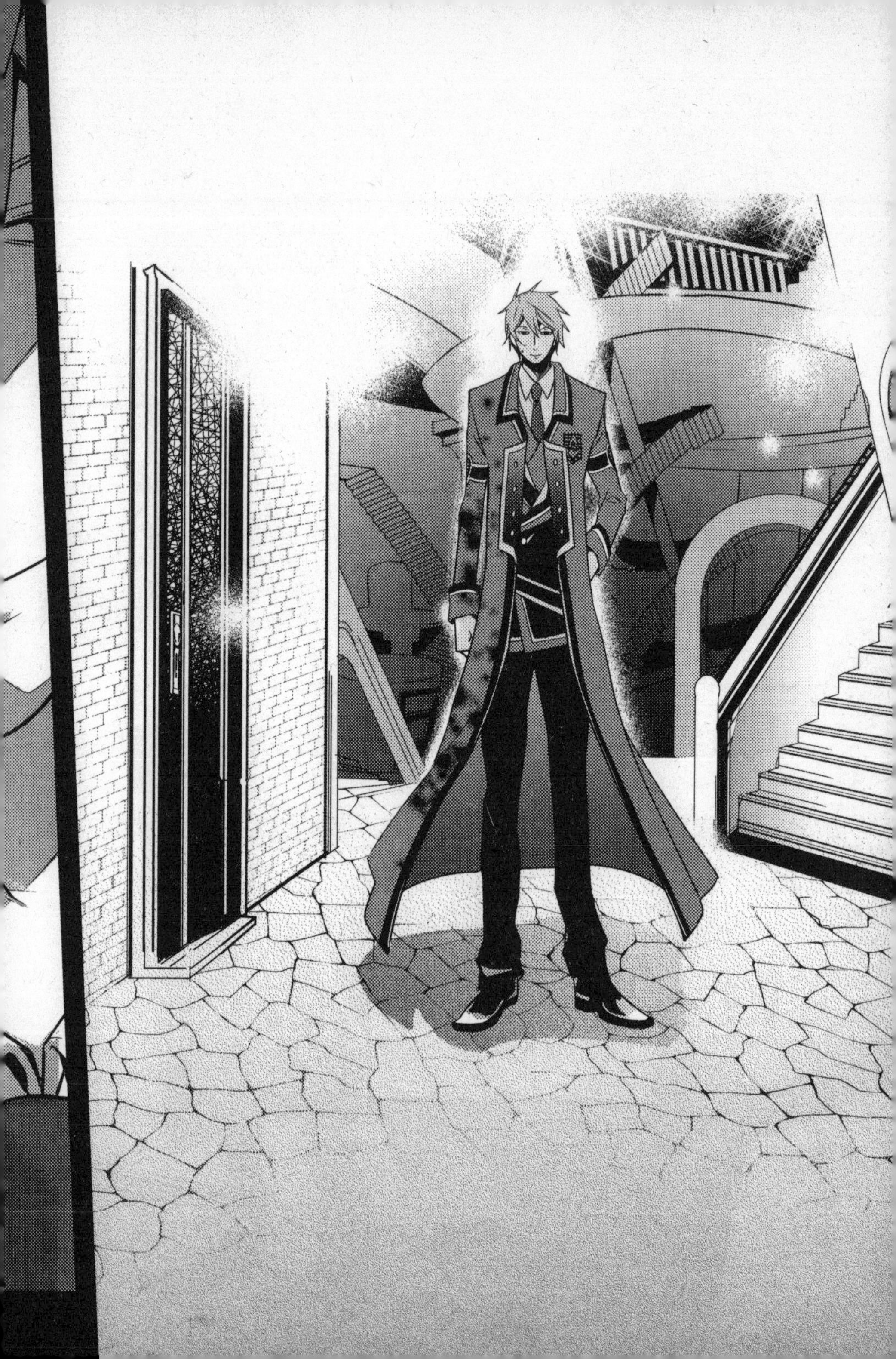

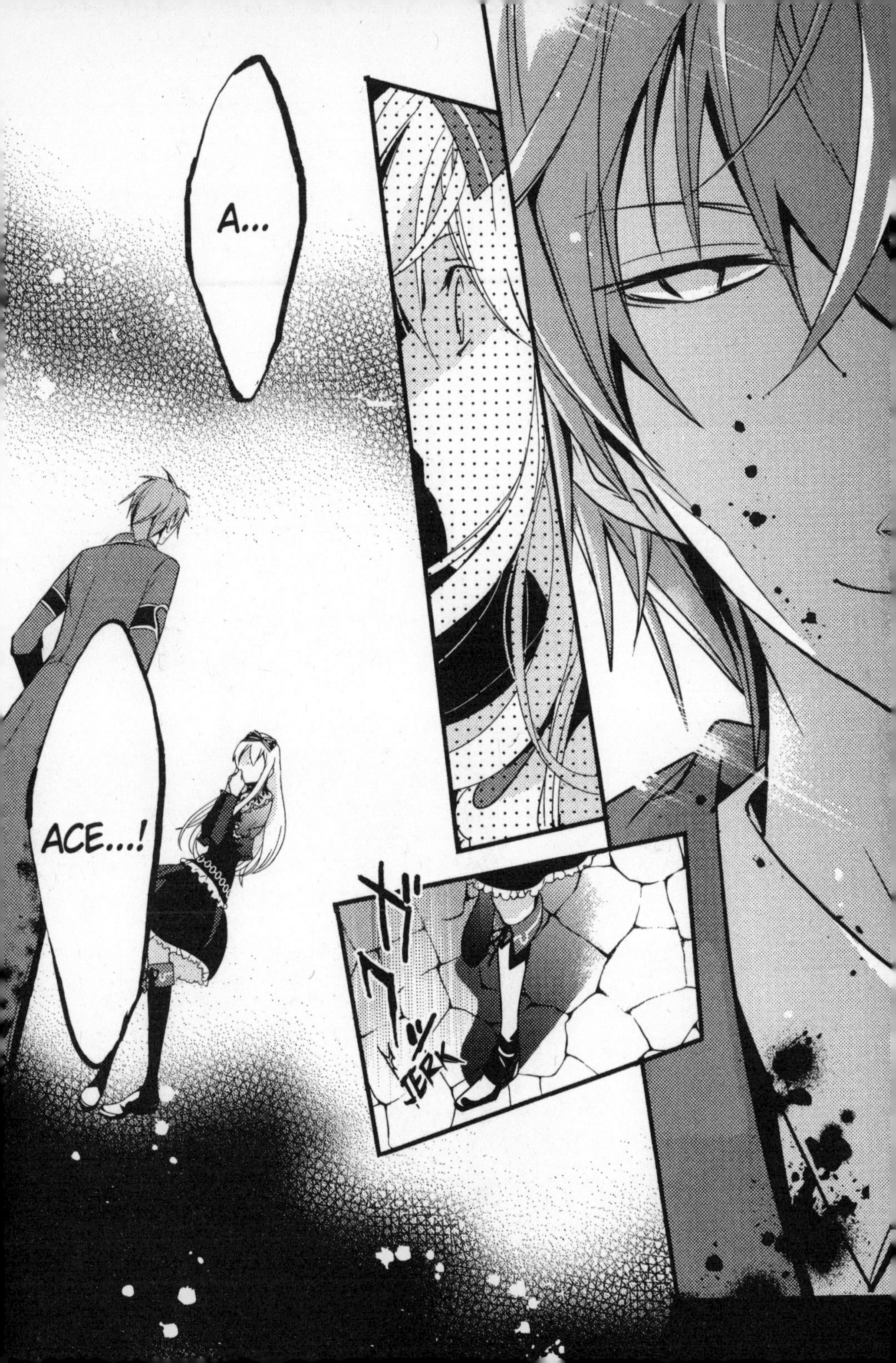
ガクッ
JERK
A...
ACE...!

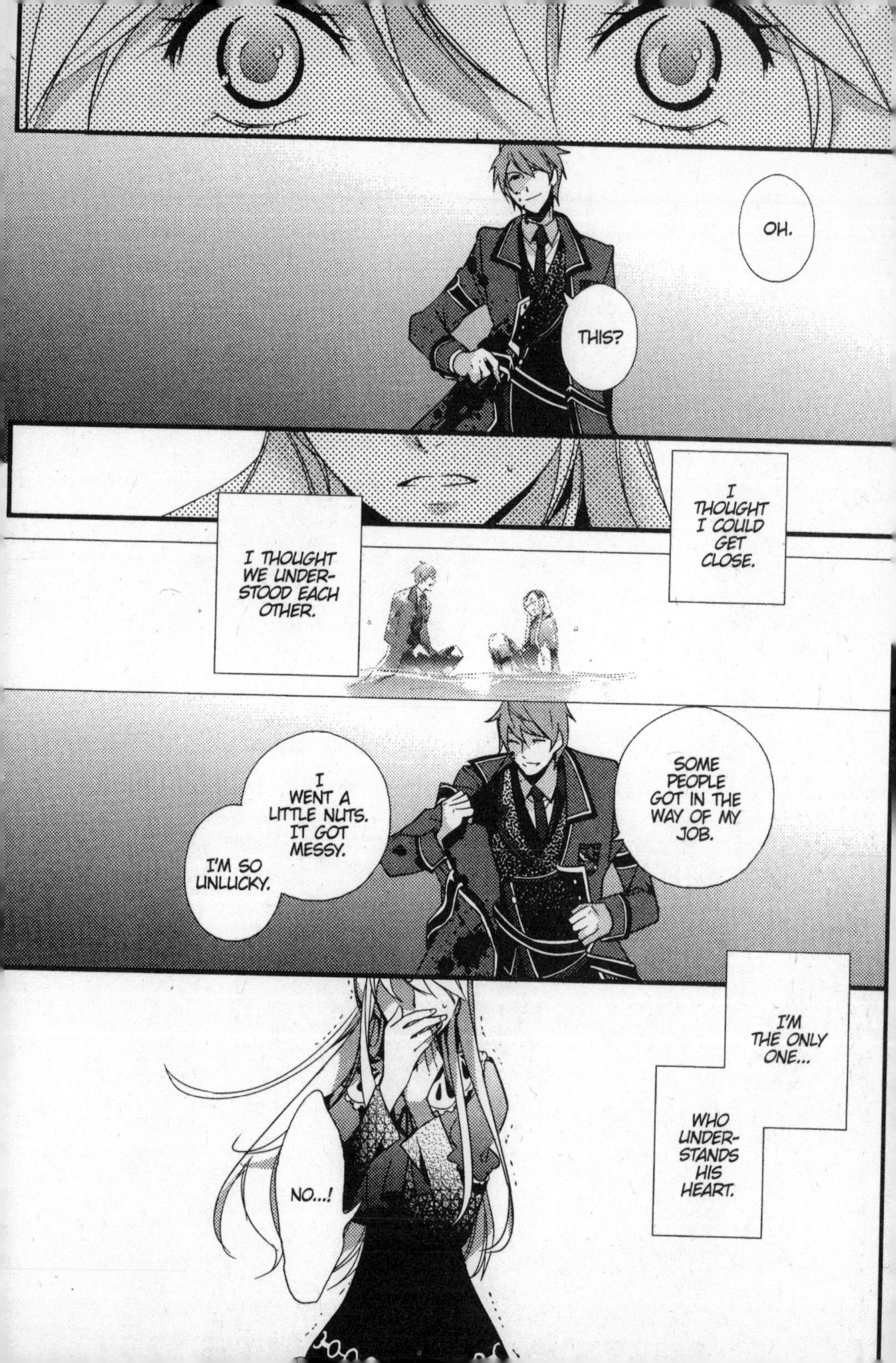
OH.
THIS?
I THOUGHT I COULD GET CLOSE.
I THOUGHT WE UNDERSTOOD EACH OTHER.
SOME PEOPLE GOT IN THE WAY OF MY JOB.
I WENT A LITTLE NUTS. IT GOT MESSY.
I'M SO UNLUCKY.
I'M THE ONLY ONE...
WHO UNDERSTANDS HIS HEART.
NO...!

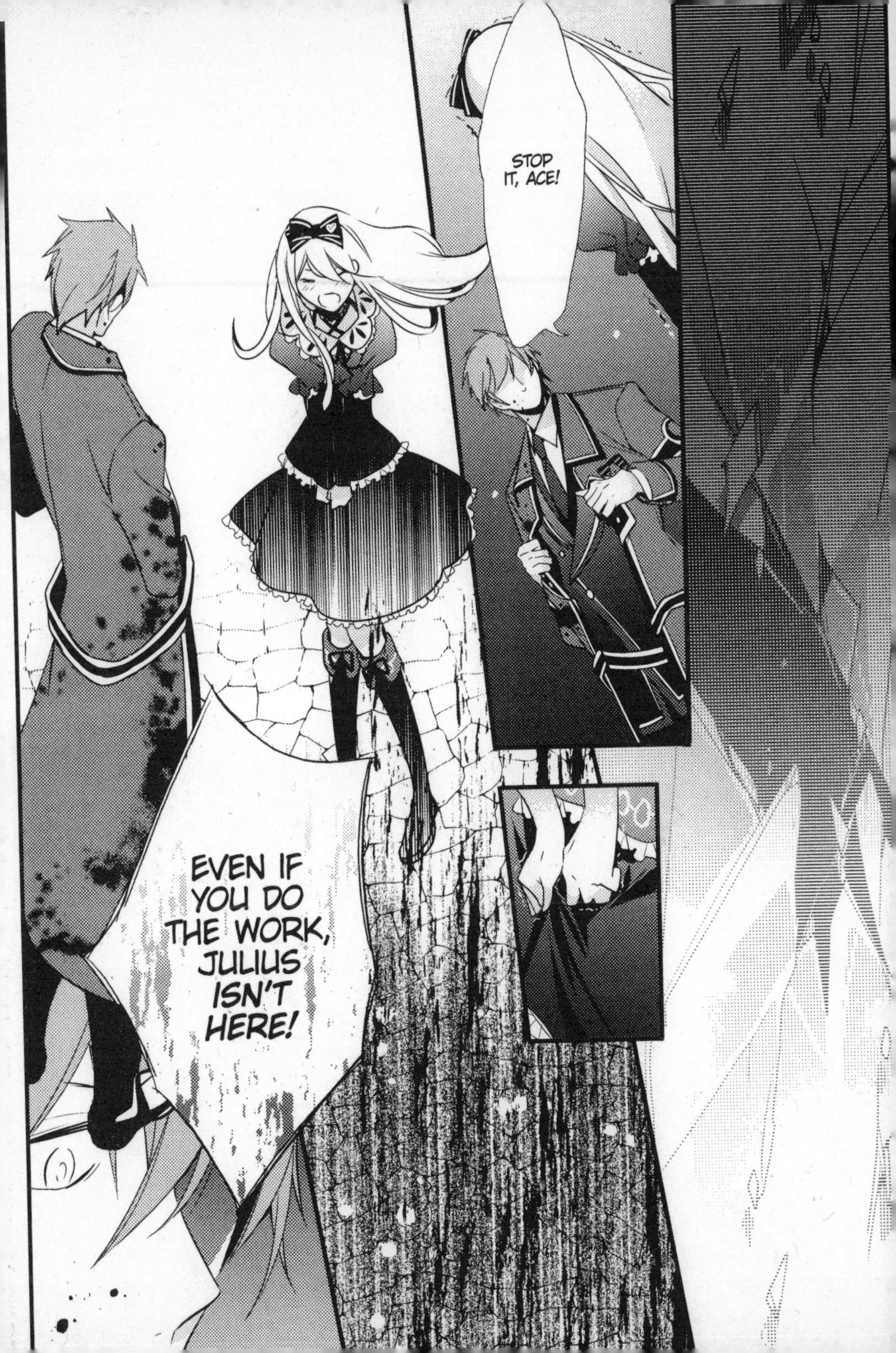
STOP IT, ACE!
EVEN IF YOU DO THE WORK, JULIUS ISN'T HERE!

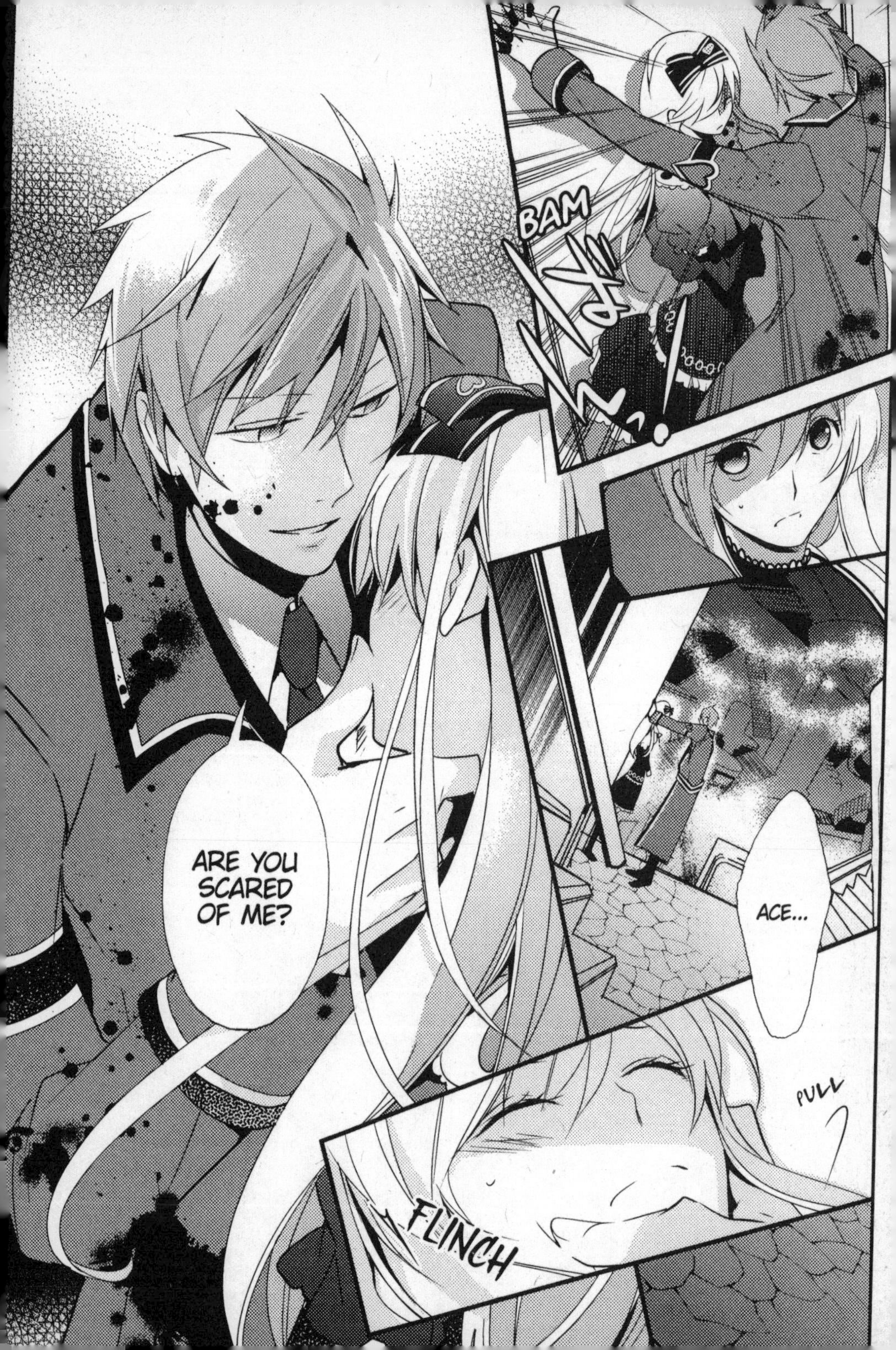
BAM
ACE...
PULL
FLINCH
ARE YOU SCARED OF ME?

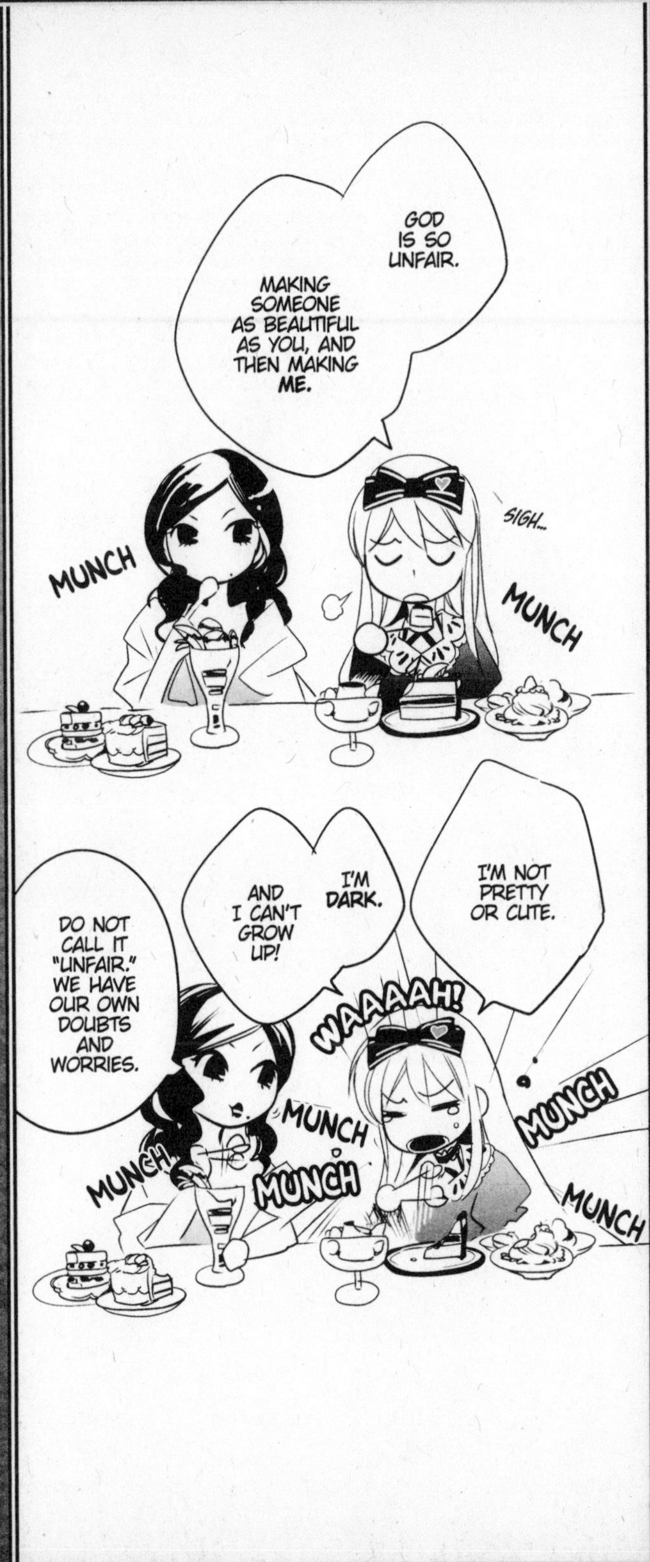
GOD IS SO UNFAIR.
MAKING SOMEONE AS BEAUTIFUL AS YOU, AND THEN MAKING ME.
SIGH...
MUNCH
MUNCH
I'M NOT PRETTY OR CUTE.
I'M DARK.
AND I CAN'T GROW UP!
WAAAAH!
MUNCH
MUNCH
DO NOT CALL IT "UNFAIR." WE HAVE OUR OWN DOUBTS AND WORRIES.
MUNCH
MUNCH
MUNCH

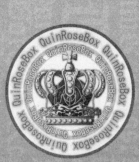

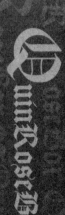

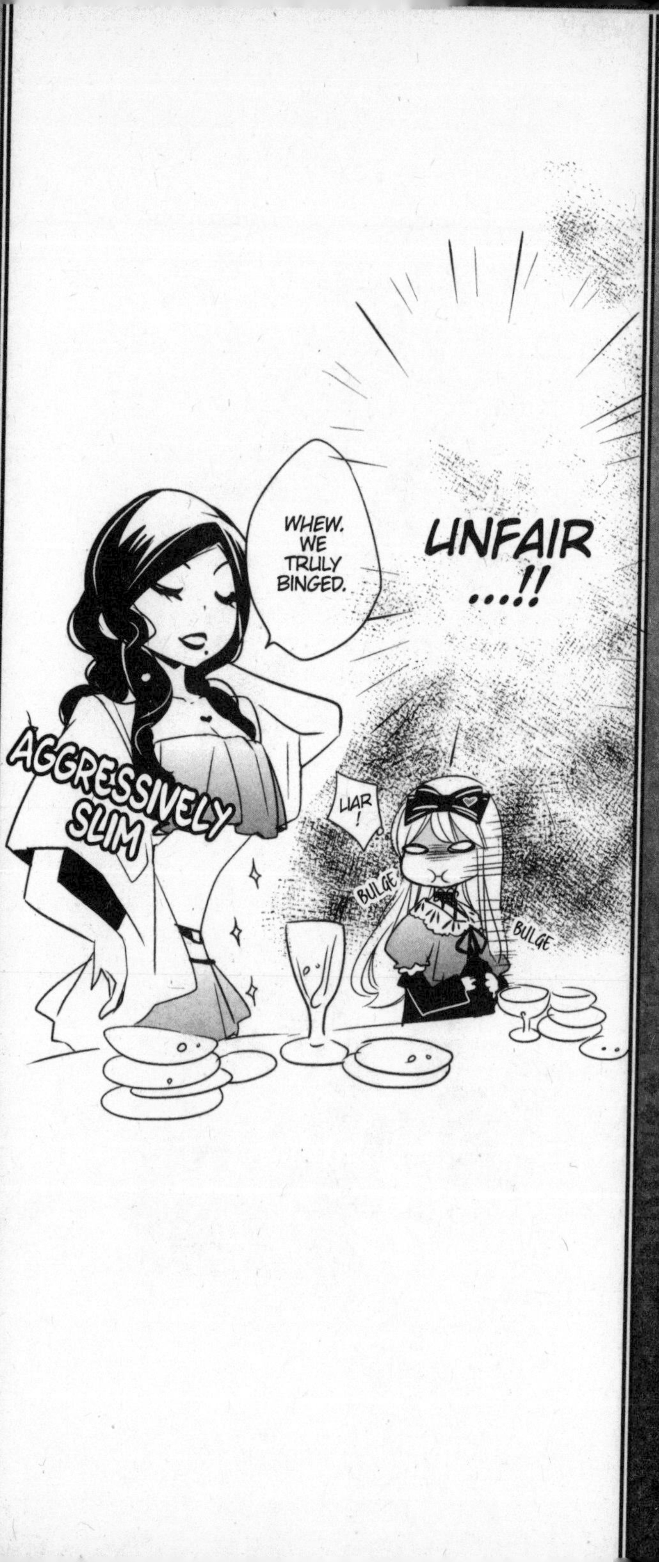
UNFAIR
...!!
WHEW. WE TRULY BINGED.
LIAR!
BULGE
BULGE
AGGRESSIVELY SLIM

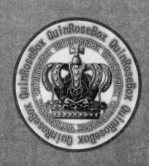

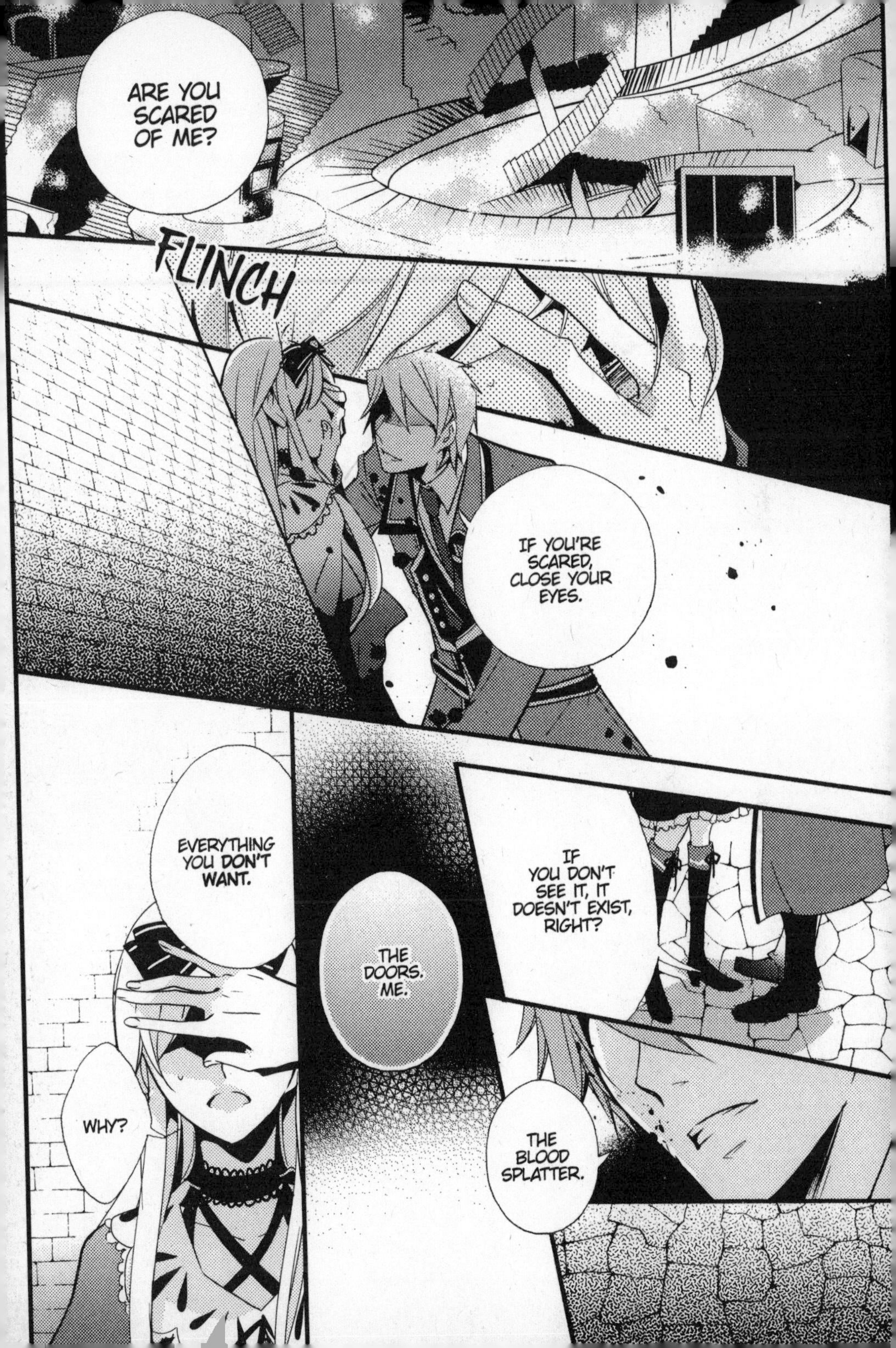
ARE YOU SCARED OF ME?
FLINCH
IF YOU'RE SCARED, CLOSE YOUR EYES.
IF YOU DON'T SEE IT, IT DOESN'T EXIST, RIGHT?
THE BLOOD SPLATTER.
THE DOORS. ME.
EVERYTHING YOU DON'T WANT.
WHY?

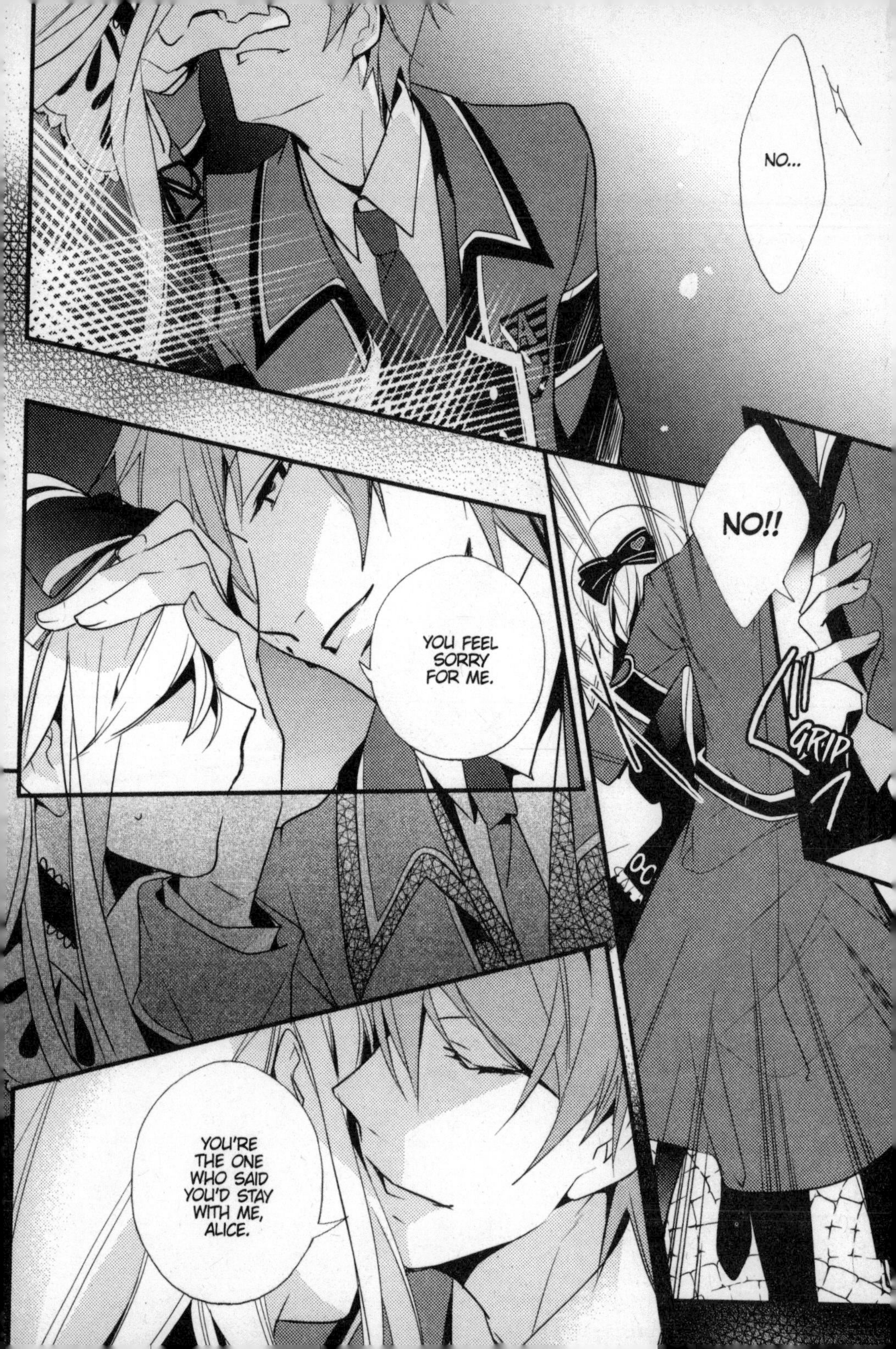
NO...
NO!!
GRIP
YOU FEEL SORRY FOR ME.
YOU'RE THE ONE WHO SAID YOU'D STAY WITH ME, ALICE.

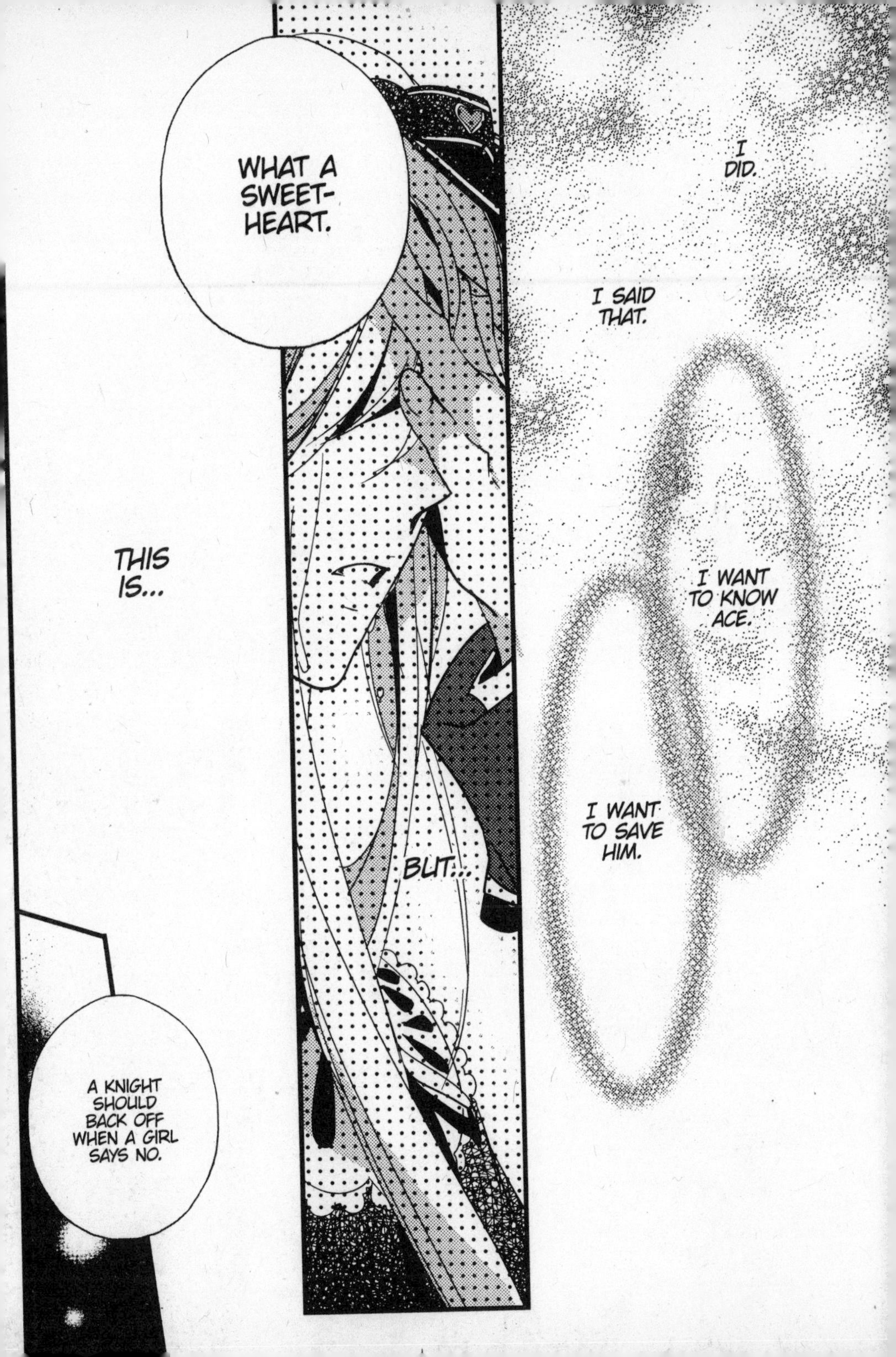
I DID.
I SAID THAT.
I WANT TO KNOW ACE.
I WANT TO SAVE HIM.
WHAT A SWEET-HEART.
BUT...
THIS IS...
A KNIGHT SHOULD BACK OFF WHEN A GIRL SAYS NO.

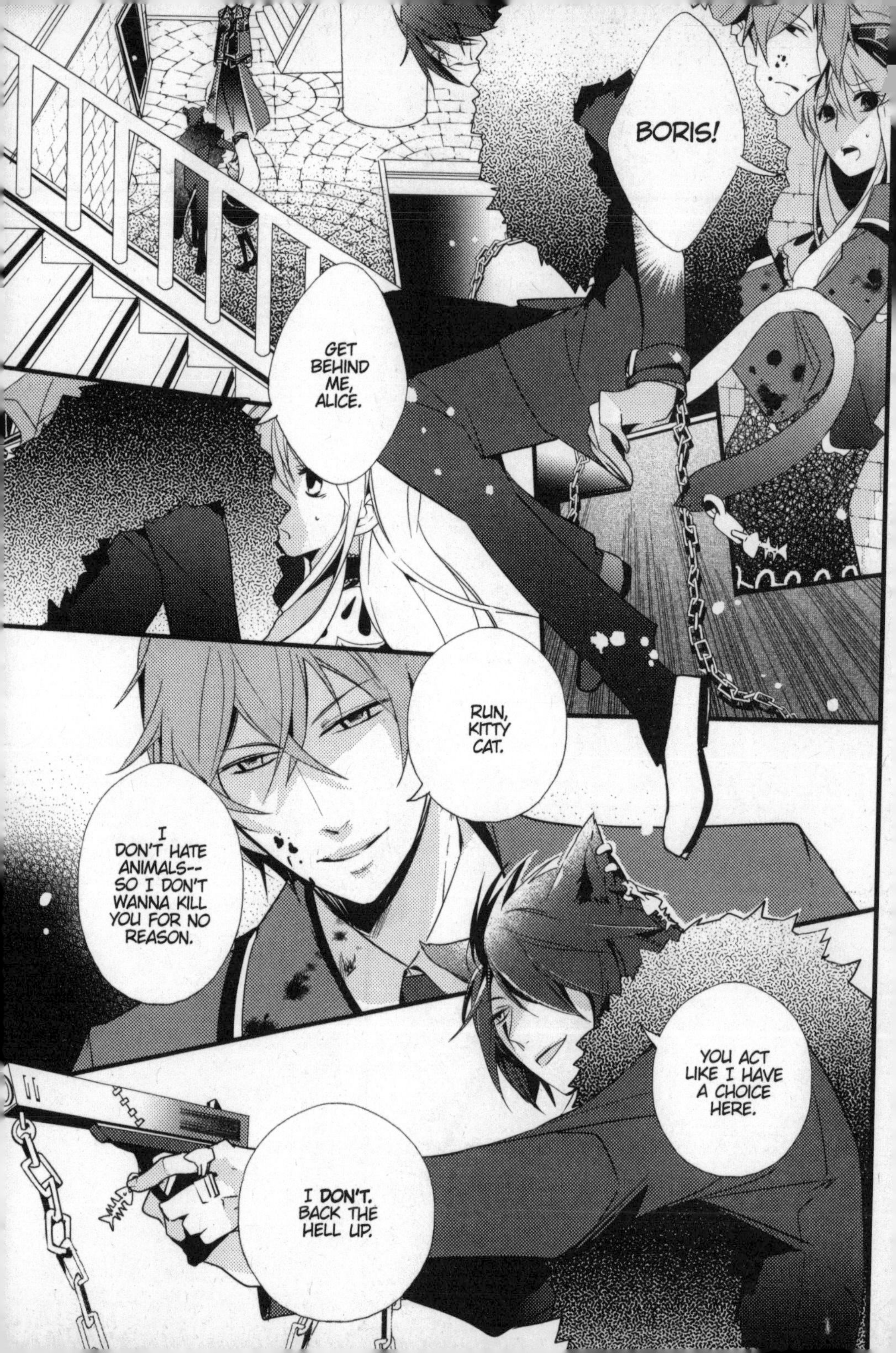
BORIS!
GET BEHIND ME, ALICE.
RUN, KITTY CAT.
I DON'T HATE ANIMALS-- SO I DON'T WANNA KILL YOU FOR NO REASON.
YOU ACT LIKE I HAVE A CHOICE HERE.
I DON'T. BACK THE HELL UP.

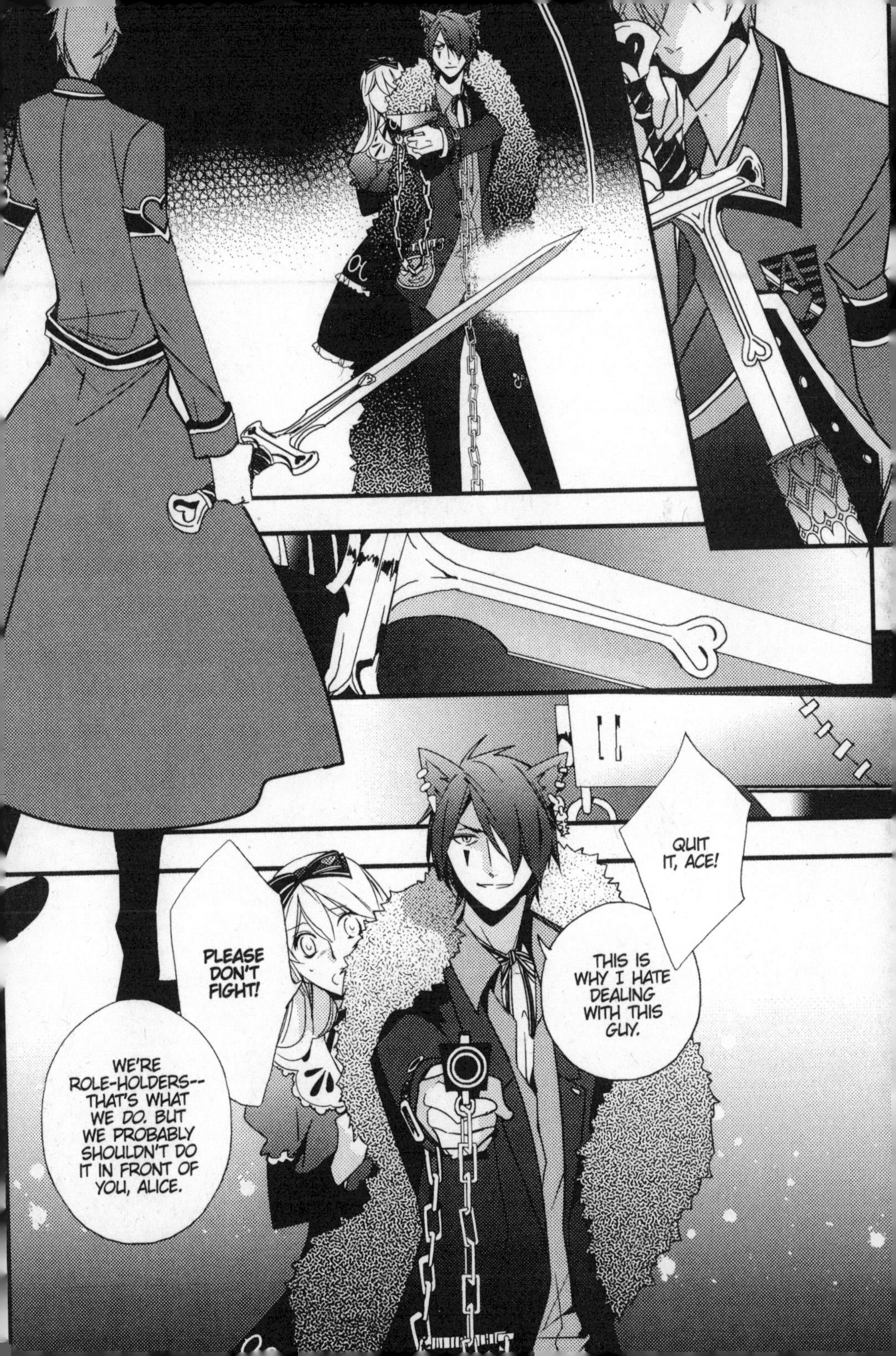
QUIT IT, ACE!
THIS IS WHY I HATE DEALING WITH THIS GUY.
PLEASE DON'T FIGHT!
WE'RE ROLE-HOLDERS-- THAT'S WHAT WE DO. BUT WE PROBABLY SHOULDN'T DO IT IN FRONT OF YOU, ALICE.

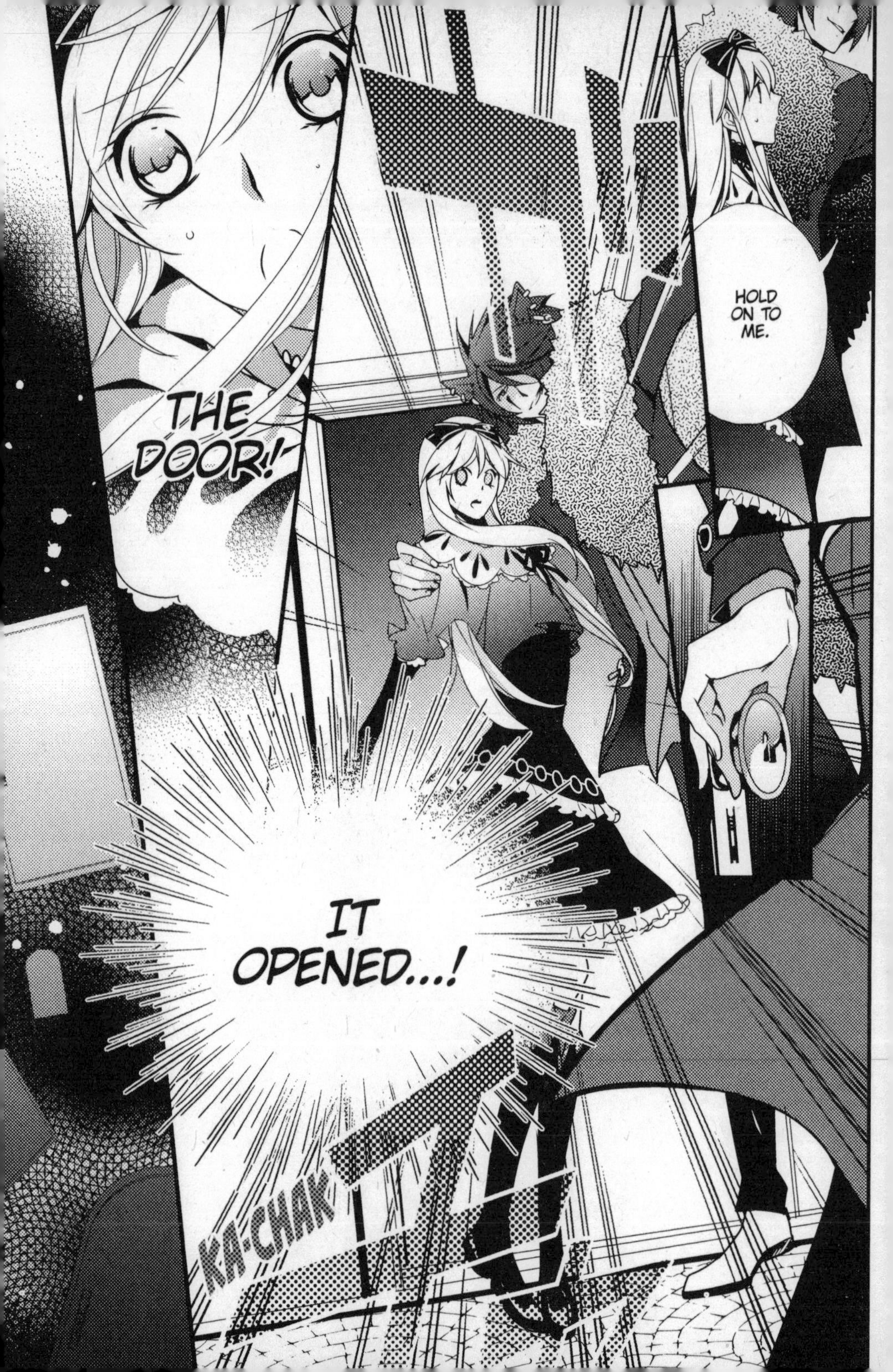
HOLD ON TO ME.
KA-CHAK
THE DOOR!
IT OPENED...!

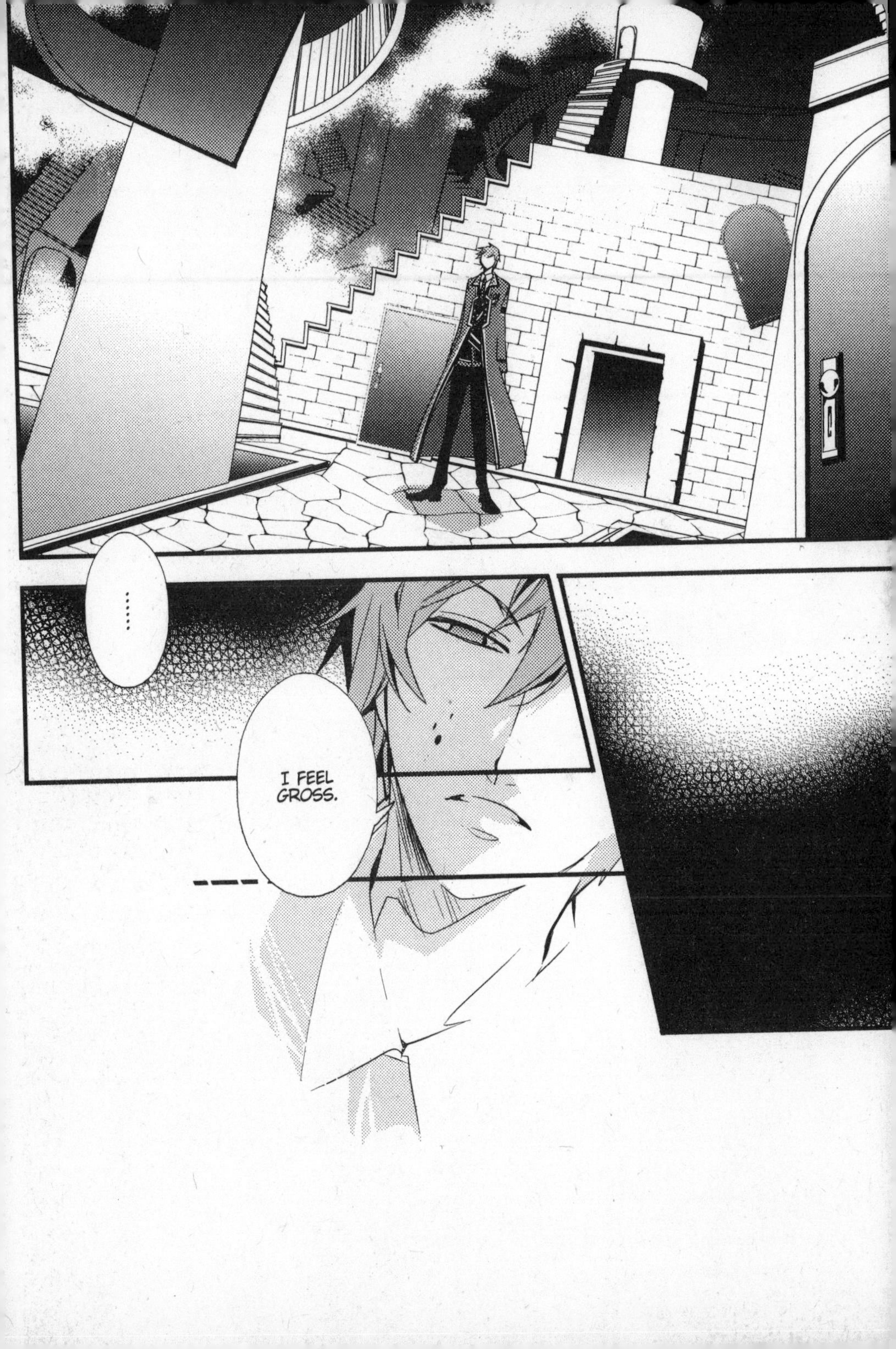
......
I FEEL GROSS.

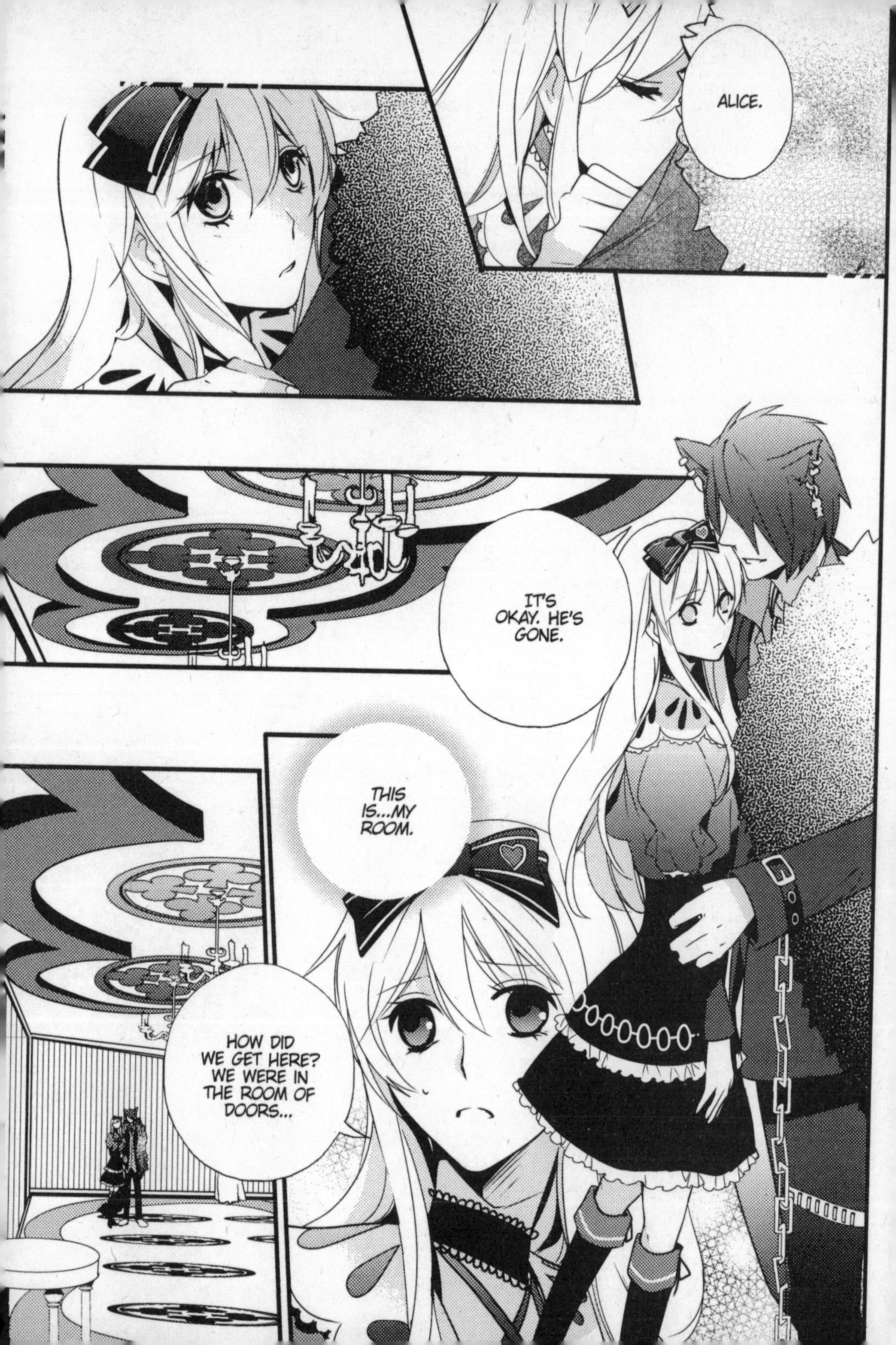
ALICE.
IT'S OKAY. HE'S GONE.
THIS IS...MY ROOM.
HOW DID WE GET HERE? WE WERE IN THE ROOM OF DOORS...

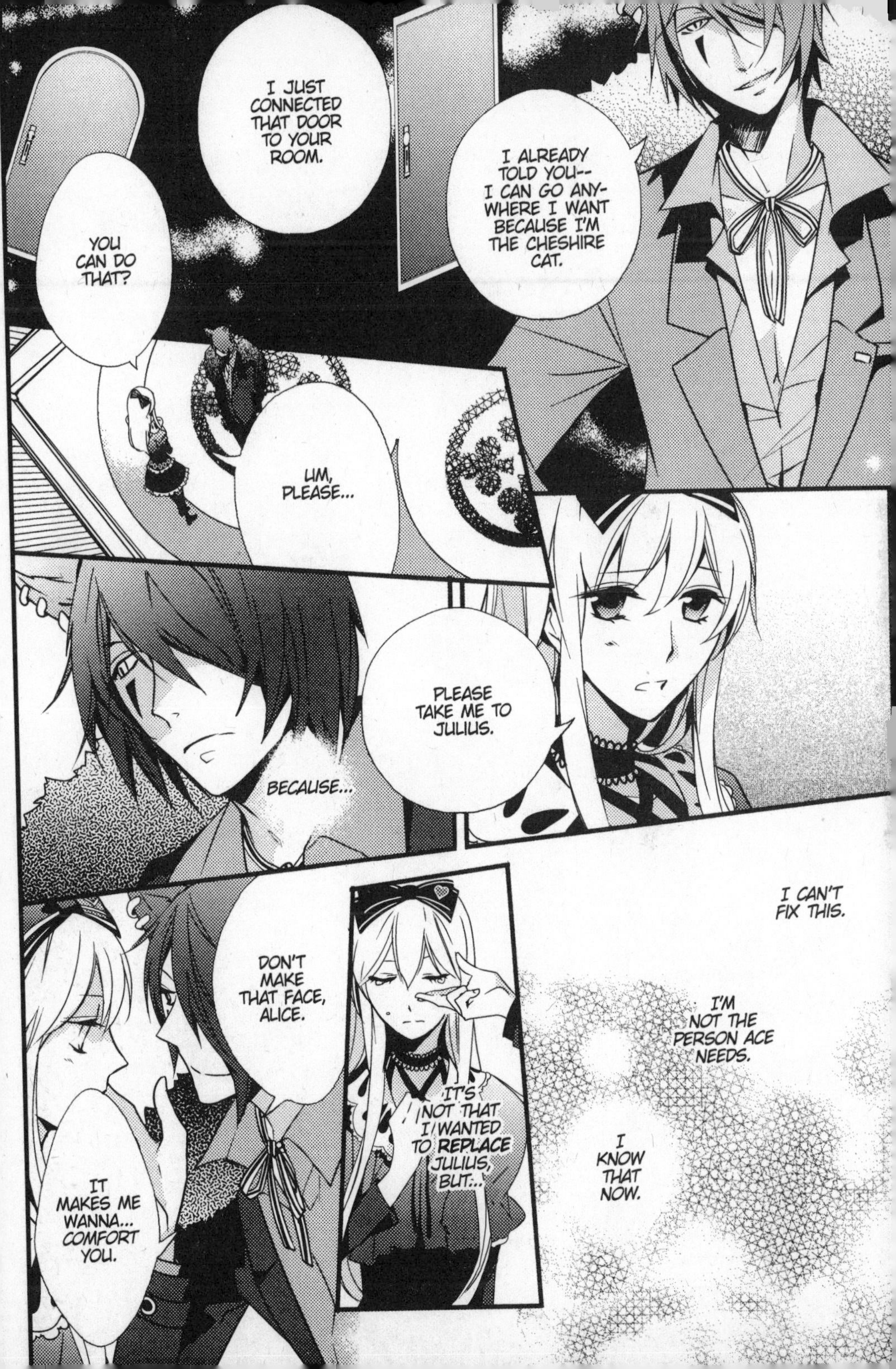
I JUST CONNECTED THAT DOOR TO YOUR ROOM.
YOU CAN DO THAT?
I ALREADY TOLD YOU-- I CAN GO ANY-WHERE I WANT BECAUSE I'M THE CHESHIRE CAT.
UM, PLEASE...
PLEASE TAKE ME TO JULIUS.
BECAUSE...
I CAN'T FIX THIS.
I'M NOT THE PERSON ACE NEEDS.
I KNOW THAT NOW.
IT'S NOT THAT I WANTED TO REPLACE JULIUS, BUT...
DON'T MAKE THAT FACE, ALICE.
IT MAKES ME WANNA... COMFORT YOU.

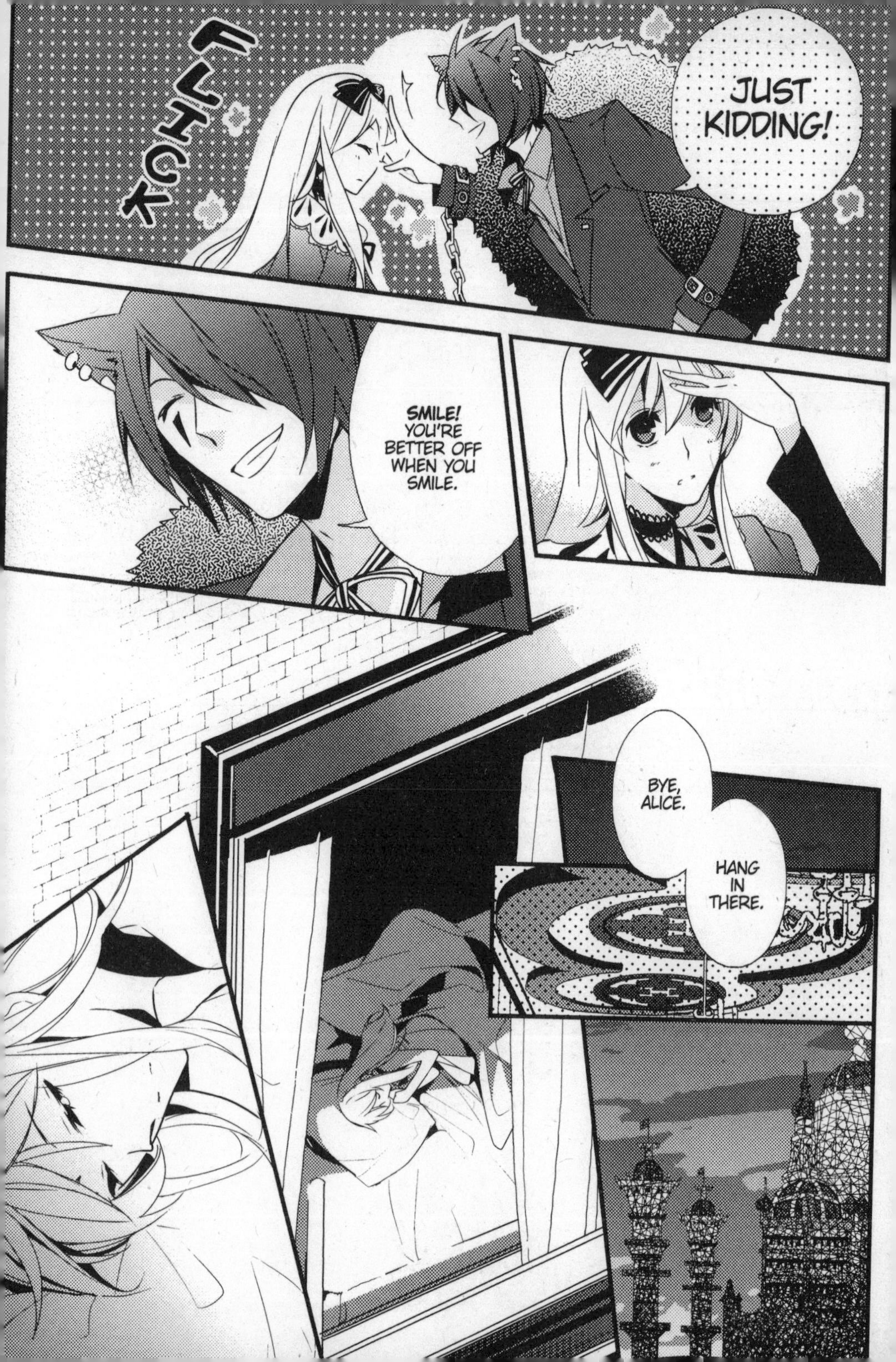
JUST KIDDING!
FLICK
SMILE! YOU'RE BETTER OFF WHEN YOU SMILE.
BYE, ALICE.
HANG IN THERE.

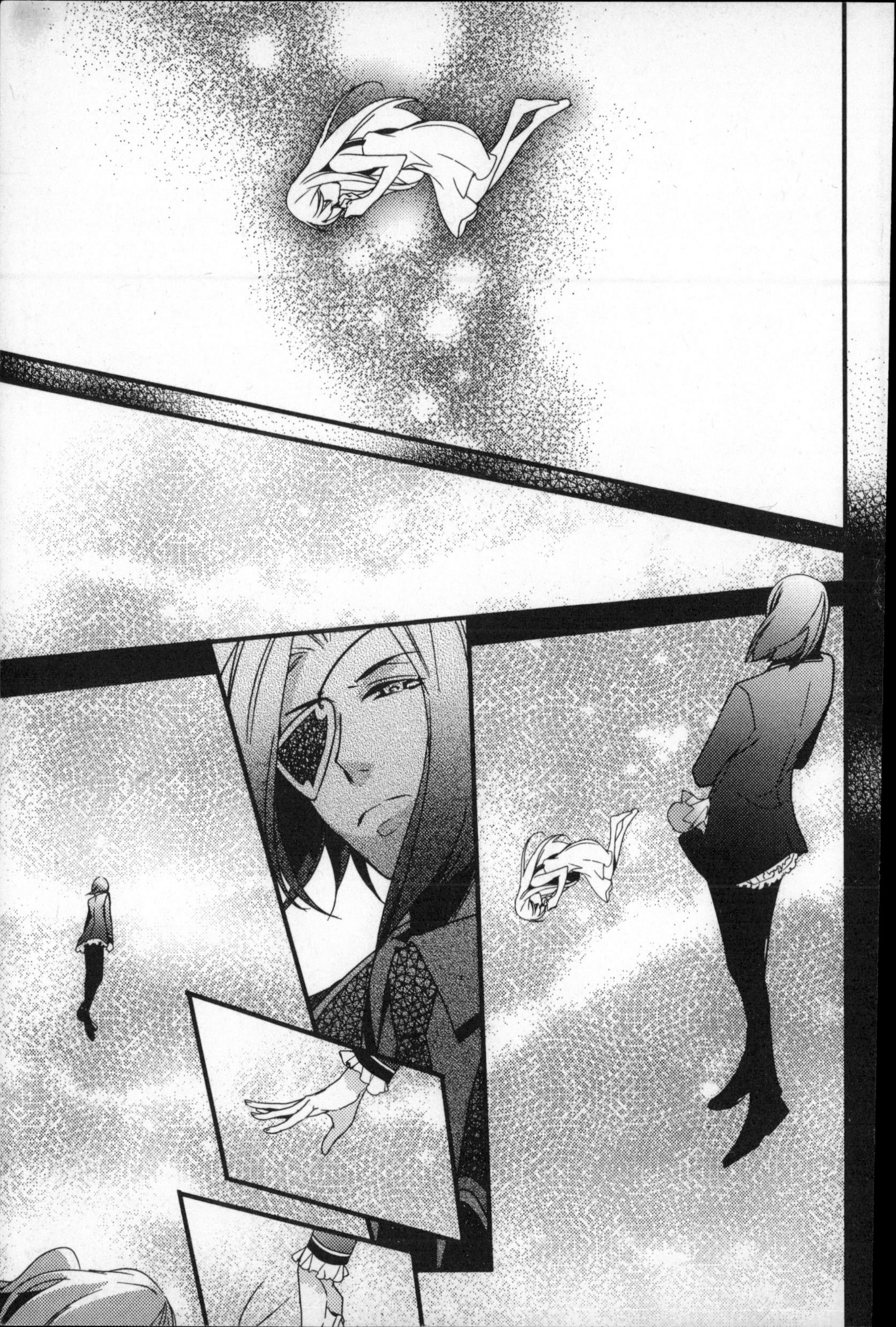

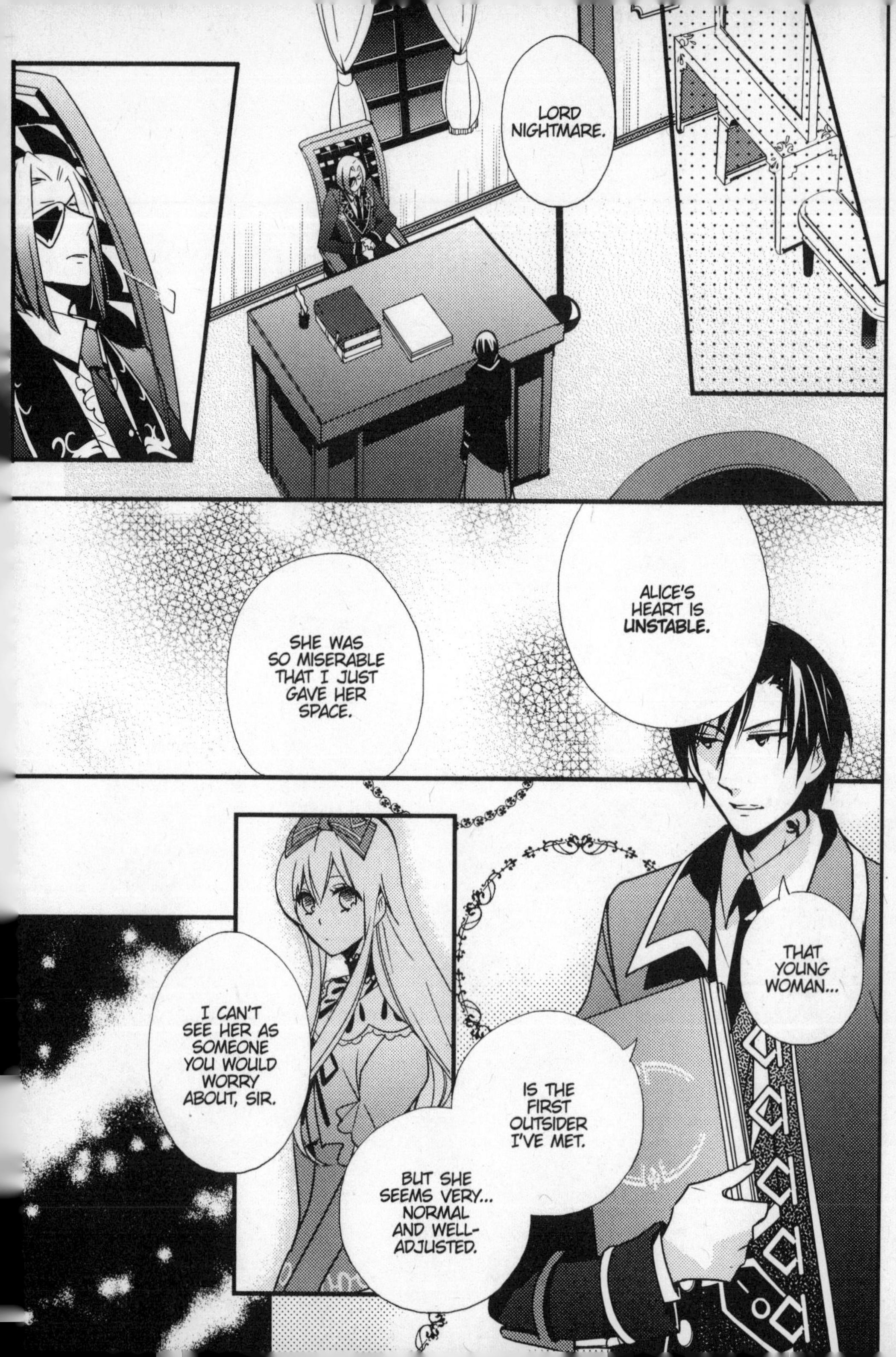
LORD NIGHTMARE.
ALICE'S HEART IS UNSTABLE.
SHE WAS SO MISERABLE THAT I JUST GAVE HER SPACE.
THAT YOUNG WOMAN...
IS THE FIRST OUTSIDER I'VE MET.
BUT SHE SEEMS VERY... NORMAL AND WELL-ADJUSTED.
I CAN'T SEE HER AS SOMEONE YOU WOULD WORRY ABOUT, SIR.

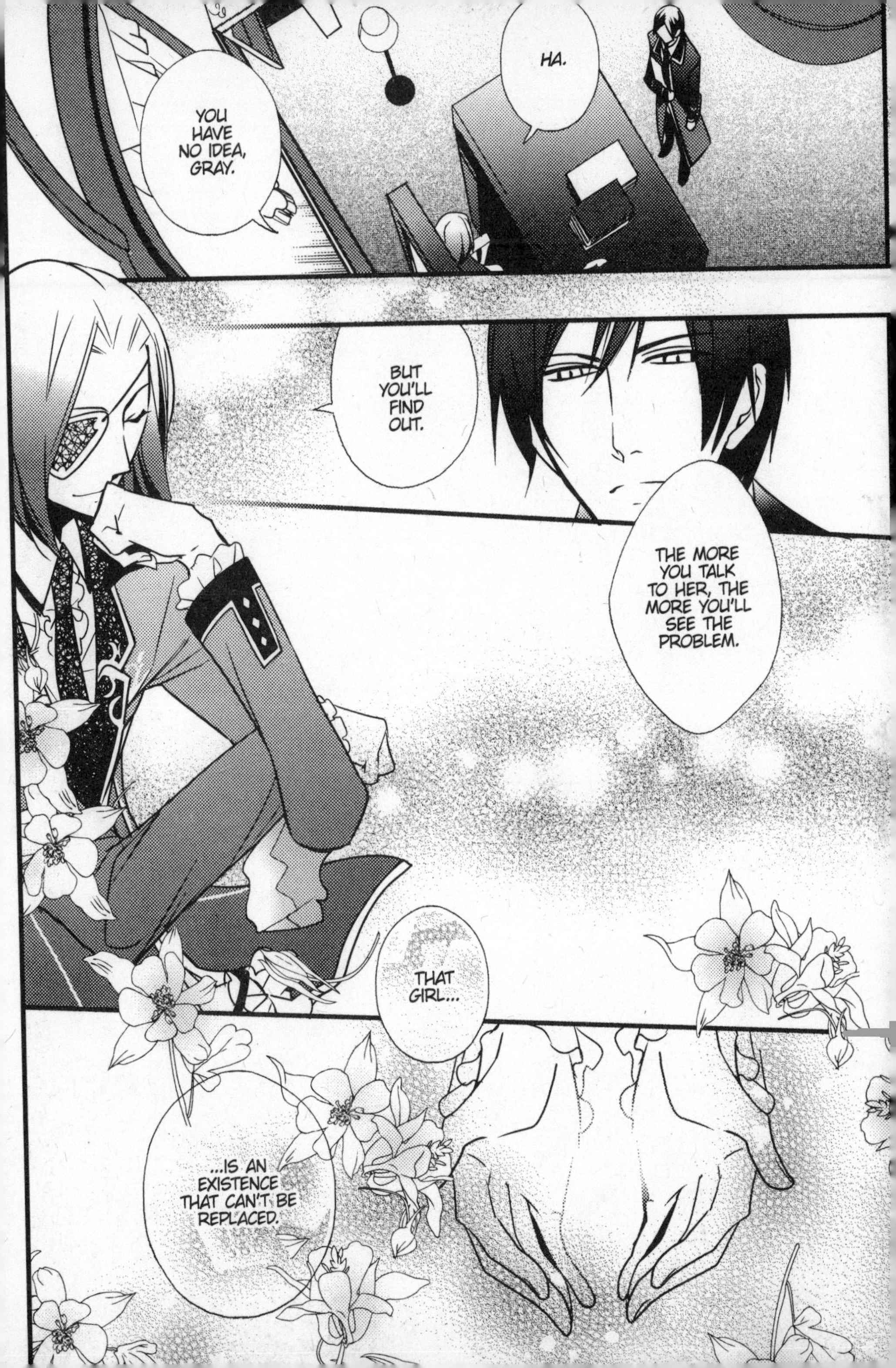
HA.
YOU HAVE NO IDEA, GRAY.
BUT YOU'LL FIND OUT.
THE MORE YOU TALK TO HER, THE MORE YOU'LL SEE THE PROBLEM.
THAT GIRL...
...IS AN EXISTENCE THAT CAN'T BE REPLACED.

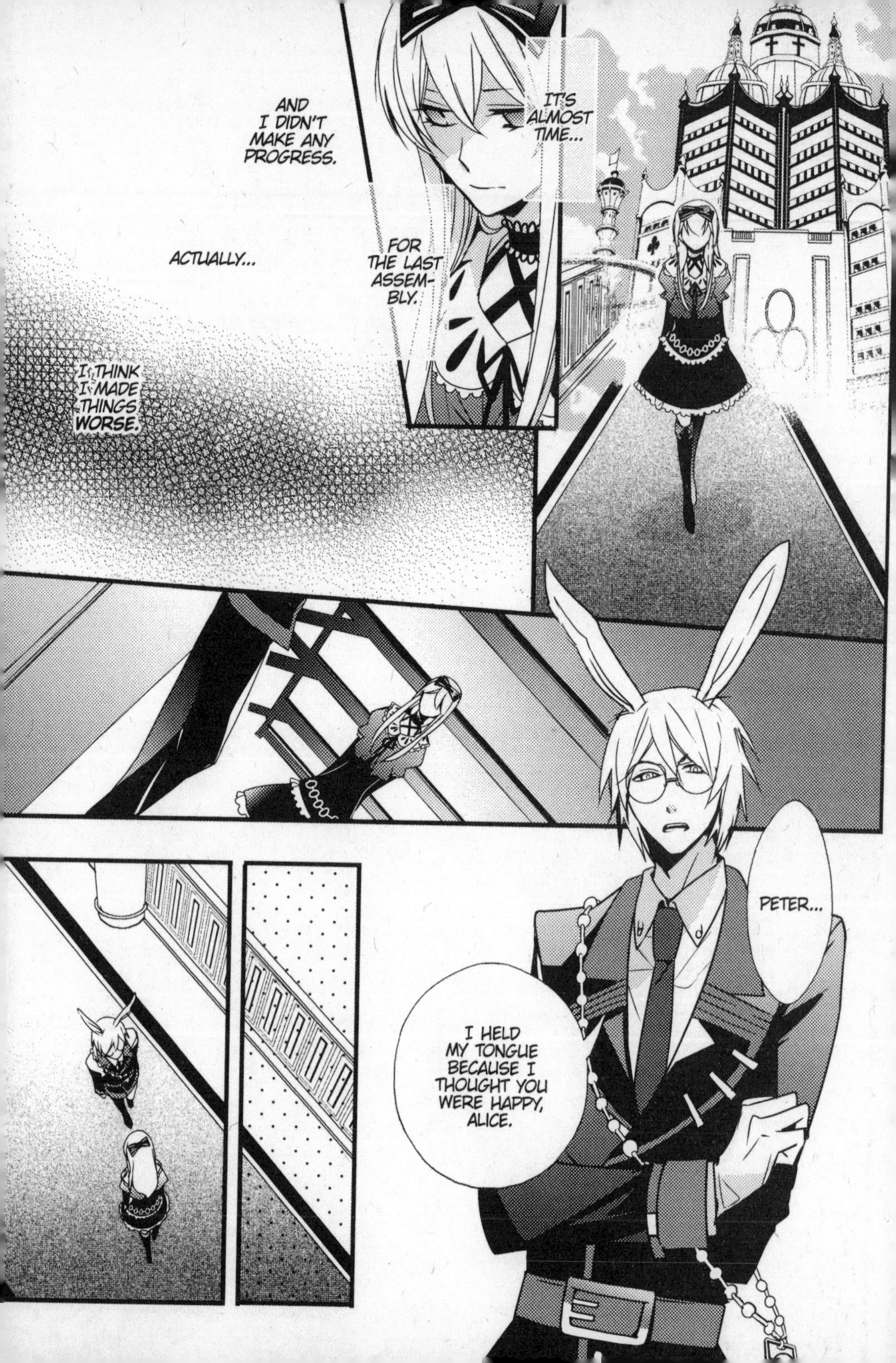
IT'S ALMOST TIME...
FOR THE LAST ASSEMBLY.
AND I DIDN'T MAKE ANY PROGRESS.
ACTUALLY...
I THINK I MADE THINGS WORSE.
PETER...
I HELD MY TONGUE BECAUSE I THOUGHT YOU WERE HAPPY, ALICE.

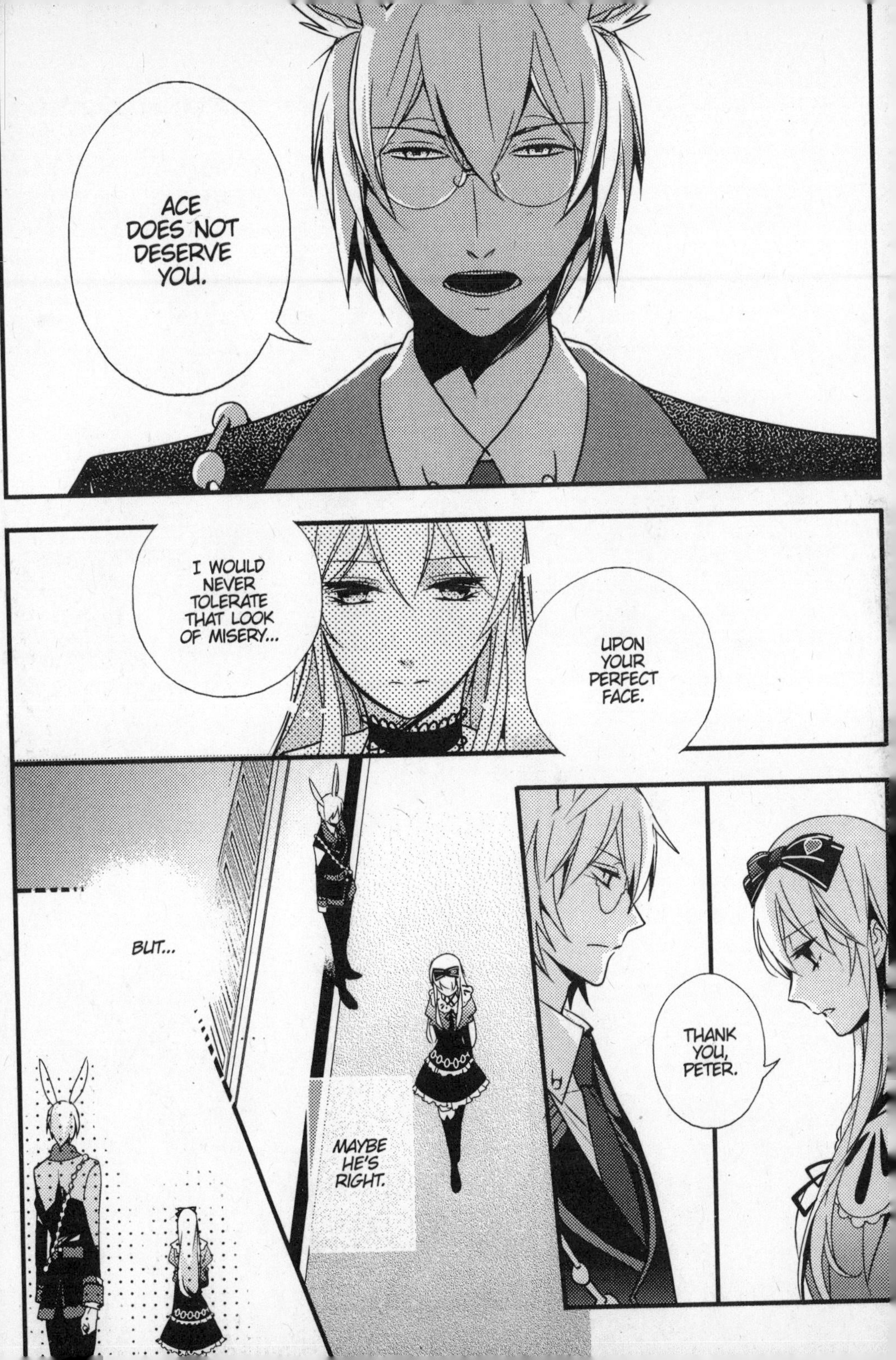
ACE DOES NOT DESERVE YOU.
I WOULD NEVER TOLERATE THAT LOOK OF MISERY...
UPON YOUR PERFECT FACE.
THANK YOU, PETER.
BUT...
MAYBE HE'S RIGHT.

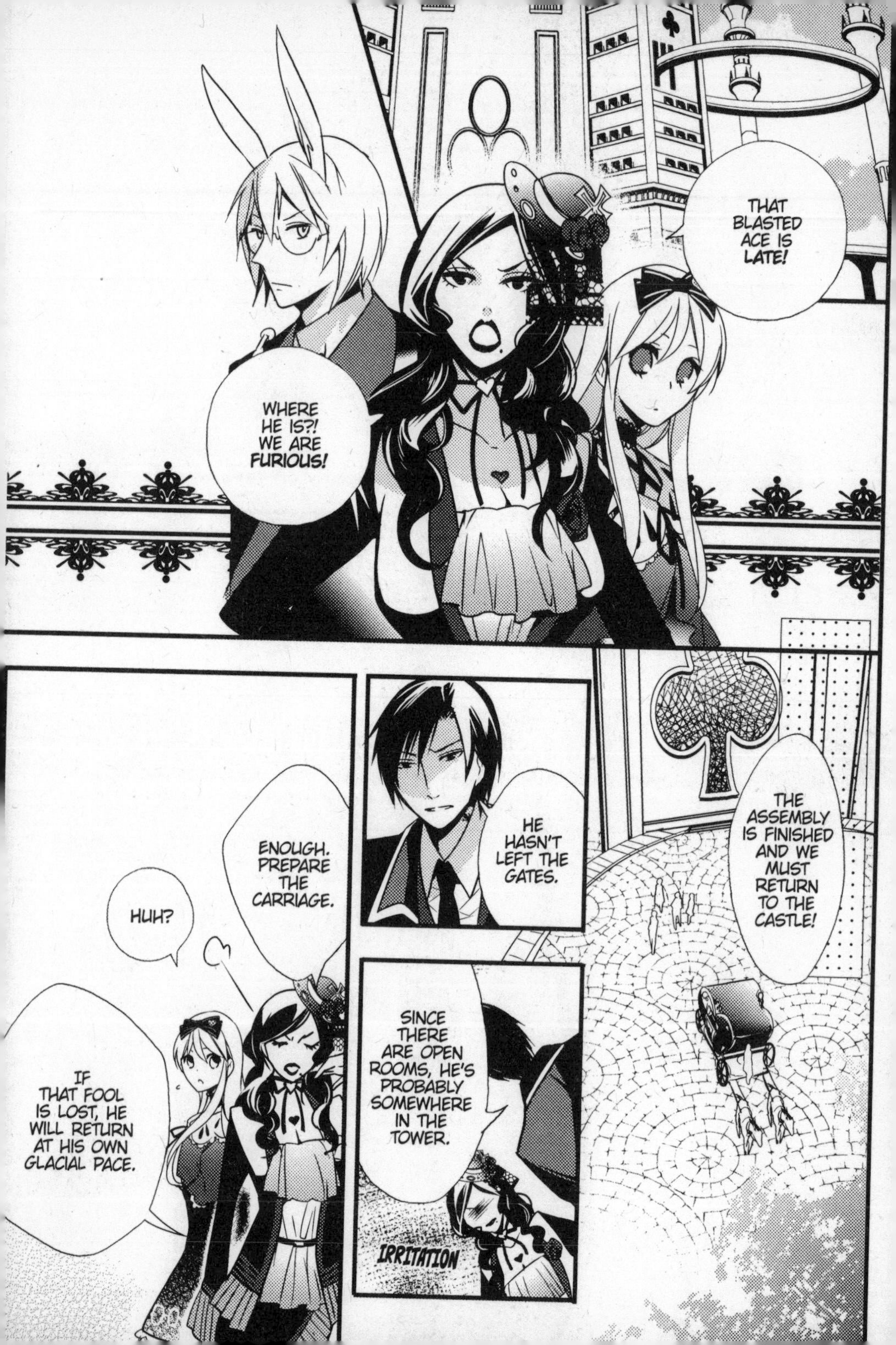
THAT BLASTED ACE IS LATE!
WHERE HE IS?! WE ARE FURIOUS!
THE ASSEMBLY IS FINISHED AND WE MUST RETURN TO THE CASTLE!
HE HASN'T LEFT THE GATES.
SINCE THERE ARE OPEN ROOMS, HE'S PROBABLY SOMEWHERE IN THE TOWER.
IRRITATION
ENOUGH. PREPARE THE CARRIAGE.
HUH?
IF THAT FOOL IS LOST, HE WILL RETURN AT HIS OWN GLACIAL PACE.

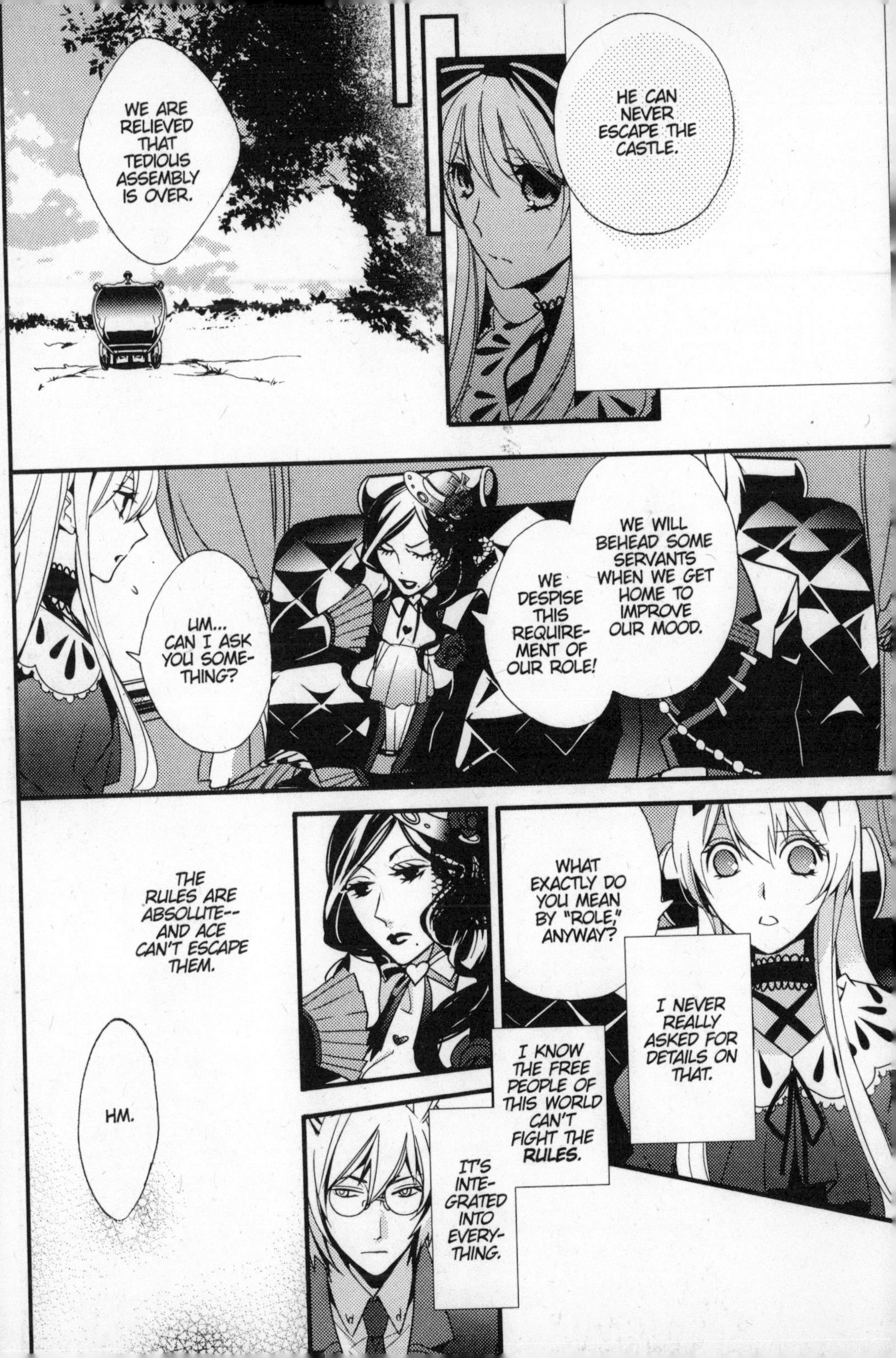
HE CAN NEVER ESCAPE THE CASTLE.
WE ARE RELIEVED THAT TEDIOUS ASSEMBLY IS OVER.
WE WILL BEHEAD SOME SERVANTS WHEN WE GET HOME TO IMPROVE OUR MOOD.
WE DESPISE THIS REQUIRE-MENT OF OUR ROLE!
UM... CAN I ASK YOU SOME-THING?
WHAT EXACTLY DO YOU MEAN BY "ROLE," ANYWAY?
I NEVER REALLY ASKED FOR DETAILS ON THAT.
THE RULES ARE ABSOLUTE-- AND ACE CAN'T ESCAPE THEM.
I KNOW THE FREE PEOPLE OF THIS WORLD CAN'T FIGHT THE RULES.
IT'S INTE-GRATED INTO EVERY-THING.
HM.

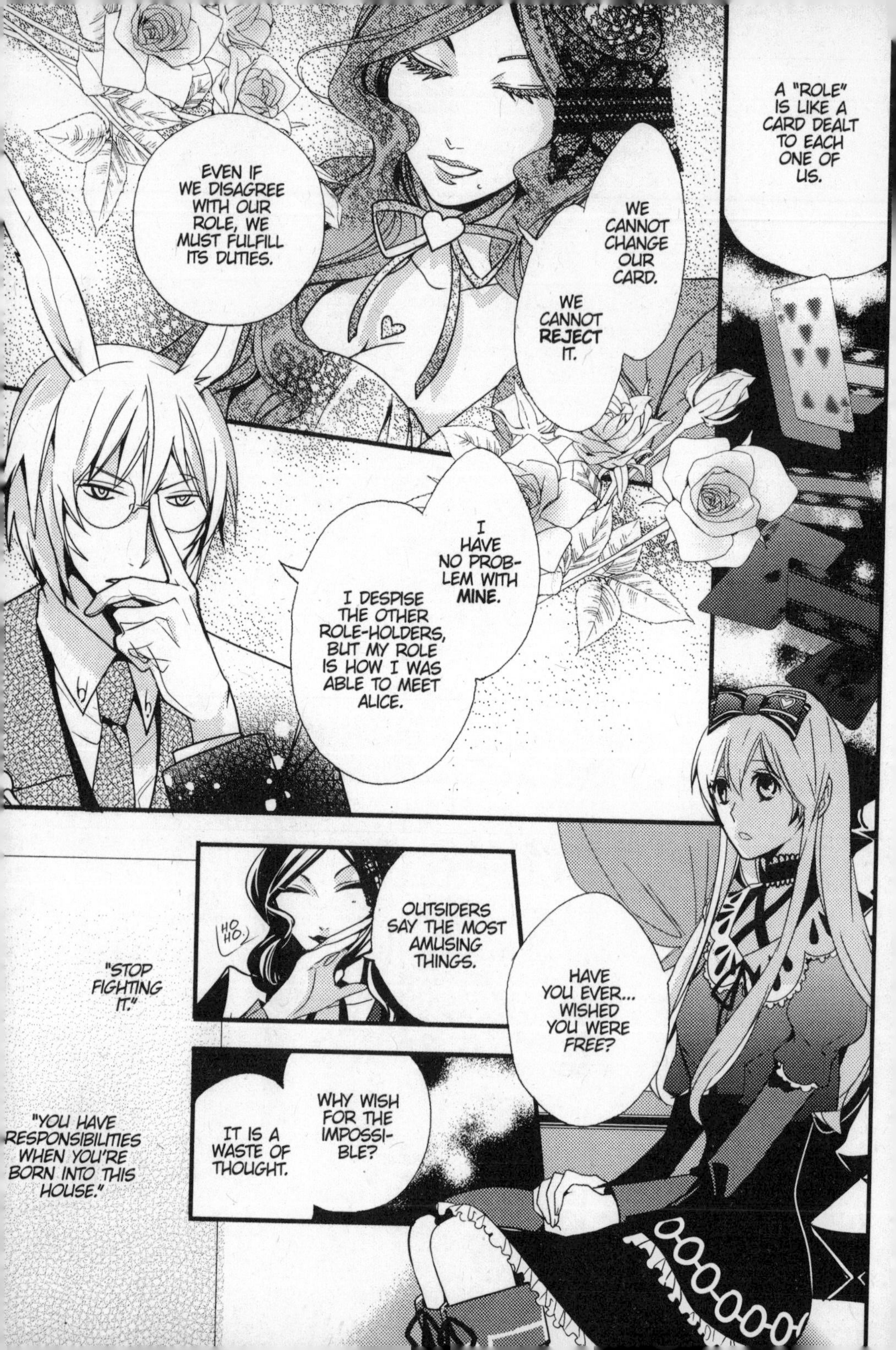
A "ROLE" IS LIKE A CARD DEALT TO EACH ONE OF US.
WE CANNOT CHANGE OUR CARD.
WE CANNOT REJECT IT.
EVEN IF WE DISAGREE WITH OUR ROLE, WE MUST FULFILL ITS DUTIES.
I HAVE NO PROB-LEM WITH MINE.
I DESPISE THE OTHER ROLE-HOLDERS, BUT MY ROLE IS HOW I WAS ABLE TO MEET ALICE.
HAVE YOU EVER... WISHED YOU WERE FREE?
OUTSIDERS SAY THE MOST AMUSING THINGS.
HO HO.
WHY WISH FOR THE IMPOSSI-BLE?
IT IS A WASTE OF THOUGHT.
"STOP FIGHTING IT."
"YOU HAVE RESPONSIBILITIES WHEN YOU'RE BORN INTO THIS HOUSE."

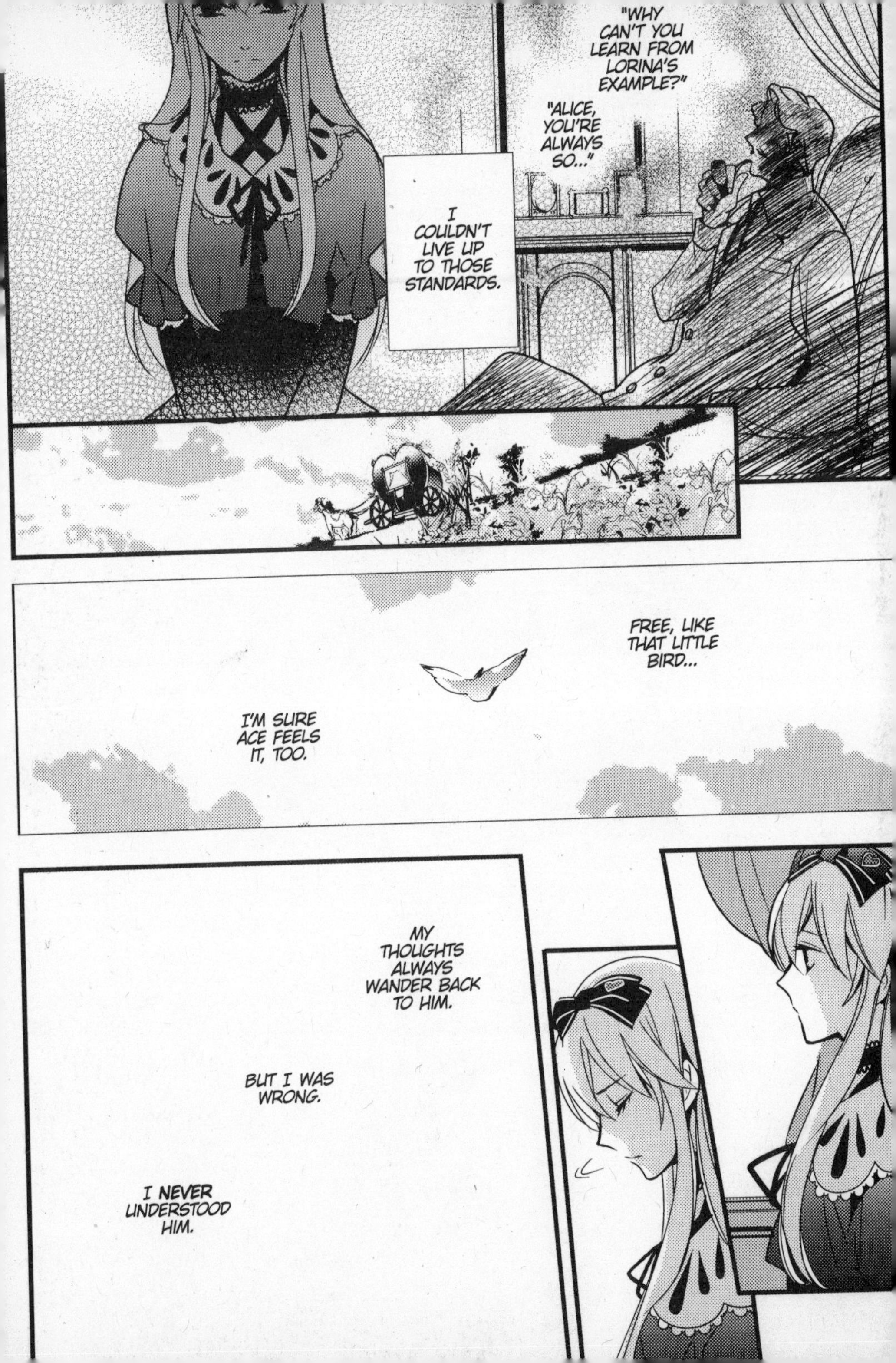
"WHY CAN'T YOU LEARN FROM LORINA'S EXAMPLE?"
"ALICE, YOU'RE ALWAYS SO..."
I COULDN'T LIVE UP TO THOSE STANDARDS.
FREE, LIKE THAT LITTLE BIRD...
I'M SURE ACE FEELS IT, TOO.
MY THOUGHTS ALWAYS WANDER BACK TO HIM.
BUT I WAS WRONG.
I NEVER UNDERSTOOD HIM.

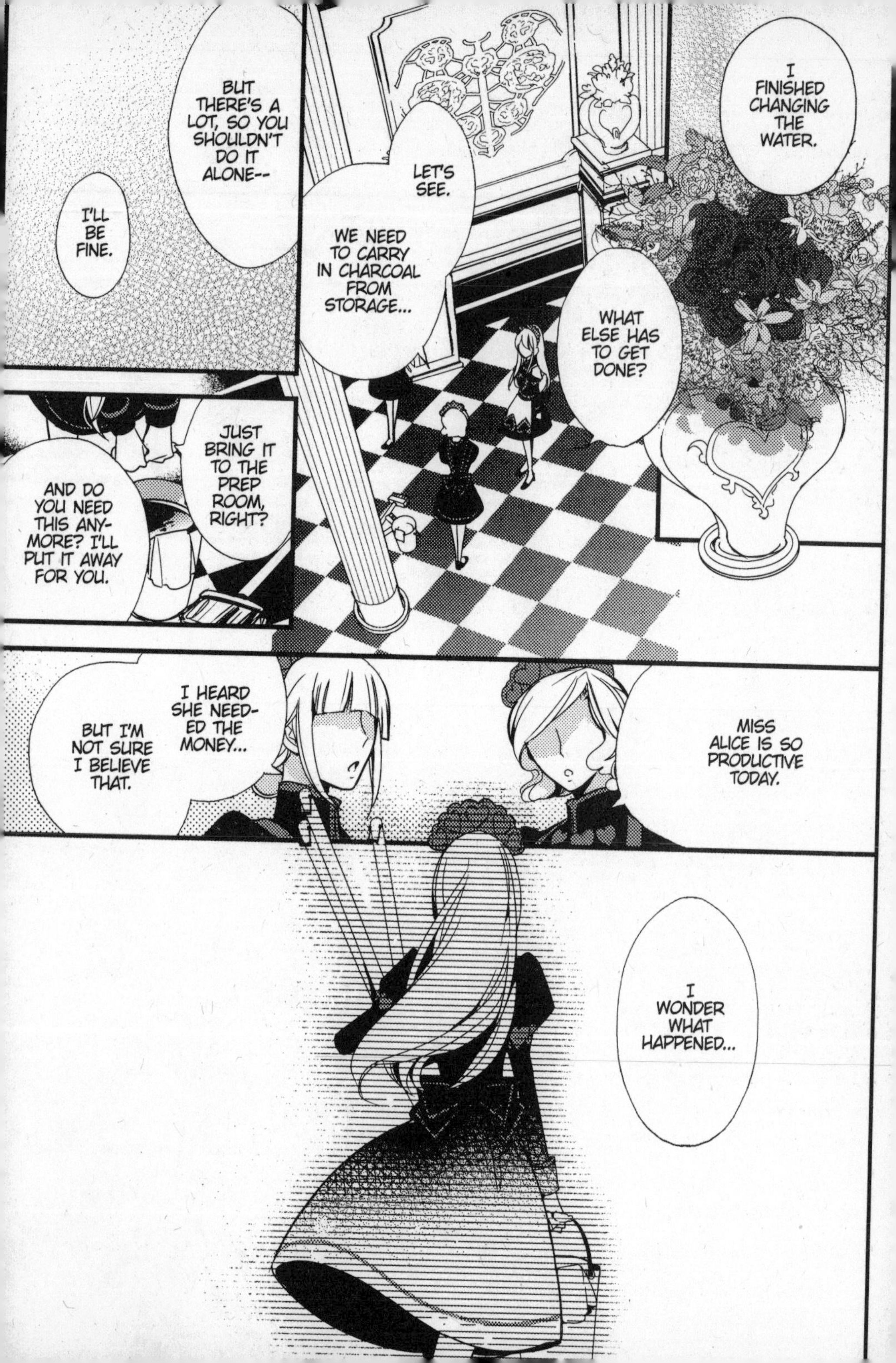
I FINISHED CHANGING THE WATER.
WHAT ELSE HAS TO GET DONE?
LET'S SEE.
WE NEED TO CARRY IN CHARCOAL FROM STORAGE...
BUT THERE'S A LOT, SO YOU SHOULDN'T DO IT ALONE--
I'LL BE FINE.
JUST BRING IT TO THE PREP ROOM, RIGHT?
AND DO YOU NEED THIS ANY-MORE? I'LL PUT IT AWAY FOR YOU.
MISS ALICE IS SO PRODUCTIVE TODAY.
I HEARD SHE NEED-ED THE MONEY...
BUT I'M NOT SURE I BELIEVE THAT.
I WONDER WHAT HAPPENED...

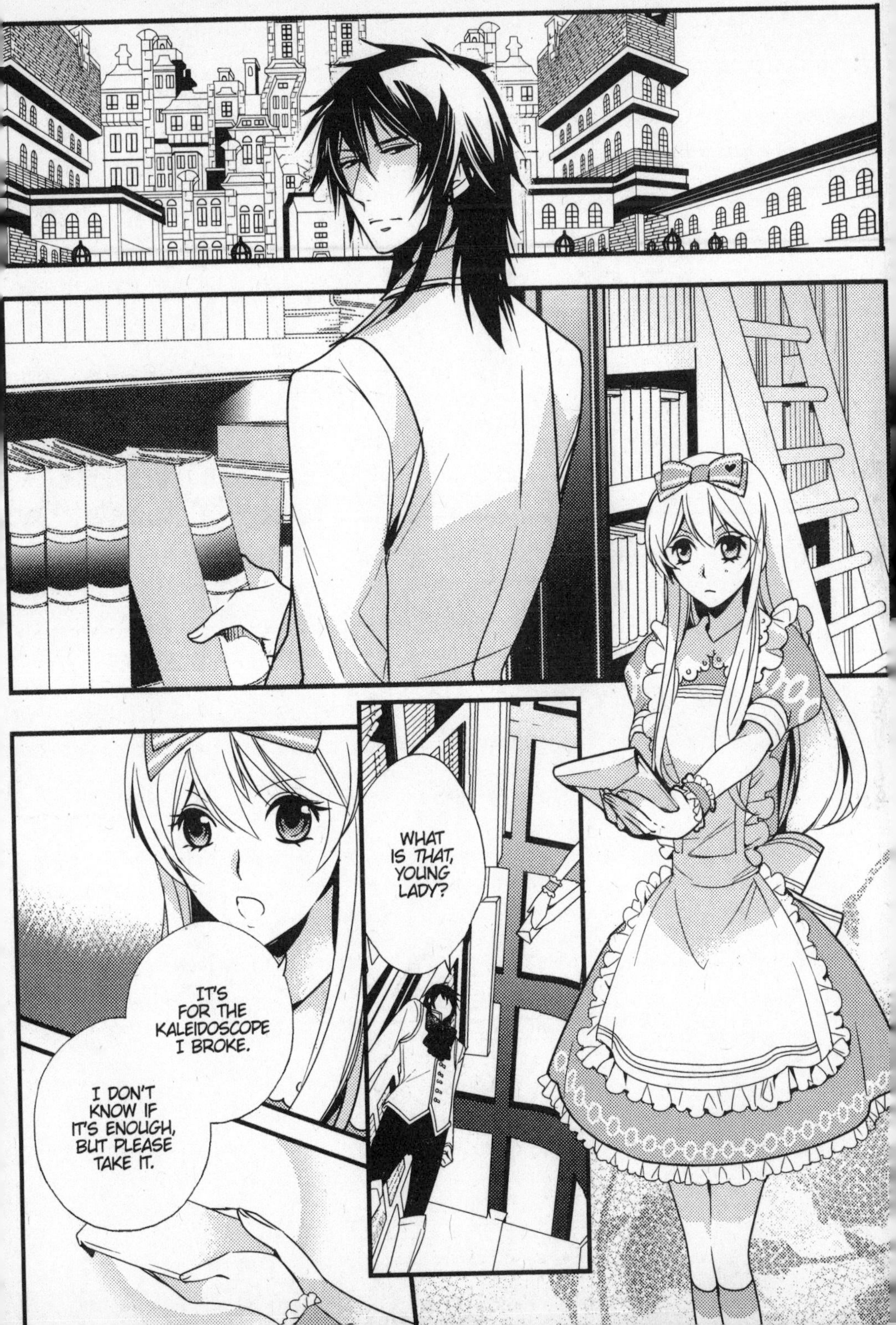
WHAT IS THAT, YOUNG LADY?
IT'S FOR THE KALEIDOSCOPE I BROKE.
I DON'T KNOW IF IT'S ENOUGH, BUT PLEASE TAKE IT.

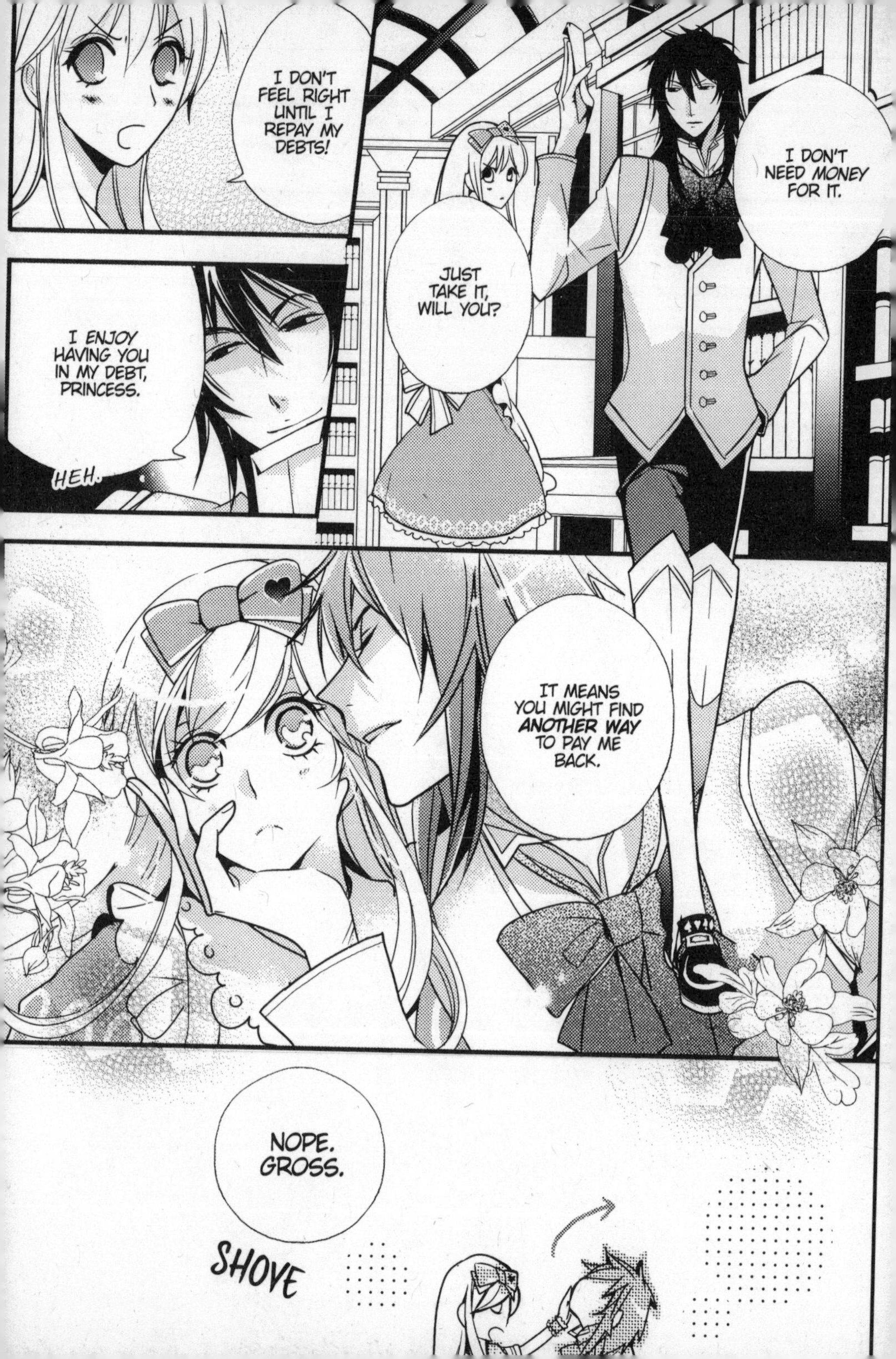
I DON'T NEED MONEY FOR IT.
JUST TAKE IT, WILL YOU?
I DON'T FEEL RIGHT UNTIL I REPAY MY DEBTS!
I ENJOY HAVING YOU IN MY DEBT, PRINCESS.
HEH.
IT MEANS YOU MIGHT FIND ANOTHER WAY TO PAY ME BACK.
NOPE. GROSS.
SHOVE

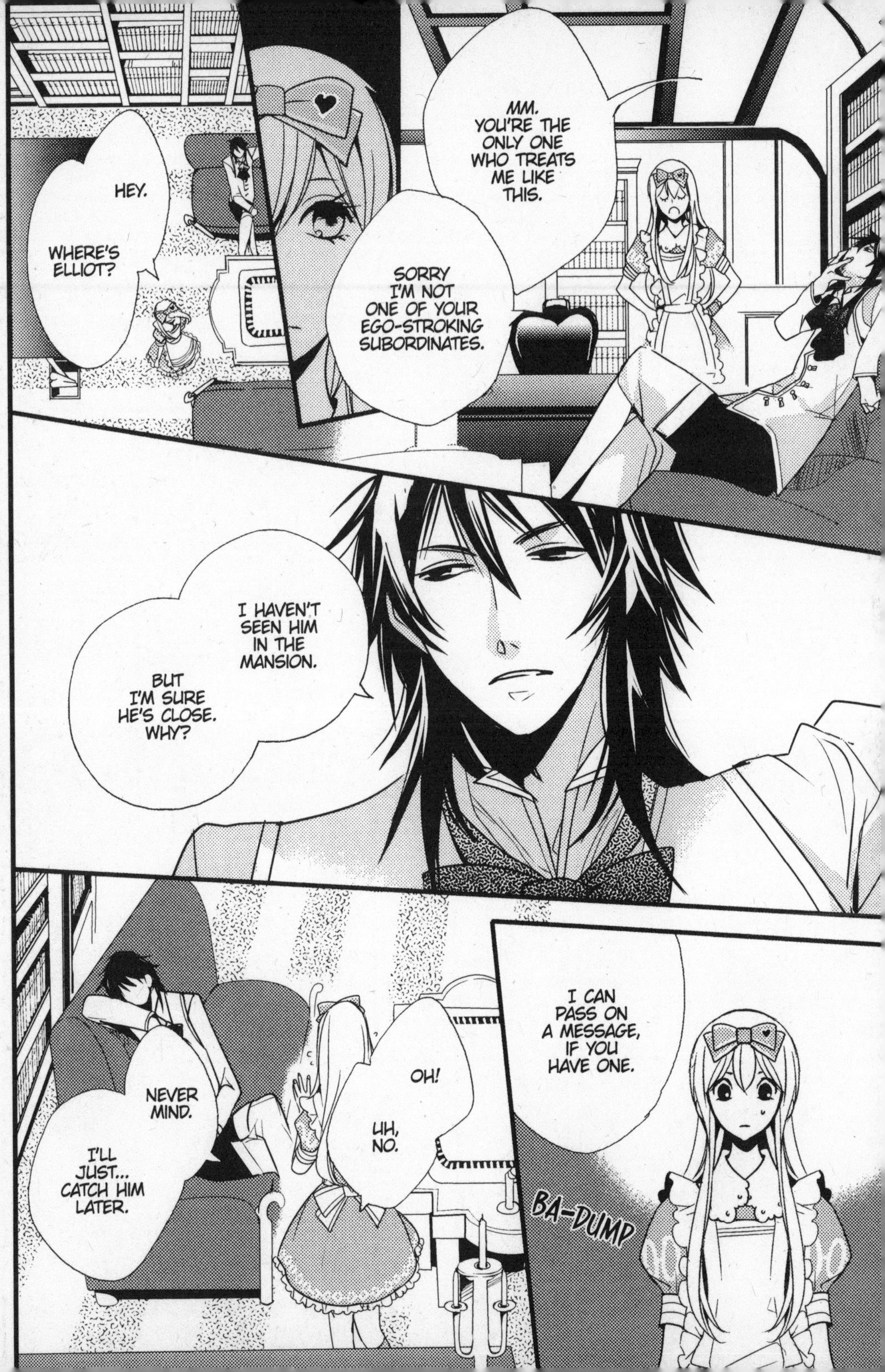

MM. YOU'RE THE ONLY ONE WHO TREATS ME LIKE THIS.
SORRY I'M NOT ONE OF YOUR EGO-STROKING SUBORDINATES.
HEY.
WHERE'S ELLIOT?
I HAVEN'T SEEN HIM IN THE MANSION.
BUT I'M SURE HE'S CLOSE. WHY?
I CAN PASS ON A MESSAGE, IF YOU HAVE ONE.
BA-DUMP
OH!
UH, NO.
NEVER MIND.
I'LL JUST... CATCH HIM LATER.

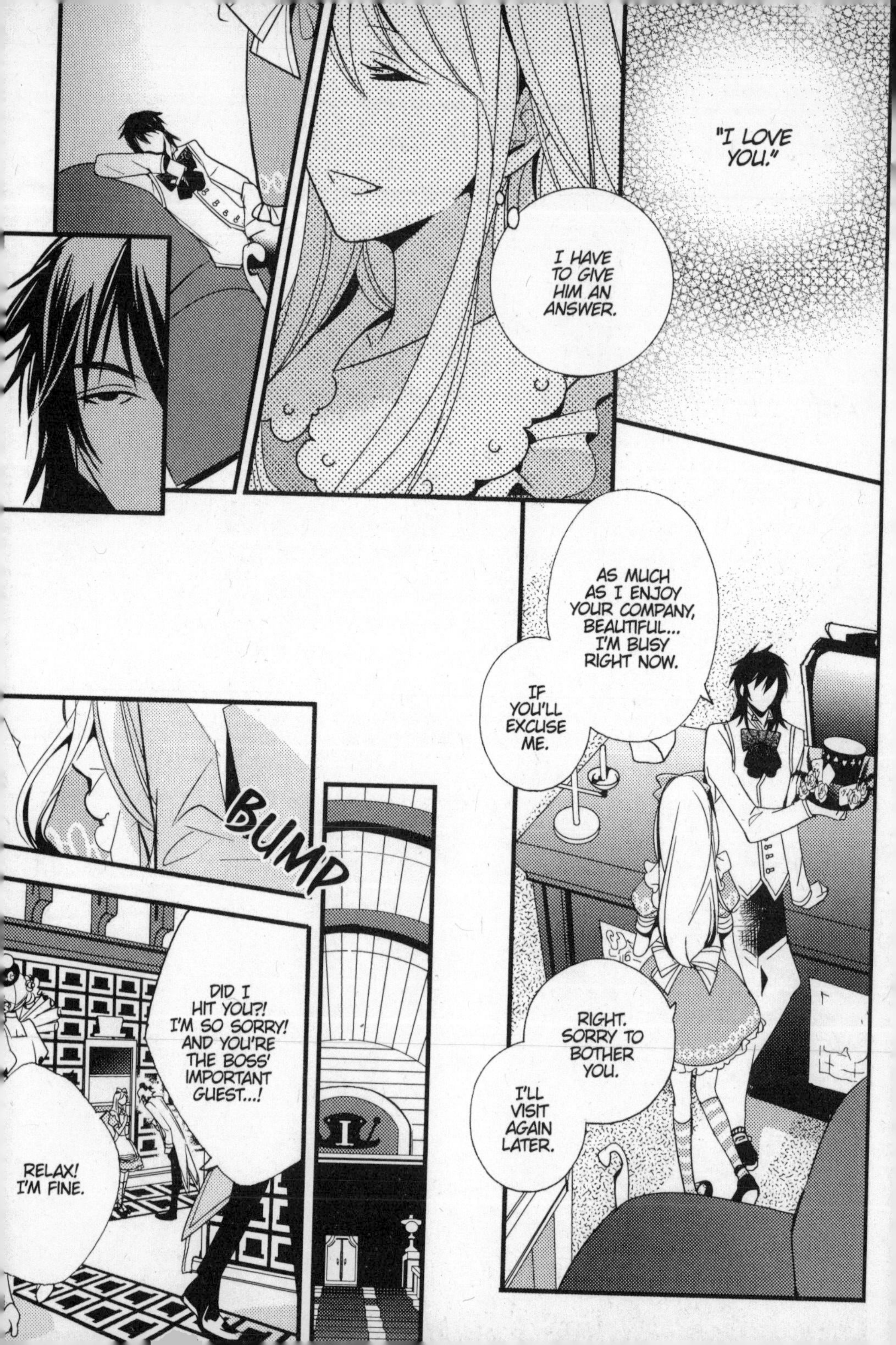
"I LOVE YOU."
I HAVE TO GIVE HIM AN ANSWER.
AS MUCH AS I ENJOY YOUR COMPANY, BEAUTIFUL... I'M BUSY RIGHT NOW.
IF YOU'LL EXCUSE ME.
RIGHT. SORRY TO BOTHER YOU.
I'LL VISIT AGAIN LATER.
BUMP
DID I HIT YOU?! I'M SO SORRY! AND YOU'RE THE BOSS' IMPORTANT GUEST...!
RELAX! I'M FINE.

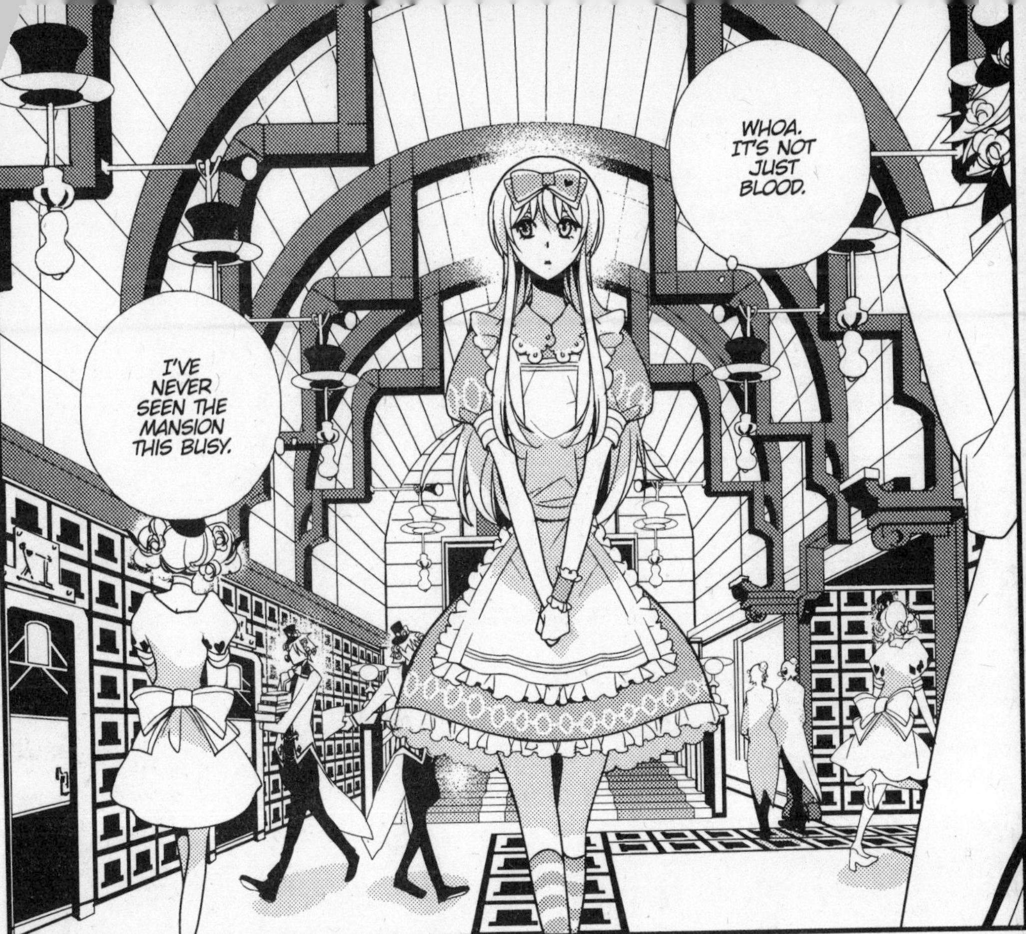
WHOA. IT'S NOT JUST BLOOD.
I'VE NEVER SEEN THE MANSION THIS BUSY.

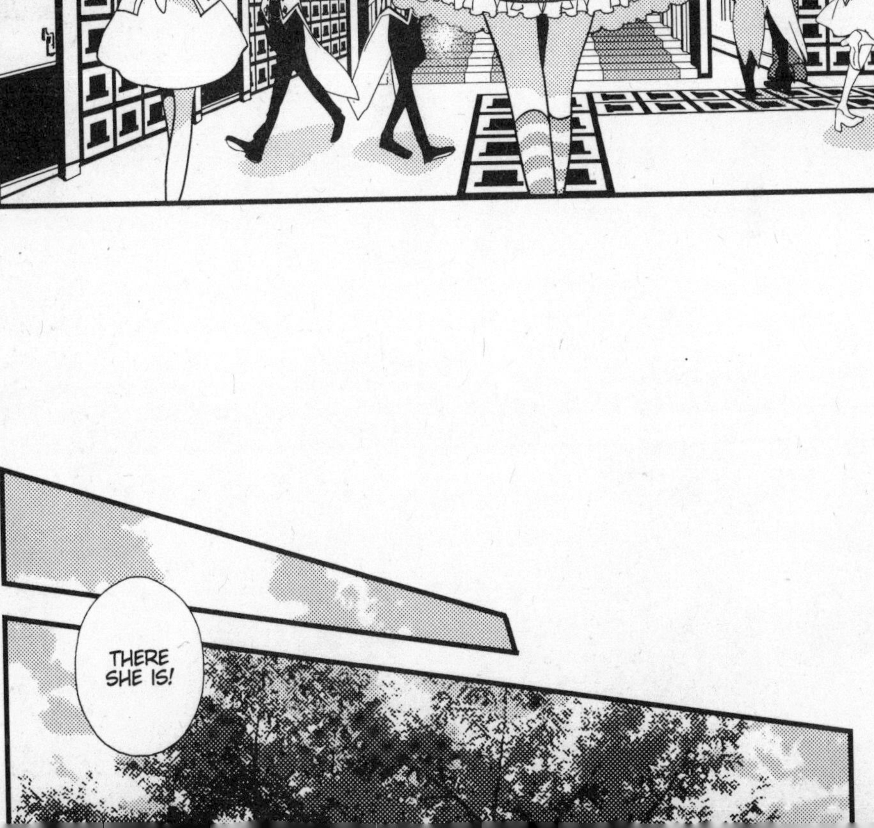
THERE SHE IS!

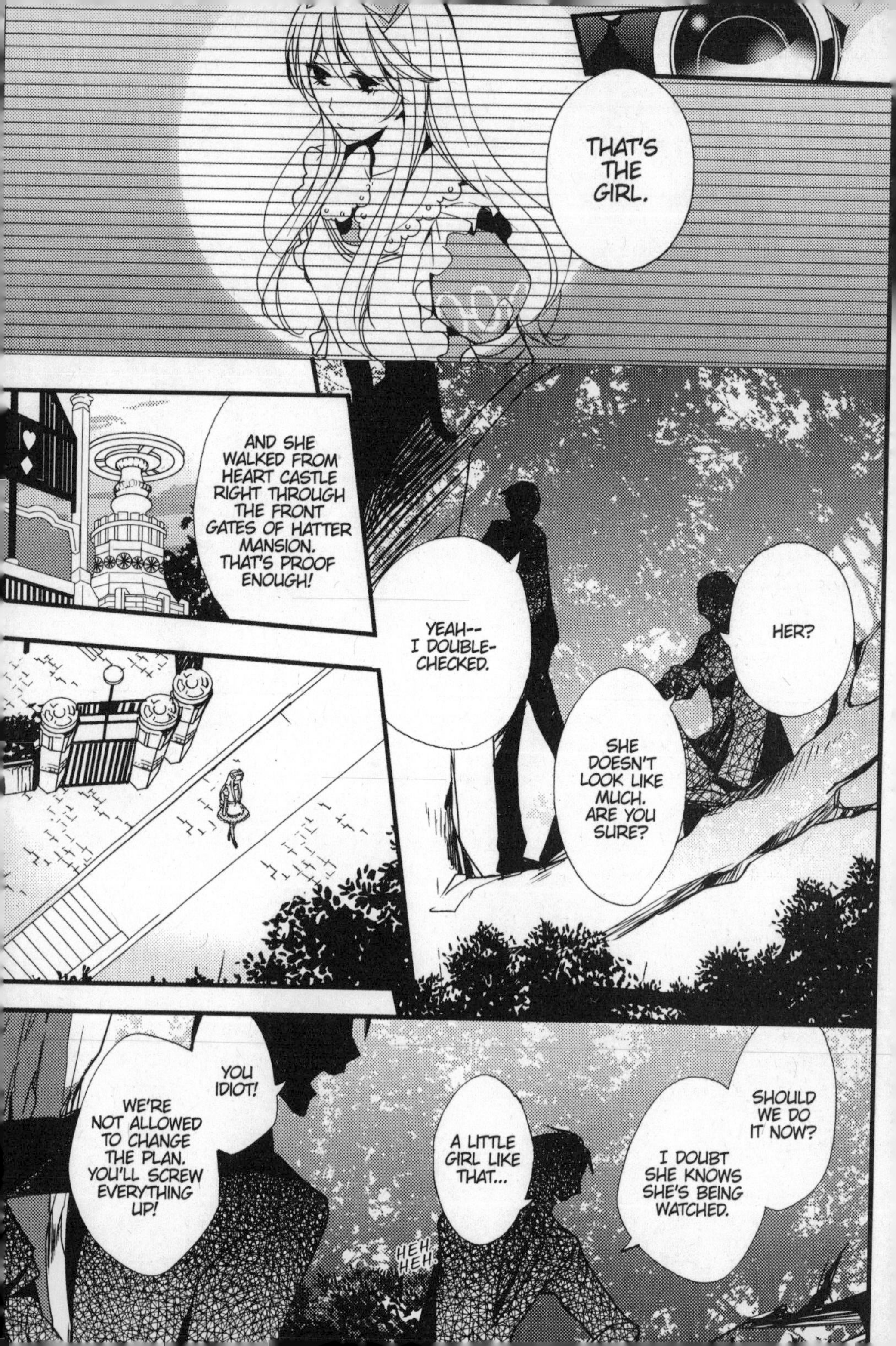
THAT'S THE GIRL.
HER?
SHE DOESN'T LOOK LIKE MUCH. ARE YOU SURE?
YEAH-- I DOUBLE-CHECKED.
AND SHE WALKED FROM HEART CASTLE RIGHT THROUGH THE FRONT GATES OF HATTER MANSION. THAT'S PROOF ENOUGH!
SHOULD WE DO IT NOW?
I DOUBT SHE KNOWS SHE'S BEING WATCHED.
A LITTLE GIRL LIKE THAT...
HEH HEH
YOU IDIOT!
WE'RE NOT ALLOWED TO CHANGE THE PLAN. YOU'LL SCREW EVERYTHING UP!

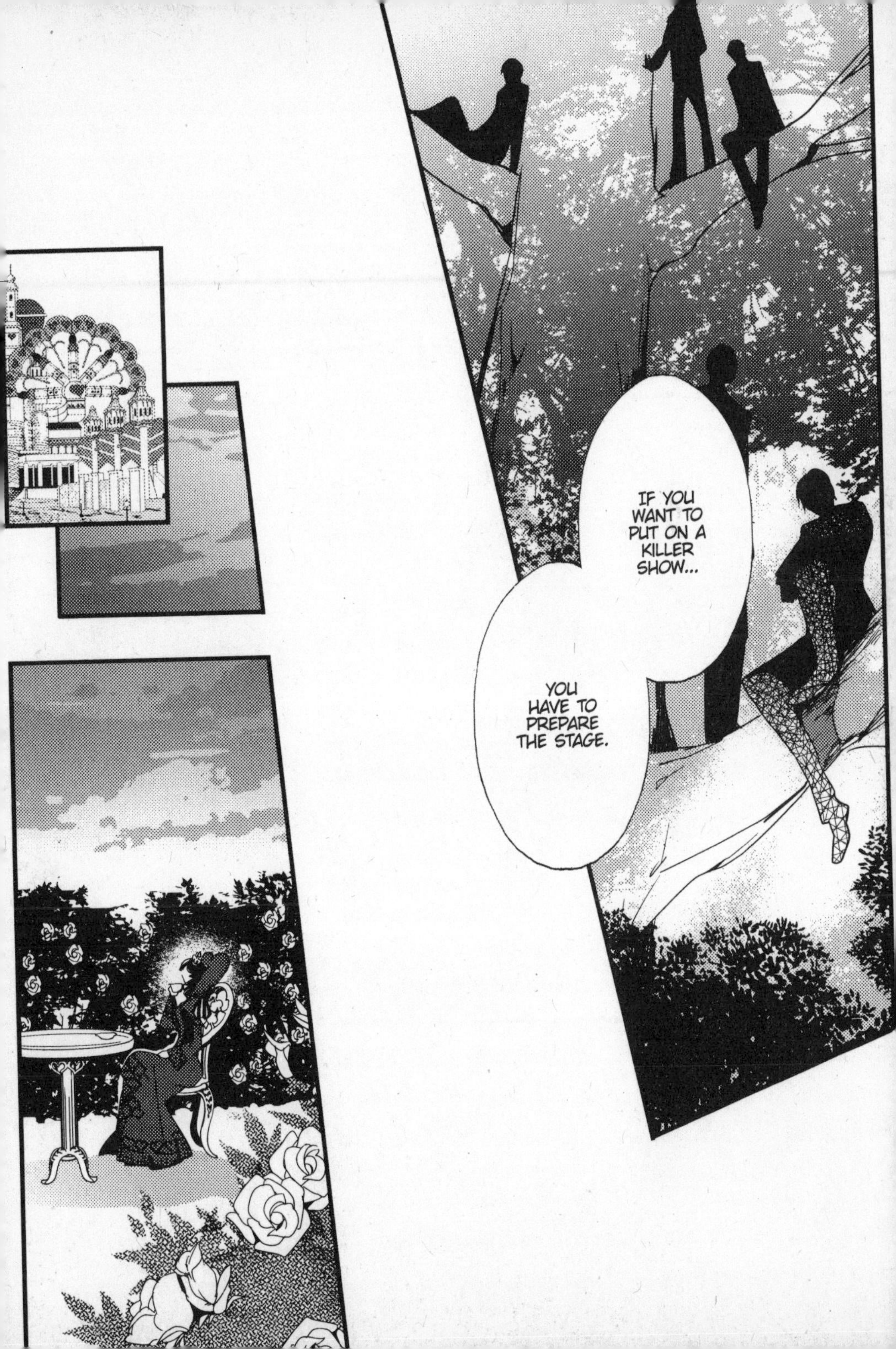
IF YOU WANT TO PUT ON A KILLER SHOW...
YOU HAVE TO PREPARE THE STAGE.

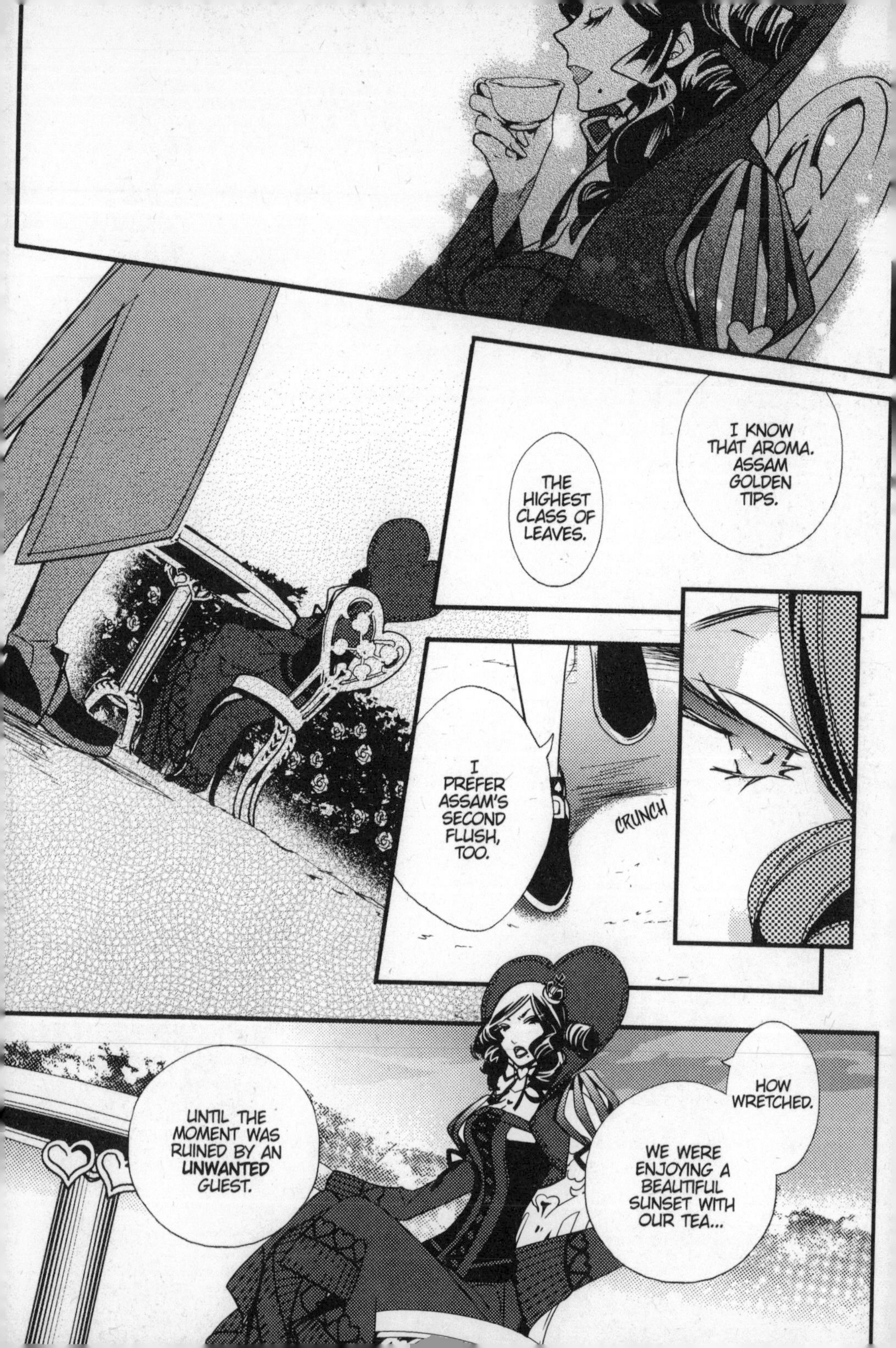
I KNOW THAT AROMA. ASSAM GOLDEN TIPS.
THE HIGHEST CLASS OF LEAVES.
CRUNCH
I PREFER ASSAM'S SECOND FLUSH, TOO.
HOW WRETCHED.
WE WERE ENJOYING A BEAUTIFUL SUNSET WITH OUR TEA...
UNTIL THE MOMENT WAS RUINED BY AN UNWANTED GUEST.

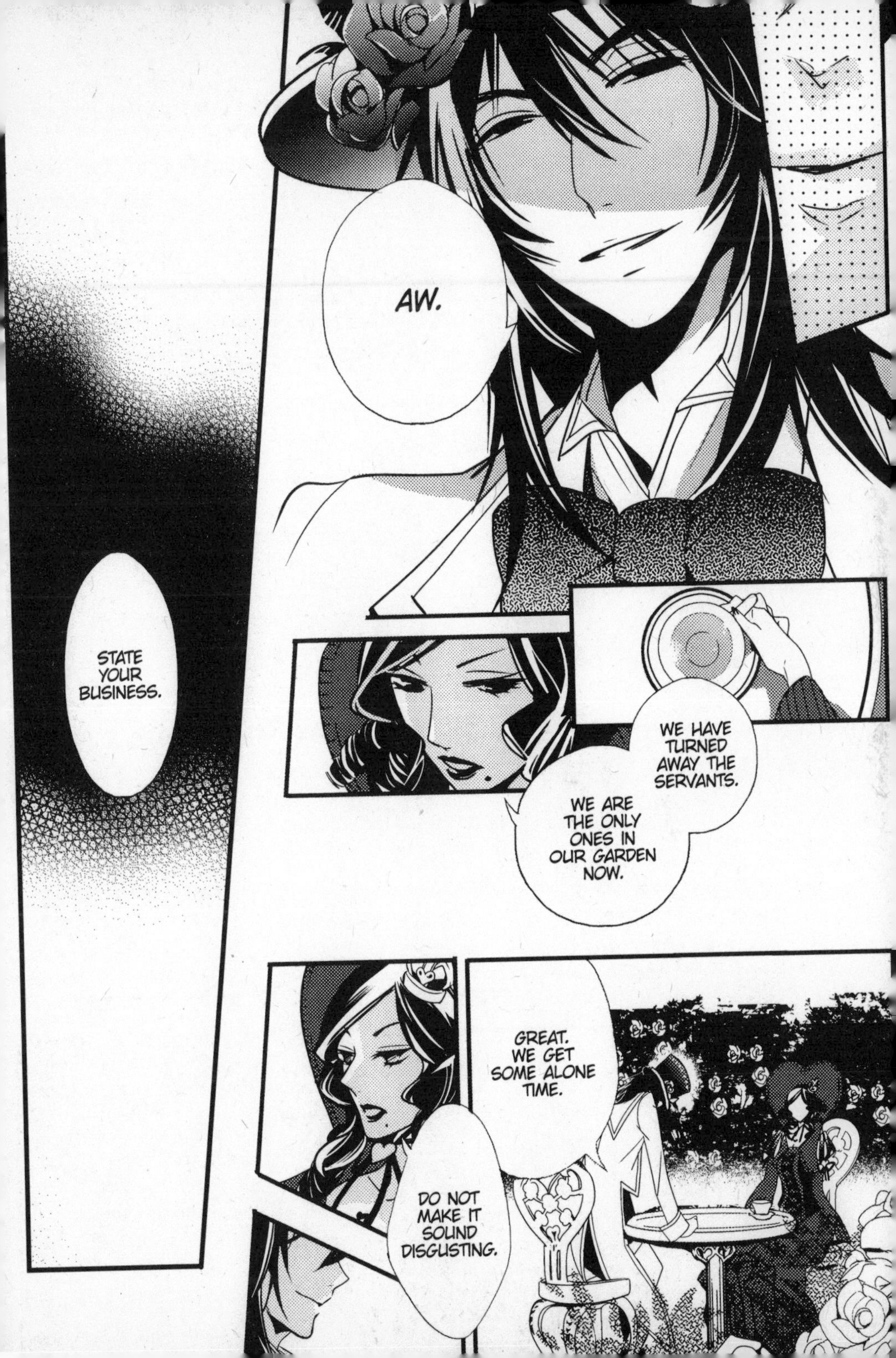
AW.
WE HAVE TURNED AWAY THE SERVANTS.
WE ARE THE ONLY ONES IN OUR GARDEN NOW.
GREAT. WE GET SOME ALONE TIME.
DO NOT MAKE IT SOUND DISGUSTING.
STATE YOUR BUSINESS.

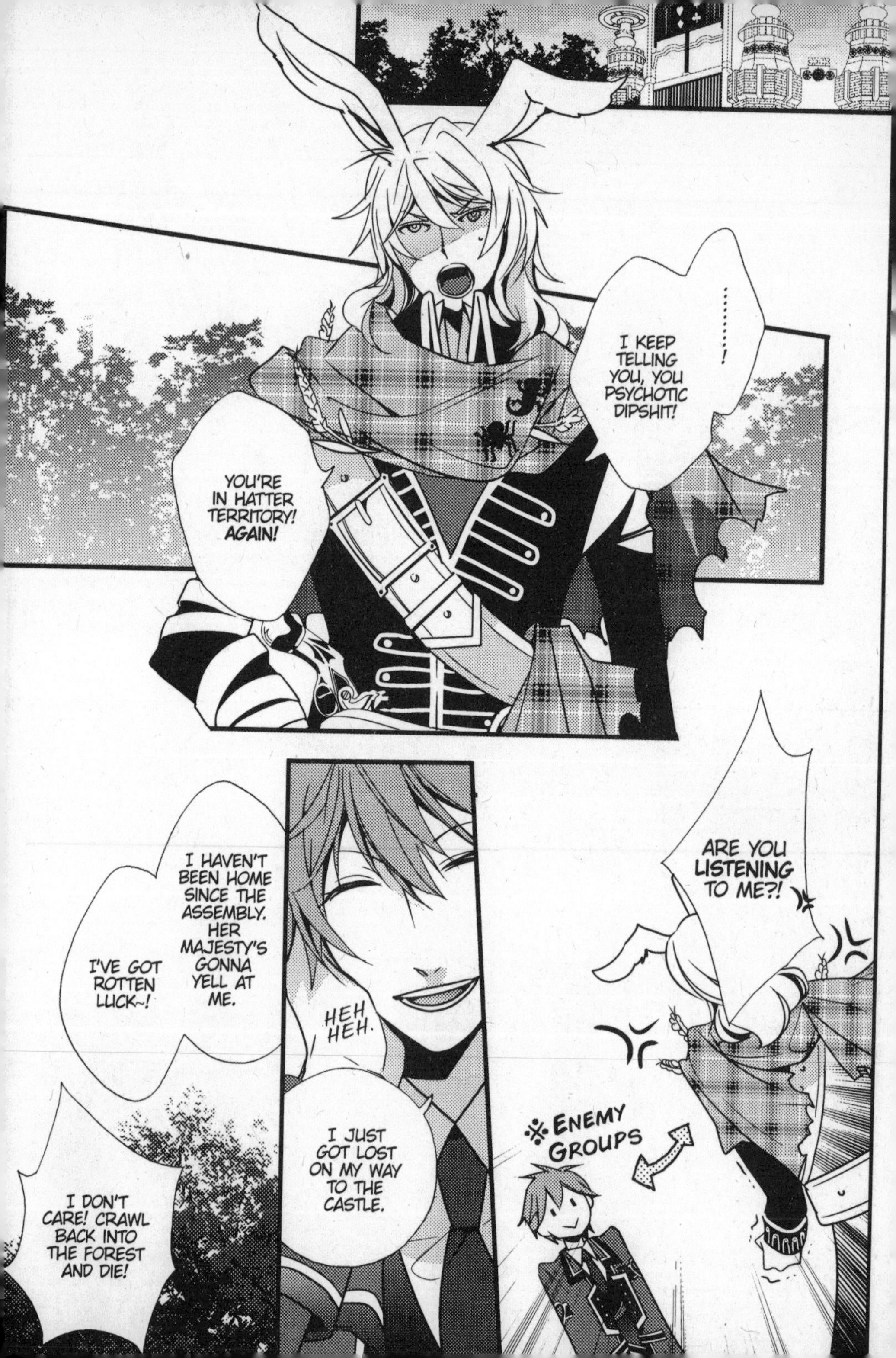
......!
I KEEP TELLING YOU, YOU PSYCHOTIC DIPSHIT!
YOU'RE IN HATTER TERRITORY! AGAIN!
ARE YOU LISTENING TO ME?!
※ENEMY GROUPS
I HAVEN'T BEEN HOME SINCE THE ASSEMBLY. HER MAJESTY'S GONNA YELL AT ME.
I'VE GOT ROTTEN LUCK~!
HEH HEH.
I JUST GOT LOST ON MY WAY TO THE CASTLE.
I DON'T CARE! CRAWL BACK INTO THE FOREST AND DIE!

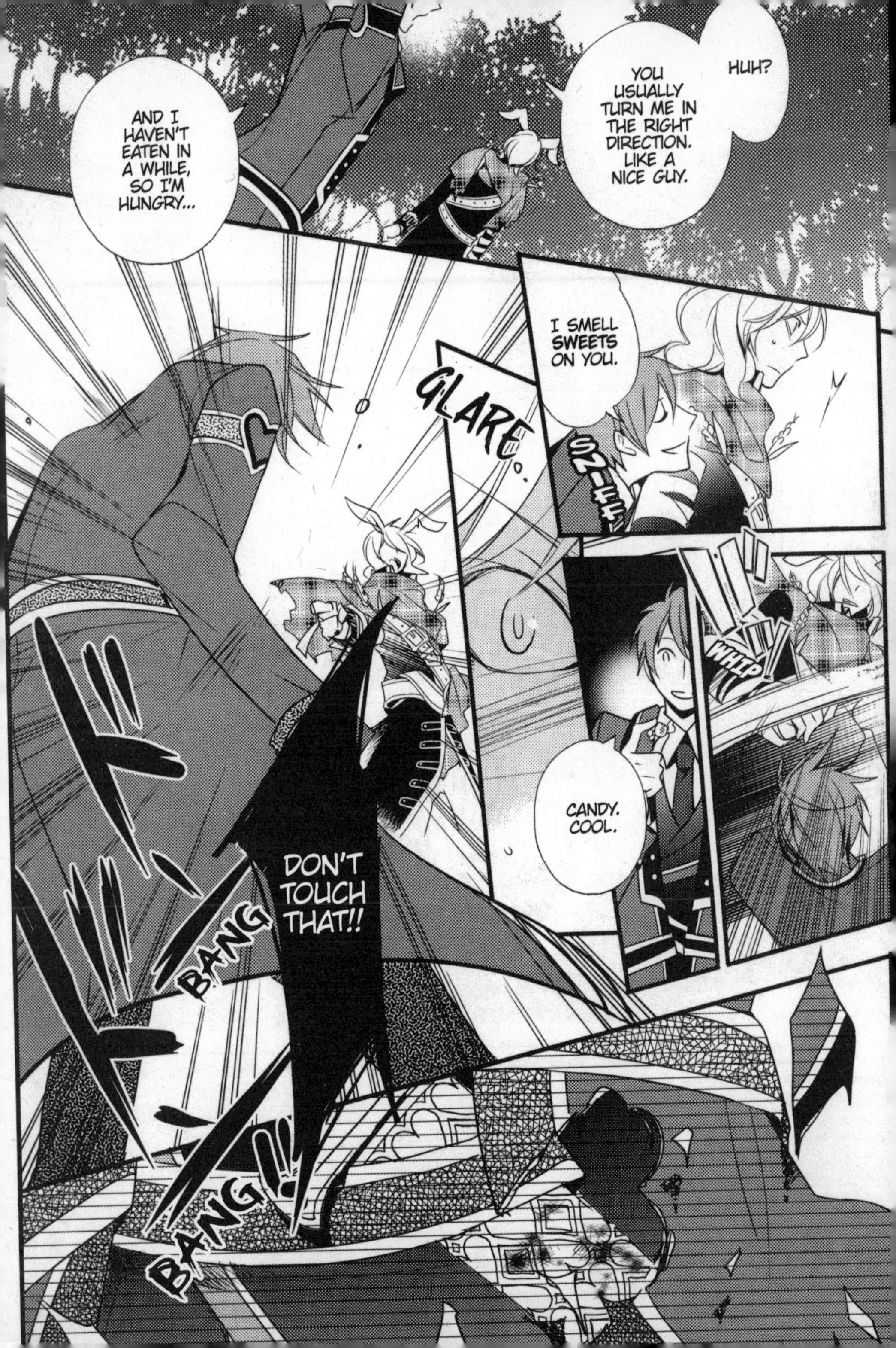
HUH?
YOU USUALLY TURN ME IN THE RIGHT DIRECTION. LIKE A NICE GUY.
AND I HAVEN'T EATEN IN A WHILE, SO I'M HUNGRY...
I SMELL SWEETS ON YOU.
SNIFF
GLARE
WHIP
CANDY. COOL.
DON'T TOUCH THAT!!
BANG
BANG!!

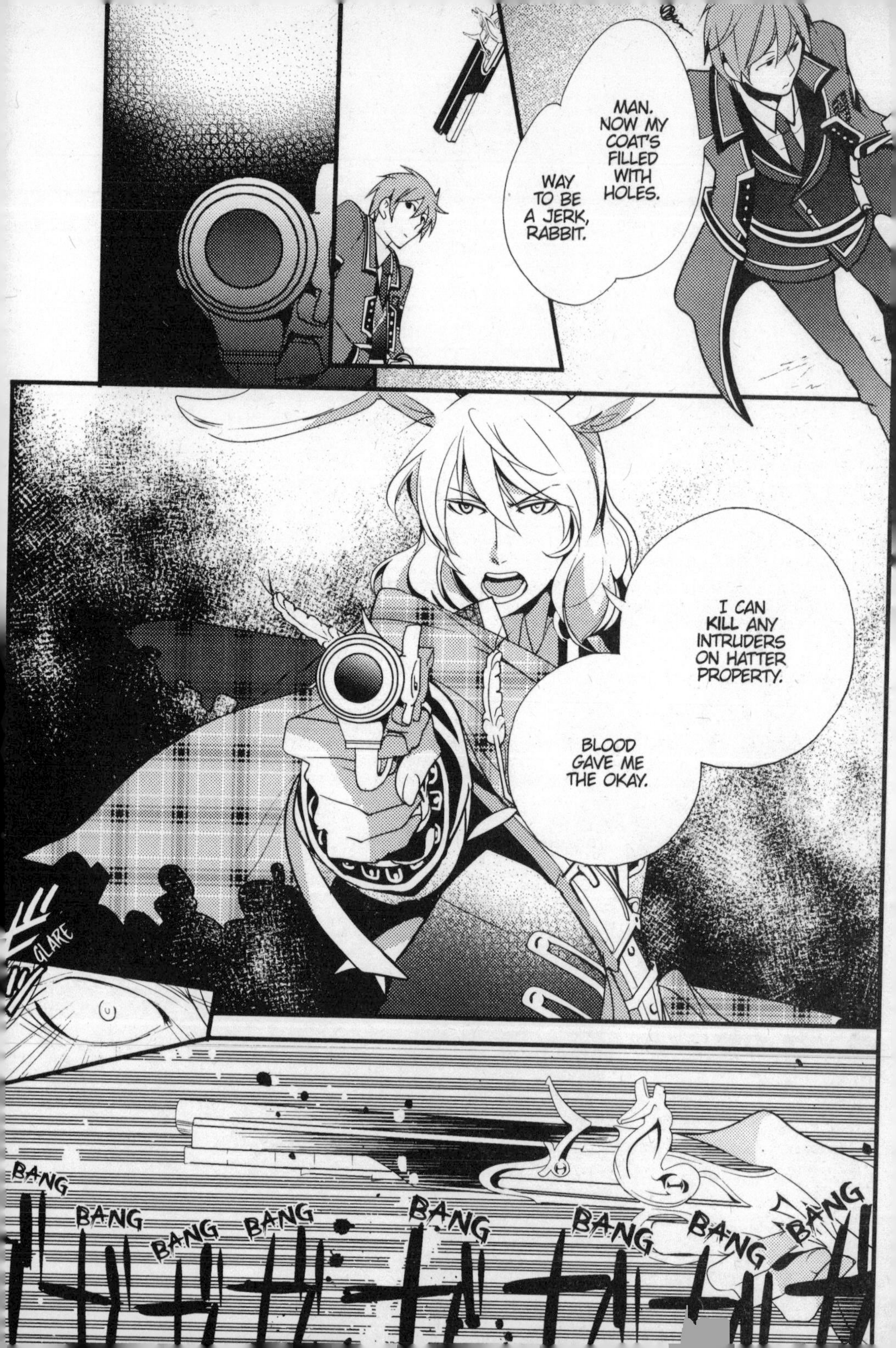
MAN. NOW MY COAT'S FILLED WITH HOLES.
WAY TO BE A JERK, RABBIT.
I CAN KILL ANY INTRUDERS ON HATTER PROPERTY.
BLOOD GAVE ME THE OKAY.
GLARE
BANG
BANG
BANG
BANG
BANG
BANG
BANG
BANG

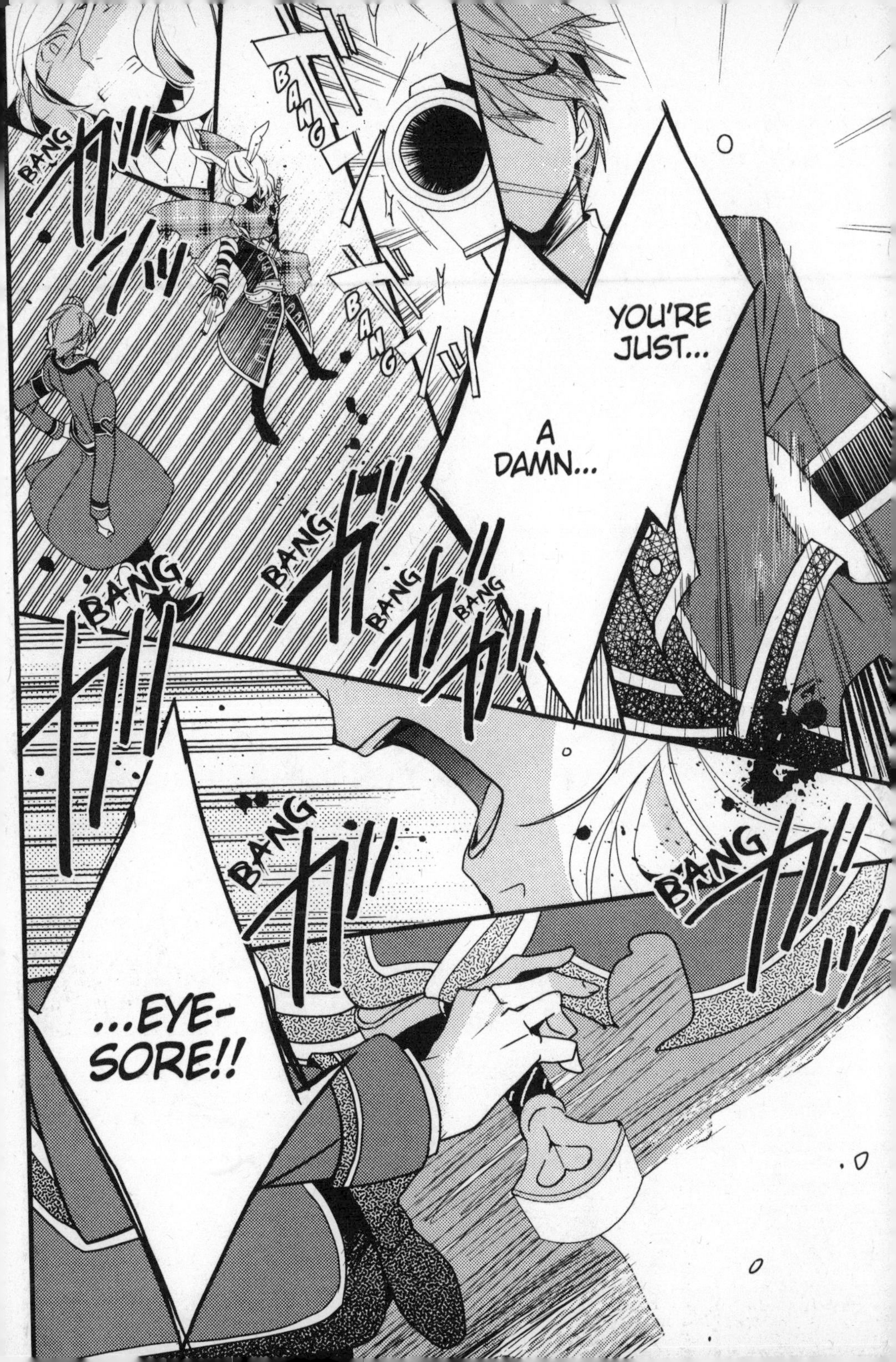
BANG
BANG
BANG
BANG
YOU'RE JUST...
A DAMN...
BANG
BANG
BANG
BANG
BANG
BANG
...EYE-SORE!!

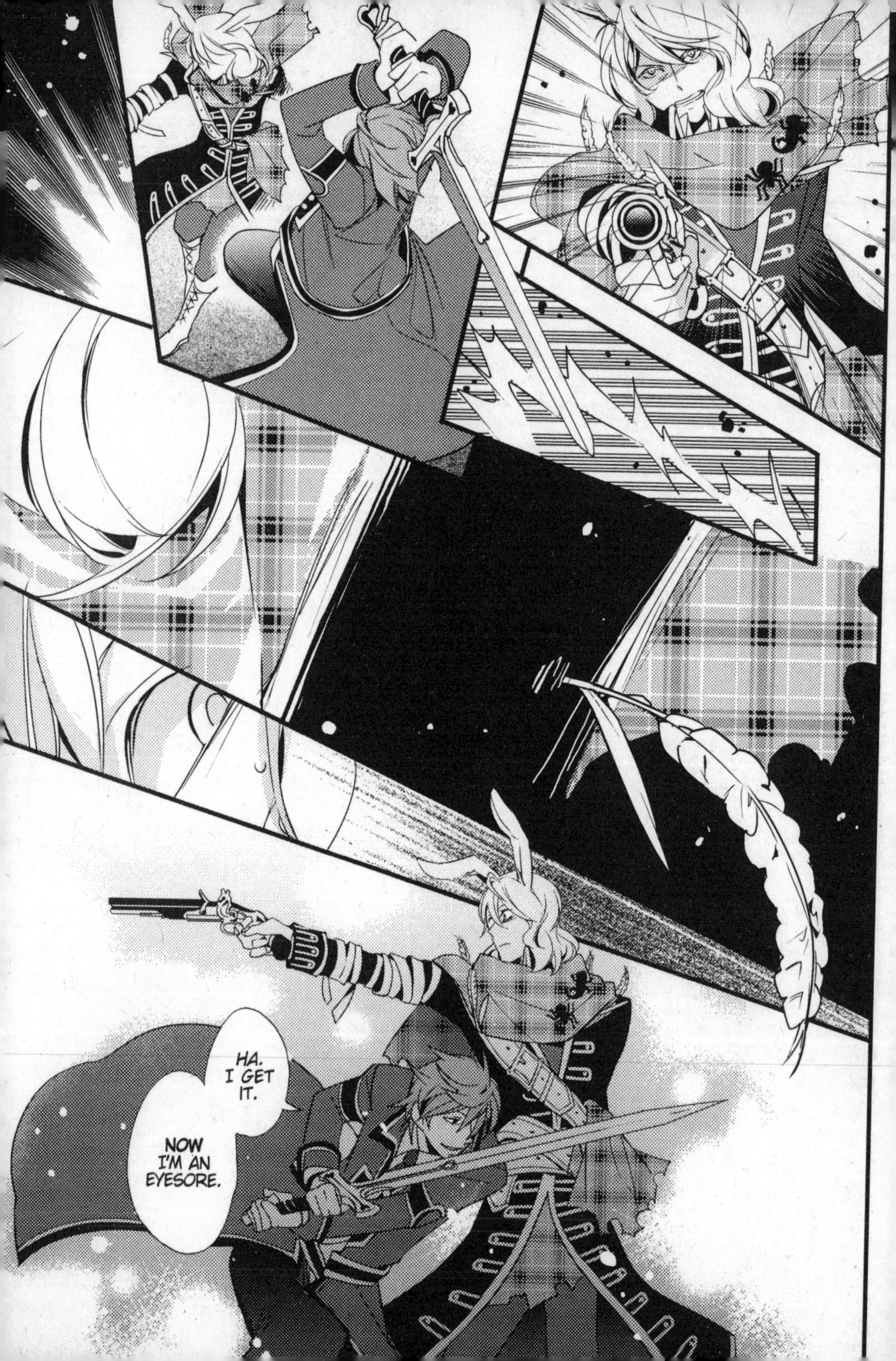
HA. I GET IT.
NOW I'M AN EYESORE.

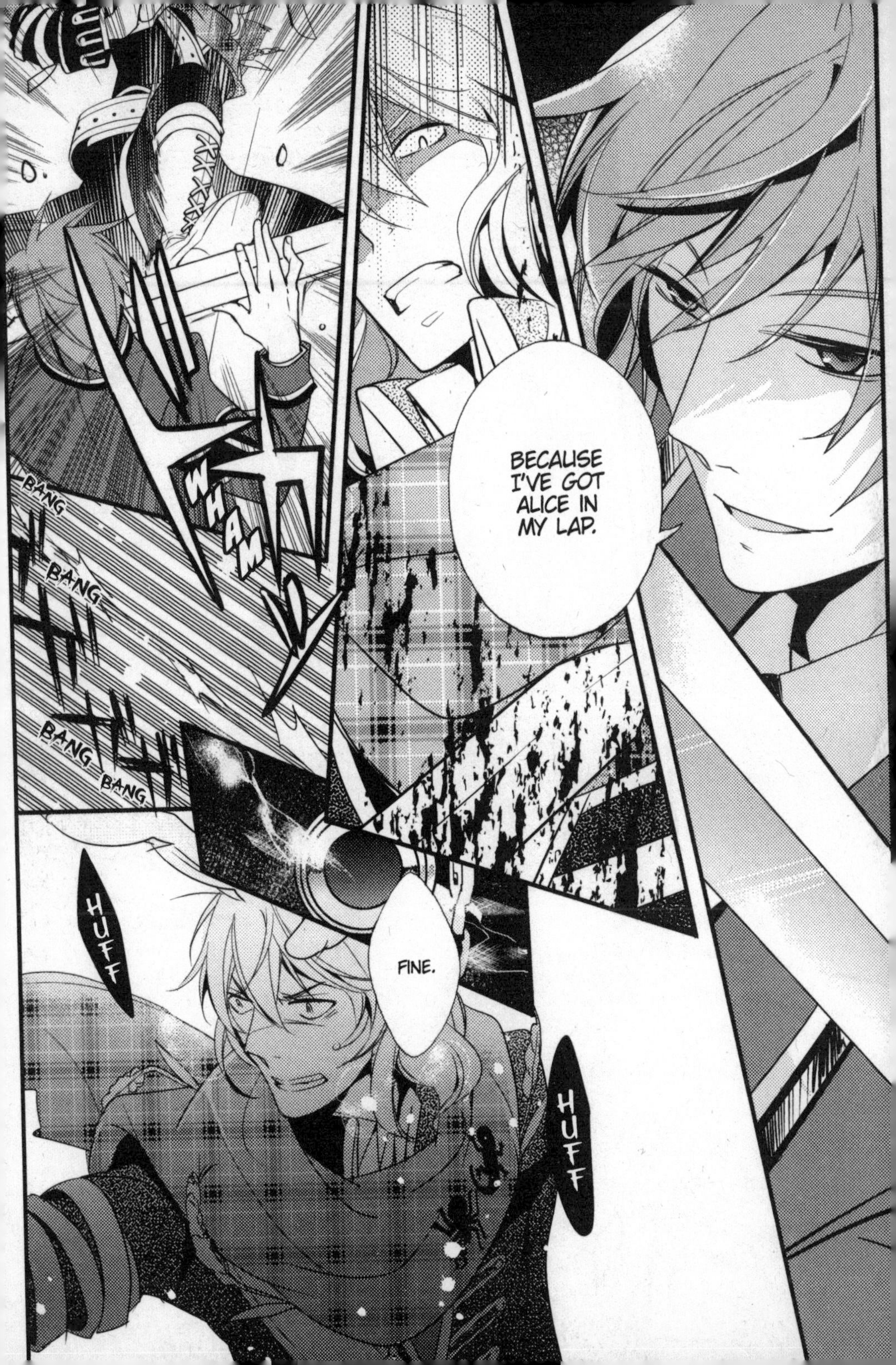

BECAUSE I'VE GOT ALICE IN MY LAP.
WHAM
BANG
BANG
BANG
BANG
HUFF
FINE.
HUFF

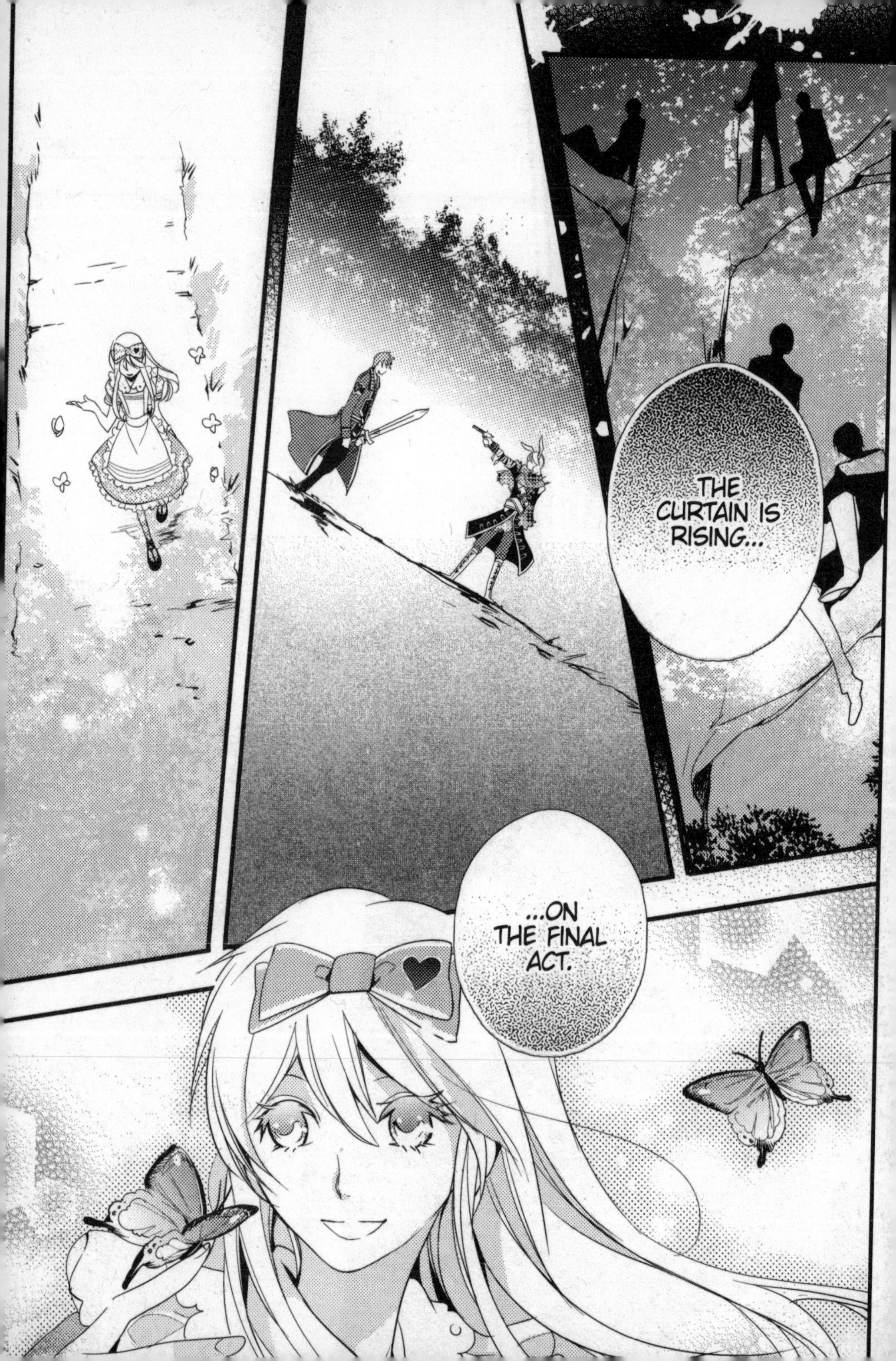
THE CURTAIN IS RISING...
...ON THE FINAL ACT.

Thank you very much!

I was working on my pages on the computer when it suddenly broke-- and all my data disappeared (...!!). Despite everything that happened, I'm glad I was still able to get the second volume to you.

It was fun to draw all the characters in the Clover assembly! I wasn't sure where I wanted each of them to appear.

Ace and Alice's relationship will come to its climax in the next volume. I'll work hard toward a happy ending, so please stick with me until the end.

❀Thank you!❀

QuinRose-sama
Publisher-sama
Taku & Tama-chan
who helped me
And especially all
you readers! Love!!

Sai Asai

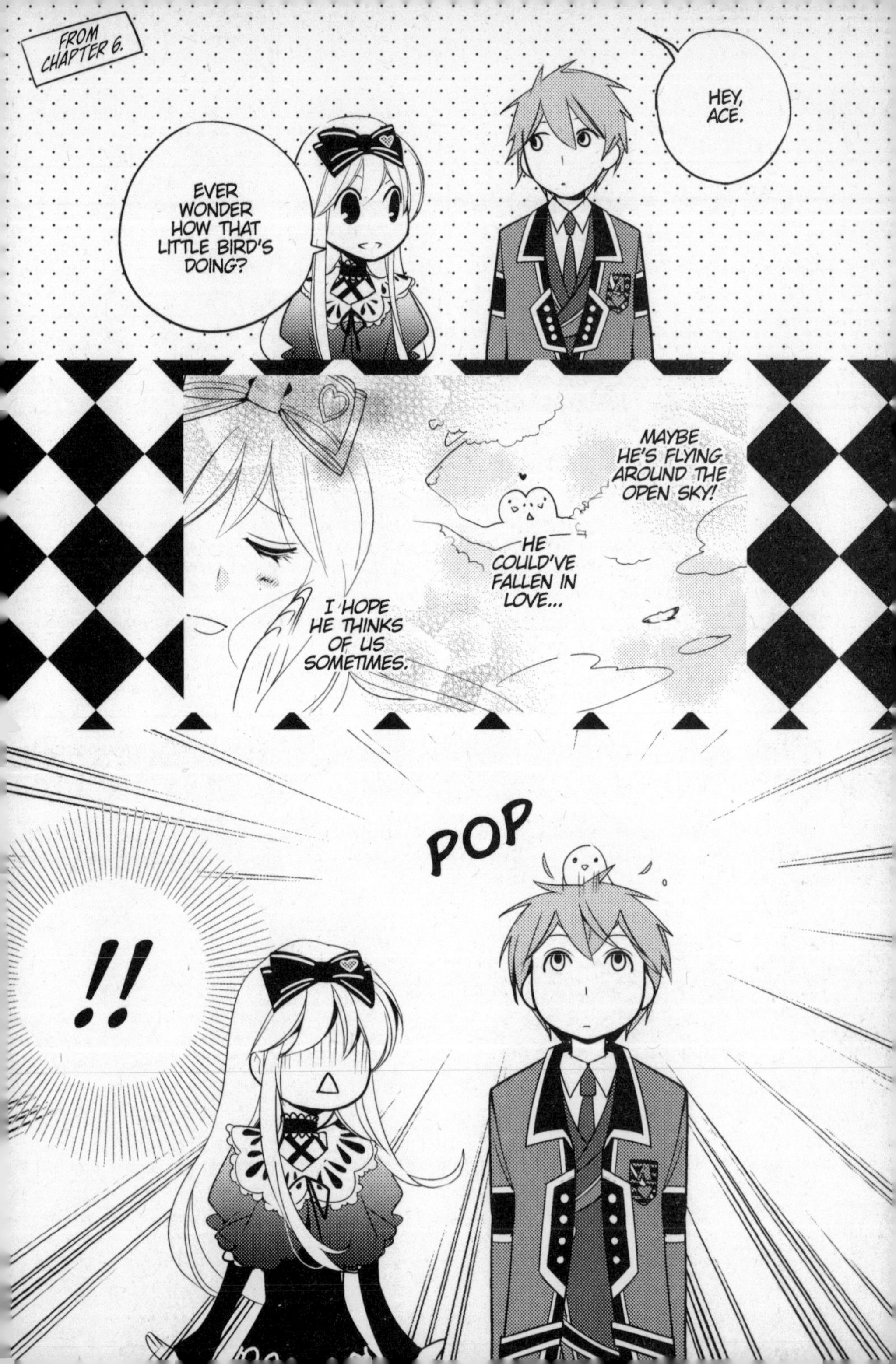
FROM CHAPTER 6.
HEY, ACE.
EVER WONDER HOW THAT LITTLE BIRD'S DOING?
MAYBE HE'S FLYING AROUND THE OPEN SKY!
HE COULD'VE FALLEN IN LOVE...
I HOPE HE THINKS OF US SOMETIMES.
POP
!!

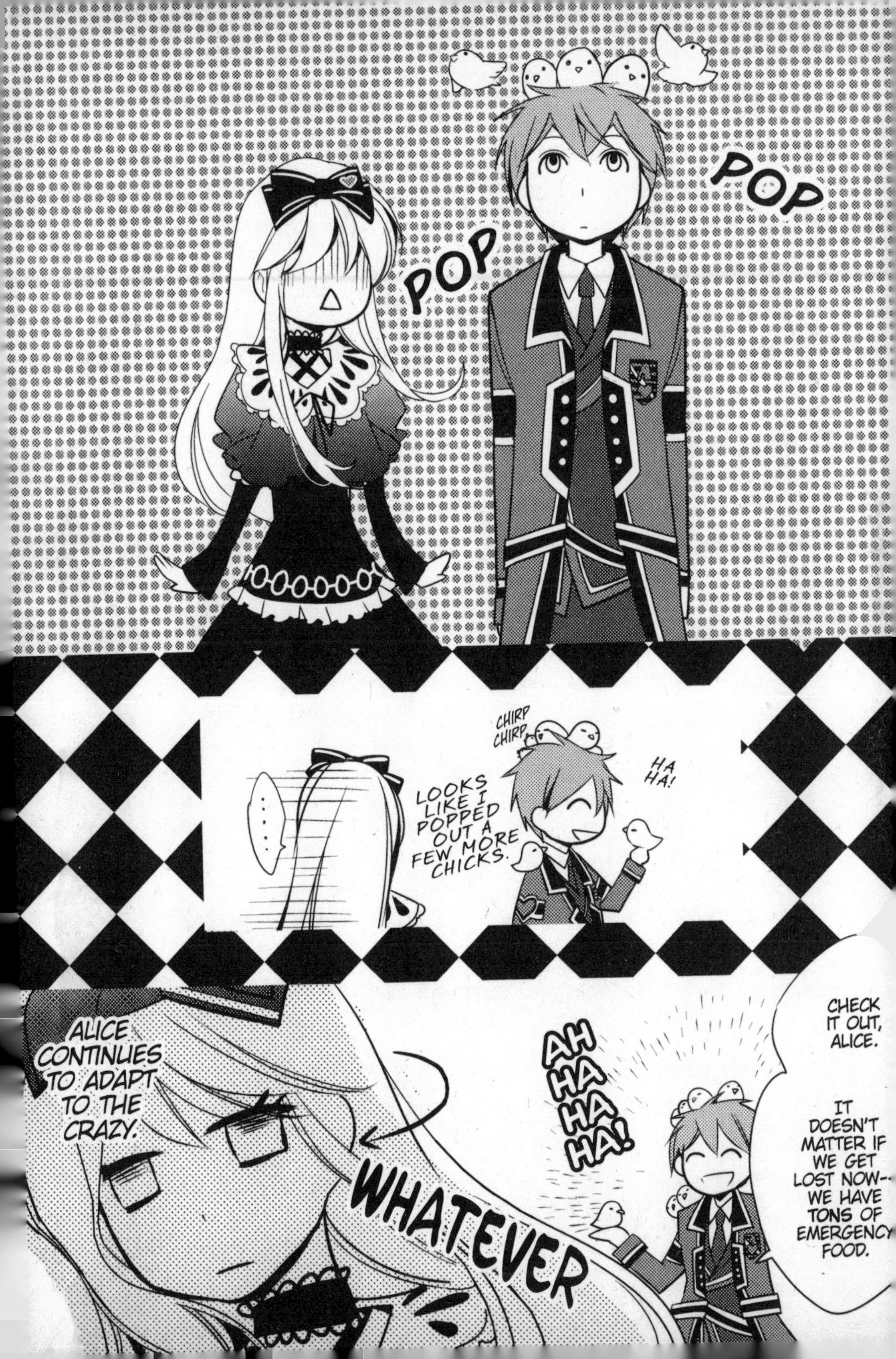
POP
POP
POP
CHIRP CHIRP
HA HA!
LOOKS LIKE I POPPED OUT A FEW MORE CHICKS.
...
CHECK IT OUT, ALICE.
IT DOESN'T MATTER IF WE GET LOST NOW-- WE HAVE TONS OF EMERGENCY FOOD.
AH HA HA HA!
WHATEVER
ALICE CONTINUES TO ADAPT TO THE CRAZY.

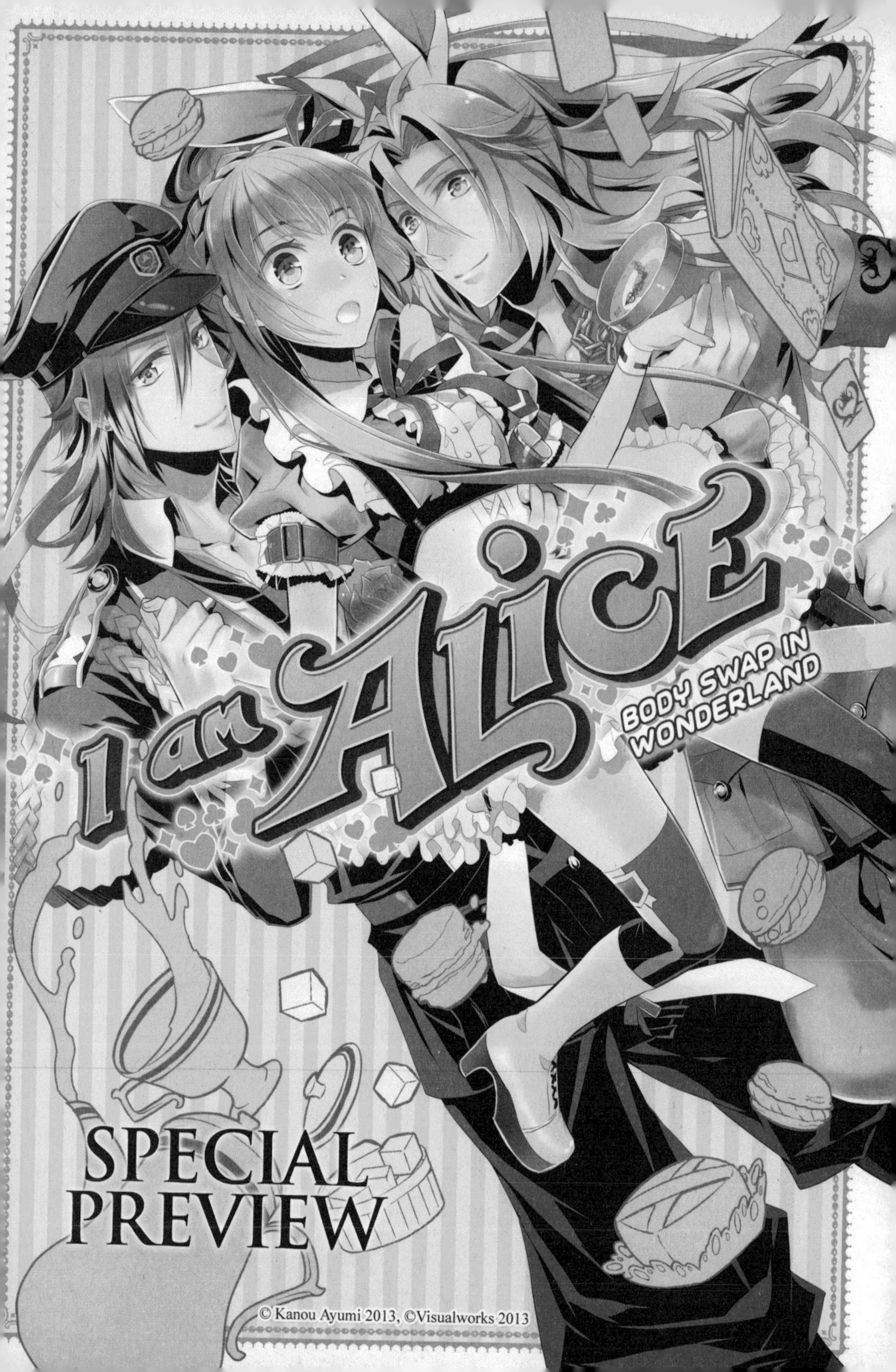
I am ALICE
BODY SWAP IN WONDERLAND
SPECIAL PREVIEW
© Kanou Ayumi 2013, ©Visualworks 2013

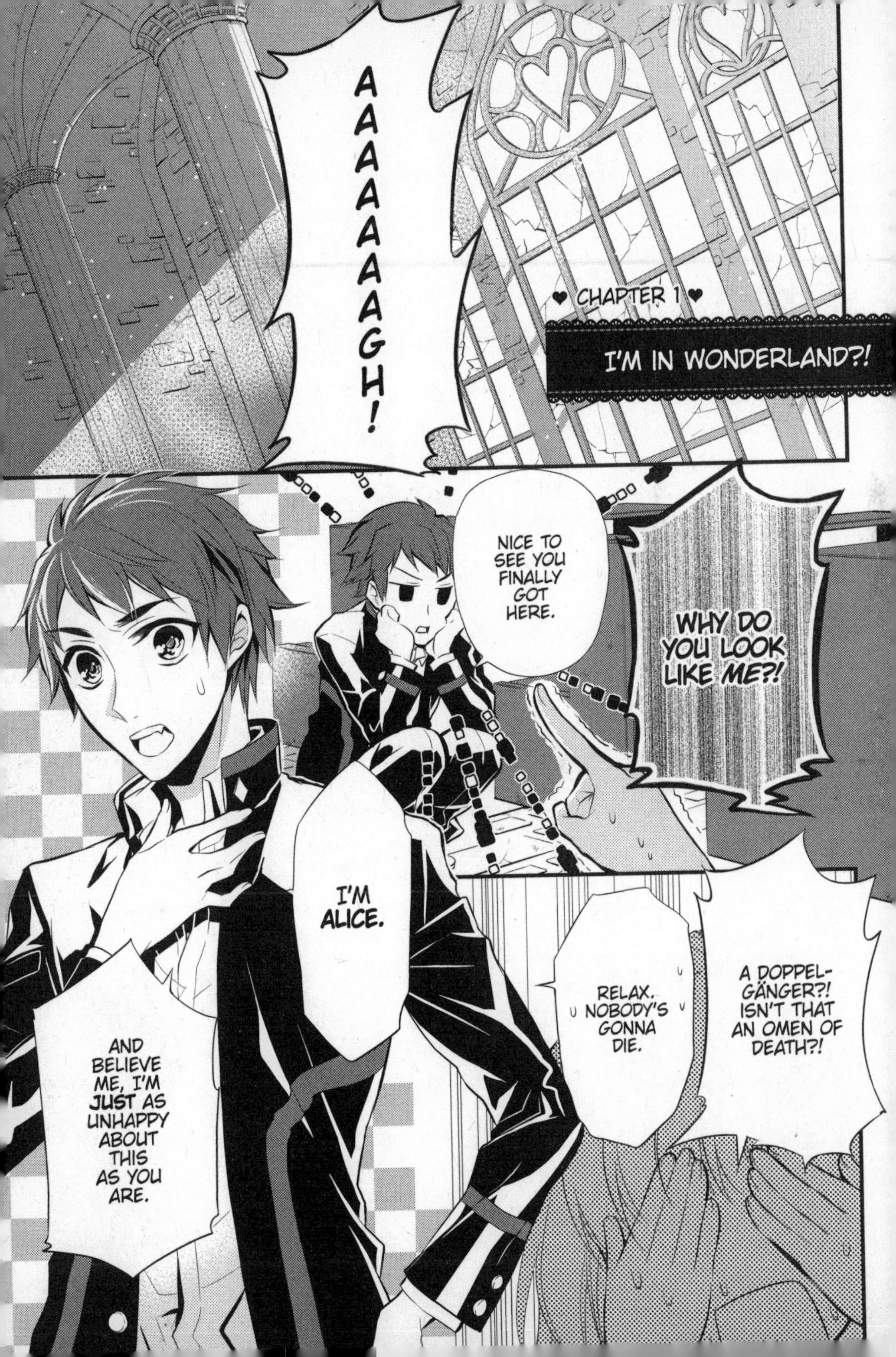
CHAPTER 1
I'M IN WONDERLAND?!
AAAAAAAGH!
WHY DO YOU LOOK LIKE ME?!
NICE TO SEE YOU FINALLY GOT HERE.
A DOPPEL-GÄNGER?! ISN'T THAT AN OMEN OF DEATH?!
RELAX. NOBODY'S GONNA DIE.
I'M ALICE.
AND BELIEVE ME, I'M JUST AS UNHAPPY ABOUT THIS AS YOU ARE.

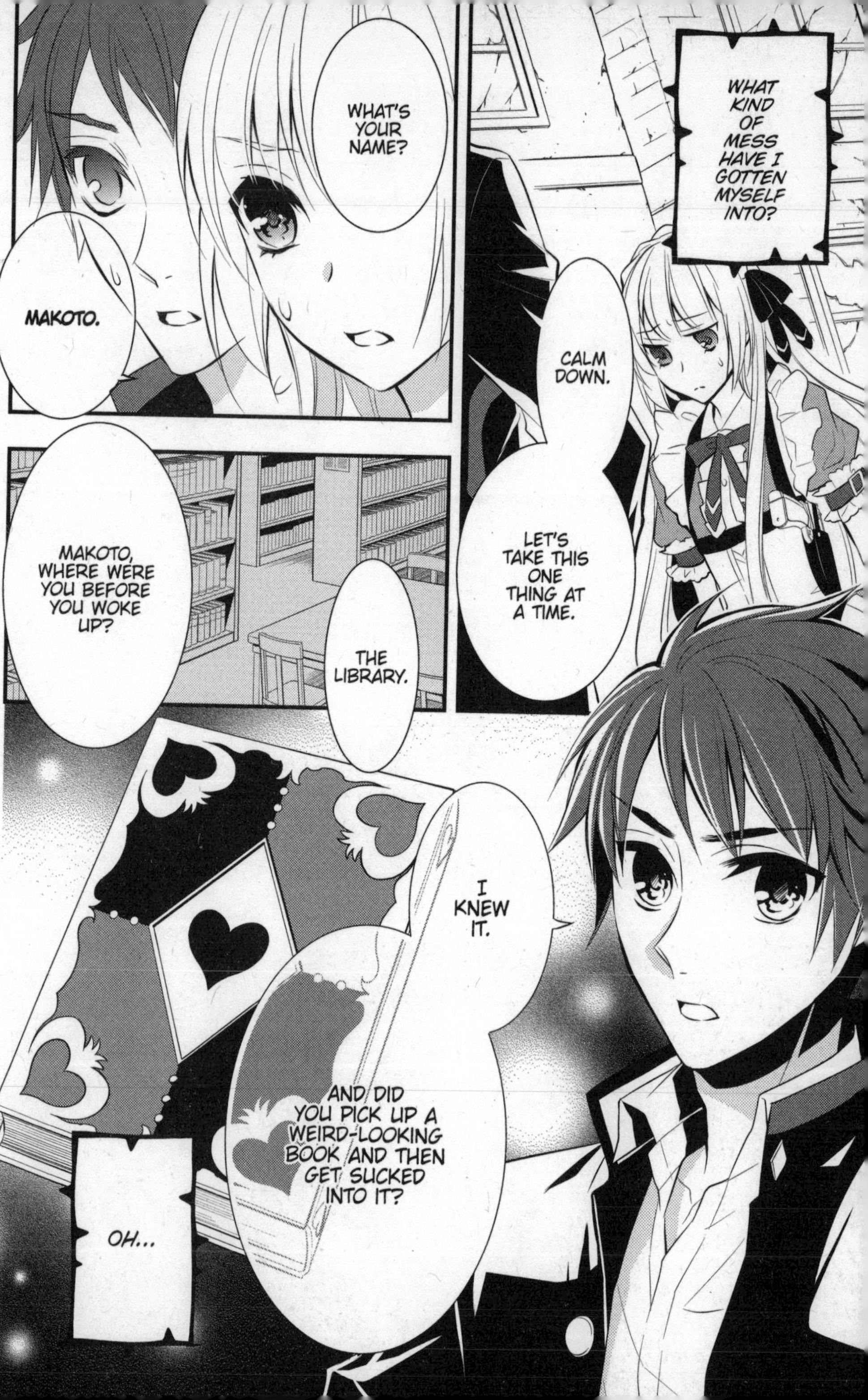
WHAT KIND OF MESS HAVE I GOTTEN MYSELF INTO?
CALM DOWN.
LET'S TAKE THIS ONE THING AT A TIME.
WHAT'S YOUR NAME?
MAKOTO.
MAKOTO, WHERE WERE YOU BEFORE YOU WOKE UP?
THE LIBRARY.
I KNEW IT.
AND DID YOU PICK UP A WEIRD-LOOKING BOOK AND THEN GET SUCKED INTO IT?
OH...

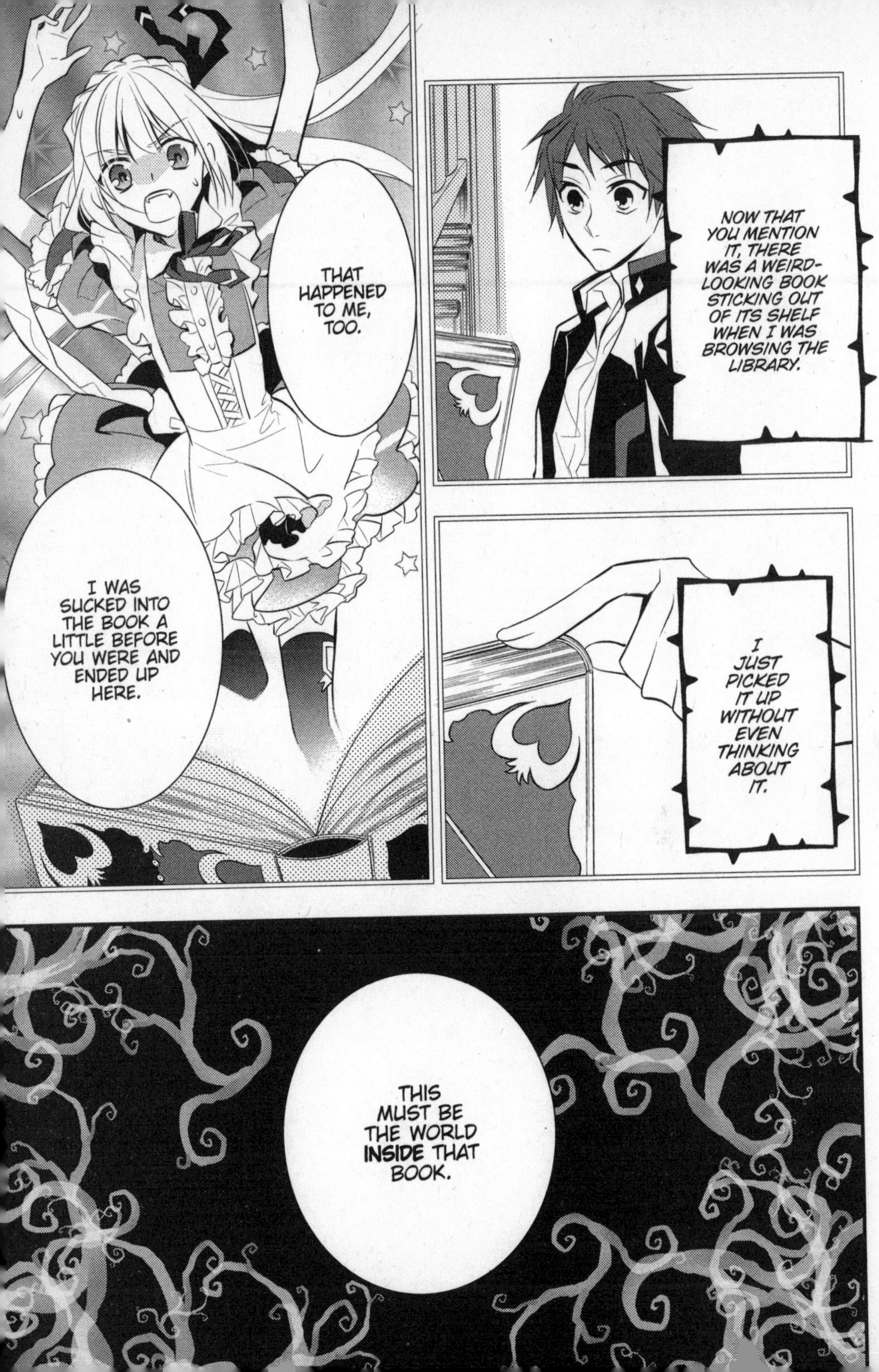
NOW THAT YOU MENTION IT, THERE WAS A WEIRD-LOOKING BOOK STICKING OUT OF ITS SHELF WHEN I WAS BROWSING THE LIBRARY.
I JUST PICKED IT UP WITHOUT EVEN THINKING ABOUT IT.
THAT HAPPENED TO ME, TOO.
I WAS SUCKED INTO THE BOOK A LITTLE BEFORE YOU WERE AND ENDED UP HERE.
THIS MUST BE THE WORLD INSIDE THAT BOOK.

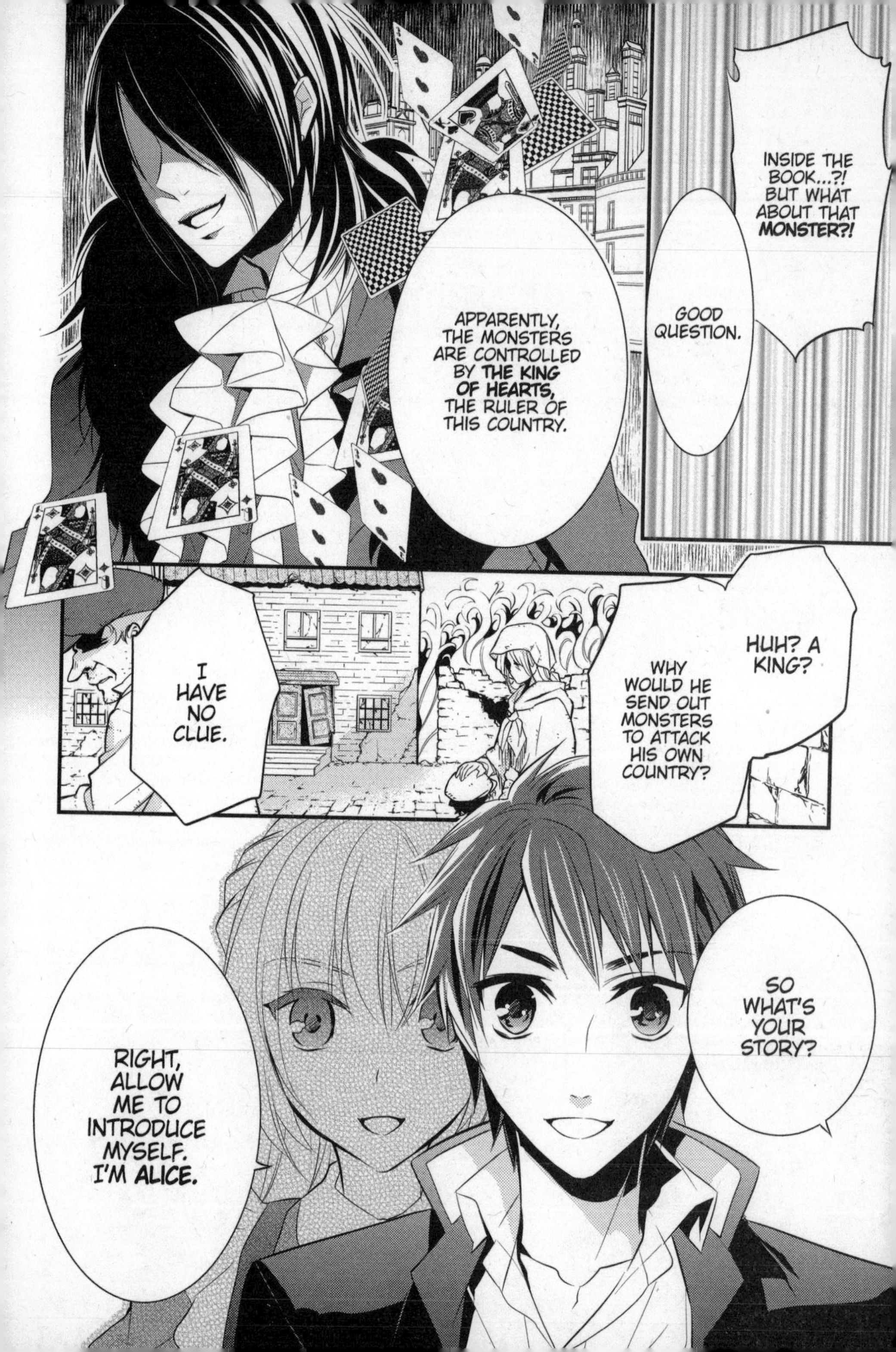
INSIDE THE BOOK...?! BUT WHAT ABOUT THAT MONSTER?!
GOOD QUESTION.
APPARENTLY, THE MONSTERS ARE CONTROLLED BY THE KING OF HEARTS, THE RULER OF THIS COUNTRY.
HUH? A KING?
WHY WOULD HE SEND OUT MONSTERS TO ATTACK HIS OWN COUNTRY?
I HAVE NO CLUE.
SO WHAT'S YOUR STORY?
RIGHT, ALLOW ME TO INTRODUCE MYSELF. I'M ALICE.

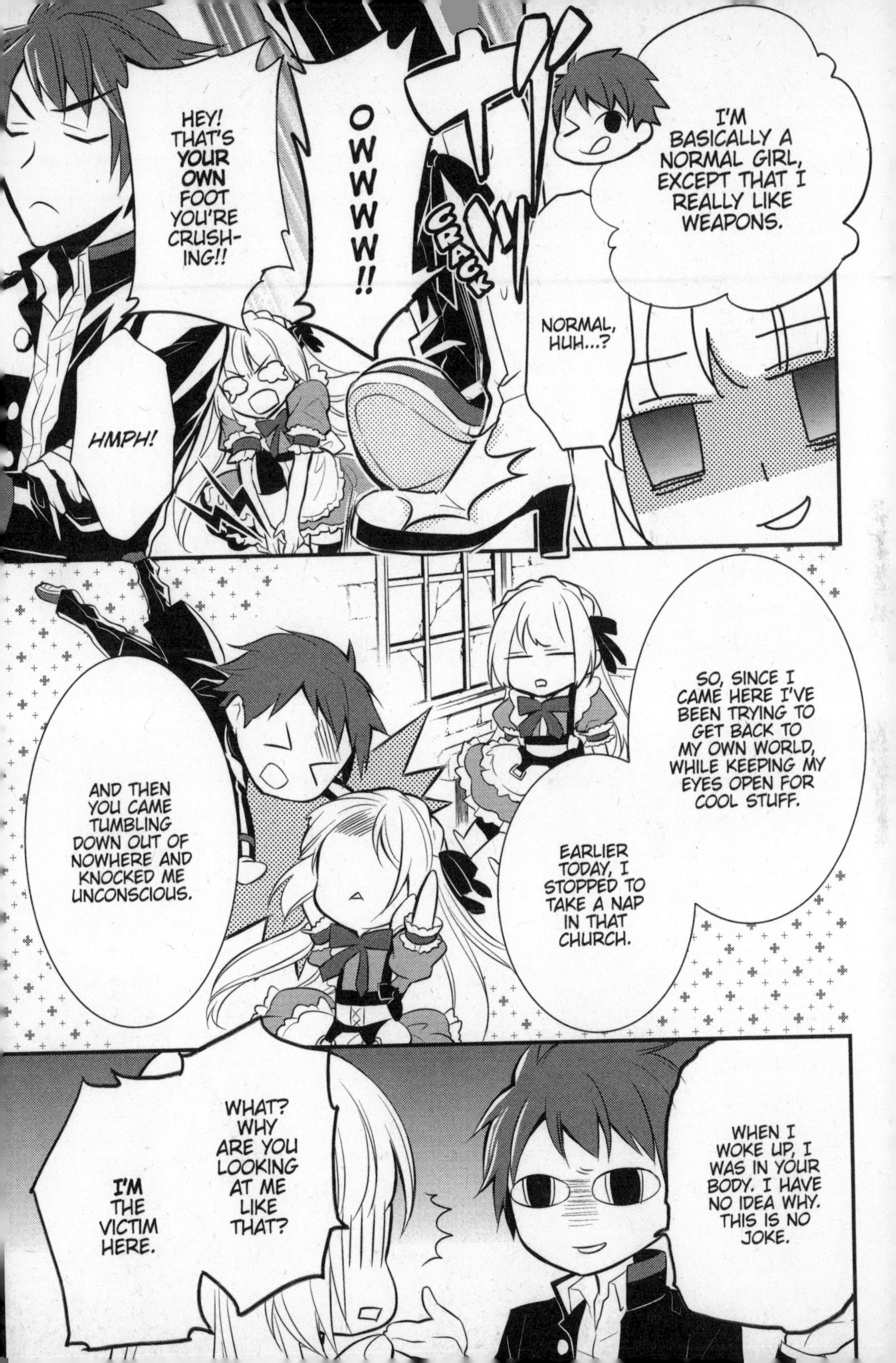
I'M BASICALLY A NORMAL GIRL, EXCEPT THAT I REALLY LIKE WEAPONS.
NORMAL, HUH...?
CRACK
OWWWWW!!
HEY! THAT'S YOUR OWN FOOT YOU'RE CRUSHING!!
HMPH!
SO, SINCE I CAME HERE I'VE BEEN TRYING TO GET BACK TO MY OWN WORLD, WHILE KEEPING MY EYES OPEN FOR COOL STUFF.
EARLIER TODAY, I STOPPED TO TAKE A NAP IN THAT CHURCH.
AND THEN YOU CAME TUMBLING DOWN OUT OF NOWHERE AND KNOCKED ME UNCONSCIOUS.
WHEN I WOKE UP, I WAS IN YOUR BODY. I HAVE NO IDEA WHY. THIS IS NO JOKE.
WHAT? WHY ARE YOU LOOKING AT ME LIKE THAT?
I'M THE VICTIM HERE.

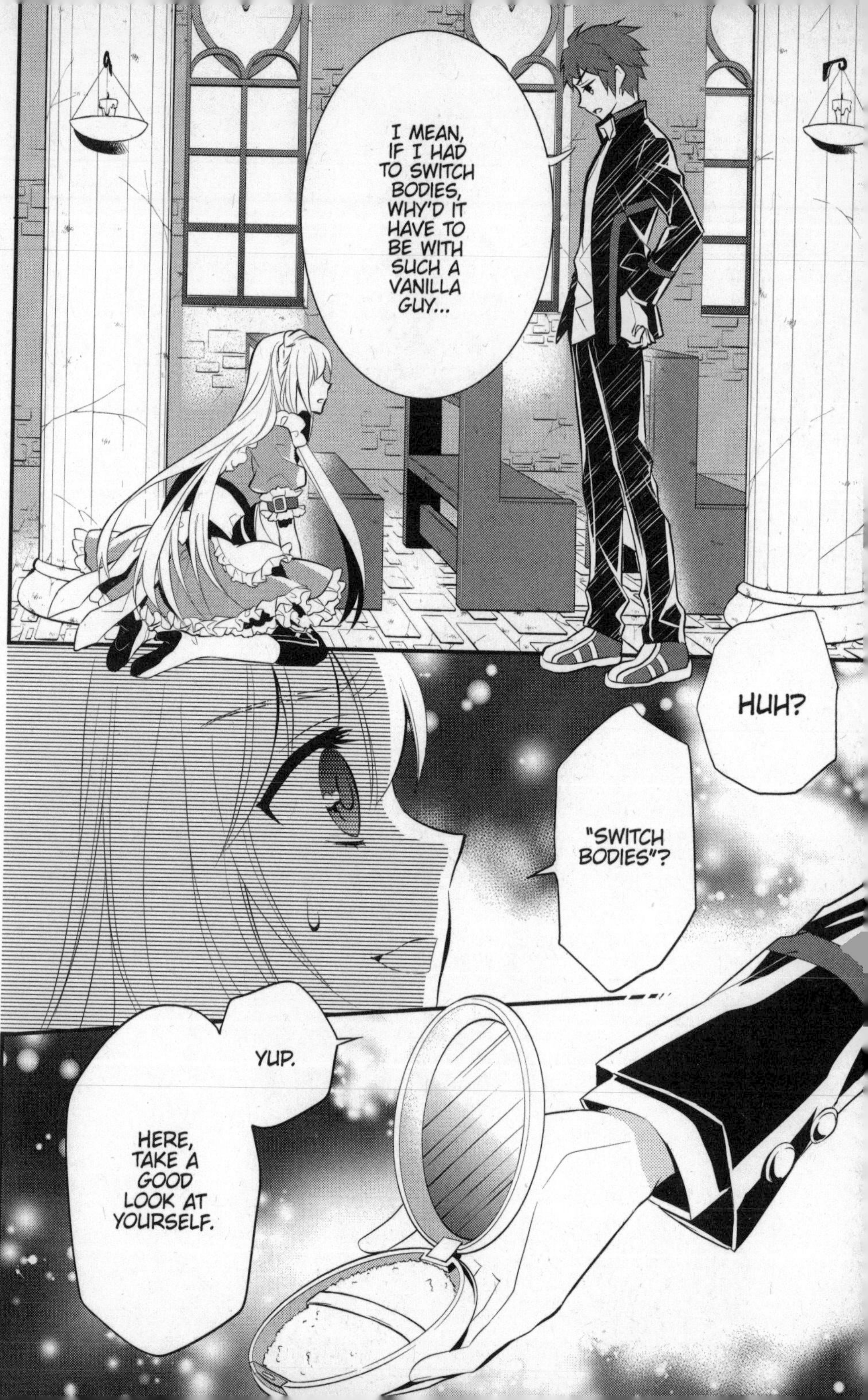
I MEAN, IF I HAD TO SWITCH BODIES, WHY'D IT HAVE TO BE WITH SUCH A VANILLA GUY...
HUH?
"SWITCH BODIES"?
YUP.
HERE, TAKE A GOOD LOOK AT YOURSELF.

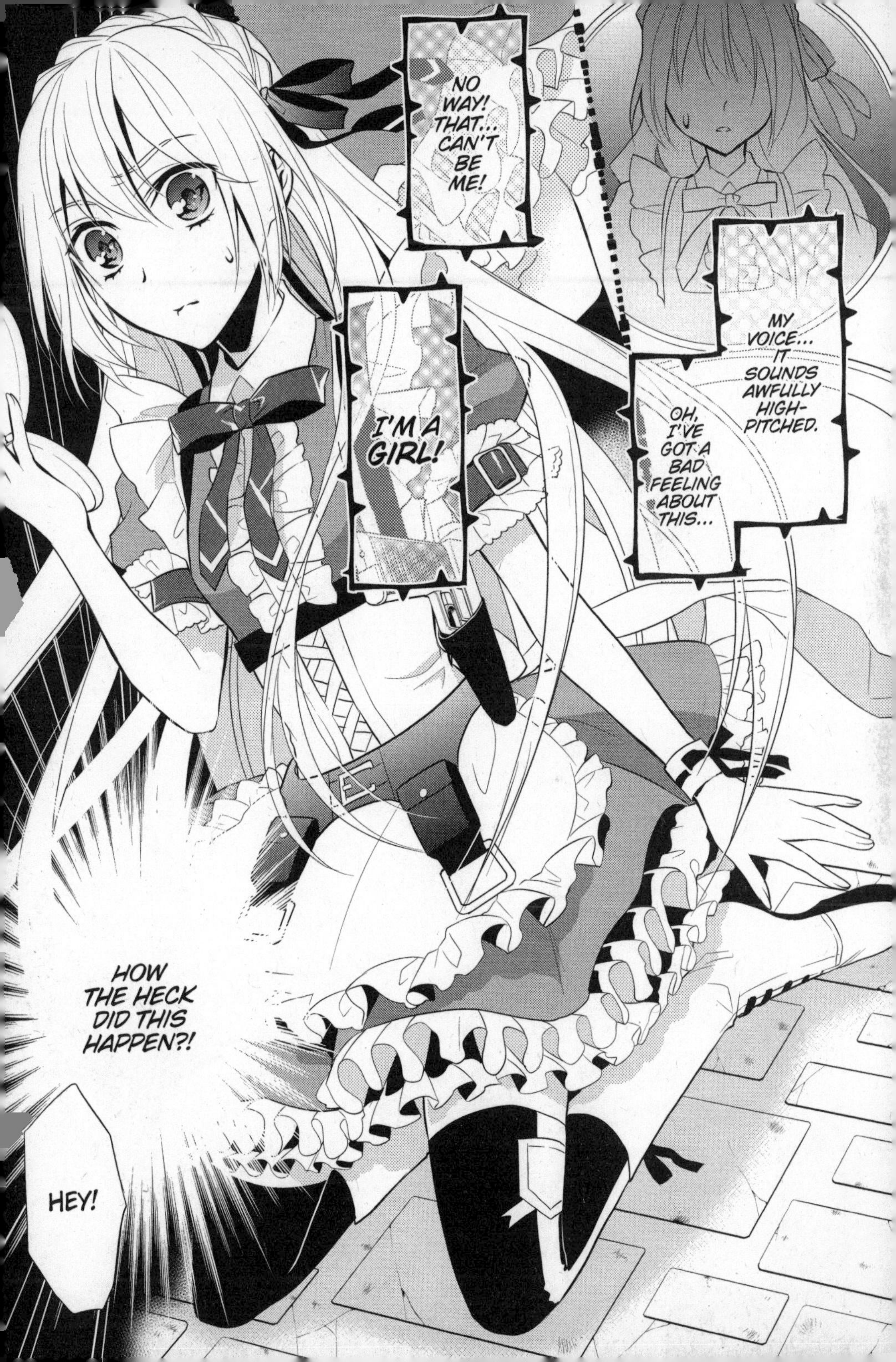
MY VOICE... IT SOUNDS AWFULLY HIGH-PITCHED.
OH, I'VE GOT A BAD FEELING ABOUT THIS...
NO WAY! THAT... CAN'T BE ME!
I'M A GIRL!
HOW THE HECK DID THIS HAPPEN?!
HEY!

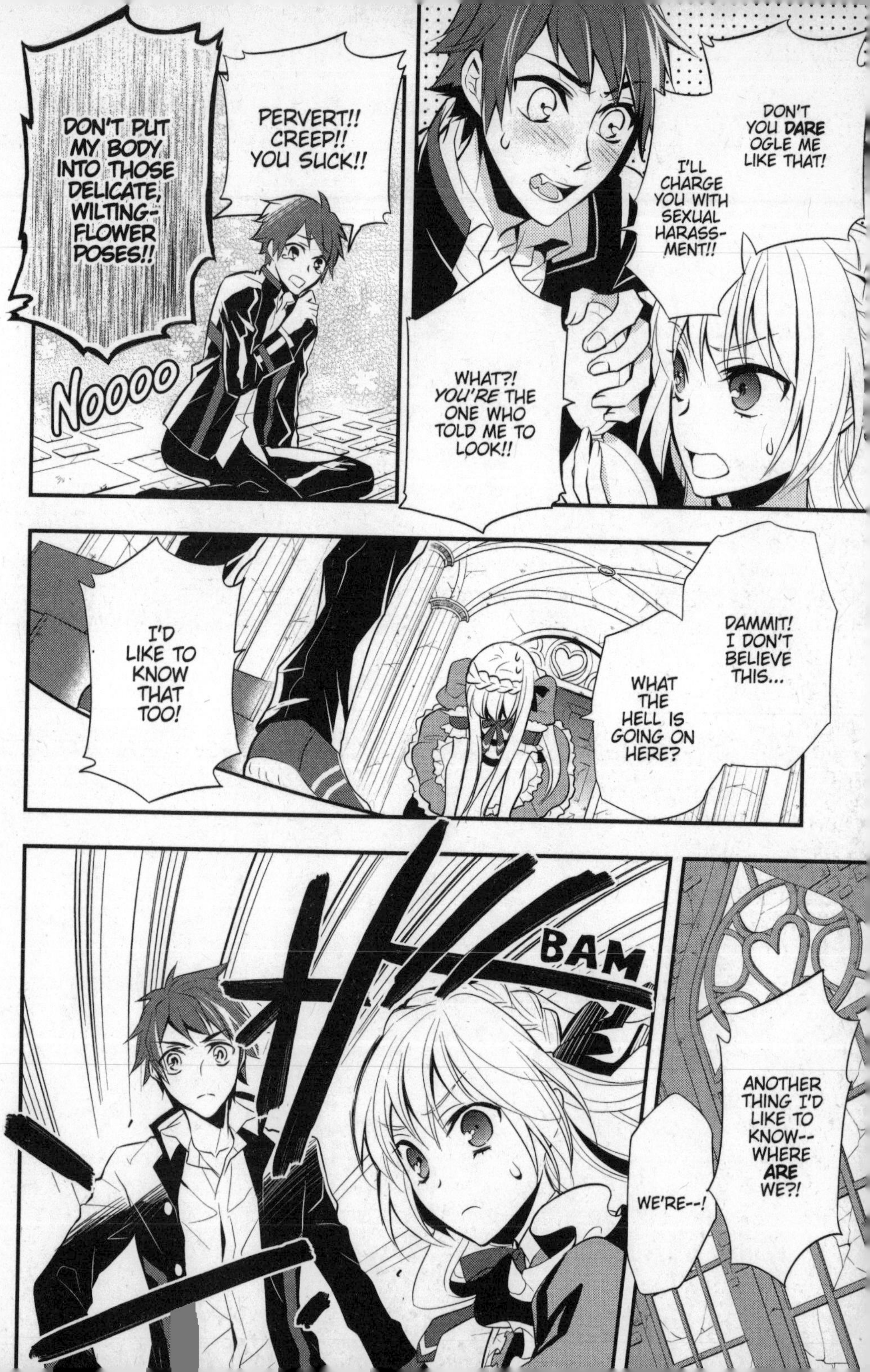
DON'T YOU DARE OGLE ME LIKE THAT!
I'LL CHARGE YOU WITH SEXUAL HARASSMENT!!
WHAT?! YOU'RE THE ONE WHO TOLD ME TO LOOK!!
PERVERT!! CREEP!! YOU SUCK!!
DON'T PUT MY BODY INTO THOSE DELICATE, WILTING-FLOWER POSES!!
NOOOO
DAMMIT! I DON'T BELIEVE THIS...
WHAT THE HELL IS GOING ON HERE?
I'D LIKE TO KNOW THAT TOO!
ANOTHER THING I'D LIKE TO KNOW-- WHERE ARE WE?!
WE'RE--!
BAM

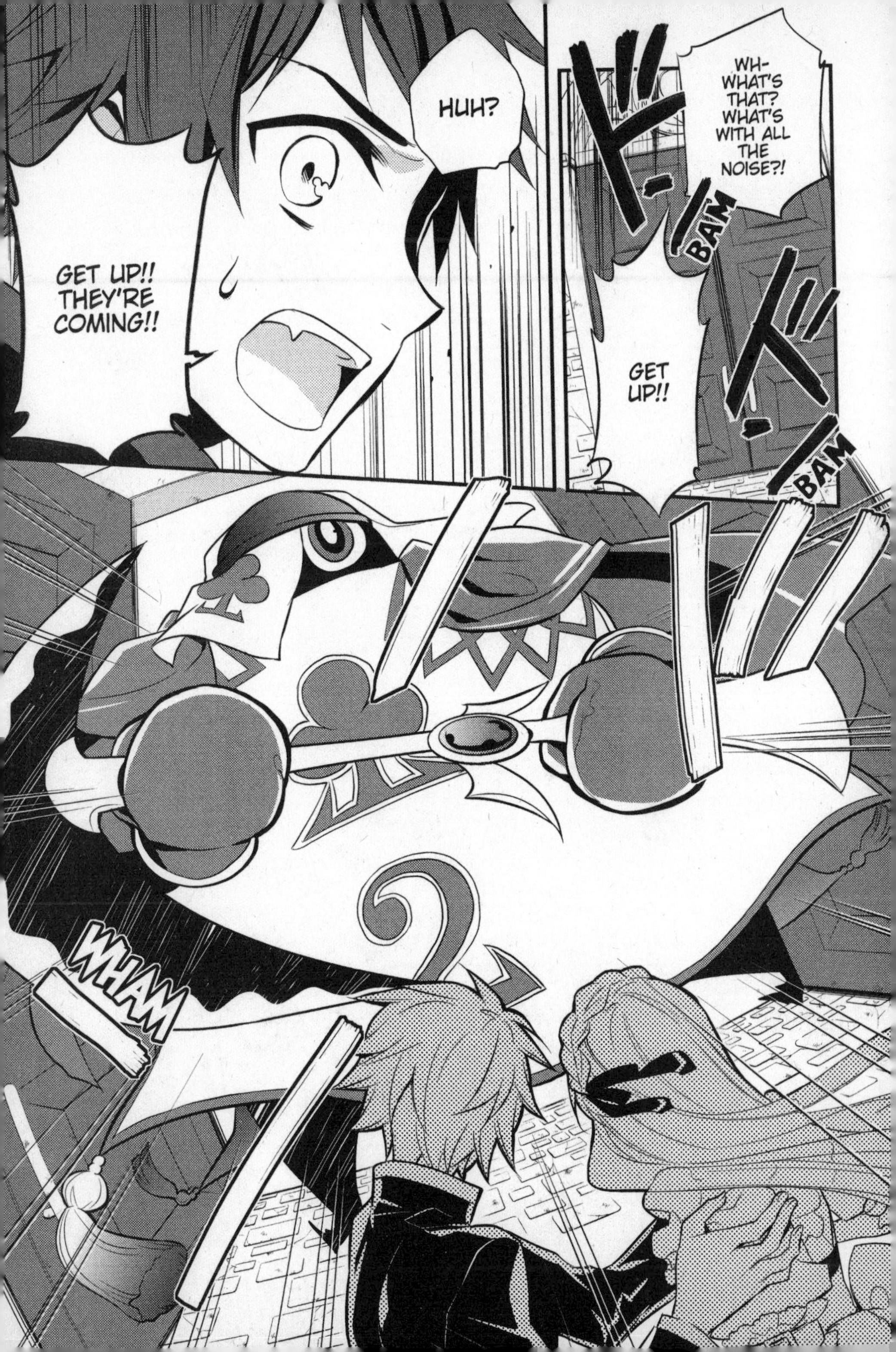
WH- WHAT'S THAT? WHAT'S WITH ALL THE NOISE?!
BAM
GET UP!!
BAM
HUH?
GET UP!! THEY'RE COMING!!
WHAM

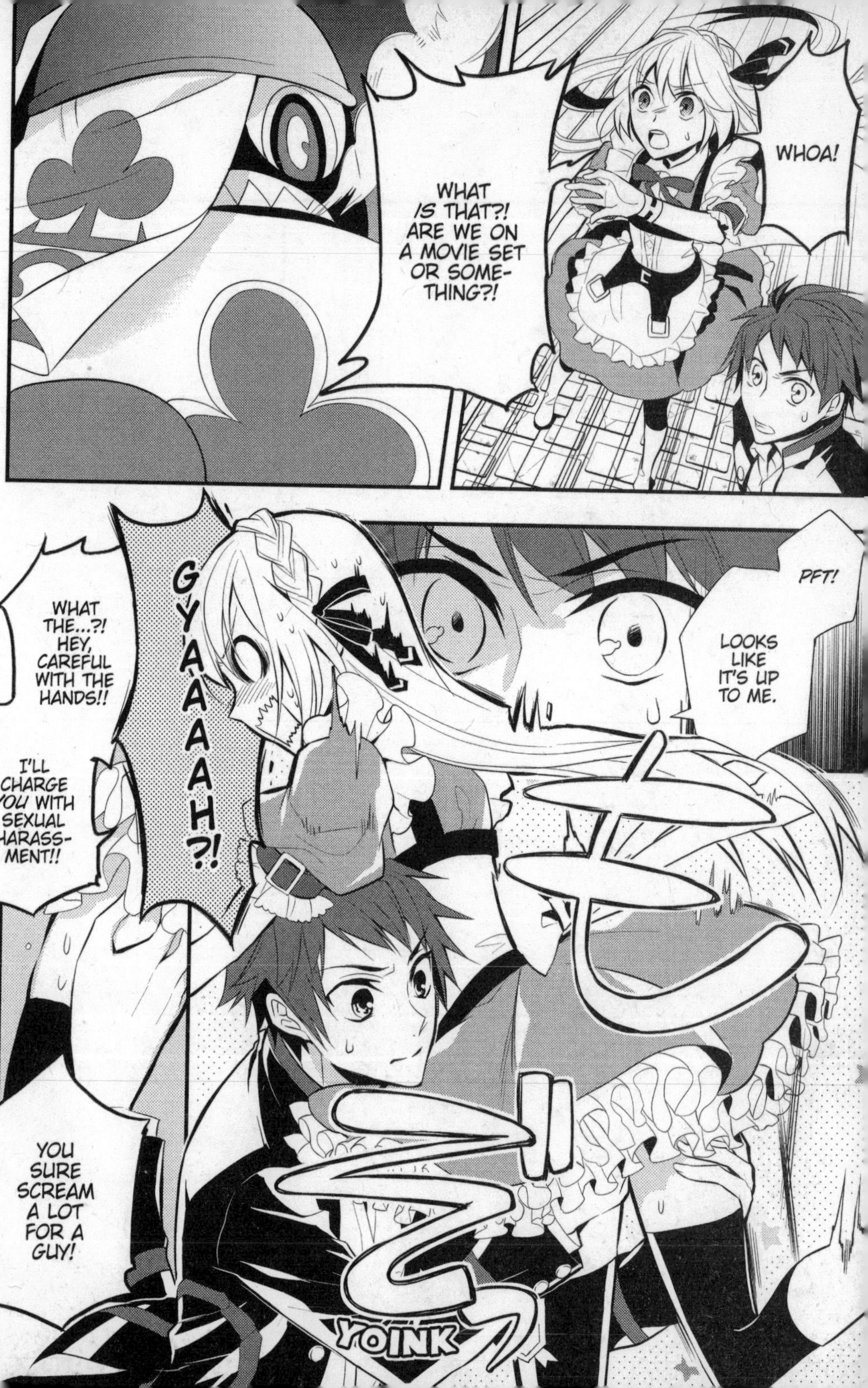
WHOA!
WHAT *IS* THAT?! ARE WE ON A MOVIE SET OR SOME- THING?!
PFT!
LOOKS LIKE IT'S UP TO ME.
GYAAAAAH?!
WHAT THE...?! HEY, CAREFUL WITH THE HANDS!!
I'LL CHARGE *YOU* WITH SEXUAL HARASS- MENT!!
YOINK
YOU SURE SCREAM A LOT FOR A GUY!

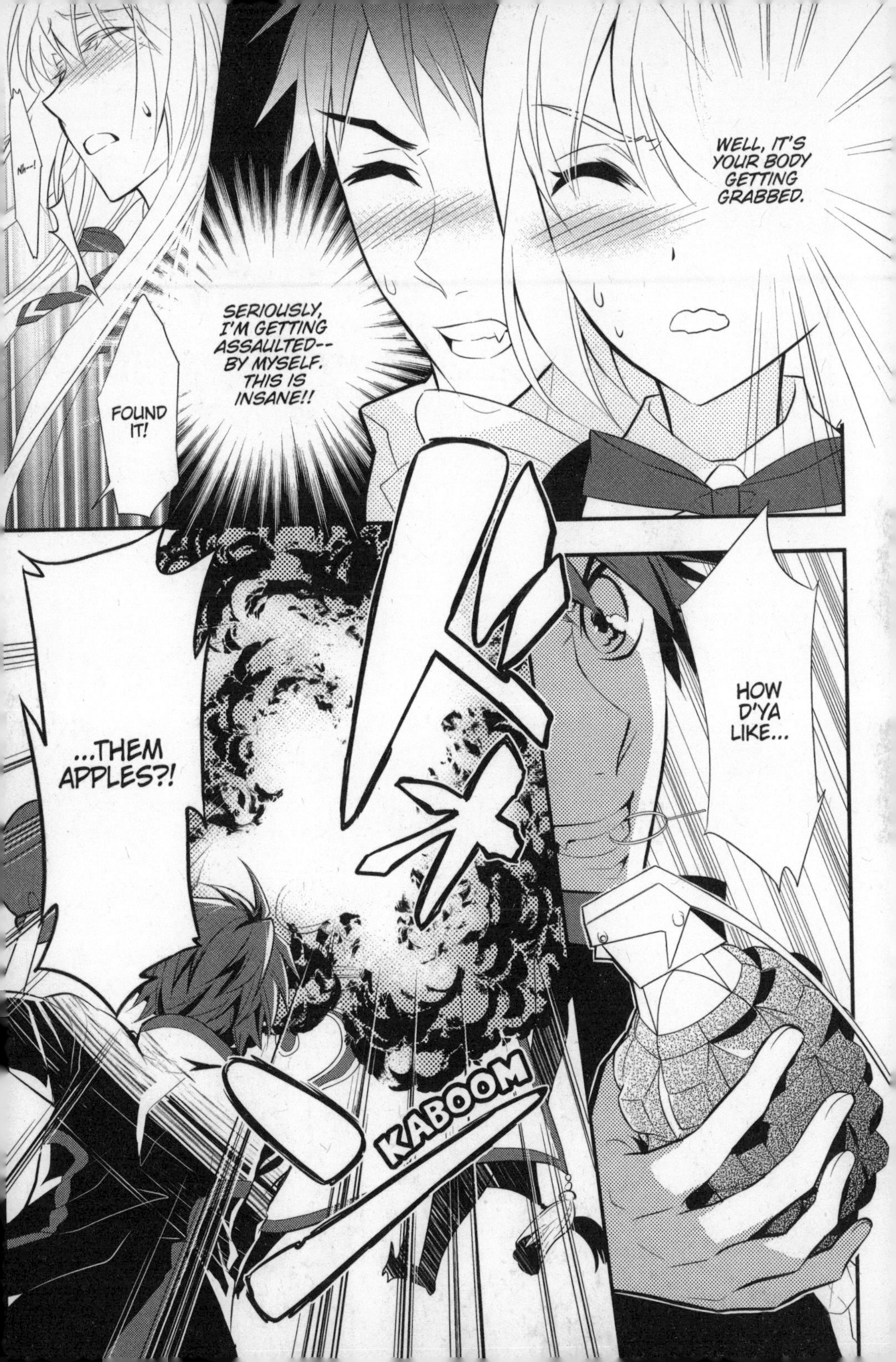
WELL, IT'S YOUR BODY GETTING GRABBED.
SERIOUSLY, I'M GETTING ASSAULTED-- BY MYSELF. THIS IS INSANE!!
Nh--!
FOUND IT!
HOW D'YA LIKE...
...THEM APPLES?!
KABOOM

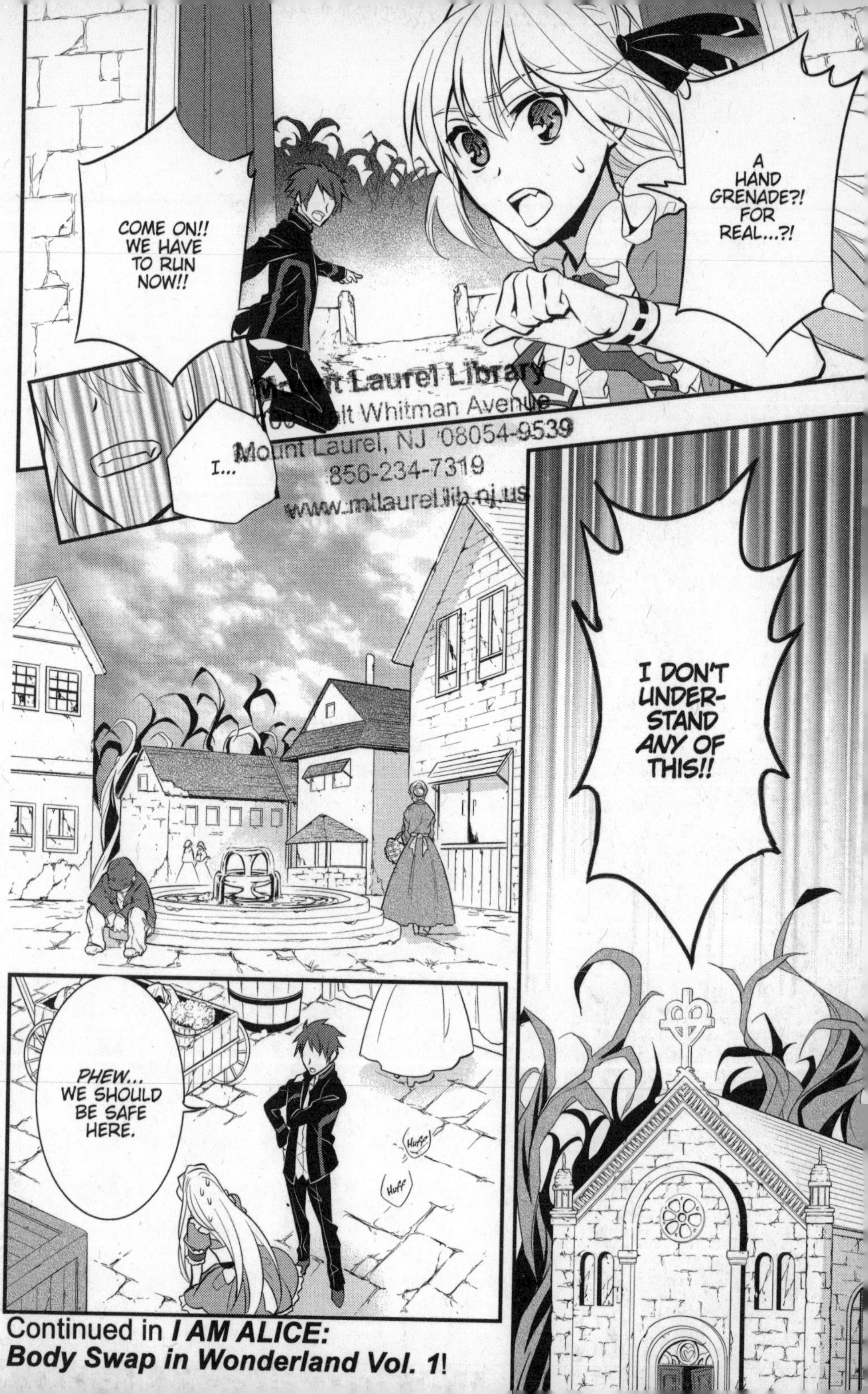
A HAND GRENADE?! FOR REAL...?!
COME ON!! WE HAVE TO RUN NOW!!
I...
I DON'T UNDER-STAND ANY OF THIS!!
PHEW... WE SHOULD BE SAFE HERE.
Huff
Huff

Continued in ***I AM ALICE: Body Swap in Wonderland Vol. 1***!

COMING SOON

OCTOBER 2014
Alice in the Country of Diamonds:
Bet On My Heart

NOVEMBER 2014
Alice in the Country of Clover:
Knight's Knowledge Vol. 3

DECEMBER 2014
Alice in the Country of Joker:
The Nightmare Trilogy Vol. 2

JANUARY 2015
Alice in the Country of Clover:
The Lizard Aide

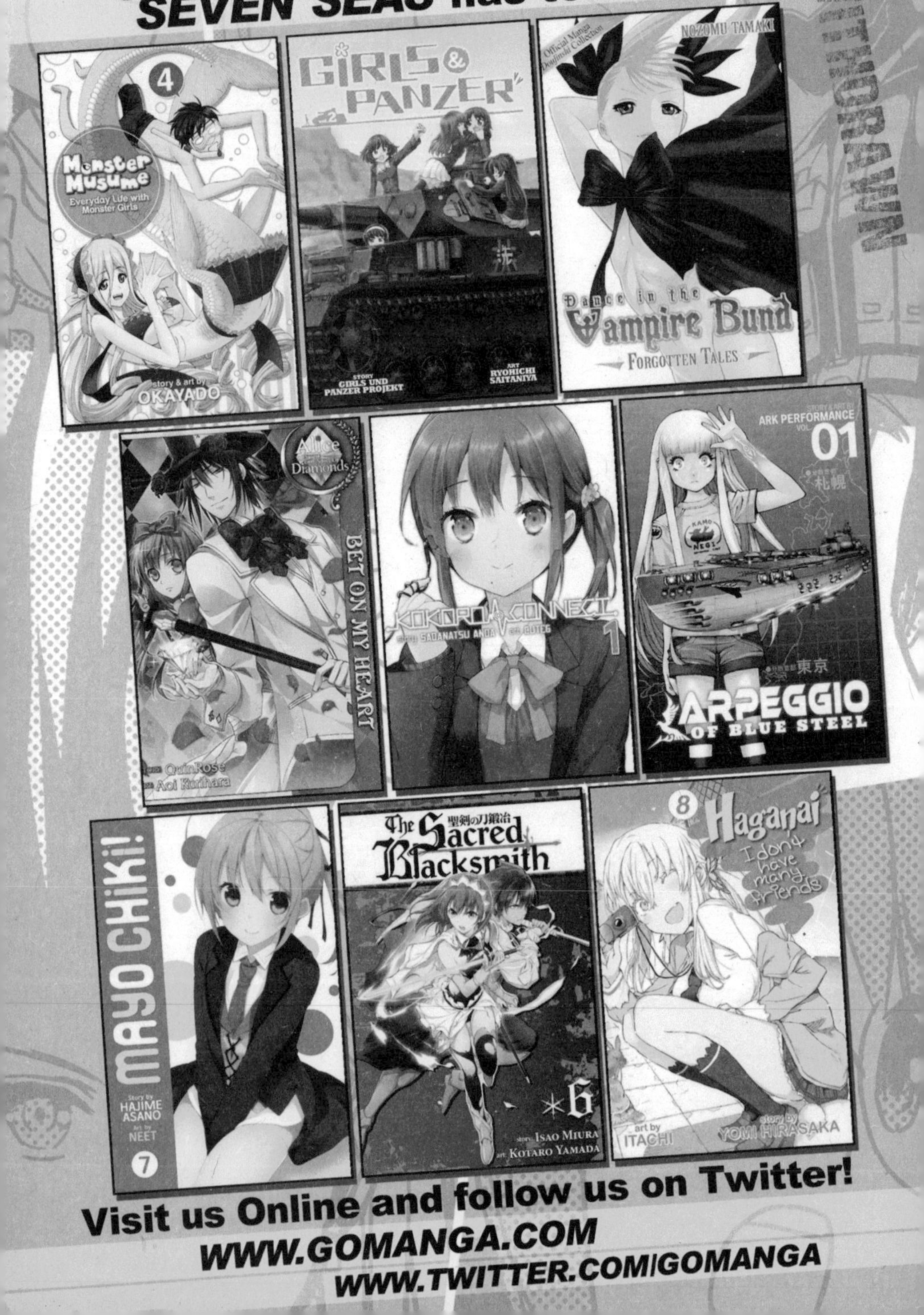
4
Monster Musume
Everyday Life with Monster Girls
story & art by OKAYADO
GIRLS & PANZER
STORY GIRLS UND PANZER PROJEKT
ART RYOHICHI SAITANIYA
Official Manga Doujinshi Collection
NOZOMU TAMAKI
Dance in the Vampire Bund
FORGOTTEN TALES
Alice in the Country of Diamonds
BET ON MY HEART
QuinRose
Aoi Kurihara
KOKORO CONNECT
SADANATSU ANDA
CUTEG
1
ARK PERFORMANCE
VOL 01
ARPEGGIO OF BLUE STEEL
MAYO CHIKI!
Story by HAJIME ASANO
Art by NEET
7
The Sacred Blacksmith
聖剣の刀鍛冶
6
story ISAO MIURA
art KOTARO YAMADA
8
Haganai
I don't have many friends
art by ITACHI
story by YOMI HIRASAKA